John Webb Probyn

Essays on Italy, Ireland and the United States of America

John Webb Probyn

Essays on Italy, Ireland and the United States of America

ISBN/EAN: 9783742846167

Manufactured in Europe, USA, Canada, Australia, Japa

Cover: Foto ©Andreas Hilbeck / pixelio.de

Manufactured and distributed by brebook publishing software (www.brebook.com)

John Webb Probyn

Essays on Italy, Ireland and the United States of America

ESSAYS

ON

ITALY, IRELAND, AND THE UNITED STATES
OF AMERICA.

ESSAYS

ON

ITALY AND IRELAND

AND THE

UNITED STATES OF AMERICA.

Reprinted from the "Revue des Deux Mondes" and the "Westminster Review."

BY

J. W. PROBYN

(handwritten annotations: John Webb)

LONDON:
TRÜBNER & CO., 60 PATERNOSTER ROW.
1868.

[*All rights reserved.*]

Ballantyne & Company, Printers, Edinburgh.

PREFACE.

THESE Essays, written during the course of the last three years, are now reprinted in a single volume, in the hope that their publication may not be without use to those who watch with interest the great events of our own time. The subjects treated of are, the Rise and Formation of the Kingdom of Italy, the Disestablishment of Ireland's State Church, and the American Civil War, which involved constitutional questions of vital importance to the cause of national self-government.

The writer must, however, venture to ask those who think it worth while to read these Essays, to bear specially in mind, while doing so, the exact date at which each one of them was written. The reason for making such a request arises simply from the extraordinary rapidity with which the changes of the present day are accomplished; for they often entirely alter, within a very brief period, the circumstances and condition of a whole country. Thus have been completely transformed, within a few months, or even weeks, the essential characteristics of a government, and the entire destinies of a people. To take a single but notable instance; one specially connected with the subject-matter of several of these Essays—Austria, but yesterday an absolute despotism, is to-day a constitutional monarchy; she is now bound to Hungary by the ties of a free and equal union, instead of oppressing the Hungarian people and trampling on their rights; she is carrying out the liberal legislation of her representative assemblies, instead of doing the work dictated to her by retrograde ministers and priests; she has quitted Italy, and officially acknowledged her newly-formed kingdom, instead of ruling two Italian provinces with a leaden hand, while thwarting to the utmost the formation of Italy's constitutional monarchy.

Thus Austria and Italy are no longer the respective representatives of bigoted despotism and of national aspirations. They now possess in common that constitutional freedom which wisely seeks to bring the prerogatives of the sovereign into harmony with the rights of the people; which strives to unite together, as necessary parts of a well-ordered government, the principle of law and the principle of liberty. That these two countries, (lately so bitter in their hostility to each other,) may go forward and prosper in their new career, is the heartfelt desire of all who believe that the adoption by them of a system based upon order and liberty, will not only bestow upon both Italy and Austria internal prosperity and freedom, but will also draw them together by the enduring ties of common interests and constant intercourse, not more productive of material welfare than of peace and good-will.

Although these great changes, effected with marvellous rapidity, have thus transformed the whole condition of these countries, still it by no means follows that it is either useless or uninteresting to recall the progressive steps by which those changes have been brought about. Rather is it well to study them; for by so doing a clearer knowledge will be gained of the past, and fresh light be obtained for guidance both in the present and the future. Special benefit will be conferred upon Austrian and Italian alike by such study; for it will bring out, in strong relief, the contrast presented by the unspeakable perils and misery brought upon Austria in the past by the blind and unyielding policy of despotism, as compared with the brighter prospects to-day held out to her by constitutional freedom; it will not less surely afford great encouragement to the citizens of Italy to persevere unto the end in working out their country's union and regeneration. That work has, in a few short years, made marvellous progress, despite innumerable difficulties — difficulties which to-day are kept alive, chiefly, if not wholly, by the hostility of those who wield the Papal *Temporal* Power, which is still upheld (as during many years past) by foreign bayonets.*

---

* That Austria and Italy are to-day numbered amongst the free and constitutional powers of Europe, is a matter for sincere congratulation : not, however, on that account are their errors to be passed over in silence. Therefore it is that their respective Parliaments must be censured for subjecting to taxation the *bonâ fide* foreign holders of their state bonds. If such holders were exempted, doubtless facilities would be given for the perpetration of frauds which would deprive the treasury of its dues. Nor can it be denied that the taxation referred to will aid in establishing an equilibrium between receipts and expenditure, thereby benefiting in the end foreign bondholders, by giving greater security and value to their investments in the public funds of Austria and Italy. Still the income-tax in question is unjustifiable, being in fact a diminution of the rate of interest promised to the foreign purchaser when the loans were brought out on the foreign money markets of Europe. Such proceedings cast a slur on the good faith of Austria and Italy. The writer, therefore, while cordially sympathising with both countries in their noble work of national regeneration, freedom, and progress, cannot hesitate to blame the parliaments of Vienna and Florence for thus unjustly subjecting to taxation the foreign holders of their state bonds.

Some additions have been made, some abbreviations effected, and some inaccuracies corrected, in the Essays reprinted in this volume. These alterations have not, however, weakened, in any appreciable degree, the general conclusions of the writer, or the facts and arguments on which they repose. If in some cases he has added proofs, recently obtained, tending to strengthen his previous opinions, he has not hesitated, in other cases, to admit that events have led him to change or modify his views.

But whatever may be the defects of these Essays, (and doubtless they are many,) the writer, in dealing with the subjects of which they treat, has earnestly sought to arrive at TRUTH alone; not without some hope that he may perchance, while so engaged, have done something to aid others also in their search after that "pearl of great price."

J. W. PROBYN.

CONTENTS.

	PAGE
Milan and Venice since the War of 1859: Translated from the *Revue des Deux Mondes* of October 1865,	1
Italy, Venice, and Austria: Reprinted from the *Westminster Review* of July 1866,	42
Italy and the War of 1866 (Custoza, with a Map): Reprinted from the *Westminster Review* of April 1867,	94
Two Temporal Powers (the Anglican Church in Ireland and the Roman Church in Italy): Reprinted from the *Westminister Review* of January 1868,	184
The Church System of Ireland and Canada: Reprinted from the *Westminster Review* of April 1868,	254
The United States Constitution and the Secessionists: Reprinted from the *Westminster Review* of April 1866,	283

MILAN AND VENICE SINCE THE WAR OF 1859.

Translated from the "Revue des Deux Mondes" of 1st October 1865.

THE peace of Villafranca (1859) gave freedom to Milan, but left Venice under foreign rule. Thus were suddenly separated two Italian cities, which for nearly half a century had been united under the government of the same German power. Six years have passed away since that unexpected separation took place. What are the respective conditions of Milan and Venice at the close of this short but significant period? That is a question which facts (collected together during frequent and prolonged stays in the north of Italy) enable me to answer with the assurance of bringing to bear on this important subject, information that will interest the friends of the new kingdom of Italy, whether French or English. The contrast afforded by the material prosperity of Milan, as compared with the suffering and languor against which Venice struggles, is not, however, the only object of these pages. Examples are not wanting to teach us the life-giving power of freedom, and the death-like effects of servitude. I desire, whilst pointing out a contrast so striking and so sad, to set forth also the points of resemblance, the similarity which may be remarked between Milan and Venice as regards their moral and political vitality. I wish to invite attention to the Italian character, exposed, as it were, to a double trial; here in the best, there in the worst circumstances. If these facts and recollections afford ground for believing that Venice, when set free, will prove herself able to tread, like Milan, the path of progress, my object will be attained, and my conclusion be complete; for while a severe rebuke will thus be inflicted upon Austria, solid encouragement will at the same time be given to the young Italian nation.

I.

In order thoroughly to appreciate the progress accomplished by Milan, some account must be given of the state of that city during the last years of Austrian rule. I shall never forget the impression produced upon me by the general aspect of Milan when I visited it for the first time, in October 1853. The unquiet and suspicious looks of the Austrian sentinels gave one the idea that the enemy was at the very gates. The sentinels had, however, good reason to be on the watch, for the enemy was in possession of a far more formidable position; he was within the city itself. The enemy was the entire population. I soon remarked that the Austrians and Italians were never to be seen in the same café. I learned that they never met in the boxes of the Scala, or in private houses. An Austrian officer could not enter a room, without the Italians, who might happen to be there, instantly quitting it. But while the inhabitants of Milan thus proclaimed their detestation of Austrian despotism, the Viennese government was not slow in redoubling its rigour against those whom it styled "the seditious Milanese," (*les frondeurs de Milan.*)

One day I was loitering about in front of the magnificent cathedral, changing my place leisurely from time to time, the better to see the thousand details of the Duomo, when suddenly an Austrian sentinel came up to me, and gave me to understand by his gestures, accompanied by German phrases, (of which I comprehended not a word,) that I must no longer continue thus sauntering about. He seemed to fancy there was something revolutionary in the proceeding. Accordingly, I took myself off. Half an hour later I came upon one of the gates of the city, and the thought struck me that I would take a look at the neighbourhood outside. I was on the point of passing through the gateway, when my passport was asked for; I had left it at the hotel. As that necessary document was not forthcoming, I had to give up my country walk. From that day I never again separated myself from my passport. Having determined on a visit to the lake of Como,

I took good care to procure the *visé* necessary for that hour and a half's railway journey: unfortunately, though duly furnished with the *visé*, I forgot to take into account the rain, which obliged me to let two days go by before going on my trip. At length, on the third morning, a bright and sunny one, I started. About half-way, passports were asked for, and I gave up mine with the utmost confidence; five minutes afterwards the official came and told me that I must return to Milan, as my passport was not in order. The *visé*, it appeared, was only good for forty-eight hours, which had expired the evening before. I was obliged to leave the railway carriage, and was consigned to the custody of a Croat soldier—the ugliest of his race. The idea of having him as a travelling companion back to Milan led me to make a last effort to soften the official, who, after some hesitation, allowed me to go on to Como; not, however, until I had given a solemn promise, which I kept religiously, to return within three days.

In 1859, some two months after the war, what a difference! On a beautiful September day I entered Lombardy, having crossed the Swiss frontier without even showing my passport. On arriving at Milan, I found the city holding high festival. Bells were ringing, crowds filled the streets bedecked with flags, the whole population was astir. Citizens and soldiers, nobles and plebeians, municipal authorities and private persons; in a word, all, from the highest to the lowest, had a frank and joyous look. They were laughing, talking, and discussing aloud political matters. As for me, I stared, walked about, and listened. More than once I looked up at the great Cathedral to make quite sure that I was in that same Milan which had formerly worn so gloomy an aspect, each one of whose citizens seemed to have something of a conspirator's look about him. What had come over these seditious Milanese? (*ces frondeurs de Milan.*) I asked one of them the question. "To-day," said he, "are coming here the deputations from central Italy on their way to Turin, there to present to the King their votes of annexation." "Are you pleased," I asked, "to be under the government of Victor Emmanuel?" "Pleased! I should think so," replied the Milanese. Then he added, "Is not our most pressing interest the formation of a kingdom of North Italy capable of opposing Austria, unfortunately left in possession of Venetia?" We talked thus freely in the open street, on the very spot, just in front of the Palace, where I had awakened, during my first visit, the suspicions of the Austrian sentinel, while quietly contemplating the Cathedral.

The arrival of the deputations was hailed with transports of joy by the Milanese. In the evening, the city and the Cathedral were illuminated. The theatre of the Scala re-echoed with enthusiastic shouts of applause upon the appearance of the deputations. The enthusiasm was of that pure and heart-stirring kind begotten by the first inspirations of freedom newly bestowed upon a people who had long been oppressed.

The next day I presented to one or two Milanese my letters of introduction, and so had the pleasure of entering, for the first time, into Italian society. The welcome I received was full of courtesy and cordial kindness. Politics were, as might be expected, the principal, indeed almost the only, subject of conversation. Every one discussed freely and earnestly, without, however, overstepping the limits of good manners or good sense. That which struck me above all, and pleased me much, was the practical and sensible way in which the questions of the day were dealt with. I heard no propounding of abstract propositions. No one talked about the "rights of man," the origin of the social state, nor of any other of those abstractions which are well enough in philosophical disquisitions and during times of leisure. No one took interest in anything except the urgent questions of the day, such as the application of the constitutional system to Italy once emancipated. I have had many opportunities of associating with the Milanese, thanks to the charming kindness, free from all pride, which they lavish (the word is not too strong) upon foreigners whose stay is sufficiently prolonged to enable them to become acquainted with the society of Milan. My first impression has always been strengthened as regards the manner in which the Milanese treat political questions. I have joined in many discussions, some of which were very animated: the subject of them was always one of immediate and serious practical importance, such as the more or less extension of the suffrage, the relations to be established between the Church and the State, the limits of power to be accorded to the central and to local authorities, the prompt and surest remedies to be applied to brigandage. From what I have seen and heard in other parts of Italy I can affirm that it is not only in Milan that is to be found this happy tendency; rather is it a characteristic trait of the national mind. Much, therefore, may be hoped of a society which gives such proofs of good sense. It could not otherwise have effected in so short a time that which has been accomplished, and have already raised itself in no slight degree above the degradation of the past. It is a great misfortune to a nation when its statesmen and the leaders of its public opinion, instead of turning their attention to practical matters, allow themselves to be carried away by merely general theories and purely abstract questions. The Italians thoroughly understand the danger of abstractions; they seem to agree in recognising (contrary to the received opinion of some other countries) that our modern societies are not like a sheet of blank paper, on which may be written what best pleases the theorist; but rather do they resemble a contest in which the claims of rival interests, ideas, and facts, often very diverse and even opposed, must be met and adjusted by seeking to effect that which is practically best.

The general election which took place in the beginning of 1861 gave me an opportunity of seeing how the Italians fulfilled that important function of constitutional life. I was present at several public meetings preceding the day of election. The discussions were free and animated, both as regards the candidates and as to political matters generally. Similar discussions filled the public papers without any official interference of any kind whatever. I neither heard nor read anything which could shock a friend of order and liberty. Milan, containing about 250,000 inhabitants, is divided into five electoral colleges or districts, each represented by one member, and containing each from 1500 to 2000 electors.* Every college or district has several large halls or rooms, where the voting takes place. The suffrage is not universal in Italy, but limited, as in England. The National Guard was on duty at the polling places. All the electoral operations took place with the greatest regularity and amidst the most complete order. The electors voted in perfect freedom, without its being possible for any one to know for which candidate any given elector recorded his vote.† In the interior of the halls, even when full, reigned the most perfect quiet; indeed, silence was preserved almost without interruption. The general aspect of the town was as orderly as can possibly be imagined; in truth, these seditious Milanese (*ces*

* Both population and electors have increased since 1861.
† There is no nomination-day in the Italian electoral proceedings. A most complete and simple form of secret ballot is used in the parliamentary and municipal elections throughout the Italian kingdom, as was the case in Piedmont from 1848-59, under the constitution granted by King Charles Albert in March 1848. It is this same constitution which has been extended by his son and successor, Victor Emmanuel, to the whole of Italy.

frondeurs de Milan) had become the most peaceable of people. The fact is, that knowing, as I do well, what English elections are, I could not but admire the quiet, the order, and, above all, the absence of corruption which characterised the elections of Milan, and did its citizens such great honour.*

If the political state of a country, and the practical working of its political machinery, deserve special attention when seeking to form a correct idea of that country's condition; it is, nevertheless, true that there are also other subjects of the greatest importance which ought to be closely studied; as, for instance, the question of public instruction. That is a matter of the utmost importance in all countries, but especially in those which boast of being free, whose citizens have a large share in the direction of public affairs. Whoever sincerely loves free institutions ought to be the decided and active friend of popular instruction. Only by making it sound and effective, by spreading it in all directions, and by watching carefully over the spirit which directs it, can the edifice of a nation's liberties be established upon an enduring foundation. This truth has not escaped the Italians, and the Milanese especially have set themselves to practise it with an earnestness that deserves the highest praise.

The municipality of Milan appointed a commission, in 1860, composed of six very competent persons, to examine the state of popular education in

* The same is true of the general election of 1865, which the writer witnessed at Florence and in its neighbourhood.

that city, and to report upon it. That report, very detailed, and most carefully drawn up, was presented to the town-council on 6th May 1861. It showed that the number of scholars was, in 1859, 6100, and that in the beginning of 1861 they had increased to 6700; that the school accommodation had also increased in the same period from 84 school-rooms to 100; and that several of them which were not well arranged had been replaced by others which were much superior. The commissioners, whilst admitting this improvement, earnestly called the attention of the town-council to reforms still required, and to the standard which ought to be aimed at. They observed that the material condition of many schools left much to be desired; they insisted on the necessity of constructing more spacious and commodious localities, instead of hiring houses whose arrangements were but little adapted to meet the requirements of a school. They wished the salaries of the masters and mistresses to be augmented, besides giving them a regular increase of 100 francs every five years. They set forth the necessity of forming a superior school for young girls, as well as one for perfecting their education. In proposing these reforms the commission remarked that the development of instruction was the surest guarantee of the prosperity of the country; it therefore demanded, with a view to carry out such a work, that no sacrifice should be spared. The municipality hastened to follow the excellent advice of the commission, and to realise the greater part of the reforms suggested. It recast the system of instruction, and gave it fresh life by the application of the newest and most accredited methods of teaching. It still continues to push forward in the same direction. A few statistics will suffice to show what progress has been made in Milan, since 1861, in the matter of popular instruction :—

PRIMARY SCHOOLS.

	13 Boys' Schools.	9 Girls' Schools.	Total.
1862–63	4849 pupils	2986 pupils	7835
1863–64	5202 ,,	3480 ,,	8682
1864–65	5359 ,,	3645 ,,	9004

Thus, in these schools, 22 in number, (13 for boys, and 9 for girls,) there were 9004 pupils in 1864–65, as compared with 6100 in 1859 to 1860.

Milan has, besides, three schools for technical instruction, (*scoule techniche,*) a superior institution of the same character, two gymnasiums, two lyceums, and two normal schools. All these schools and institutions are free. The elementary or primary schools are maintained at the expense of the municipality, and are entirely under its control. The government bears a part of the expense of the other establishments, and has a voice in their management. There are, besides, evening schools and festival schools, (*scoule festive,*) that is, schools opened on Sundays and certain saints' days. The evening schools were first instituted in 1861 by the municipality; they are frequented by men and lads of all ages, who come for instruction after their day's work. These schools are open from the middle of October to the end of

May. The numbers attending these evening schools amounted in 1864 to 1684. The "scoule festive," or festival day schools, established towards the close of 1862, are of the same kind as the evening schools, with, however, this difference, that the former are exclusively for young girls and women of the working-classes; while the latter (the evening schools) are only for boys, lads, and men. The scholars of the festival schools assemble on Sundays and certain saints' days, from one to four in the afternoon. In 1864 the number of girls and women who took advantage of these admirable institutions amounted to 1156. The evening and festival schools are free, being maintained at the expense of the municipality, which alone has the direction and care of them.

At the close of 1864 Milan possessed not less than 44 schools, containing 200 school-rooms, 275 teachers, and 12,695 pupils, as given in the following tabular statement:—

	Class-rooms.	Teachers.	Pupils.
22 primary schools	132	162	9,004 [*]
8 evening schools	27	37	1,684
8 festival schools	22	22	1,156
3 professional schools	10	31	483
1 superior girls' school	3	8	95
1 normal school (men)	3	7	65
1 normal school (women)	3	8	208
44	200	275	12,695

[*] Two additional facts are not without interest. The numbers attending the primary, evening, and festival schools at the close of 1864 were, as given above, 11,844; in November 1865 they had increased to 13,057. The numbers attending the infant schools had increased at the same time from 1200 to 2684.

The infant schools, which depend wholly on private charity, although under government control, were seven in number in 1864, and contained 1200 children between the ages of two and six years old.

The city of Milan has increased its budget of public instruction from 100,000 francs allotted to it in 1859, to 564,000 francs in 1864. There is no town in Europe which can show a like increase for such a purpose in the same space of five years. In one of the most populous quarters of Milan, there is now constructing a vast school building, which will not cost less than one million francs. The municipality proposes to construct others to meet the wants of their city, whose scholars increase year by year. These facts and figures are striking proofs of the zeal and perseverance with which the civic authorities labour to insure and to advance the moral well-being of the people committed to their charge, as well as of the eagerness with which the Milanese take advantage of the means of instruction thus offered to them.

I did not, however, content myself with reading the reports addressed to the municipality of Milan on the subject of their popular schools. I wished to look yet more closely into them, and to examine them for myself. Thanks to the kindness of more than one member of the School Commission, I was enabled to visit several of the elementary boys' and girls' schools, and also two or three of the evening schools. I remained two, three, and sometimes even four hours in each school, hearing the pupils read, and seeing them write, listening to the lessons given in grammar and geography, and myself examining them *vivâ voce* in different branches of popular instruction. I was very satisfied with the general condition of the schools, with the progress, order, and good conduct of the scholars. Thanks to the obliging kindness of a lady inspector, I was enabled to visit twice, with her, one of the festival schools, and there, also, I could not but admire the sustained attention with which the pupils profited by the opportunity afforded them of gaining instruction.

It is not the municipality only, but some of the *élite* of the Milanese society which lends its aid to the development of popular instruction. Such participation on the part of the rich is excellent in itself, it is also a very favourable testimony to the actual state of the community, and a pledge full of hope for the future; for it is evident that if the rich thus interest themselves as regards the poor, they will understand better the desires and wants of the working classes, while the poor, on the other hand, will naturally be led to regard their wealthy fellow-citizens with kindly feelings, and will get rid of everything like distrust. The different classes of society will thus become united by the durable tie of common affection. The poor and the rich will feel themselves to be members of the same body, children of the same country, and the nation will thereby find itself stronger, more capable of internal development, and therefore more able to resist foreign aggression.*

But however great the interest which attaches to the moral progress made by Milan under the auspices of freedom, its material progress also merits attention and inquiry. The first thing which strikes all observers are the changes which have been effected in the city, and its enlargement. In one of the most populous quarters of the Lombard capital, that between the Porta Nuova and the Porta Garibaldi, large streets have been opened up which bear the names of Solferino, Ancona, Castelfidardo, and Marsala. Two new bridges, named Pioppette (Little Poplars) and Castelfidardo, have been built over the canal which surrounds the city. Not to take up time with details, I will content myself with mentioning the construction of the fine Victor Emmanuel Gallery, which is to unite the Cathedral Square with that of the Scala, and with the large and new streets adjacent to those squares. The execution of this project will sweep away the narrow and tortuous streets which encumber the centre of the city and impede the circulation of air, light, and traffic; it will at the same time make the Cathedral Square worthy of that magnificent building. The plan of this vast and useful work has been made by an architect of Bologna, Signor Mengoni; its execution

* Since 1864-65 this important work of popular education has continued to progress in every way, and bids fair to place the Milanese people high on the list of well-educated communities.

has been undertaken by an English company, which tendered for it to the municipality of Milan. On the 7th March 1865, King Victor Emmanuel laid the first stone of this magnificent gallery, which bears his name. Despite very bad weather, a great crowd was assembled, anxious to witness the inauguration of works which will make the capital of Lombardy one of the prettiest cities in Europe.* As such undertakings cannot, however, be carried on without incurring great expense, the immediate consequence of these fine projects is an increase of taxation; it must not, however, be forgotten, that they give work and occupation while increasing the circulation of money; and there is good reason for believing that under the direction of a free government they will have the effect of rendering more brilliant the future of Milan.

Within the last five years the number of hotels, inns, and restaurants has been doubled. Since 1863 one of the finest railway stations on the Continent has been opened. A handsome new street, named Prince Humbert, now, leads from this terminus into the city, piercing the old ramparts near the public gardens, which have been much extended and improved since 1859. The Museum of Natural History, which faces one side of the gardens, has also been greatly enlarged during the last two or three years. In this neighbourhood are forming the new streets

* The gallery has since been completed, and is certainly the handsomest construction of the kind in the world.

Montebello, Parini, and Carlo Porta, the latter so called after the Milanese poet of that name.*

The abolition of the petty internal custom-houses which, by their thousand vexations, formerly impeded the development of Italy's material interests, and the great extension of the network of Italian railways since 1859, have given everywhere to the internal commerce of the Peninsula an activity hitherto unknown. Milan has naturally had its share of the general benefit; still it is difficult to find exact data as to the progress which has been made by the commerce and industry of the city. I have only been able to get at comparatively few details worthy of notice in the documents, only too few in number, relative to the commerce of Milan. In the report of the civil administration laid before the communal council on the 28th November 1864, it is said that the produce of the house tax had yielded 19,693 francs more in 1864 than in the previous year. This increase came from the additional number of houses, whose rental had increased by 613,259 francs between 1863 and 1864. The produce of the taxes upon the commerce of the city had also augmented, the matters subject to impost having yielded about one million of francs more in the latter than in the former year. It was absolutely the same in the case of all the other taxes, and this result was due to the mere increase of commodities subject to taxation, for (at the time

* This paragraph was accidentally omitted in the original article.

referred to, 1863 and 1864) the taxes themselves had undergone no change whatever.

Another document, the report of the Milan Chamber of Commerce, especially pointed out the unexpected extension of the spirit of association since 1860. It signalled the formation of six joint-stock companies, and of five limited liability companies, in the province of Lombardy. One of these societies deserves special mention, namely, the one formed for the construction of dwellings for the working classes, and for the building of public baths and wash-houses. Established in 1861, with a capital of 350,000 francs, which has since been augmented, it has already constructed working men's houses to the value of 500,000 francs. These dwellings are situated in the new streets of San Fermo and Montebello, and form in great part the new square which bears the latter name. The object of the society is to give the working classes commodious and clean house accommodation at a moderate rent. According to its statutes, the society cannot declare a dividend of more than 4 per cent. All monies accruing over and above that profit must be employed in the construction of new dwellings destined to the same object. This society has already made much more than 4 per cent., and has been most successful in every way. Benefit or Mutual Aid Societies have also grown in numbers and importance during the last few years. These inestimable associations (which anticipate distress, which tend to produce and propagate habits of economy and saving, and which establish the happiest bonds of union between individuals and families) are now so general that the report of the Chamber of Commerce for 1863 says, that almost all the persons belonging to the classes who live by personal or manual labour have become members of one or other of these societies.

Freedom has thus assured to Milan material as well as moral progress. It has not less contributed to develop those charming and pleasant social relations which are nowhere more agreeable than in the capital of Lombardy. Thus the stranger finds in Milanese society a kindness which never fails, a cordial and unaffected hospitality. There is, however, one reproach to which the Milanese lay themselves open. The richest and the most aristocratic among them have the disagreeable habit of using generally and constantly in ordinary conversation the common patois or dialect of the country. That the people should converse in it is no matter of surprise; that is the case in all countries. Now, this dialect is composed either of barbarous words peculiar to itself, or of words belonging to the beautiful Italian language, which are mangled and horribly disfigured. The educated classes of cities like Turin and Milan, which justly boast of being at the head of the Italian movement, will do well to follow the example of good society in Naples, and leave the patois or dialect of the country to porters and uneducated peasants. Is it indeed asking too much to beg of the Milanese to banish from amongst them this last badge of the divisions and bondage of Italy, and henceforth to use only their rich national tongue, that almost divine language, the sweetest and the most musical spoken by any European community? Let my good friends of Milan pardon me for being so outspoken, for I cannot consent to keep back either praise or blame. I can, however, most truly say, that never shall I forget the many and happy days which I have spent in their midst; above all, those bright hours of peace and joy in which Milan first tasted the ennobling pleasures of freedom.

II.

It was during that same autumn of 1859, in which I had seen Milan so full of attraction and life, that I found only sadness and silence in Venice. It appeared like a city of the dead. Its people mourned in bitterness of heart the vanished hope of freedom—a freedom that seemed already within their grasp. An incident which occurred at the time paints to the life the condition of Venice in the summer of 1859.

There lived together a Venetian widow and her son, whom his mother loved tenderly. Her only cause of anxiety was the fear of his getting into trouble with the Austrian government, for the young man was an ardent patriot. The poor woman had so often beheld the hopes of Venice vanish away, that she had almost ceased to believe in the deliverance of her country. When her son told her of hopeful signs, she shook her head sadly, and contented herself with praying in silence for her beloved and unfortunate Venice. The great events of the spring and summer of 1859 kindled anew the ardour of the young man. It is easy to imagine with what animation he related to his mother every particle of news which reached him during that eventful period. Still she believed not; it seemed too good to be true. At length, one day the son came rushing into his mother's room, and cried, "Come, mother, come quickly! from a neighbouring roof I will show you the fleet of our deliverers, the flag of France!" They hastened forth, and when, in the far distance, the poor woman saw the French men-of-war, she raised to heaven her eyes full of tears, and said: "Merciful God, I thank thee! at length I believe indeed in the deliverance of my beloved Venice." The next day came the news of that peace which left Venice to Austria.

Who on that account has a right to blame France? If France did not do all she promised in 1859, she yet did much. To speak plainly, we are still too near those unequal contests, sustained by Poland and Denmark abandoned to their fate, to give an Englishman the right to blame France for not having completed the work she undertook in 1859. At any rate, she spent both blood and treasure for the Italian cause. If I have narrated, as I heard it, the little story given above, it is with the sole object of showing how bitter was the disappointment of Venice, and how deep still is her grief.

Of all the Italians whom I have known, the Venetians are those who display most patience. It is they above all whom I have heard say: "Let not Italy risk everything upon the stroke of some rash attempt; we know that our king and our brothers will not fail to come to our aid when a propitious occasion presents itself, when strikes the appointed hour." The Venetians are right. If young and ardent patriots occasionally throw themselves into a hopeless struggle against their oppressors, that is no cause for wonder; but the more experienced and sensible among them ought to use all their influence to prevent such mistakes being committed, for mistakes they are. Venetians, one and all, ought to reserve themselves for the last great effort which, one day or another, will assuredly bring with it the triumph of the Italian cause.

The general aspect of Venice at the present time (1865) is of the saddest; its population wears a sombre look, and there is a singular absence of young men. It is to be accounted for by the fact that thousands of the young generation have quitted their country in order to settle in the Italian kingdom, whose army numbers some 14,000 Venetians in its ranks. Along the Grand Canal and elsewhere, the palaces fall more and more into ruin, and can be bought at a very low price. Everything indicates a decaying city. The beautiful old palace of the Foscari is turned into a barrack, an ample proof of the amount of respect felt by Austrian rulers for the great memories of the past, so dear to Venetian hearts. The ancient Queen of the Adriatic has become one of the most mournful cities in Europe.

The carnival is now but a thing of the past. Since 1859, operas, illuminations, and balls have disappeared. Festivities find no place in public or in private life. The only demonstrations which interrupt the national mourning are those by which the Venetians protest against the rule of the Germans. Sometimes they take an amusing form; as when, for example, the pigeons of St Mark are seen, some fine morning, flying about with tricoloured wings, to the great scandal of the Austrians. The Venetians have invented various ingenious modes of celebrating the national fêtes of Italy; such as the birthday of King Victor Emmanuel, the giving of the Italian constitution, the celebration of the victories of Magenta and Solferino. Sometimes fireworks displaying the Italian tricolour shoot across the evening sky from one place or another; sometimes the early dawn reveals upon the walls placards in which the Venetians hail Victor Emmanuel as their king, offer him their homage, or express their sympathy and good-will to their brother Italians. Thereupon the Austrian police take the field in hot haste; ladders, poles, pails of water, are brought quickly to bear on the obnoxious placards; they are mercilessly attacked, and ere long utterly destroyed.

The Venetian character is naturally open and good-humoured. In the cafés, at balls, fêtes, and places of public resort, strangers easily made acquaintance with the inhabitants of Venice. Now all is changed. The Venetians regard with suspicion those whom they do not know. Such a change is by no means astonishing; for spies are to be found everywhere plying their vile trade under a thousand disguises. Before 1859 they covered the whole of Italy, with the exception of Piedmont; to-day unhappy Venetia alone is left to them, and there they literally swarm. It is therefore very difficult to examine, on the spot, the condition of Venice. The authorities are always on the watch; and any stranger who prosecuted inquiries, and frequented Venetian society (or rather the ghost of it which still survives), would not be allowed to remain long in the city.

I cannot describe better the state of Venice than by saying that it is exactly that of Milan previous to 1859; the same tyranny and the same hatred, the same suspicion on one side, and the same irritation on the other; the same absolute separation at all times, and in all places, between the Austrians and the Venetians; the oppressors and the oppressed. Often have I heard from the traveller just come from Venice such language as the following:—" How beautiful are the Venetian buildings and remains! but what a city of the dead! how miserable it must be to live there!" Such exclamations are naturally uttered by every one who visits such admirable specimens of art, in a city which suffers the bitter degradation of servitude. I will, however, cease to dwell upon such sentimental sorrows, and proceed to show from facts and material results what is the condition of Venice. Their testimony is yet more convincing than the voice of complaint.

A recent report of the Venetian Chamber of Commerce gives, in Austrian florins, the value of the exports and the imports of the port of Venice from 1860 to 1864. The Austrian florin is as nearly as possible two francs and a half. The report is dated 31st January 1865, and gives the following returns:—

	Imports.	Exports.
1860	48,864,500 florins	21,233,220 florins
1861	39,145,189 ,,	16,982,508 ,,
1862	33,359,948 ,,	12,945,225 ,, .
1863	28,346,973 ,,	13,245,641 ,,
1864*	26,108,012 ,,	12,822,272 ,,

Amongst the trades which contributed, according to the report of January 1865, to this great decay of Venetian commerce, that of glass manufacture must be specially mentioned. The president of the Chamber of Commerce, speaking of it, says:—"This industry falls off notably, and is in danger of complete ruin, unless the government comes to its rescue." The same is true of other branches of industry and commerce; as, for instance, soaps, jewellery, and hardware, metals wrought and unwrought, colonial produce and drugs, cheeses, and animals for butcher's meat. There are, however, some exceptions to this general decline, as in the case of the wood trade, colours and colouring material, hemp and cordage.

* In 1865 and 1866 the imports and exports were :—

	Imports.	Exports.
1865	22,596,102 florins	12,741,044 florins
1866	22,184,750 ,,	12,482,222 ,,

This latter year (1866) was the last of Austrian rule, as the Austrians evacuated Venice 19th October 1866.

The Venetian Chamber of Commerce also published in January 1865 a report of the number and tonnage of the vessels which entered and cleared out from the port of Venice from 1859 to 1864. These statistics are an irrefutable proof of the ruin which appears in store for this unhappy city. The President of the Venetian Chamber of Commerce says:—
" From the war of 1859 dates a period of decay in Venice so rapid, that it is probably impossible to find a like example in the history of our commerce."

VESSELS ENTERED.*

	1859.	1860.	1861.	1862.	1863.	1864.
Vessels	4,581	4,250	3,788	3,382	3,292	3,123
Tonnage	537,285	436,416	364,792	332,413	312,275	301,337

VESSELS CLEARED OUT.*

Vessels	4,466	4,251	3,756	3,295	3,241	3,093
Tonnage	519,241	450,980	375,015	336,483	310,968	303,539

Thus, in five years there has been a diminution of 1458 vessels and 235,948 tons entry; and of 1373 vessels and 215,702 tons of exit. While Venice†

* In 1865 and 1866 there were—

	1865.	1866.
Vessels entered	3,078	2,866
Tonnage	291,679	304,696
Vessels cleared out	3,101	2,813
Tonnage	296,416	299,329

The Venetian coasting and river trade, which in 1858 was valued at 36,000,000 florins, had fallen in 1865 to 15,600,000 florins.

† The following facts and statistics given by a correspondent of the *Indépendance Belge*, of the 3d May 1866, are worth recording: " Venice has a population of about 118,000, and a garrison of about 8000 or 9000. It is a free port, and the capital of a province of

MILAN AND VENICE SINCE THE WAR OF 1859. 27

has had such cruel losses inflicted upon it, Genoa has doubled its commerce in six years, and the port of Naples is not sufficient for its growing trade.

Though the resources of Venice diminish, its taxes grow heavier. Savings banks and benefit societies are few and far between in Venetia ; no wonder, therefore, that want increases. Austria maintains herself in that province by means of an army of 150,000 men resting on the famous Quadrilateral. The fortifications of Venice itself have been considerably augmented since the war of 1859. The Venetian territory has been covered with numerous strategic works. The necessity of being always on the watch produces in Austria financial difficulties of the most serious kind. The fact is, that Venetia is a heavy burden upon the government of Vienna—a burden which is exhausting the resources of the empire. Without Venetia, every one knows, even at Vienna, that Austria would be without doubt richer and stronger, for she would be able to reduce considerably both her army and her expenditure. Indeed, if the true frontier between Italy and Austria, that of the Alps,

2,500,000 inhabitants. . . . Do you wish some statistics which will show you better than all arguments the decay of this city, which ought to be a centre of pleasure and business, and which might have increased visibly since Italy is free, just as Naples and Milan have increased in population and riches ? I will take an article of daily consumption (butcher's meat), and I will compare the statistics of 1860 and 1865 :—

	1860.		1865.
Imports	3,489,356 florins	...	1,897,348 florins
Exports	394,410 ,,	...	266,727 ,,
Consumption	3,094,946 ,,	...	1,630,621 ,,

Is it necessary to enumerate the miseries hidden beneath these figures ?"

were wisely accepted in accordance with the natural order of things, not only would an end at once be put to the hostility which exists between the two countries, but there would, moreover, spring up between them a trade equally beneficial to both. Austria could thus at a single stroke diminish her military expenditure and augment her commerce. Now, on the contrary, Italy (who if mistress of her national territory would be occupied solely with the development of her agriculture and industry) is ever on the look-out for an opportunity by which to set Venetia free; she holds herself ready to rise whenever an offer to aid her in that work is made by an enemy of Austria. How everything would be changed if this latter power undid, of her own accord, the chains of Venice, which weigh so heavily on Austria herself! Much indeed is said of the strategic necessity which obliges Austria to hold the line of the Mincio, and the Germans themselves not unfrequently assert it. Such a pretension is altogether exaggerated, and on the part of Austria it is a mistaken idea. The Italians number, with Rome and Venetia included, about 25,000,000; the German confederation numbers 44,000,000; Austria, without Venetia, 32,000,000. Between these German and Italian lands rises the barrier of the Alps. It is really impossible to discuss seriously the claim made by the stronger power, to possess on the other side of that great Alpine barrier a province naturally belonging to its weaker neighbour, on the ground of the danger to which the former and stronger power would be exposed, by the province in question belonging to the latter and weaker power.

If, on the other hand, the question of right be examined, it must be remembered that the possession of Venetia by Austria has its origin in the iniquitous act committed at Campo Formio in 1797 by the first Napoleon, at that time the republican general of revolutionary France. The Congress of Vienna but re-enacted the selfsame injustice when it permitted Austria to seize again upon Venetia in 1815. Moreover it must not be forgotten that the Austrian and English generals, when they sought in 1813 to raise Italy against Napoleon, actually declared in their proclamations to the Italian people, that the allies wished only to deliver Italy "from the iron yoke of Bonaparte, and to restore her to herself." Assuredly, then, Venetians and Italians have good reason to protest; assuredly right is on their side—right as clear as ever appealed to the tribunal of public opinion.

Treaties and right of possession forsooth! Is this indeed the moment (1865) for Austria and her friends to make use of like arguments? Where are the treaties which bound Holstein and Schleswig to Denmark? The possession of those provinces by the Danish monarchy is numbered, not by tens, but by hundreds of years. Are these ancient title-deeds of Denmark to the possession of the Duchies of the Elbe inferior to those of Austria touching Venice, which had their origin in an act of modern injustice committed by the republican general of a revolutionary power? Is the manner in which the Danish government has treated the Duchies alleged against Denmark? Certainly that government has not been without its faults; but any one who reflects upon what the government of Vienna has done, and still continues to do, in Hungary and Italy, can see nothing but a cruel mockery in the idea of Austria's sending an army to deliver Schleswig and Holstein from Danish rule. Those who wish to know how that great German power acts in its non-German provinces, let them make themselves acquainted with the trial known as the "procès Saint-Georges,"* which took place in Venetia in the summer of 1862; or with the cause which led to the imprisonment of those Venetian ladies, Mesdames Labia, Calvi, and Montalban. Before playing the liberator on the banks of the Eider, would not Austria do well to renounce her work of oppression on the banks of the Mincio? The fact is that, so long as she insists upon holding Venetia, so long will she be relatively weak,

---

* In the summer of 1862 the police arrested at Verona a traveller going to Turin, and seized upon him a paper attributed to the famous secret Venetian committee. The names of 40 persons were on the list, 35 being those of respectable citizens, nobles, men of business, and lawyers, the other five were simple miscreants. Englishmen will hardly believe the truth of this affair, but it is simply this, that the traveller seized was no other than one of the Austrian police, disguised for the purpose, and the paper a forgery. The accused were tried, not before a civil, but a military tribunal. The spirit in which the proceedings were carried on may be judged by the shameful means used to begin them. After several months of trial and captivity, the accusation broke down in the case of all but five, two of whom were finally acquitted on a second trial before the superior military tribunal, and three condemned to 10, 12, and 16 years in irons; they left for the fortress of Lubiana in February 1864. Such was this famous case known as the "procès

so long will her policy be vacillating and inconsistent. It is only by disencumbering herself of such a dead weight as Venice, and by coming to terms with Hungary, as she seems inclined to do at present, that Austria can become truly constitutional and really strong. Argument, right, and interest, even that of Austria herself, plead in favour of a plan which shall separate Venetia from the government of Vienna. Such separation is the only reasonable method that can be employed for putting an end to the actual suffering, and even the material decay of Venice. With regard to the proposal of Austria, that this Italian province should send representatives to the Reichsrath of Vienna, it will ever receive the same refusal as would be given by the people of Innspruck to a proposal on the part of the Italian government to send representatives to the parliament of Florence. As for the writer, having himself seen Milan rejoicing in her freedom, and Venice mourning in grief and misery, he cannot but express

---

Saint-Georges," of which fuller details are given in a publication entitled "La Venetie en 1864," published in Paris, by L. Hachette et Cie. But it was upon the spot, in Venetia itself, that the author of the publication referred to informed himself of this and other facts, which prove how deplorable is the state of this Italian province, and how oppressive is the rule of its foreign taskmasters. The gentler sex also come in for a share of the delights of Austrian rule. The Countess Labia, having gone to mass in St Mark's dressed in mourning on the 6th of June, the anniversary of Cavour's death, was arrested. She refused to pay the fine imposed for this high crime and misdemeanour, and was therefore punished with imprisonment. Madame Calvi and the Countess of Montalban have undergone the same punishment after a trial which seems to have formed a pendant to the one described above as originating in the seizure of one of the Austrian police disguised as a traveller.

his ardent desire that the hour of deliverance may speedily come to the ancient city of the Doges—that hour when her people, freed from a foreign yoke, shall celebrate with boundless joy the union of Venice to Italy.

The principal features of the contrast offered by the actual condition (1865) of these two Italian cities (Milan and Venice) have now been laid before the reader. In the former of these two capitals is to be seen a contented and prosperous population earnestly labouring to develop all that constitutes their moral and material welfare. The increase of commerce, the construction of new houses, hotels, streets, and public buildings; the formation of several new societies for carrying out useful public undertakings,—all attest present prosperity as well as confidence in the future. Schools are multiplied, and pupils flock to them; benefit societies, whose object is at once appreciated by the working classes, spring up in various parts. Such are the sure signs of real progress. The municipality of Milan, freely elected, displays the most praiseworthy activity, in accordance with the desire of its constituents. Political elections are carried on in perfect freedom, accompanied with the utmost order. Complete liberty is allowed to the press as well as to public meetings. At the same time it would be difficult to find a city where the general security is greater, where the police and administration are better. Its inhabitants are ready to make all the sacrifices demanded by their country's necessities. Their devotion to the great national work, to-day being carried on throughout Italy, and their attachment to her honest king, knows no limits. Such is the actual condition of the Lombard capital, which Austria found so difficult to govern and so impossible to satisfy. Never has constitutional liberty gained a more complete or striking victory.

But Venice! Not only are the signs of prosperity wanting, but at every step are to be seen the saddest proofs of decay. Palaces are falling into ruin, commerce diminishes year by year, as does also the number of vessels entering and leaving the port; primary education hardly exists, beggary and theft continually increase. The population is united in a common hatred against the foreign government which rules. In vain does that government offer to Venice a participation in the new Austrian system, inaugurated by the patent of February 1861; she will have none of it; she only asks that the foreigner should quit her territory. So long as he remains there the Venetians will never cease to show their abhorrence of the government of the Emperor Francis Joseph, and their attachment to that of King Victor Emmanuel. Neither the menaces nor the offers of Austria will ever produce any effect on the unanimous resolution of the Venetians. Seized upon by an act of crying injustice, held down by force, plunged in misery, Venice is at once a shame and a weakness to Austria. So long as this union, which violates every principle of justice, is maintained, so long will it continue to bear the same bitter fruit.

Let us suppose for a moment that the war of 1859

had restored Venice to freedom, that she had been, like Milan, united to the mother country, or at least to a constitutional kingdom of North Italy. In that case, would not the Venetians have made the same progress and accomplished the same reforms as the Milanese? Would not popular schools have seen the number of their pupils increase year by year? Would not new schools have been erected to satisfy the popular demand? Would not the municipality of Venice have done its utmost, like that of Milan, to push forward the work of instruction so worthy of a free people, and so absolutely necessary to their welfare? Would it not have furthered public works for the material improvement of the city? Would there not have been formed in Venetia, as in Lombardy, various joint-stock and limited companies for carrying out enterprises of public utility? Under a free national government, would not the commerce of the port of Venice have increased, as has been the case with Genoa and Naples?

Perhaps the enemies of Italy will reply that the Venetians are too frivolous, too little united among themselves for such a result to be probable; that they are only capable of vexing and embarrassing their Austrian rulers, but by no means worthy of liberty; that they are wholly incapable of self-government and of prospering under a system of freedom. The first argument that suggests itself in answer to such allegations is, that all this was said of the Milanese previous to 1859;—whereas the facts contained in this essay touching Milan prove how completely those who made such assertions were mistaken. But there is something more to be added in reply—it is this: that Venice gave proof of what she was capable before 1859; that it is not so very long since she manifested to the world what she was, and what she could do when mistress of herself. From March 1848 to August 1849 the Venetians became free, after having endured for fifty years a foreign yoke. What use did this people, now accused of frivolity and effeminacy, make of that brief period of independence? They began by selecting as their chief a citizen of Venice, who united political intelligence to the noblest natural qualities—Daniel Manin. His government was one of freedom at home, while displaying both diligence and ability in the presence of foreign complications. Is there need to recall the heroic defence which terminated that short but memorable period of Venetian liberty? Assuredly a people who have achieved such things have sufficiently proved that they are worthy of freedom. If they could act thus in the midst of a revolution, after half a century of bondage, what will they not do under a national government which shall bestow upon them all the blessings of order and of liberty?

There is yet another fact which strikingly proves that the Venetians are capable, now as ever, of making sacrifices for their country's cause. Some 12,000 or 14,000 of them have exiled themselves, despite all the efforts of the Austrian authorities, and have enrolled themselves in the ranks of the Italian army. At the same time, Austria obliges the province to furnish its contingent to the Austrian army. Thus Venetia undergoes a double conscription — the one obligatory, the other of her own free will for the cause of Italy. And yet there are persons who blindly maintain that the Venetians are degenerated, and are unworthy of liberty; that Italians will not fight, that their country is a land of the dead. In answer to such accusations we point, on the one hand, to those proofs of vitality still to be found in Venice, enthralled though she be, and, on the other, to Milan, to-day in the full enjoyment of freedom. Let the friends of Italy take courage. Venice remains worthy of a better future; she awaits without faltering that day which shall yet realise the prediction of Manzoni :—

> "Non fia loco ove sorgan barriere
> Tra l'Italia e l'Italia, mai più!"

> "No more shall any spot be found where barriers rise to sever Italian from Italian soil—henceforth, for ever!"

Let me be permitted to add one word more, after having thus expressed my confidence in the future of Venice. An Englishman thus praising the work which is to-day being accomplished in Italy, might fairly be accused of injustice if he did not recognise the great share which France has had in bringing about that result. Doubtless she did not intervene in the war of 1859, declared by Austria against Piedmont, in order to form a single nation out of the different states of which Italy was composed. France only wished to construct, against the return of Austria, the barrier of a kingdom of North Italy. But was not even that an immense benefit to Italy, a real triumph for the cause of liberty and right? Where would Italy and Piedmont be to-day if France had given in 1859 only the aid of words and despatches, the effects of which were made manifest in the case of Poland and of Denmark? If that only had been done, would not Italy still mourn to-day as Poland mourns? Would not Piedmont have suffered the same misfortunes as Denmark, despite that admirable Piedmontese army which did such good service in the Crimea, but which was numerically so small as was that of Denmark? Thanks to France, such misfortunes have been averted. Her part in the creation of Italian liberty has then been so noble, that England should cordially recognise it, and support with earnest sympathy the work thus begun.

June 1868.

The writer has great pleasure in placing at the end of this translation of his article, published in the *Revue des Deux Mondes* of 1st October 1865, the following interesting letter signed A. H. L., and inserted in the London *Times* of 27th February 1868. It bears testimony to the moral and material progress which has already commenced in Venice since the departure of the Austrians in October 1866. The friends of Italy will hail with joy this promise of a brighter future, this dawn of a happier day; as yet, indeed, but "a day of small things," still assuredly a day not to be despised.

TO THE EDITOR OF "THE TIMES."

27th February 1868.

"SIR,—You and your correspondents in Italy have, of late, passed severe, though perhaps not unmerited strictures, upon the Italian Government and upon the Italian Chambers. But let us be just to the Italian people. I need not point out the singular moderation and good sense which they have shown in times of great difficulty and under grave provocation. You have done them full justice in this respect. I am desirous of calling your attention to the social and moral progress which is taking place in Italy, and which is less known to your readers, as it is with political matters that your correspondents are naturally most concerned. For the last two months I have been residing in Venice, and an acquaintance with persons of all classes in that city has enabled me to collect a few facts upon this subject which, in justice to the Venetians, should be made known.

"Since the departure of the Austrians, in the autumn of 1866, schools have been opened by the municipality in all the parishes of the city, and are now frequented by about 3800 children of both sexes. Other schools will be speedily added. Sunday-schools, for girls who cannot attend on week-days, and infant schools, have also been established. An institution for the education of female teachers already contains ninety pupils. Night schools have been founded by gentlemen connected with the liberal professions in the eight districts of Venice. The municipality has since undertaken to support some of them. They are divided into inferior and superior schools, and are attended by nearly 2000 pupils, including about 1000 adults, working-men who resort to them after their day's labour. The most distinguished professors of Venice give gratuitous lessons there every evening, and the progress made by the mechanics is most remarkable. The schools are admirably conducted, the rooms large, clean, and well-aired.

"A reading-room, open every evening, and a lending library in connexion with it, for the benefit of working-men and poor prisoners, was established about eight months ago in the quarter of San Giovanni Laterano. Members pay the small entrance-fee of one halfpenny (five centesimi). The books are lent for fifteen days, and are well selected, including translations from the works of J. S. Mill, Smiles, Ellis, Chambers, Macaulay, &c. Above 1500 volumes had been lent at the end of the year, and among the applicants for them were members of all the different trades, and many common soldiers.

"Two co-operative stores, upon the English system, have been opened for working-men. Shares, representing something more than £300, have been taken up by 450 associates, and the experiment is answering so well that other shops are to be opened in different parts of the city.

"People's banks, upon the German system, and savings banks, have also been founded.

"A technical school, in which instruction is given in the various branches of science, including political economy, has been established in the old convent of San Giovanni Laterano, and is furnished with laboratories and scientific collections. It is frequented by a large number of pupils, some of whom assist the professor in teaching reading, writing, and arithmetic to evening classes of adults. A technical school of commerce, on a large scale, including instruction in the commercial laws of all countries, and in the languages of Europe and the East, is about to be opened in the Palazzo Foscari.

"The societies for mutual help (benefit societies) which existed during the Austrian rule, but which were then only allowed to squander their money in masses, funerals, and festivities, are being reorganised and turned to good and useful purposes. Already several of the corporations—such as the gilders, carpenters, smiths, &c.—have formed themselves into such societies, and have placed themselves under statutes framed upon the English model. They include, at present, about 2700 working-men.

"There are gratuitous evening lectures for the people, in which the principal professors of Venice lecture upon political economy and other branches of science, and read the best Italian classics, illustrating and explaining them by commentaries on history, constitutional law, and public economy.

"The foundation of all these institutions is due to the professors and representatives of the middle class in Venice, and the names of Dr Errera and Professors Luzzatti, Namias, and Gera deserve special mention in connexion with them. They have received of late the support of the municipality. It would be well for them and for their country if the inheritors of the great historic names of the Venetian Republic, who form the upper or aristocratic class of Venice, were to think less of frivolous amusements, and to associate themselves heartily with the promotion of these good works.

"I may mention that a company has been formed for building docks upon a large scale in Venice, and that negotiations are in progress for the establishment of a line of steamers between the city and Alexandria, and other parts of the East. Other projects for the development of the resources and for the improvement of Venice are being carried out, under the direction of the active and public-spirited prefect, Signor Torelli.

"The progress which I have described as taking place in Venice extends to other cities and towns in Italy, especially in the north. All this has been done in the first year of liberty. Scarcely twelve months ago, any attempt to introduce real knowledge among the people, and to improve their condition, would have been treated by the Austrian rulers of Venice as a political crime. Dr Errera was condemned to ten years' imprisonment—two and a half of which he had passed in solitary confinement, when he was liberated on the transfer of the Italian provinces—mainly for attempting to introduce those institutions which he has now helped to establish.

"That there is discontent in Italy—discontent with the manner in which the affairs of the country are administered—there can be no doubt. With a perfectly free press and absolute liberty of speech, that discontent finds ample expression; but those who imagine that there is any desire on the part of the Italians to return to their old divisions, and to give up that national unity which alone can make them a great people, altogether mistake the popular feeling. It may suit the French, who are naturally irritated at seeing a young nation enjoying those liberties of which they have been deprived, to misrepresent the present state of feeling in Italy; but there is no Italian, except the veriest boor of the Neapolitan provinces, who would not spurn with indignation the suggestion of returning to that miserable priestly and political tyranny which has reduced Italy to the condition of ignorance and degradation from which she is now surely, though slowly, emerging. The choice is not now between a united Italy and a divided Italy, but between monarchy and republicanism. The decision of the Italian people will depend upon the patriotism and wisdom of Italian statesmen, and not a little upon the policy of France.—Your obedient servant,

"A. H. L."

ITALY, VENICE, AND AUSTRIA.*

Reprinted from the "Westminster Review" for 1st July 1866.

1. *Recueil des Traités, Conventions, et Actes Diplomatiques concernant l'Autriche et l'Italie.* 1703-1859. AMYOT, Editeur, Rue de la Paix, Paris.
2. *Documents et Pièces Authentiques laissés* par DANIEL MANIN, Président de la République de Venise. *Traduits sur les Originaux et Annotés* par MME. PLANAT DE LA FAYE. Furne et Cie, Editeurs. Paris. 2 vols.
3. *Mémoires de Daniel Manin.* Par M. HENRI MARTIN. Furne et Cie, Editeurs. Paris.
4. *La Vénétie en* 1864. Librairie de L. Hatchette et Cie. Paris.
5. *La Prima Legislatura del Regno d'Italia; Studii e Ricordi di Leopoldo Galeotti, Deputato al Parlamento.* Firenze. 1865.

THE condition of Italy during the first half of the present century seemed to forbid the idea of its ever becoming one united kingdom. Yet not only

* This article was completed just before the actual commencement of hostilities between Prussia and Austria in June 1866.

has such a kingdom been formed, but it has received official recognition from all the governments of the world, with but one exception. The work is not, however, completed, inasmuch as portions of the Italian soil are still in the possession of foreign powers. Its completion is the one engrossing object to which all the efforts of the statesmen and people of Italy are alike directed. They aim avowedly at excluding all foreign rule and influence from the Peninsula, substituting in their place a purely national government, presided over by a sovereign of the nation's choice.

The more closely this important work is examined, the clearer does it become that it alone offers a reasonable hope of bestowing upon Italy the blessings of order and of freedom, increasing thereby most materially the general security and peace of Europe. This may be shown both by the failure of French supremacy in Italy, under the first Napoleon, to attain these objects, and also by the yet more signal failure of Austrian supremacy, which succeeded to that of Imperial France. It is yet further proved by the results which have sprung since 1859 from the formation of the Italian Constitutional Monarchy. Results obtained, despite the innumerable difficulties arising from the continuation of the Austrian rule in Venetia, and from the intricate problems involved in the solution of the Roman question.

From the commencement of the present century up to the year 1814 the supremacy of France was established throughout Italy in one form or another by the Emperor Napoleon. The introduction of his celebrated code of laws and a generally enlightened system of government did much to improve the condition of the country. But the burdens of the conscription and of heavy taxes (not with a view to national freedom, but for the prosecution of wars arising from the insatiable ambition of the Emperor), rendered the Italians weary of a rule which was after all but that of a foreign power. The other nations of Europe viewed this *de facto* possession of Italy by France as unjust in itself and as dangerously increasing French preponderance. Nor can this discontent of Italy and of Europe be deemed other than just and natural.

Upon the fall of Napoleon, the treaties of Vienna professed to undo that which had been done in Italy by the French revolutionary wars and those of the empire. The Neapolitan Bourbons were restored to the thrones of Naples and Sicily. The Papal authority was re-established throughout the States of the Church. The house of Hapsbourg-Lorraine was reinstated in Tuscany. The kingdom of Sardinia, incorporated into the French empire by Napoleon, again appeared as an independent state. Lombardy was replaced under the sway of Austria.

To this general rule of restoring the old order of things, an exception, deserving particular notice, was made in the case of Venice. For centuries she had been an independent republic, and was so still in 1796, when Bonaparte commanded the French republican armies in Northern Italy. Having revolutionised the Venetian government, he established over it a so-called

Protectorate. In the following year he handed over Venice and all her territory, as far as the Adige, to Austria, by the treaty of Campo-Formio, which was signed on the 17th October 1797. His government had, in a despatch dated the 29th September, expressly ordered him not to give up Venice to Austria, and had spoken of the "shame of abandoning" to that power the Queen of the Adriatic. The Directory, however, after some hesitation, ratified this act of their general, who thus, to suit his own purpose, blotted out the old republic from the map of Europe, and incorporated her with the Austrian empire.

Again, by the treaty of Presbourg, in 1805, Napoleon separated Venice and all its territory from Austria, and so united Venetia to that northern Italian kingdom, over which he placed, as viceroy, his stepson, Eugène Beauharnais.

Had the statesmen assembled at Vienna in 1815 been true to their own principle of undoing the work of their arch-enemy Napoleon, they would have restored, if not the Venetian republic, at least an independent state of Venice. Instead of doing so, they united Venice to Lombardy, thereby creating the Lombardo-Venetian kingdom, which they gave to Austria. Thus the republic of Venice was once again incorporated with that empire, and thus the statesmen who framed the treaties of Vienna renewed the flagrant act of robbery and injustice perpetrated at Campo-Formio by Bonaparte, of whose system they professed to be the uncompromising opponents.

This policy was rendered the more obviously unjust

by the language addressed to the Italians in December 1813, and in March 1814, by the allied Austrian and English generals, who, while then endeavouring to drive the French from Italy, sought to win the Italians to their standard. The Austrian general, Count Nugent, commences his proclamation, "To the peoples of Italy," dated Ravenna, 10th December 1813, with these words: "You have been sufficiently oppressed,—you have groaned beneath a yoke of iron. Our armies are come into Italy for your deliverance!" In his enthusiasm for Italian freedom he does not hesitate to add further on the following sentence: "You must all become an independent nation." General Bentinck, the commander of the English forces, in his proclamation dated Leghorn, 14th March 1814, declares, amongst other things, that "we do not ask you to come to us; we ask you to make good your own rights, and to be free!"

Yet the Austrian and English statesmen at Vienna, when they had full possession of Italy, disregarded those stirring promises of independence and freedom addressed by the generals of their allied sovereigns to the Italians, re-enacted Bonaparte's violent spoliation of Venice, and riveted at Vienna the chains forged at Campo-Formio. Thus were broken the promises of liberty held out to Italians when the allies sought to rouse them to arms against the French; and thus the special defenders of legitimist principles endorsed the lawless wrong of France's revolutionary general.

Surely these facts must have escaped the memories of English writers and speakers, when, after the conclusion of the war of 1859, they made Napoleon III. the object of their sarcasms and attacks, because he failed to carry out *his* promise to free Italy from the "Alps to the Adriatic."

The Congress of Vienna effected, in fact, no other change in Italy than that of substituting for the rule of Napoleon the supremacy of Austria. Lombardy and Venetia were now hers. Entrenched within the famous Quadrilateral, her will was law to the petty Italian courts, each of whom aped the manners and customs of their powerful brethren of the Holy Alliance. Such was the result brought about by the Austro-English allies, whose commander-in-chief, Count Nugent, had called upon you "frank and courageous Italians to effect, arms in hand, the restoration of your prosperity and your country. You will do it so much the more effectually, as you will be aided to repulse whoever opposes this result. You must all become an independent nation." Has Garibaldi himself ever asked for more? Are the legitimists of Europe aware that the demands of Italy's popular hero are but identical with the promises of the Austrian generalissimo? Count Nugent's proclamation thus concludes: "Show your zeal for the public welfare, and your happiness will depend on your fidelity to those who love you and defend you. In a short time your lot will cause envy, your new condition will excite admiration.

"By order of Count NUGENT.

"RAVENNA, *December* 10, 1813."

What that new condition did excite will best be gathered from the history of the next thirty years or more which terminated in the great uprising of 1848.

An acquaintance with the state of Italy, from 1815 to 1859, is absolutely necessary to all who would rightly understand how the formation of the present kingdom of Italy has been brought about. Without that knowledge, which alone gives the clue to the final result, nothing but blunders and confusion can ensue, arising either from absolute ignorance or from mistaking some momentary or trivial circumstances (which may have had a temporary influence on the course of events) for the real causes which have resulted in the establishment of the Italian constitutional monarchy of which Victor Emmanuel is the chosen ruler. Such knowledge will also demonstrate clearly the reason why Venetians and Italians are unanimous in demanding that Venetia should become an integral portion of the kingdom of Italy.

The years which elapsed between the conclusion of the treaties of Vienna in 1815, and the era of Italian reforms and revolutions in 1847 and 1848, are amongst the saddest in the history of Italy. The courts avowed ultra theories of divine right, and carried out the complete repression of all popular demands. The arm of military power, sometimes their own, sometimes that of Austria, crushed every effort to oppose, or even mitigate, the severity of the rulers. The press was stifled by a rigid and benighted censorship. Arbitrary power of every kind was employed to restrain the dreaded might of intelligence and thought. A system of espionage was ever at work to detect all who sought to ameliorate the condition of the country or reform its institutions; nor were those who pursued these objects by efforts the most legitimate, treated more leniently than those who sought to effect them by means the most violent. The rulers were leagued together for the oppression of the people, and the people were united by a common hatred against the tyranny of the rulers. First in one part and then in another of the Italian Peninsula revolutionary movements broke out. Sometimes so formidable were they as to necessitate the intervention of Austrian armies to prevent the overthrow of the dynasty attacked. Such was the case in Sardinia and Naples in 1821, in Parma, Modena, and the Papal States in 1831. But, throughout the whole period, smaller movements were continually recurring. Thus the list of sanguinary repressions, and of their victims increased together, and with them increased the hatred of the people to Austria and to the princes whom her arms and policy upheld. Vainly did the great powers attempt by the Congress of Laybach in 1820, and by that of Verona in 1822, to maintain tranquillity in Italy by propping up the system established by their diplomacy at the Congress of Vienna. "There was," says an Italian, writing of these sad times, "scarcely a year which did not see many executions in some one or other of our provinces; but, amongst the record of our sufferings, the years 1831, 1833, 1837, 1841, and 1844 will remain, more than all others, engraven in characters of blood." In a letter written to a friend in 1832, the *then* young and unknown Cavour says:—

"Pressed upon one side by Austrian bayonets, and on the other by the excommunications of the Pope (Gregory XVI.), our condition is truly deplorable. Every free exercise of thought, every generous sentiment is stifled, as if it were a sacrilege or a crime against the State."

The Marquis Massimo d'Azeglio, who died at the beginning of this year (1866), one of the most able and upright public men of the day, thus defines Austria's Italian policy in his pamphlet, entitled "La Politique et le Droit Chrétien:"—"The system adopted by Austria, since 1815, reduces itself to this, to kill Italy, morally and politically, in order to reign in her place." He also relates an anecdote of himself, which illustrates to what an extent Austria carried her dictation. When a young man, prosecuting his studies in Rome, in the year 1820, he was sent for one day by the Governor, Monsignore Bernetti, and questioned upon political matters. The suspicions entertained about him having been proved utterly groundless, the Governor said to him, —"Cavaliere, this affair displeases me, it is odious, but what can we do? *Austria forces us;* the Duke of Modena sends us notices; they are stronger than we are." The Marquis d'Azeglio goes on to say how surprised he was at the embarrassed manner and apologetic tone of the Roman Governor. Such language but proved to him how utterly prostrate was Italy beneath the all-pervading influence of Austria.

A young Milanese nobleman, an intimate friend

of M. d'Azeglio, known as hostile to the Austrian rule, was, says M. d'Azeglio, sent for one day by the chief of the police, who politely warned him of the danger he incurred by mixing himself up with political matters, and then added :—"Good God, Signor Count! you are young, rich, noble, and amiable, why do you mix yourself up in such troubles? Are you afraid of the ballet-girls of the Scala? The Emperor is fond of young people, and wishes them to amuse themselves. What is wanted of you is very easy; lend yourself to it with a will, and listen to my advice." Well may M. d'Azeglio add :—"If Europe knew all that has been done in Italy to beat down the strongest minds, to sear the conscience, to darken the intellect, great would be her surprise at seeing that virtue, sound judgment, and magnanimity still live amongst us."

Such, then, was the new condition of Italy which was to "excite admiration;" such were the fruits of that Austrian supremacy in Italy established by the Congress of Vienna. Yet amidst this conflict engendered by misrule; despite proscription, exile, imprisonment, and death, patriotic aspirations and liberal opinions continued to gain ground. At length the rulers, unable to stem the swelling current, yielded in a degree to demands which they could no longer resist. Some of the princes were only actuated by fear, mingled with crafty designs, others were influenced by timid hopes, united to worthy motives.

Thus it was that, in 1847, Pius IX., recently elected

to the Papal throne, promulgated a general amnesty. Iniquitous courts of so-called justice were abolished; unpopular public functionaries were removed; commissioners for carrying out reforms were named; the municipal system was sensibly improved; and soon the name of Pio Nono became the rallying-cry of Italian patriots.

Such a course pursued at Rome produced an immediate effect at Turin, Florence, and Naples. Early in the following year (1848), Constitutional Governments were inaugurated in all four capitals.

What occurred in Venice is characteristic of the Austrian system of government. The Venetians, headed by Daniel Manin (one of the purest and the most enlightened public men of our own or any other time), to whom Tommaseo and other of their fellow-citizens united themselves, reminded the Austrian authorities of the various liberties and reforms promised to the inhabitants of the Lombardo-Venetian kingdom ever since 1815; liberties which had never been granted—promises which had never been fulfilled. They kept carefully within the prescribed legal means of making known their wishes, both in reference to what had been promised in 1815, and also as regarded further reforms much needed. The result was, that every concession was refused, and both Manin and Tommaseo were thrown into prison. The former relates what took place in these words:—

"I asked the Austrian government to execute, and to cause to be executed, the laws which it had itself given, and to keep the promises it had made ever since 1815; to accord the reforms demanded by the wants and wishes of the populations, and by the spirit of the times. The government replied by throwing M. Tommaseo and myself into prison, as well as others who had written in the same sense."

As in Venice, so in Milan, the course taken by the Austrian authorities was that of violent repression. Not until the revolution of March 1848 in Vienna itself had shaken to its foundation the throne of the Hapsbourgs, did its officials yield in any degree to the demands of the Venetians and the Milanese. Thus it was manifest that nothing but the direst necessity could wring from the German rulers of Northern Italy any concession of even the commonest justice. Hence followed the natural consequence, that the inhabitants of Venice and Milan, once in possession of power, drove out their foreign masters, and proclaimed their own freedom.

Every Italian, of every shade of political opinion, felt assured that the freedom of Italy, whatever form that freedom might assume, could only be secured by the expulsion of the Austrians from the Peninsula. So surely as they remained in any part, so surely was all hope of the permanency of Italian liberty a mere delusion. Subsequent events confirmed only too fully this opinion, and proved that the maintenance of German rule to the south of the Alps is certain destruction to the freedom of Italy. But to effect this vital object of driving out the hated foreigner, the co-operation of all Italians, governors as well as governed, was absolutely necessary. The people of

Italy, therefore, headed by the leading men of every state in the Peninsula, insisted upon all their princes forming an active alliance for the expulsion of the Austrians. But the princes, with the exception of Charles Albert, King of Sardinia, were opposed to the war against Austria. Pius IX. declared that, as head of the Church, he could not appeal to the sword; he allowed, however, at first, volunteers from the States, and some regular regiments under General Durando, to join the national forces against Austria. But in little more than a month, on the 29th April 1848, he pronounced an allocution, in which he repudiated all partnership with those who were fighting against the Austrians in Northern Italy. From that hour he lost both his influence and popularity. This act put an impassable gulf between the Italians and Pius IX. Henceforth his course was vacillating. After various ministerial changes, the unfortunate Count Rossi became Prime Minister. He was assassinated in November 1848, as he mounted the stairs leading to the Legislative Chamber. Shortly after the commission of this foul crime, perpetrated by an unknown hand, the Pope fled from Rome, and went to Gaëta, in the Neapolitan dominions. The Roman Republic was immediately established, but was soon overthrown by the arms of then republican France. The French restored the Pope to his temporal power, for the maintenance of which their soldiers have ever since been necessary. But the Papal Cabinet ever refused to carry out the reforms and ameliorations constantly insisted on by the

French Government; it ever followed the counsels of Austria, and rejected those of France.

The Grand Duke of Tuscany disliking, both from reasons of policy as well as from family connexion, the war against Austria, yet allowed his soldiers and subjects to join in it. The assent he gave was reluctant, and the support feeble. Suddenly he quitted his dominions, without telling even his own ministers of his intention of doing so; nor did he return to Florence until his States had been occupied by Austrian troops. They maintained order while he abolished the constitution and drove the Tuscan patriots into exile.

Ferdinand II. of Naples acted in accordance with the two main principles of his statecraft, falsehood and treachery. On the 7th of April 1848, he issued a proclamation, in which he said:—

"The lot of the common country is about to be decided on the plains of Lombardy! Every prince, every Italian people, is bound to hasten thither to take part in the conflict which ought to secure the independence, the glory, and the freedom of Italy. As for us, we intend to co-operate with all our forces by land and sea, with our arsenals, with all the riches of the nation, &c., &c.

(Signed) "FERDINAND."

The Neapolitan king accordingly ordered his fleet to sail for Venice, to aid the Venetians, who had just flung off the Austrian yoke; but he sent secretly a note to the admiral to be opened near Ancona, *absolutely forbidding* him to undertake anything *hostile to the Austrians*. The same precautions modified the royal commands touching the Neapolitan land forces, ostensibly sent to North Italy to take part in the war of Italian independence. This is but a sample of the habitual perfidy of Ferdinand II. of Naples. Not long after he succeeded in getting rid of constitutional freedom at home. Instantly he recalled his forces from Northern Italy, and employed them in crushing out liberty in his own dominions, and in hunting down its friends, whether republicans or constitutionalists. It was after this fashion that the Neapolitan Bourbon "co-operated with all his forces by land and sea to secure the independence, the glory, and the liberty of Italy."

Charles Albert, the King of Piedmont, was the only one of the Italian sovereigns who was sincere in the war against Austria. But he had been so inconsistent and so vacillating in the early part of his life—was so open to the charge of mere personal ambition—was so suspicious and so suspected, that he never won the full confidence of the Italians. He was, however, throughout the war brave, loyal, and sincerely devoted to the cause of Italian independence, but he possessed little capacity as a general. At the commencement of the campaign he was, however, successful: he took Pischiera, one of the fortresses of the Quadrilateral; beat Marshal Radetzky at Goito, on the 30th May 1848, and drove him across the Adige. But the Austrian Marshal received reinforcements, and succeeded soon after in gaining the upper hand. He drove Charles Albert out of Lombardy, retook Milan, and compelled him on the 9th of August 1848 to sign the armistice of Salasco, by which the King of Piedmont consented to give up all he had gained beyond his own frontiers, and to recall his fleet from the Adriatic, where it was aiding the Venetians, under Daniel Manin, against the Austrians. In the following year (1849), Charles Albert again declared war against Austria. Ill-prepared for the conflict, his army, commanded by the Polish general Chrzanowski, was defeated by Radetzky at Novara, on the 23d March 1849. The king abdicated immediately, quitted Italy, and died in exile not long after. He was succeeded on the throne of Piedmont by his son Victor Emmanuel, who thus began his reign on the battlefield which had just witnessed his country's defeat and his father's abdication.

While the cause of national liberty was falling in all parts of Italy, Venice, under the guidance of her noble chief, Daniel Manin, still carried on the contest against Austria. Those who desire to become fully acquainted with the whole truth concerning Venice,* its government and condition, from March 1848 to August 1849, when engaged in defending its ancient rights and liberties, of which it had once again possessed itself; those, too, who desire to form a just appreciation of the statesmanlike ability and exalted patriotism of her great citizen Daniel Manin, should read his memoirs, written by M. Henry Mar-

---

* The republic of Venice was proclaimed 22d March 1848; the next day were published the names of those who formed the government, of which Daniel Manin was chosen President.

tin, the able historian of France; they should, above all, study "the authentic papers left by Daniel Manin," which have been arranged and translated by Mdme. Planat de la Faye, with all the accuracy and care worthy of so interesting and noble a subject. There will be seen with what self-sacrificing devotion the Venetians, high and low, rich and poor, vied with each other in carrying on the defence of their common country; how the feuds of past ages were buried never to rise again ; how amenable they were to the authority of their chosen rulers—they whose hearts were fired, then as now, with inextinguishable hostility to the stranger's hated rule; how joyfully and eagerly they encountered privations, sufferings, and death, in the cause of their country's freedom ; how they added to patience endurance, and to endurance courage, in their reiterated efforts to undo the wrong done to them at Campo-Formio, and endorsed at Vienna. Isolated, unaided, beset without by a powerful foe, wasted within by famine and disease, they maintained for long months the unequal struggle ; not until the last extremity did they yield, then only did they cease the desperate strife ; and so fell Venice, after an heroic defence worthy of her ancient renown.

On the 27th August 1849, whilst the Austrians defiled through the deserted streets and past the closed houses of the conquered city, Daniel Manin went forth into exile, and in exile died. But his name is engraven in imperishable characters upon every Venetian heart—it is had in everlasting remembrance throughout Italy's dominion, from the eternal snows of the Alps to the sunny shores of Sicily.

To this illustrious citizen of Venice, as to the wronged and noble country of his birth, may well be applied the lines of Manzoni —

> "Dove già libertade è fiorita,
> Dove ancor nel segreto matura,
> Dove ha lacrime un' alta sventura,
> Non c'è cor che non batta per te."—MANZONI.

> "Wherever freedom has already blossom'd,
> Wherever in secret it still matures,
> Wherever a sublime misfortune calls forth tears,
> There, there is no heart that does not beat for thee."

With Venice fell the last hope of Italian liberty. Piedmont had been crushed by Novara's terrible defeat. Austria and Austrian influence were now all-powerful. Lombardy and Venetia, with the quadruple fortresses of the Quadrilateral, were again in her absolute possession. Her troops occupied Tuscany, and garrisoned the northern portion of the Papal States. Her counsels were supreme in the Vatican, and the French troops in Rome but maintained that supremacy. The Dukes of Modena and Parma were the devoted satellites of the house of Hapsbourg. Ferdinand of Naples eagerly obeyed all its behests, save when he added some wanton cruelty of his own special grace. Thus the liberties of Italy went down before the treachery and despotism of its princes, united to the brute force of its implacable enemy enthroned at Vienna, who stifled the last hopes of national independence in the blood and carnage of such awful deeds of violence and cruelty as those perpetrated by the brutal Haynau when the city of Brescia fell into his clutches. And so, to use, with reference to Italian freedom, the touching language applied to Venice by M. Henri Martin, in his "Life of Daniel Manin," "Again the tomb closed over the liberties of Italy, and the heavy hand of Austria sealed the stone."

Had some prophet gifted with divine foreknowledge, filled with that sacred fire which is kindled by an unfaltering belief in the ultimate triumph of justice and of right, predicted in the dark hour of the German Hapsbourg's triumph, that within 16 years an Italian kingdom, comprising 22,000,000 of inhabitants should be formed, and acknowledged by all the powers of Europe, Austria alone excepted, with what derisive incredulity would his words have been received by the myrmidons of despotism? How would they not have laughed to scorn the prediction that a king of Italy, the chief of a constitutional government, freely chosen by the nation, should then have at his command an army numbering 300,000 soldiers, and a fleet of 60 ships of war, great and small, comprising 24 ironclads? Yet all this and more, which only a few years back seemed to short-sighted humanity but an idle dream, is to-day (May 1866) a mighty reality, gladdening the hearts of all who believe in the strength of justice and of liberty, of all who glory in the triumph of a nation's freedom and a people's rights.

But why did the Italians select Victor Emmanuel

as their king? Why did they annex themselves to Piedmont and proclaim her ruler their sovereign, rather than select some other Italian prince, and unite themselves to his dominions and government? To those who reply that the victories of the allied French and Piedmontese armies in the North, and the marvellous triumphs of Garibaldi in the South, were the cause, it is sufficient to reply that those victories only gave to Italians the opportunity of proclaiming their will, and neither did nor could force them to choose this government rather than that, or this king rather than another. Nay, more, it is well known that though France aided the Italians in 1859 to strike a first blow at Austria, (which they could not have done successfully without such assistance,) yet French diplomacy was opposed to the union of Central and Southern Italy beneath the constitutional sceptre of the king of Piedmont. Why, then, did the people of Italy make that choice? There is but one true answer to the question, all others are mere vain or dishonest subterfuges to get rid of the truth. The real reason was the conduct and policy of the king and government of Piedmont from March 1849, when Victor Emmanuel ascended the throne, to 1859, when the French-Piedmontese alliance and war gave to the Italian people the opportunity of making known their real wishes. A short *résumé* of facts will place this beyond all doubt or controversy, and will serve to recall the enlightened and patriotic statesmanship of the rulers of Piedmont, which the stirring events of the last few years have thrown into oblivion. Nor let it be forgotten that the admirable course pursued by the Piedmontese sovereign and statesmen, during the ten years alluded to, ever received the hearty support of their brave and loyal people.

Rarely has any king mounted his throne in a darker hour than that in which Victor Emmanuel ascended the throne of Piedmont in March 1849. Her military power had been broken by the defeat of Novara. Her finances were disordered by an unsuccessful war. A portion of her territory, and the half of her chief fortress of Alessandria, were occupied by the Austrians. A heavy war indemnity was the price to be paid for their withdrawal. The people, irritated by disasters, were in a mood to commit any rash folly at the instigation of violent counsellors. All was confusion, doubt, and anger. An implacable enemy was at the very gates of the capital; and within, were a. distracted parliament, an exhausted treasury, and an angry people.

The king confronted these dangers, and finally overcame them; neither by craft nor by violence, but by good faith, honesty, and firmness. In the proclamation announcing his advent to the throne, he invited his people to aid him in consolidating the free institutions of the country. He returned quickly to his capital from his camp, and there swore fidelity to the constitutional liberties granted by his father, Charles Albert, in March 1848. He kept his oath, and never swerved from its letter or its spirit. His very people and parliament in their irritable mood, in their little experience of free government, furnished him with occasion, or at least with a plausible excuse, for overthrowing the constitution. The honest sovereign would not avail himself of it. He hastened to summon to his councils one whose name was but another word for rectitude and spotless patriotism, Massimo d'Azeglio.

Meanwhile, Austria plied all her arts. She spoke smoothly. Her terms of peace should be softened, her pecuniary demands lessened; but could not his Piedmontese Majesty get rid—quietly, gradually, if he would, but at any rate get rid—of the Constitution? He rejected the insidious counsels, spurned the proffered bribe, signed the disastrous treaty, paid the heavy indemnity, preserved his people's rights, and kept his royal word. Austria never forgave it; his country never forgot it. From that hour it was that Victor Emmanuel gained the well-earned title of "the honest king," "*il re galantuomo,*" and from that hour Italy knew where she could find a leader whom she could trust. Great was the debt of gratitude she then incurred, and at no distant day right well was that debt discharged. In the time of her deepest distress, Italy found the King of Piedmont, alone among Italian princes, true to his people and to his word—alone he gave a refuge to her exiled sons, alone resisted her German oppressor, alone preserved the ark of her liberties:

"In te sol uno un raggio
Di nostra speme ancor vivea."—MANZONI.

"In thee alone a solitary ray of our hope yet lived.'

Therefore was it that in the day of her national triumph Italy would have none other for her king.

Thus amid gloom and danger was laid the foundation of Italy's future freedom by the honest policy of an honest prince. The accomplishment of that freedom was worked out by a master-mind, which had long employed all its vast powers in the study of the political questions both of our own and of other days.

In the year 1832, a young Piedmontese of enlightened opinions was for a short time put under arrest by his suspicious government on account of his liberal views. Writing about the matter to a lady friend, he says:—" I thank you for the interest you take in my disgrace, but believe me I shall make my way all the same. I am very ambitious, and when I am minister I hope I shall justify it; for in my dreams I already see myself minister of the kingdom of Italy." Viewed in relation to the *then* state of Italy, these words, written in 1832, must have seemed indeed but idle dreams; read *now* by the light of accomplished facts, they seem rather the prophetic utterance of genius, for he who wrote them was none other than Camillo Cavour.

When 1848 arrived it found him amongst the ardent friends of a wise liberty. He had studied closely, thought deeply, and travelled much. He loathed the foreign supremacy which for more than thirty years had sought to stifle all liberty and thought in Italy, and had deprived her of all power. But his well-balanced intellect perceived that violent deeds and utopian schemes could give her no relief. The model he studied was England. With eager interest he followed her political course, which avoiding alike useless change and stereotyped immobility, reformed what needed reformation, and altered her laws to meet the requirements of the age.

Such was the statesman who, in October 1850, first became a Cabinet minister in the Piedmontese Government, of which Massimo d'Azeglio was the president. The story runs, that when the Prime Minister mentioned Cavour's name to the King, he said, smiling:—"If Cavour once enter the Cabinet, he will soon be master." It was true, and D'Azeglio knew it, but he was one of that noble type of men to whom the public welfare is the one supreme consideration, compared with which all mere personal questions are as nothing. If another proved more capable than he in directing the national policy, it but afforded him joy, for he loved his country incomparably better than he loved himself.

It would indeed be most unjust to the statesmen, neither few in number nor ordinary in intellect, who sat in Piedmont's parliament, to represent Count Cavour as alone worthy of mention during the years which elapsed between 1850 and 1859. Indeed, he would himself have been the first to protest against such a view. Yet, none who have studied the home and foreign policy of the court of Turin during this important period, can fail to see that Cavour's was the master-mind that ruled, that shaped the policy so wisely pursued, and guided his country through innumerable difficulties to the high destinies of a glorious future.

The Piedmontese government determined, by a system of enlightened reforms, ecclesiastical, political, and financial, to get rid of abuses, to consolidate the free institutions of the state, and to improve the condition of the people. The Siccardine Laws, so called from one of the ministers, Count Siccardi, who proposed them, abolished the old right of asylum, and the special ecclesiastical tribunals before which alone priests could be tried. Thereby was established the equality of all, whether layman or ecclesiastic, before the law. Another measure, brought forward by Cavour himself, abolished certain religious communities, chapters of collegiate establishments and other benefices, whose members were not positively ministering to the spiritual wants of the people, by preaching, by educating youth, or by attendance on the sick and poor. The revenues possessed by these bodies were handed over to an ecclesiastical commission, which allotted a small portion of them to the life-maintenance of the members of the suppressed establishments. The rest was divided amongst the parish priests, formerly paid out of the exchequer, the clergy of the island of Sardinia, where tithes had been abolished, and those ministers who, though engaged in laborious parish duties, were ill paid. Considerable sums were also obtained from the property belonging to abbeys, benefices, and bishoprics, which had until then been exempt from taxation. These funds were also handed over to the Ecclesiastical Commissioners, and distributed in a manner similar to that just stated. The law, brought forward by the government, making marriage a civil contract, as in France and Belgium, was approved by the Lower House, but was thrown out by the Senate. It has very recently passed the two houses of the Italian parliament at Florence, and forms one of the many wise measures voted by the legislature of the Italian kingdom to the great benefit of the country.

Popular education was carefully improved, and every effort made to put it into effective operation throughout the whole land. Statistics which appeared in 1863 showed that Piedmont was in advance of all other parts of Italy in this most important branch of the public welfare; then came Lombardy; Tuscany being much behind the two provinces just named; while the rest of Central Italy (Parma, Modena, the Roman Legations, Umbria, and the Marches) was in a far worse condition: that of Southern Italy and Sicily, after a century of Bourbonic rule, reaching such a climax of ignorance and neglect that something like nine-tenths of the population could neither read nor write. A few facts, towards the close of this article, will show what strenuous exertions are being made, under the present constitutional government of Italy, to remedy so sad a state of things.

The question of the liberty of the press presented peculiar difficulties in a country like Piedmont, so new to free institutions, and having powerful and despotic neighbours, who were specially jealous of such liberties. The policy adopted was that of allowing ample freedom in the discussion of all home affairs, but as regarded foreign affairs, especially with reference to the rulers and governments of other countries, some check was placed on the freedom of the press.

While developing and facilitating the construction of railroads, ordinary roads, canals, and other public works, Count Cavour particularly occupied himself with a series of able financial measures. A decided advocate of free-trade, it was upon that great principle that he based his financial reforms, which did so much to augment the resources of the country and to develop its wealth. The manner in which he framed and carried out those measures signally displayed the power with which he grasped a great principle, and the skill with which he applied it. He further endeavoured, by liberal commercial treaties, to diminish the impediments to commerce, and to facilitate the progress of free-trade.

While carrying out this progressive policy, the government of Piedmont, with equal generosity and wisdom, offered an asylum to those whose fidelity to the rights and liberties of Italy had caused their banishment from all other parts of their unhappy country. Thus Piedmont became to every Italian patriot the refuge of the present and the hope of the future. Such a system of policy as that briefly described won for Piedmont the ever-increasing admiration and sympathy of every free and intelligent man in Europe. Her internal order, her wise reforms, her enlightened progress, contrasted splendidly with the mingled tyranny and anarchy which afflicted all other parts of Italy. Every day proved more clearly the fact that *there*, where foreign bayonets were *not*, and there alone throughout the whole Peninsula, was to be seen an Italian people enjoying all the blessings of order and of freedom.

Yet not without difficulty was this admirable policy pursued. The extreme radicals said the government did not go far enough—accused it of weakness, of duplicity. The extreme reactionists cried out that the ministers were mere revolutionists in disguise, and declared religion and the state alike in danger. Austria, and the whole tribe of Italian courts who followed in her wake, did their utmost to impede such a policy. Well they might; for it was undermining their power far more effectually than the plots of conspirators or the theories of republicans. But Piedmont's great minister went steadily on, overcoming (sometimes by prudent tact, and sometimes by skilful boldness) all opposition at home, while baffling at every turn, with incomparable skill, the hostile diplomacy of Austria.

Thus matters were progressing, when, in 1854, England and France declared war against Russia. The clear intellect of Cavour at once saw what course Piedmont ought to pursue, and how much Italy's cause would gain by an active alliance with the Western powers. The king fully concurred in Cavour's policy. Eighteen thousand men were accordingly sent to the Crimea, where the soldiers of this free Italian state proved by their discipline, no less than by their valour, that they were worthy to fight side by side with the armies of France and England.

Many members of both of the extreme parties opposed this policy of Cavour's. It was, however, supported by a decided majority both of the nation and of the parliament, as it was also by the noble exile of Venice, Daniel Manin, who declared " that in serving under the flag of Italian redemption, our soldiers who fight in the Crimea are not the soldiers of the province of Piedmont, but of Italy."

The early termination of the war prevented the Italians gaining as much from it as they had hoped. Nevertheless, their cause had made decided progress through Piedmont's active alliance with the Western powers. Not only did the Piedmontese ministers sit at the Congress of Paris on equal terms with those of the five great European monarchies—not only did they there plead the cause of Italy, and expose its intolerable condition, but they obtained from the representatives of England and France the official acknowledgment that it required speedy amelioration. The Russian minister also adhered to that opinion. It was clear that after such authoritative declarations the actual state of Italy could not long endure unchanged. It was indeed intolerable. The leaden despotism which oppressed the whole land, Piedmont alone excepted, was annihilating both order and liberty. The cruelties of tyranny goaded the people on to revolutionary violence, and drove many to take part in conspiracies. Some, indeed, maddened at the sight of their country's sufferings, sought revenge by assassination, that execrable crime which is the scourge alike of the victim it attacks and of the cause which it espouses.

The nature and the fruits of forty years of Austrian supremacy in Italy were now laid bare to the world. Such a condition, brought into direct contact, as it was, with the freedom and good government of Piedmont, threatened not only the peace of Italy but of Europe. If left unchanged it could not fail to bring about a violent conflict. Yet the powers assembled at the Congress of Paris were unable to find any practical remedy; they confined themselves to protests and protocols, which cost nothing and which effected nothing. The opportunity was lost, and with it, as soon was seen, the hope of an enduring peace.

It was in this year, 1856, that Daniel Manin, now fast sinking into the grave, wrote:—" All the sovereigns of Italy, except the King of Piedmont, are hostile to the Italian cause; that simplifies the question, and distinguishes it from the state of affairs in 1848, when it was necessary to respect the interests of princes *soi-disant* favourable to the cause of independence."

The Congress of Paris left face to face the freedom of Piedmont and the despotism of Austria. Around the one was gathered all the love of the hot Italian race, and around the other all its bitterest hate. Old distinctions faded away as men of every party rallied closer around Piedmont's king. To him Manin bade his countrymen to look. Garibaldi desired no better lot than to fight under his banner in a national war.

Politicians of the right, the centre, and the left supported the constitutional monarch. On him was bent the wistful gaze of all Italians—of those who had shared with his father the victory of Goito and the defeat of Novara; of Tuscans who had followed Montanelli to the field of Curtatone; of Venetians who had toiled with Manin in the heroic defence of Venice; of Romans who had fought under Garibaldi in the memorable siege of Rome; of Neapolitans who had languished for years in the dungeons of the lying Bourbon; of Sicilians burning with hatred and crying for vengeance against the same evil rule. Such a condition of Italy only served to increase the ill-feeling between Turin and Vienna; it but added fuel to the fire which was soon to burst out into another European war; it but hastened on the irrepressible conflict between freedom and despotism.

At length, in March 1857, diplomatic relations were broken off between Piedmont and Austria. The Piedmontese government urged on the fortifications of Alessandria. The people gave it their eager support. The storm was evidently gathering, when suddenly the appalling attempt of Orsini on the life of the French Emperor in January 1858, fixed upon Paris the attention of Europe. The French government appealed to its foreign neighbours to prevent such criminal attempts in future. That of Piedmont expressed its full intention to do so, but pointed out that such criminal deeds sprung from the exasperation produced by the intolerable state of Italy. Such, despite the repressive acts of his government, appears to have been the view of the Emperor Napoleon. At least, in his interview with Count Cavour at Plombières in the autumn of that year, 1858, he appears to have expressed a determination not to abandon Piedmont if she were attacked by Austria.

At length the memorable year 1859 arrived, and with it Napoleon's expression of regret to the Austrian minister at Paris that the relations of the two courts were not as good as they had been. Victor Emmanuel, in his speech at the opening of his Parliament a few days later, declared "that he was not insensible to the cry of agony which arose to him from so many parts of Italy."

Then followed the marriage of his eldest daughter to Prince Napoleon. Austria augmented her forces in the Lombardo-Venetian kingdom. Piedmont replied by additional military preparations. War was imminent. Diplomacy made impotent efforts to avert it; but it was now too late. On the 19th April 1859, the Viennese government addressed its ultimatum to that of Turin. It was rejected without hesitation. The Austrian troops at once crossed the Ticino and invaded Piedmont. The despotic statesmen of Vienna hoped by one fierce blow to crush the last refuge of Italian liberty; but France came to the rescue, and by her powerful aid the invader was driven back. Nor can any later shortcomings and faults of French diplomacy take from the great and generous people of France the glory of having defended free Piedmont against despotic Austria, and so struck a mighty blow for the cause of Italy's freedom. With what marvellous perseverance, courage, and skill, the Italian people, guided by the genius of the great Cavour and the patriotic ardour of Garibaldi, followed up that blow, is known to all. It does not fall within the scope of this article to relate that part of Italy's modern story; suffice it to say, that within eighteen months Victor Emmanuel was proclaimed King of Italy, and immediately conferred upon her citizens the rich blessing of constitutional liberty and a really national life. To those, then, who ask the reason why the Italians—when the occasion presented itself —selected the King of Piedmont as their sovereign, and annexed themselves to his dominions, the simple reply (obvious enough to all but those who *will* not see) is, that the cause of such a choice sprung from the admirable and patriotic policy pursued by Victor Emmanuel and his government from 1849 to 1859. That policy, despite innumerable obstacles, was initiated and carried out with a firmness, consistency, and wisdom which will reflect eternal honour upon Piedmont's courageous and honest king, upon her gifted statesmen, upon her free parliament, upon her brave and loyal people.

Turning now from other portions of Italian soil, let the reader fix his attention upon Venetia, whose lot was left unchanged by the events of 1859, and which to-day (May 1866) demands justice in tones that cannot be silenced, re-echoed as they are by the millions of armed and united Italy. Nor will the old pleas of her German taskmaster in favour of his leaden rule avail him any more, for they are now met by this crushing reply—Schleswig-Holstein! Since the formation of the Italian kingdom Europe has had presented to it a remarkable contrast in the condition of two well-known cities situated in the north of Italy. On the one hand, Venice has continued, after as before 1859, beneath the rule of Austria, that great German power to whom she was handed over, despite all her remonstrances, by the acts of Campo-Formio and of Vienna; on the other hand, Milan has been released from that same German rule, and become an integral portion of the Italian constitutional monarchy. It is interesting to examine, by the aid of facts, the respective condition of these two cities during the few years which have elapsed since 1859. [The contrast offered by the progress and freedom, alike moral and material, of Milan under the rule of the Italian national government; as compared with the commercial decay, the servitude, and the discontent of Venice under Austrian rule, has been fully set forth in the preceding essay on "Milan and Venice since the war of 1859." The writer begs to refer the reader to that essay, instead of again repeating here those same facts and statistics, taken from it and inserted in the article on "Italy, Venice, and Austria," as contained in the *Westminster Review* of 1st July 1866.] Yet not from Milan alone come proofs in support of Italy's righteous cause, to the confusion of her calumniators. A brief glance shall now be given at what is going on in Naples, the beautiful capital of Southern Italy. There the education of the people was in the grossest state of neglect previous to 1860. Since that date both the municipality and individuals have striven earnestly to amend a state of things so hurtful and dangerous to the public welfare.

In 1862 there were already in operation 263 elementary schools, comprising day schools for boys and girls, and 19 evening schools for boys, lads, and men. The total number of pupils amounted to 10,500.

In 1865 the total number of schools was—

Boys' day schools	251
Girls' day schools	202
Evening schools	129
Infant schools	22
Schools on Sundays and fêtes for girls and women	16
	620
Private schools, not under the care of the municipality, for poor boys and girls	370
Total,	990

The number of pupils amounted to 39,611. In 1865 the municipality expended 510,216 francs on popular education. Besides these elementary schools, there have been established superior ones in which some 800 pupils obtain a more complete education. Two normal schools have also been established, in which at present 40 young men and 160 young women are being trained up as teachers.

In March of this year (1866) the correspondent of the *Journal des Debats* says:—

"The distribution of prizes among the pupils of the elementary schools in the Theatre del Fondo, by the heir to the throne, Prince Humbert, was one of the ceremonies by which was celebrated on the 14th of this month the king's fête. Here more than elsewhere the instruction of the people is a question of capital importance; its progress is therefore followed with the liveliest interest. This year it has surpassed all expectations. Amongst the pupils who had most distinguished themselves were men of the people of from forty to fifty years of age, mingled with children of eight years old."

The writer of this article himself visited the schools of Naples some eighteen months back. Nothing could surpass the eagerness with which boys, lads, and men were then flocking to the evening schools after a hard day's work. Little fellows of nine to fourteen years old were to be seen sitting beside their own fathers, or mingled with grown men of their own family and friends, all diligently at work, reading, writing, learning arithmetic, or the rudiments of geography. The quickness with which they learn is marvellous, and is only outdone by their desire to acquire knowledge.

Naples is to-day as remarkable for the absence of beggars as it used to be famous for the swarms of them. The formation of a good police, the introduction of gas, of various sanitary measures, and other good municipal arrangements, have greatly improved the condition of the city. Much, however, remains to be done, for it must take years to civilise and to bring into thorough order the towns and country of the Neapolitan provinces, which long years of Bourbon misrule had converted into an Augean stable of ignorance, pauperism, brigandage, and vice.

In Palermo had been established 27 schools in

1861; there are now 78. Those of Bologna have also increased considerably. Indeed, throughout Italy, the government, the municipalities, and individuals have done their utmost to push on the all-important work of popular education, and still continue to do so. The general result is thus given by Signor Galeotti in his interesting volume entitled "La Prima Legislatura del Regno d'Italia," published in 1865:—

Boys' and girls' elementary schools	30,321	Pupils	939,234
Evening schools	3,576	,,	123,581
Infant schools	1,774	,,	80,819
	35,671		1,143,434

The government, the municipalities, and individuals are spending annually, says Signor Galeotti, 12,122,515 francs on elementary popular instruction.

The Italian government has, during the six years of its existence, spared neither labour nor money in promoting the material interests of the country. A well-planned network of railways has been formed, and is being rapidly executed. Turin is now united by a continuous line, *viâ* Milan, Bologna, and Ancona, to the port of Brindisi, in the extreme south-east of the Peninsula. Other important lines—such as that which crosses the Apennines, connecting Bologna and Florence, and that between Naples and Rome—are now in operation; while others of great importance are being constructed as quickly as possible.

Not less diligence is being shown in the matter of ordinary roads, chiefly in the southern provinces, which greatly need them. Ports, harbours, bridges, canals, and lighthouses are being made or repaired. Industrial societies and public companies are growing in numbers and prospering, the government and the municipalities favouring and aiding them in every way.

The parliament has already done very much in the vast and intricate work of administrative, legislative, judiciary, and monetary reform. Previous to 1860, the country was divided into seven separate states, whose rulers endeavoured to keep the Italian people as much divided as possible. They fostered all the local jealousies, prejudices, and petty interests to the utmost, and impeded by their custom-houses, their different coinages, their varying systems of administration, law, and usage, the union, liberty, and progress of Italy.

The enlightened and beneficent work of the constitutional government which now rules has been, on the contrary, that of overthrowing local prejudices and interests for the sake of promoting the general welfare. It has broken down separating barriers, and united, both materially and morally, these common children of a common country. In this double work of demolition and reconstruction, the parliament and people of Italy have displayed patience and prudence, mingled with earnest and persevering efforts to found upon just and wise principles a good and enduring system of government. If much remains to do, yet assuredly very much has been already done, and the work continues to progress.

The general state of Continental Europe, and the peculiar condition of the Italian kingdom, with foreign powers still in possession of portions of its territory, and with a powerful enemy encamped within the famous Quadrilateral, has necessitated the creation and maintenance of a large army and fleet; the Italians not wishing to have as their only available weapon against foreign foes that moral support, that thunder of despatches and articles, whose aid proved so ineffectual in the recent cases of Poland and of Denmark. This necessary military work has been accomplished, so that the Italian nation is to-day able to vindicate its just claims with something more than moral force to sustain them.

But all these vast undertakings have severely taxed the financial resources of the country, which have not had time in six years to grow in proportion to the immediate outlay necessitated by so many and such important demands. Hence the deficits and financial difficulties of the moment. It is, however, a mistake to suppose that they present anything like hopeless embarrassment. There is nothing but what time, economy, and prudence can surely put right, Space will not allow this interesting and important subject to be dealt with in the present article. But those who desire to form a true idea of Italy's financial difficulties and financial resources, of the great work she has done and is doing, cannot do better than study Signor Galeotti's work, "La Prima Legislatura del Regno d'Italia." There assuredly they will find the full confirmation of the saying attributed to

Cavour—"If Italy wishes to be free, she must pay, pay, and pay again." But there they will also learn that if much remains to be done, vast has been the work already accomplished; that rulers and people are alike determined to shrink from no sacrifice required for the completion of Italian union and independence; that they possess in themselves and in their country resolution and resources sufficient to overcome the difficulties and the dangers yet to be encountered in completing the glorious task. The might of freedom, justice, and right is on their side, and though dark and stormy be the present hour, (May 1866,) though to-day the sky be black with the thunder-clouds of imminent war, theirs shall be the final victory. It is but the history of all struggles for liberty that the world has ever seen. It is but the universal law, that no great and good object can be attained or carried out, by nations or by individuals, without costly labour and exertion. There can be no freedom unless the price for obtaining it be paid, no leaving the house of bondage save by signs and by wonders, no entering into the promised land without toiling through the wilderness of privation and of suffering—in a word, no redemption without sacrifice.

As to the attitude of Italy at the present hour, it is but that which would be assumed by every other nation in the like circumstances. She finds Austria and Prussia on the point of coming to blows over their Danish spoils, and the latter willing to enter into an Italian alliance. The occasion is unique; for hitherto the vast majority of Germans have been in favour of aiding Austria to retain possession of Venetia, whenever that possession has been endangered. The National German Assembly at Frankfort, in 1848, where there was full freedom of vote and voice, presented the spectacle, at once ludicrous and shameful, of declaring that Germany ought to possess itself of Schleswig-Holstein, but should at the same time support Austria in maintaining her hold upon Venetia.

There are those who talk of the necessity of the frontier of the Mincio as a protection to Germany. Frontier! Necessity! What frontier have Germans left to Denmark? What forbearance have they manifested for Danish necessities? Have they not taken even to the uttermost farthing? In this matter German Powers have pronounced judgment without mercy against their weaker neighbour; therefore judgment without mercy shall be their portion. Let the facts of the case be looked to. The German Confederation numbers 44,000,000; Austria, without Venetia and the Italian Tyrol, 32,000,000; Italy, with those two provinces, rather more than 25,000,000. Between these German and Italian lands rises the great barrier of the Alps, (like the Pyrenees between France and Spain,) yet the more powerful retains possession of a large province of Italy to the south of the Alps as being necessary to German security; and *that* after the conduct of Germany towards Denmark in the matter of Schleswig-Holstein.

If it be said that the Italian kingdom has no claim to Venetia, because that province has never belonged to the kingdom of Italy, it is sufficient to reply, first, that the desire of Italians to possess Venetia is only the echo of Venetian longing to be united to Italy; next, that Venetians and Italians only ask for Venetia that which Austria so loudly demands for the Duchies of the Elbe—freedom to choose their own sovereign.

Let it also be remembered that Italy did not create the present danger of war now (May 1866) so imminent; she has but taken advantage of her German oppressor's quarrels to assert her own rights by negotiation, or by arms, as the case may be. To those who advise her to wait she replies by asking: Until when? Until German Powers have made up their differences? Until it suits those who, in full possession of all their rights and liberties, find their business affairs deranged by Italian demands for the like blessings? Are not such advisers the very same as those who told Italy in 1859 that she had nothing to gain by war? Or shall she wait until *moral force* delivers Venetia from Austrian rule? Italians surely may be pardoned if they are sceptical about the efficacy of such aid, considering what a broken reed it proved to Poland and to Denmark. It was not mere moral force, able despatches, and eloquent writing, but far sterner work, that gave Italy her present position, her fleet, her artillery, and her army of 300,000 men. To-day she relies on bringing them to bear upon the work of completing her deliverance at a time when the two great German Powers are in hostile array against each other.

Experienced Piedmontese generals and officers, men not given to boasting, not blinded by enthusiasm, men who know what military matters are, both by practice and in theory, have the greatest confidence in the Italian army, in whose formation, training, and discipline they have borne a large part, having made it the subject of their most earnest labours. To such a force must be added the tens of thousands of volunteers who are flying to arms with the devoted enthusiasm of those who believe themselves called to fight for all that a people holds most dear. Time, with its stern facts, alone can prove whether, as the writer believes, the chiefs of the Italian army are justified in their confidence; but woe to the enemy that comes to do battle with Italy's sons in the belief that he has but an easy victory to win. Italians are under no delusion as to the power of their formidable foe; that foe had best not undervalue those who, from their gallant king to the youngest conscript, from the hero of Caprera to the most youthful of his volunteers, are *one* in their devotion to the sacred cause of their country's freedom; who know that to-day the question for them and Italy is nothing short of this, "To be, or not to be?"

There are some who, as usual, suspect France of waiting to aggrandise herself at Italy's expense. France, for service done, made the Alps her boundary between Italy and herself. History will no doubt give full weight to whatever may be urged against that proceeding, but it will assuredly admit that there was much to justify it. Sound policy and justice alike forbid France to change the boundaries of her south-eastern frontier, and that double motive will doubtless prevent her from tarnishing the lustre of those triumphs which marked the memorable campaign of 1859, bright as they are, not so much with the questionable glare of mere military achievement, as with the imperishable glory of a kindred nation's freedom and a kindred people's rights. Not to the elected of millions, but to those who claim to be the special depositories of the divine right of kings, to the Hohenzollerns and to the Hapsbourgs, the world must turn if it would contemplate the most recent example to be found of a policy which has not scrupled to break down treaties, to belie promises, to use alike violence and fraud, for the attainment of its own ends at the expense of its feeble neighbour. Such, in the Danish question, was the statecraft common to the royal and imperial monarchs enthroned at Berlin and Vienna, who are not sovereigns by the national will, not offsprings of universal suffrage, but whose boast it is that *they* reign by right divine, that *they* rule by the grace of God!

It remains only to say a few words upon a subject much talked of latterly, which is, however, by no means new—that of the cession of Venetia to Italy by negotiation. This has long been desired by various English diplomatists and statesmen, not only in the interest of Italy, but in that of Austria and of Europe. It is interesting to see what was being said and proposed on this subject in the troubled years 1848 and 1849, more especially as all subsequent events have amply proved the wisdom and foresight of those who advocated such an arrangement.

In May 1848, Sir Ralph Abercromby, the English minister at Turin, in a despatch to Lord Palmerston, then Foreign Secretary, points out that, should Austria completely reconquer Lombardy and Venetia, they would always be a cause of heavy and permanent expense. "If Austria," he writes, "could for once make up her mind to negotiate honestly for the evacuation of those provinces and the recognition of the new constitutional kingdom of North Italy, in consideration of an advantageous pecuniary arrangement, she would certainly find the most liberal intentions, both in this country, (Piedmont,) and in the provinces which are uniting themselves to it." Having spoken of the great value to be attached to a prompt and satisfactory solution, he concludes with these words: "But, in order to be satisfactory, it is indispensable that the Austrians evacuate Italy, and recognise its complete independence. Any other solution would but serve to prepare for the future new insurrections and new conflicts."

Upon the 3d June 1848, Lord Palmerston, in a very able despatch to M. de Hummelauer, endeavours to persuade the Austrian minister of the necessity of giving up Venetia as well as Lombardy, chiefly on the ground of the cost and difficulties in which Austria would be involved if she undertook to re-establish her power over those provinces, and, when re-established, the impossibility of maintaining it, except at great expense, and by the costly means of the permanent employment of a large military force. He expresses the willingness of the English government to interpose its good offices between Piedmont and Austria, provided that the arrangements already accorded in the case of Lombardy were extended by Austria to that part of the Venetian territory which should be agreed upon between the two parties.

Again, on the 9th October 1848, after the recovery of Lombardy and Milan by Austria, Lord Palmerston, writing to Lord Ponsonby, the English minister at Vienna, again points out the insuperable obstacles which prevent that power from holding Lombardy, except as a conquered province, and its therefore becoming a burden and a source of weakness to Austria. He says that the hatred of the Lombards towards her might well lead them to ask foreign aid against her, and that if such aid led even to a general war, it might well end in Austria losing all her Italian possessions. The despatch terminates thus :—

"Thoroughly disposed as the friends and allies of Austria might be to aid her if she were menaced in her own proper and legitimate existence in Germany, there exists on the subject of her pretensions to impose a yoke on the Italians so general a feeling of their injustice, that this feeling might well have the effect of leaving Austria with very little aid in the case of a similar war."

Another most remarkable despatch of Lord Palmerston's is that of the 11th of November 1848, addressed to Lord Ponsonby, at Vienna. The English Foreign Secretary again refers to the inextinguishable hatred of the Lombards to Austria ; he impresses on the Cabinet of Vienna that the policy of ceding Lombardy could now be adopted by the imperial and royal government without loss of prestige or honour, inasmuch as the arms of Austria having been completely victorious, and being in full possession of that province, such cession would be regarded as an act of wise and generous policy, springing from the purely voluntary determination of Austria. He goes on to remind the Viennese statesmen that the government of France might soon change hands, as it actually did, on account of the presidential election then pending; that French policy might assume in the future a much more active part as regarded foreign affairs; that a war against Austria for the liberation of North Italy would always be pleasing to France, in certain circumstances; and he then asks: "Could Austria be certain that even the sympathy of Germany would follow her in her efforts to force again her yoke on the Italian nation?" He further says, most truly, that the principle of nationalities to-day, (1848,) the rallying-cry of Germany, is in itself a protest against Austrian rule in Italy: then adds, that the principle of prescriptive right is scarcely more favourable to Austria, because, although good as regards certain parts of Lombardy, which, like the Duchy of Milan, had long been fiefs of the empire, it was equally strong in favour of the republic of Venice.

"This State," says the despatch, "has played a considerable part in history during nearly fourteen centuries of liberty, whilst the title of Austrian possession only remounts to the treaty of Campo-Formio, (1797,) by which General

Bonaparte handed over to her (Austria) Venice, and to those of 1815, which once again placed Venice in the possession of Austria."

Never, in the course of his long and remarkable career, did Lord Palmerston display more far-sighted sagacity than in his Austro-Italian despatches of 1848-49. Never have predictions been uttered which subsequent events more completely ratified. It is curious to reflect that it was at that very time the fashion to call him a mere meddler, and to decry his policy with a persistency as ignorant as it was unjust. Had his wise counsels been followed in the years referred to, immense would have been the gain, not only to Italy, but to Europe and to Austria.* As he so justly pointed out to this latter power, her Italian possessions have been nothing but a source of embarrassment and disaster. They have been the scene of that oppressive and cruel rule, from 1849 to 1859, which alienated from Austria the sympathy of all lovers of freedom and of justice. They cost her the blood, the treasure, and the disasters of that latter year, when, left without an ally, she was brought into the utmost peril. They are the reason why, at this very hour, an Italian army of 300,000 men, and a fleet more powerful than her own, menace the southern

* No one more constantly and consistently supported the policy of effecting a complete separation between Italy and Austria than Sir James Hudson, who so ably represented England at the court of Turin from January 1852 to August 1863. He rightly believed that the absolute severance of those two countries, and the formation of an independent and free Italian kingdom would be beneficial alike to Austria and Italy.

frontier and ports of Austria, when she needs all her strength to oppose the policy and armaments of Prussia. Had the statesmen of Vienna wisely followed Lord Palmerston's advice, given seventeen years ago, and consented to the formation of a northern Italian kingdom, with an Alpine frontier, running somewhere between Trent and Bolzano, and including Venetia within its limits, Austria would have escaped all the disasters and difficulties of the last fifteen years, and, would not see Italy to-day arrayed in hostility against her. Indeed, the gain would have been greater still; for commercial interests and intercourse would, long ere this, have sprung up, and necessarily drawn together in friendly relation Italy on the one side, and Austria, with Germany, upon the other. Instead of the ruinous expenditure caused by the creation and maintenance of enormous armaments of every kind, a lucrative commerce would now be enriching both countries, and erasing the old feelings of hatred engendered by past wrongs.

It was in April 1848 that Daniel Manin, then President of the Republic of Venice, wrote the following lines, in an official despatch addressed to the French and English governments: "Venise affranchie ne saurait donner de l'ombrage. Venise autrichienne serait une honte pour le présent et un embarras pour l'avenir:" "A free Venice can give no offence: an Austrian Venice will be a present shame and a future embarrassment." The world, and especially Austria, know to-day, (May 1866,) how true those words were and are. Happy would it have been, judged only as matter of policy, (or even from a mere money-point of view, without entering into higher considerations,) had the wise and far-sighted advice of England's minister been followed, and that "future embarrassment" been got rid of—happy for Italy, happy for Europe, and happy for Austria herself.

As to the claims of Venetians to settle freely their own future, they have the support alike of policy and justice; more especially after the conduct of Germany, and particularly that of Prussia and Austria, in the question of the Duchies of the Elbe. To every sophism urged by Germans, Austrian or other, for the maintenance of German rule in Italy, there is to-day this short but unanswerable reply, *Schleswig-Holstein*. Let statesmen and diplomatists be well assured that there can be no lasting peace until Germans and German powers cease to hold Italian provinces beneath their yoke. To patch up a peace, leaving those provinces in such thraldom, is a worse evil than setting them free by immediate war.

If Austria were once again to have Italy in her power as completely as in 1850, not only would it be a calamity to Italy but to Europe, for so surely would it entail a lengthened period of conflict and revolution, so surely would it bring in its train such years as 1848 and 1859. Upon such a basis there can be no enduring peace for Europe. Those, then, who prize that rich blessing, those who uphold order and justice, no less than those who love freedom, are interested in delivering every portion of Italy from foreign rule.

Those who would maintain it are favouring that which does but lay up countless and certain stores of future disorder, revolution, and war.

The cause of Italy is the cause of liberty and order, of right and justice, of all that is held most dear by every people under heaven, of all the most precious among temporal rights that man can claim or God bestow; therefore the voice of every free nation, and especially that of England, (the ancient cradle, the island home of liberty and law,) should be raised in support of Italy's just claims—that most beautiful of southern lands, so long oppressed by the curse of tyranny and the miseries of anarchy. There, to-day, are to be seen a patriot king, a free parliament, a brave army, and a noble people, all equally devoted to the sacred cause of their country's freedom; there the millions of enfranchised Italy, without distinction of rank or age, are united in an heroic determination to deliver, once for all, their native land from foreign thraldom, and prepared to seal her freedom with their blood:—

> "Già le destre hanno strette le destre;
> Già le sacre parole son porte:
> O compagni sul letto de morte,
> O fratelli su libero suol."—MANZONI.

> "Already right hands by right hands are grasp'd;
> Already the sacred words are utter'd:
> Either companions on the bed of death,
> Or brothers on a free soil."

It may be that even such a sight will fail to move those who proclaim cheapness to be the highest good, the desire of all nations, who never rise above the business point of view, who have no thought, save for material interest and personal loss or gain, who know no higher law than that of buying in the cheapest market and selling in the dearest, who hold no book so sacred as the ledger, who, in their blind devotion to the golden idol of their worship, forget the Divine claims of justice and liberty, of a nation's freedom, and a people's rights.

But whoever has faith in those mighty principles, whoever believes that they are the God-given heritage of all mankind, will turn with deepest sympathy to Italy's brave sons, who, rallied around their chosen king, are "to-day (1866) soldiers, that they may be to-morrow the free citizens of a great country."* To them will be given an earnest "God-speed" wherever justice reigns; for them the free men of every land and of every clime will raise to Heaven the heartfelt prayer, "May God defend the right."

* It is well to remind the reader that these words are taken from the proclamation of Napoleon III., dated Milan, 8th June 1859:—"Ne soyez aujourd 'hui que soldats; demain vous serez les citoyens d'un grand pays."

ITALY AND THE WAR OF 1866.

Reprinted from the "Westminster Review" of April 1867.

1. *Documenti Diplomatici presentati al Parlamento dal Ministro degli Affari Esteri, il* 21 *Dicembre* 1866. Firenze: Eredi Botta, Tipografi della Camera dei Deputati.
2. *Relazione Ufficiale dell' Arciduca Alberto, sulla Battaglia di Custoza.*
3. *Rapporti sulle Operazioni Militari del* 23 *e* 24 *Giugno*, 1866, *del Generale Lamarmora.*
4. *La Guerre de* 1866 *en Allemagne et en Italie.* Par W. RUSTOW, Colonel de Brigade. Genève et Paris: Joël Cherbuliez, éditeur.
5. *Rapporto del Vice-Ammiraglio Tegethoff, sulla Battaglia di Lissa.*
6. *Relazione sull' attacco di Lissa e sulla battaglia navale del* 20 *Luglio*, 1866. "Gazzetta Ufficiale." Firenze, 3 Agosto 1866.

AMONG the memorable events of the last twenty years, those of 1866 hold no secondary place; for by their instrumentality the unity of Germany has been founded and that of Italy well-nigh completed. They have called into existence, under the direction and government of Prussia, a united northern Germany, possessed of vast and varied resources, upon whose government and people it alone depends to turn those resources to good account. Nor does it seem improbable that this new power will ultimately attract to itself the states to the south of the Main, and thus end in forming that united fatherland which has only existed hitherto in the aspirations of its children. This great change has been brought about in no slight degree by a diplomacy, often unscrupulous in the means it employed for attaining its ends, and by the war originating in the quarrels of Prussia and Austria over the spoils of the Danish monarchy, whose integrity they had bound themselves by treaties to respect. Thus the new Germany of to-day has had its immediate rise under auspices which find but little favour with those who desire that a great and worthy end should be pursued by no less worthy means. It will, however, be matter for congratulation if this sin of origin be redeemed by the establishment in Germany of a political system based upon sound principles of order and of freedom. That the Germans should succeed in bestowing upon their fatherland such a system, and prevent its becoming little else than a mere military despotism, is to be desired not only for the sake of their own country, but also for that of the progress, the liberties, and the peace of Europe. It is time that Germany, inhabited by a people admirably instructed and endowed with so many excellent qualities, should no longer be stultified by the rivalry of its princes, or, as in days past, by the political craft and imperious will of a Nicholas of Russia; on the contrary, Germany, placed in full possession of its just influence, should bear its part in promoting the advancement and civilisation of the world in the matter of political self-government and in questions of international policy, as well as in the regions of thought, science, and literature, in each of which it holds so leading a position. That such a result may spring from the new-born unity of Germany, is the heartfelt wish of those who desire not only the welfare and progress of their own land, but also that of other countries, being, as we all are, members of the same body, the common children of a common humanity.

While the events of the past year have thus done so much towards realising a united Germany, they have all but completed the great work of Italian unity, which not ten years ago seemed but an idle dream. To the south of the Alps is to be seen a spectacle which has for centuries been the desire of the noblest and the most gifted of the sons of Italy, and which is at length realised to-day—that of their country freed from* all foreign rule, and her destinies consigned to the hands of a purely Italian government, the offspring of the nation's will, and the responsible guardian of its rights. To see a whole country thus re-

* The French occupation of Rome ceased in December 1866, but was resumed in October 1867. The circumstances under which that re-occupation took place are discussed in the next (4th) Essay.

stored to the possession of itself after having been for centuries sacrificed to the greed of foreign ambition, or to the selfish ends of its own petty rulers, is a result full of present good, and pregnant with hope for the future. It may well attract the thoughtful study of all who watch with profound interest the spectacle offered by the triumphs and the failures, the successes and the errors, the excellences and the defects, the struggles (sometimes effectual and sometimes the reverse) of Italians striving, amidst many difficulties, to establish order in the place of despotism, liberty in the place of anarchy, national independence in the place of foreign domination. To Englishmen this spectacle, which Italy offers to the world at the present time, is especially interesting, inasmuch as she has selected the principle of constitutional freedom as the means for effecting this mighty change in her internal condition—a principle which has secured to England the unspeakable blessing of a wise, a well-ordered, and a progressive liberty. Indeed all, to whatever country they belong, who are sincerely attached to that or any other form of free self-government, should give Italy their cordial support in her arduous and patriotic task; unless, indeed, despite all their loud profession of attachment to constitutional freedom, they would sacrifice its triumph to that despicable policy whose supporters proclaim that the receipt for the greatness and prosperity of their own country is the weakness, the division, and the misgovernment of their neighbours. How despicable that policy is, becomes clear enough to each of us when we see it adopted by others. Thus Englishmen are fully alive to its unworthiness when they hear a certain class of French politicians speak with undisguised ill-will of Italian or German unity and freedom; on the other hand, its unworthiness becomes not less obvious to Frenchmen when they remember how a certain class of English politicians desired and predicted the breaking up of the United States, the wish being father to the thought. But every true friend of progress and civilisation should protest against this despicable and odious policy, begotten of petty jealousy and the narrowest selfishness, absolutely opposed to all that is elevated and generous, utterly unworthy of nations who boast that they are great and who call themselves Christian.

To give a truthful sketch of what has taken place in Italy during the year 1866 is the object of the present article; yet such a sketch must necessarily be, at the best, imperfect; for the events of which it treats are too near to allow of all their details being fully known, and the feelings they excited are still too vivid to admit of a perfectly calm and impartial estimate being formed of those events and of their results. Whoever, then, seeks to make himself acquainted with them must for the present be content with an approximative judgment as to the share of praise or blame to be bestowed upon the Italians for their conduct during the past year, and upon their leading men, whose arduous task it has been to direct the nation's destinies at this decisive moment of the nation's history. It should, moreover, be borne in mind, when dealing with this subject, that Italy is no longer an oppressed nationality, but has now her place among free nations. Those, then, who have been faithful to her just cause in days gone by, and who still desire to do it real service, will not now dwell so much upon the cruel wrongs she has suffered in the past, as upon the work to be done in the present. Nor can they render greater service to Italy than by pointing out honestly what they believe to be both her merits and her faults; knowing that if she is to reap all the fruits to be obtained by the just restitution of her rights, it must be by a truthful examination of all that is good and all that is bad within her body politic, of its strength and of its weakness. Such a process has assuredly its unpleasant as well as its pleasant phase; but it issues in this great good, that if faithfully persevered in, evils are exposed and corrected, impending dangers are pointed out and averted, and the nation is gradually formed to that vigorous public life and power of self-government whose fruits, if slow in their growth, are sure and enduring. A nation, trained up in such a school, will often surprise the world by passing safely through some formidable crisis in which its enemies predict its inevitable ruin; it will, like the government and people of the United States, know how to maintain its constitutional rights against the armed attacks of a violent and misguided minority; it will, as did England and Belgium in the years immediately following 1848, preserve its freedom when despotism and reaction crush the liberties of neighbouring nations; or, again, like those two countries during the year 1848 itself, it will maintain in all their integrity its laws and institutions when the storm of revolution, sweeping over a whole continent, overthrows governments which form the beau-ideal of those who prefer the rule of an intelligent despot to the self-government of an intelligent people.

During the first two months of 1866, Italy, in common with the rest of Europe, had little or no belief that the wrangling of Prussia and Austria would terminate in a resort to arms. The Italians were busy about matters of a very different kind: they were debating what reductions could be made with safety in their army, so as to improve the financial condition of the country. Among other projects for its amelioration there had been formed that of an "Association," or "National Subscription," for diminishing the public debt. At its head was no less a person than the king's cousin, Prince Eugène de Savoy Carignano. The means by which the society was to carry out its project formed the subject of much public discussion; but as time passed on, and the irritation increased between Berlin and Vienna, the government, press, and people of Italy followed with continually increasing watchfulness the diplomatic war between the two German governments, each of whom, by the middle of March, was accusing the other of making armed preparations. By the end of the month the armaments of Austria in Bohemia, and the counter armaments of Prussia, had fairly aroused the attention of the Italian public. The press advised the Government to keep a watchful eye upon what was going on in central Europe. "We cannot sufficiently recommend to our statesmen," wrote the *Perseveranza* of Milan on the 26th of March, "that prudent audacity which holds itself ready for every eventuality, ready to seize every occasion that may be favourable to the completion of the national destinies, without compromising itself by useless demonstrations." This influential and moderate organ of the Italian press, which, up to that time, had had but little belief in war breaking out between Austria and Prussia, continues in the same article to express its belief "that perhaps the day is not far distant when fortune will smile on Italy, offering her a means of triumphing over her adversary." The Italian and Prussian governments entered into negotiations with a view to concert a common action in case of war. General Lamarmora, the head of the cabinet of Florence, conducted the negotiation with ability and success, thus adding another important service to the many he had already rendered to the cause of Italy. In his despatch of the 3d of April, the General states the double object of the alliance, and the principles upon which it was based, according to the views of the Italian government. It was—"1°, To maintain, if necessary by arms, the proposals made by his Prussian Majesty for the reform of the federal constitution in conformity with the wants of the German nation; 2°, To obtain the cession to the kingdom of Italy of Italian territories subject to Austria." As to the principles upon which the alliance was based, the Italian statesman declares it to be that of German and Italian nationality for the furtherance of liberal institutions in Germany and Italy. It is indeed earnestly to be desired that such may be the final result of the Prusso-Italian alliance, and war to the north as well as to the south of the Alps. The concluding portion of the despatch runs thus:—

"Piedmont began in 1859 the work of liberating the Italian soil, with the noble aid of France. We trust that that work may be completed at no distant time by Italy— perhaps in a war of independence, fought side by side with that power which represents the future of the German people, in the name of an identical principle of nationality. Amongst the solutions which, in these last years especially, have been proposed as regards the Venetian question, this more than any other would enable us to remain consistent with our political and international position, and would preserve our national alliances, even the most distant. We shall, besides, be happy to aid Prussia in resisting the designs of the Austrian Empire, by placing herself resolutely at the head of the German national party, by calling together that Parliament which has been for so many years the desire of the nation, and securing in Germany, as has been done in Italy, the progress of liberal institutions, by the exclusion of Austria."

It is pleasant to see Italy thus pushing Prussia, as it were, into the path of progress, and bidding her remember that her real work was not mere self-aggrandizement, nor the humbling of a rival, but the far nobler one of uniting Germany together, and endowing her with a great national system, at once liberal and progressive. Nor can the correctness and elevation of these ideas of the cabinet of Florence be denied, if a large and comprehensive view be taken of the wants and aspirations of the German people; although it must be owned that the course pursued by Prussian statesmen and Prussian diplomacy during the last three or four years has often been such as to dishonour the cause of German nationality and progress.

As regarded Venetia, the policy of the Italian ministers was perfectly consistent with the declarations continually and publicly made during the last six years by Italians of all classes and of all parties. Ever since the formation of the Italian kingdom, the government and the people, the parliament and the press, had made no secret of their determination to unite Venetia to the new kingdom, a union eagerly desired by the people of that province. They were willing enough to compass that end by negotiation and indemnity; but if such means were not opened to them, they avowed very frankly that they should make use of other means whenever the occasion presented itself. Austria, on the other hand, refused to come to any terms touching the cession of Venetia. It was hers by the treaties of 1815, and she intended to keep it. She cared nothing for the fact of Venetians having had no voice in those treaties, which, after the fashion of Campo-Formio, blotted out the ancient Venetian state from the map of Europe, and handed it over to Austria, because it seemed good to the conquerors that it should be so. In vain the wisest friends of Austria advised her to yield; she refused. They gently reminded her of her recent policy with regard to Denmark and the Duchies of the Elbe; she turned a deaf ear to all such remonstrances. They warned her of the danger of a conflict in which she ran the risk of being attacked at the same time by Prussian ambition and Italian patriotism; she pointed to her army and to the Quadrilateral. She had trusted to them in 1859, and the result was Solferino; but that lesson was not enough. Again she trusted to them in 1866, and the result was—Königgrätz.

This attitude on the part of Italy and Austria respectively takes away all real interest from the question which of the two powers first armed. The exact point of time at which the respective armaments commenced, or Italian negotiations with Prussia began, furnishes admirable ground for diplomatic fencing. Two skilful practitioners in that art would be able to sustain a very able and almost endless defence of their respective clients upon such a question. But similar discussions have but little value as regards the real cause of the hostilities which broke out to the south of the Alps. That cause was the possession of Venetia by Austria. It was the question of treaties as against national independence. On the one side were the artificial rights created by the treaties of Campo-Formio and of Vienna, which for their own purposes disposed, each in their own way, of a people who had enjoyed centuries of a great and glorious independence, without deigning to consult that people; on the other was the mighty sentiment of national liberty, the profound conviction that the stranger must be ejected from every part of Italy, if Italy were to be indeed free. That conviction arose from no mere abstract principle, but from the bitter experience of centuries. The occupation of some portion or portions of Italy by one or more foreign powers was ever giving rise to the intervention of others. Germany, France, and Spain had made her the battle-field of their endless quarrels about Italian possessions. Her neighbours fomented her internal discords. Her petty governments were perpetually invoking the aid of the stranger to suit their own purposes. Such had been the fate of Italy up to the end of the eighteenth century; the nineteenth has beheld her first under the dominion of imperial France, next under that of the Hapsbourgs. The curse of foreign domination had eaten into her very soul, and had aroused a deep and universal hatred of the stranger's rule, such as is known to those alone who have been subjected for long years to its galling yoke.

At length, the Italian policy inaugurated by Napoleon III. in 1859—a policy which, despite all its shortcomings, was truly noble, and really worthy of the ruler of a great people—gave Italy the opportunity of establishing her national independence. She turned that opportunity to such good account that friends and foes remained equally astounded at the results. The quarrels of the two German powers, who had hitherto united in oppressing her, offered her, in 1866, an opportunity of completing the work of her unity and freedom. She hastened to seize upon it by forming an alliance with Prussia against Austria. A more compact and better-united Germany, under the direction of the Hohenzollerns, was the object of Count Bismarck; the completion of Italian independence was that of the government and people of Italy. Austria determined to oppose both. She tried to break down the newly-formed alliance by disarming in Bohemia and arming to the full in Venetia. But the Prussian statesman was not the man to be blinded by so transparent a manœuvre. He demanded a complete disarmament on the part of Austria on her southern as well as on her northern frontier. The latter refused, upon which all three powers placed their respective forces on a war footing. France, England, and Russia endeavoured to bring about a Congress for the settlement of the three questions in dispute,—that of the Elbe Duchies, of Venetia, and the reform of the German Bund. Prussia and Italy accepted the proposal, the terms of which were carefully drawn up, so as not to wound the susceptibilities of Austria. This latter power, however, declined the proposal, unless a formal promise was given beforehand that the Congress "should exclude from its deliberations every combination which should tend to give to any one of the states to-day invited to the Congress a territorial aggrandisement, or an augmentation of power." With such questions pending as those of Schleswig-Holstein and Venetia, such a proposition simply rendered all negotiation useless. The three intervening powers, France,

England, and Russia, naturally took that view, and the proposed Congress fell to the ground. Austria, confident in her military strength, preferred an appeal to arms.

On the 20th of June 1866, the King of Italy put forth a proclamation declaring war against Austria. In so far as it referred to the monarch's past devotion to the cause of Italian independence, to his desire to liberate Venice, to his determination to seize again the sword of Goito, Palestro, and San Martino, the proclamation was suited to the occasion; but to refer in such a document to the armaments that had been made by Austria was a mistake. It was fitting enough that that question should be discussed in the despatches of diplomatists, but it had really little to do with the cause of the war, which arose from the desire of the Venetians to be united to Italy, and the determination of the Italians to effect that union, thereby completing their national independence. Austria was determined to prevent that work; Italy was equally determined to accomplish it. All the rest was a mere secondary question of time, policy, and opportunity. The ministers of the crown were, therefore, ill-advised in touching upon the question of armaments in a proclamation which bade the nation rally around the soldier-king, and called his people to arms in the name of the liberties and independence of their country.

Never did such an appeal meet with a more unanimous and enthusiastic reply from an entire people. The Parliament received with shouts of applause the announcement that war had been declared against Austria. The Senate and the Chamber hastened to vote the special powers demanded by the government. The ranks of the army were speedily filled up by soldiers eager to bear a part in the war universally regarded as the final and victorious struggle for the independence of Italy. The National Guard hastened to bear its part in the national armament. The *bureaux* for the enrolment of the volunteer corps were literally besieged by the youth, chiefly of the middle and lower classes, proud to enrol themselves under the command of Garibaldi. Among the young men of the upper classes, those who had quitted the army hastened to return to the military service; many of those who had never entered it volunteered as common soldiers. Thus it was that some twenty or more young Neapolitans of rich and noble families entered in a body the regiment of the Guides. That of the Lancers of Aosta, quartered at Milan when the war broke out, received into its ranks over eighty recruits, all of whom were members either of the aristocracy or of the wealthy families of the Lombard capital. Nor were the two Italian provinces still subject to foreign rule behindhand in responding to their country's call. Upwards of 2000, belonging to the strip of territory which was then still garrisoned by the French in the interest of the Papal temporal power, joined the ranks of the regular army or those of the Garbaldians; and among them were to be found not a few members of rich or aristocratic Roman families. The number of Venetians in the

Italian army before the war amounted to about 14,000—a number further increased in 1866 by those who, escaping across the frontier, took up arms for the redemption of Venice, whose sons were still animated by that spirit which had led them eighteen years before to struggle single-handed against the return of Austrian despotism, with a devoted courage, not the less heroic because it was unsuccessful. Italians of every class vied with one another in sacrificing whatever was most dear to them in their country's cause; their lives, their wealth, their children, were freely devoted to the final and complete liberation of their native land from foreign thraldom.

Yet, noble and heart-stirring as was this spirit of patriotic devotion and self-sacrifice which burst forth throughout the length and breadth of the land, it was not without its defects and dangers. That it should have begotten a feeling of general confidence was right and natural; but that it should have passed beyond that limit, and produced overweening assurance, was much to be lamented. The young and high-spirited nation had the courage and enthusiasm of youth, but it had also its presumption. Of this charge the Italians cannot be acquitted; and it is all the more to be regretted, because their cause was as righteous and as pure as ever roused a people to arms. There were many amongst them who drew in bright colours the future exploits of their army and navy, and some even talked of marching to join the Prussians at Vienna. They forgot that it would have been both good taste and good policy not to have talked overmuch beforehand of what they were *going* to do. They were guilty of no slight fault, which brought with it its own punishment. Yet, in justice it must be added, that the fault arose not from underrating their foe, but from the confidence arising from a deep conviction of the justice of their cause, and from the knowledge that the whole nation was prepared to support it by every possible sacrifice; truths which led them to overlook the fact that courage and devotion, even in support of the most just of quarrels, must be united to good administration and able leadership in order to secure victory. Soldiers may be brave, and do their duty well, as did those of the young Italian army; but to gain battles they must be led by a chief who is not only upright and courageous, but who is also capable of planning a campaign skilfully, and of executing it well. Sailors may be as devoted as those on board the *Palestro*, who preferred to follow the example of their gallant captain, and perish with their ship rather than abandon her, and so run the risk of her being captured by the enemy; their officers may be as gallant as the one on board the *Re d'Italia*, who, when the enemy approached to seize the flag of the sinking vessel, only thinking (even in that terrible moment) of his country's honour and his own duty, fired on the advancing foe, then tore down his ship's flag, and fastened it around his body, that, thus preserved from the enemy's hand, it might with him be saved or with him find a watery grave. Yet fleets manned even by such men will fail to win victories if placed under a commander in whom they feel no confidence, and whose conduct justified only too well the absence of that feeling on the part of those who served under him.

The lesson which the Italians have received has been a bitter one; but it has not been without good effects. They are themselves the severest critics of their own failures during the brief campaign of last year. They search resolutely into the causes of their defeats. In so doing they are right. It is the only honest and manly course—the only one worthy of a free people, who, instead of seeking to hide from themselves the truth as to past failures, are wise enough to study them and learn by them, so preparing the way for success in the future. Thus it was that England repaired, towards it close, the series of blunders which marked the opening of the Crimean campaign, and showed in the power and promptitude with which she overcame the formidable Indian rebellion a year or two later, that the severe lessons of the Russian war had not been studied in vain. So, too, the government and people of the United States, whose mistakes and failures at the beginning of the war against the Southern Secessionists afforded matter of much pleasantry to their European critics, finally succeeded in forming a powerful and efficient military organisation, which annihilated their enemy, changed foreign ridicule into something very like fear, and gave the laughers good reason to meditate upon the homely proverb, "He laughs best who laughs last."

When the war broke out, Italy was able to bring

at once into the field rather more than 200,000 men ready to carry on active operations against the Austrians in Venetia. This force was divided into two armies of about equal strength, one of which, commanded by General Cialdini, had its head-quarters at Bologna, in order to operate on the Lower Po; while the other, under the orders of General Lamarmora, was destined to attack the Quadrilateral on the line of the Mincio. This latter army was composed of the 1st *corps d'armée*, commanded by General Durando; the 2d by General Cucchiari; and the 3d by General Della Rocca. The head-quarters of these three corps were respectively at Lodi, Cremona, and Piacenza before the actual outbreak of hostilities; their forward movement towards the Mincio was directed by the King in person and by General Lamarmora when the war actually broke out. Prince Humbert, the heir to the throne, and his brother, Prince Amadeus, accompanied the army of the Mincio, and took an active part in its operations; the eldest brother commanding the 16th division of the 3d *corps d'armée*, and the second a brigade of the 3d division of the 1st corps. The two young princes proved themselves true scions of the fighting House of Savoy, and displayed on the hard-fought field of Custoza that intrepid courage which has ever distinguished the warrior race from which they spring.

To General Lamarmora's army was thus assigned the arduous task of making a direct attack against the most formidable military position in Europe by crossing the Mincio between the fortresses of Peschiera and Mantua, in order to take possession of the cluster of hills which occupy the north-west corner of the Quadrilateral, and command the plain lying between the Mincio and the Adige. The object of this movement was to cut off Peschiera from the three remaining fortresses of Verona, Legnago, and Mantua, placing at the same time the Italian forces in possession of the hills just mentioned, so as to establish them solidly in a strong position capable of being successfully defended against all attacks which might be made upon it by the Austrians issuing out of Verona. That done, the army of General Cialdini, whose head-quarters were transferred to Ferrara at the outbreak of hostilities, was to cross the Po and march northward upon Rovigo and Padua, or else form a junction with General Lamarmora, as circumstances might direct.

On the morning of the 20th June 1866, notice was given to the Austrians that, at the expiration of three days, active hostilities would be commenced. On the 22d, General Lamarmora's head-quarters were at Canneto; that night they were advanced to Cerlungo, close to Goito, which lies on the right bank of the Mincio. Orders were given to cross that river, which formed the boundary between Venetia and the Italian kingdom, on the following morning, the 23d June. The troops which performed that operation were those of the 1st *corps d'armée*, commanded by General Durando (with the exception of the 2d division, under General Pianell, which remained on the right bank in the neighbourhood of Peschiera, to observe that fortress); and the 3d *corps d'armée*, commanded by General Della Rocca; together with the reserve division of cavalry, under General de Sonnaz.

As to the 2d *corps d'armée*, commanded by General Cucchiari, two divisions, those of General Cosenz and Nunziante, remained on the right bank of the Mincio, and were pushed forward towards Mantua, to watch that strong place. The two other divisions of Generals Angioletti and Longoni did not cross the Mincio until the morning of the 24th, but took no part in the action of that day.

The 1st and 3d *corps d'armée*, which alone were engaged in the battle of Custoza of the 24th June 1866, were composed of the following divisions:—

1st *corps d'armée*, General Durando:
    1st division, General Cerale.
    2d division, General Pianell, ordered to remain on the right bank of the Mincio, not far from Ponti, to watch Peschiera.
    3d division, General Brignone.
    5th division, General Sirtori.

3d *corps d'armée*, General Della Rocca:
    7th division, General Bixio.
    8th division, General Cugia.
    9th division, General Govone.
    16th division, Prince Humbert.

Each division consisting of 16 battalions of infantry, 2 battalions of the bersaglieri, and 3 batteries of artillery, the actual fighting force of a division may be reckoned at 9000 men. The cavalry, under General de Sonnaz, consisted of 20 squadrons and 2 batteries, amounting to 2000 men and 12 guns.

The 1st division of the 1st *corps d'armée* was ordered to cross the Mincio on the morning of the 23d by the bridge at Monzambano; the 2d remained on the right bank, watching Peschiera; the 3d effected its passage at Molini di Volta by means of two pontoon bridges; the 5th crossed by the bridge of Borghetto.

The 7th, 9th, and 16th divisions of the 3d *corps d'armée*, and the cavalry, passed the Mincio at Goito, and the 8th at Ferri, by a pontoon bridge thrown across the river at that place.

This passage of the Mincio was effected without the slightest opposition from the Austrians, who had left untouched the regular bridges of Monzambano, Borghetto, and Goito. In consequence of this apparent inactivity of the enemy, General Lamarmora became unfortunately more than ever convinced that the Archduke Albert, who commanded the Austrian forces in Venetia, was on the other side of the Adige, and that he would offer no serious opposition to the Italian army while taking complete possession of the hills situated in the north-west angle of the Quadrilateral between Peschiera and Verona. Orders were consequently given to the effect that at early dawn on the 24th of June, the 1st, 5th, and 3d divisions of the 1st *corps d'armée* were to march as follows: the 1st division, General Cerale, by Monte Vento and Oliosi to Castelnovo, where the head-quarters of the 1st corps were to be established; the 5th division, General Sirtori, by San Rocco di Palazzolo and San

Giorgio, in Salice, to Santa Giustina; the 3d division, General Brignone, by Custoza and Sommacampagna to Sona. The 3d *corps d'armée*, with its four divisions of the 8th, General Cugia; the 9th, General Govone; the 7th, General Bixio; and the 16th, Prince Humbert, marching in the plain, or skirting the hills on the right of the 1st *corps d'armée*, were to go forward until they finally occupied the line extending from Sona to Sommacampagna, Villafranca, and Mozzecane. The cavalry were to take up their position just to the rear of the two last-named places at Quaderni.

The 1st and a portion of the 3d *corps d'armée* were thus ordered to traverse a broken hilly country within the Quadrilateral, in sight of Verona itself, in order to occupy the long line which extends in a semicircle from Castelnovo to Santa Giustina, Sona, Sommacampagna, Villafranca, and Mozzecane. And yet the Italian commander-in-chief had actually persuaded himself that the Austrians would offer no opposition to such a movement, to be effected in such a field of operation. "But this forward march," he writes naïvely, in his report of the battle, "which it seemed was only to lead simply to taking up a position, changed soon after into a serious action along the whole front of our line." As if it were the most wonderful thing in the world that the Archduke Albert, with his army in and around the great entrenched camp of Verona, should come out at a moment's notice from that stronghold and attack his adversary suddenly while on the march among the hills which General Lamarmora fondly imagined he was going to take possession of without serious opposition. Assuredly it was not to so little purpose, as the Italian commander learned to his cost, that the Austrians had been for half a century in possession of the famous Quadrilateral, had strengthened it by every means which military art could devise, and had made themselves thoroughly acquainted with every inch of its ground, with every road and byeway, river and streamlet, with every hill and valley, with every variation of its surface, with every village, cluster of houses, or solitary building situated either in the plain or among the hills.

The fact is, that the Archduke and his generals watched from their impregnable position at Verona the proceedings of their antagonists. No doubt the satisfaction of the Austrian commanders was great when they saw the Italian army of operation, rather over 200,000 strong, divided into two distinct and equal corps entirely separated from one another, thus giving the Austrians the chance of attacking each corps singly, by issuing out from their strong position in and around Verona at the moment they judged most opportune for doing so. When, then, the Archduke found that one of the Italian armies was crossing the Mincio, he determined to attack the assailants. He knew well that the Italians must detach considerable forces from their main body, as they did, in order to mask Peschiera and Mantua, thus enabling him to meet them on equal terms upon a battlefield so well known to the Austrians as that between Peschiera and Verona. If the Italians were repulsed or beaten, they had the consolation of knowing that they had a river in their rear and a hostile fortress on each flank ; if the Austrians met with a reverse they had the very different consolation of having simply to take refuge in Verona, whose multiplied defences afforded secure shelter to their retreating columns. Surely, then, a general undertaking such a movement as that which the Italian commander-in-chief attempted to execute, should have set about the task, not with the assurance that he would not be attacked, but with the assurance that he might be attacked at any moment, and that he would very probably meet with determined opposition. Nor should any reports that the Austrians were on the other side of the Adige, or appeared to be preparing no movement, have lulled General Lamarmora into security, inasmuch as the position of Verona, which is the junction of three branches of railway, and the nature of its fortifications, which make it a vast fortified camp, enabled the Austrians to change their plans at a moment's notice, according to the proceedings of their adversary, and come out upon him suddenly just when and where he least expected an attack. Such appears to be the conclusion that should have been drawn from all the circumstances of the case when duly considered either from the military point of view, or from the more homely one of common-sense.

On the afternoon of the 23d of June the Austrians commenced their advance. Early on the following morning (the 24th) their forces, consisting of the division of reserve (Ruprecht) forming their extreme right, the 5th *corps d'armée*, a brigade of the 7th corps, and the 9th corps, with their cavalry on their extreme left on the plain near Ganfardine, were in possession of the hills extending from Mongabia to San Giorgio in Salice and Sommacampagna; to the left of which latter place, in the plain below, was their cavalry supported by artillery.

Thus the Italian army on the southern portion of the hills marching in a northerly direction towards the positions which its various divisions were ordered to take up, met half-way the Austrian army, which, from the northern portion of the hills, was marching in a southerly direction. This hilly country is traversed by the little river Tione, which flows in a south-south-easterly direction.

Instead, then, of taking unopposed possession of these hills, General Lamarmora found himself unexpectedly engaged along his whole front, in the midst of them, and in the midst of a march in which baggage-trains stopped in more than one instance the advance and impeded the movements of his troops, so unhappily rooted was his conviction "that this forward movement was only to take up a position." In other words, the Archduke surprised General Lamarmora, and gave him battle precisely when the latter believed that such would not be the case. There is no other conclusion to be drawn from the Italian commander's own report. The fact redounds but little to his foresight and capacity; it proves, on the other hand, that the Archduke knew how to turn the formidable position of Verona to the best possible account, by leaving it suddenly and attacking his enemy just at the time and place in which he least expected such an attack.

The battle began on the extreme right of the Italian army about 6 A.M., and commenced by an attack directed chiefly against the 16th division, commanded by Prince Humbert. The division of General Bixio was on the left of the Prince, that of General Cugia a long way to the rear, and that of General Govone far away to the rear again. Soon after the Austrian artillery had opened fire, Prince Humbert's division was suddenly charged by a large force of cavalry. The Parma brigade, which was in front, formed quickly into squares, within one of which, that of the fourth battalion of the 49th, was the Prince and part of his staff. Twice the onslaught of the Austrian cavalry was impetuously renewed and twice repelled. The division of General Bixio deployed and joined in repulsing the various attacks of the enemy. All the efforts of the Austrians completely failed in this quarter, and severe loss was inflicted upon them. The two divisions of Generals Bixio and Prince Humbert, belonging to the 3d *corps d'armée* of General Della Rocca, maintained their positions throughout the day; nor were they again molested. As will be seen hereafter, they were most unhappily left inactive during the rest of the day, although a fierce struggle was carried on for hours along the hills around Custoza, which formed the central and decisive point of the battle.

But matters proceeded unfavourably to the Italians upon their left at Oliosi; close to which place, the first division of the 1st *corps d'armée* first came in contact with the Austrians. This division, commanded by General Cerale, instead of crossing the Mincio, as it was ordered to do, at Monzambano, descended the river to Valeggio, and crossed the river at that point, where the 5th division, under General Sirtori, was effecting its passage over the Mincio. Hence much confusion and loss of time. Besides which, the vanguard of the 5th division, on arriving at Fornelli, instead of preceding its own division in the direction of San Rocco di Palazzolo, followed the high road towards Oliosi, in front of General Cerale's division (the 1st), which was behindhand in its movement, owing to its having descended the right bank of the river in order to cross it at Valeggio. The 5th division followed the route assigned it in the direction of San Rocco di Palazzolo. Its advancing columns first came into contact with the enemy near the farm buildings of the Pernisa, close to the little river Tione, its second line occupying the heights behind, at Santa Lucia del Tione.

The 1st division, under General Cerale, advancing in column along the high road from Valeggio to Oliosi, came upon the Austrians just beyond that place on the rising ground of Mongabia. General Villarey, who commanded the foremost brigade of the Italian division, seeing the Austrians extended along his front, began quickly to deploy his troops in order to attack the enemy, when he received from his superior, General Cerale, the command to continue the advance in column, as his orders were to take up his position at Castelnovo. General Cerale, impressed with the conviction that the Austrians (as General Lamarmora, the commander-in-chief, declared) would offer no opposition to the march of the Italian army, thought that his subordinate had but to deal with some of the enemy's skirmishers. He soon found out his mistake, which cost him the lives of many brave men and very nearly his own. General Villarey obeyed the order to continue his advance in column, predicting only too truly the fatal consequences, as turning to his son, who was by his side, he said—" On nous envoie à la boucherie. Allons-nous faire tuer en gentilhomme."* Then leading on his men, the gallant officer continued his advance along the high road. The Italians moving forward in column became the focus of the fire and attacks of the enemy who was on their flanks and to their front, while they themselves, marching in column, could offer but an ineffectual resistance. General Villarey was killed, General Cerale wounded, and the Italians were finally driven back in confusion with heavy loss. General Durando, who commanded the 1st *corps d'armée*, upon learning how ill matters were going with the Cerale division, hastened to the front with the 2d, 8th, and 13th battalions of the Bersaglieri, four batteries, and the Lancers of Aosta. These troops, posted on the rising ground between Monte Vento,

---

* "They are sending us to the slaughter-house. Well, let us go and die like gentlemen."

Monte Magrino, and the Colle Lanzetta, offered an effectual resistance to the advance of the enemy. It was during this part of the battle that General Durando was wounded and had to leave the field.

But that which especially contributed to check the progress of the Austrians was the movement made by General Pianell, who commanded the 2d division. When from his position on the right bank of the Mincio, in the neighbourhood of Ponti, he perceived from the heavy and continued firing on the other side, that, contrary to General Lamarmora's expectations, a great battle had begun, he advanced towards the river, and upon finding that the 1st division was being driven back in disorder, he at once took the initiative, boldly crossed the Mincio, attacked the Austrians in flank, checked their advance, and captured a number of prisoners. In vain the Austrians directed their attacks against General Pianell's forces, admirably handled and directed by their able commander. He preserved his menacing position until seven in the evening, thus saving the extreme left of the Italian army from what might have proved an irreparable disaster, and enabling them, when they finally retreated upon Vallegio, about five P.M., to do so without pursuit on the part of the enemy. General Sirtori took command of the 1st *corps d'armée* after General Durando had been wounded and forced to leave the field. Owing to the severe repulse of General Cerale's division, the 5th—that of General Sirtori—had to fall back from the Pernisa to its second line at Santa Lucia del Tione.

Whilst this struggle was going on on the left of the Italian line from the morning until 5 P.M. against the Austrian infantry reserve of Ruprecht and the 5th *corps d'armée* of the Austrians, a yet fiercer contest raged throughout the whole day along the hills close to Custoza, which formed the central scene of action and the key of the whole position. This part of the battle was sustained first by the 3d division of General Brignone, belonging to the 1st *corps d'armée*, and afterwards by the 8th and 9th divisions of the 3d corps, commanded respectively by General Cugia and General Govone. These three divisions bore the whole struggle at the centre against the Austrian 9th *corps d'armée* and the brigade Scudier of the 7th corps.

The 3d division—that of General Brignone—was conducted by General Lamarmora himself, about 7 A.M., to take possession of Monte Torre and Monte Croce, heights which lie a little to the right of the hill on which Custoza stands. The commander-in-chief had the intention of pushing on this division to Sommacampagna, but found the Austrians in force upon the opposing heights of the Berettara, thus barring the further advance of the Brignone division. The numerous artillery of the Austrians, who covered the hills in front of the Berettara between Monte Godio and Staffalo, inflicted heavy loss on General Brignone's troops, after which they were attacked by the enemy with a view to dislodge them from Monte Torre and Monte Croce. An arduous struggle ensued, during which Prince Amadeus, who commanded a brigade of the division, was wounded while leading his men to the charge, as was also General Gozani, who commanded a brigade of the Sardinian grenadiers. After an obstinate fight General Brignone was obliged to fall back before the numerous forces brought up to the attack by the Archduke Albert, who rightly judged that the hills around Custoza formed the key of the whole position; whoever got final possession of them forced his enemy to retire. The eastern slopes of the hill of Custoza were still held by some companies of the grenadiers. These troops fought with a courage and tenacity that would have done honour to the best corps of any of the old armies of Europe. They were still in possession of their position when the divisions of Generals Govone and Cugia, ordered up by General Lamarmora, at length came upon the scene of action, which, however, they did not do, unfortunately, until after General Brignone had fallen back, about 11 A.M.

But before describing the successful counter-attack directed against the Austrians around Custoza by Generals Govone and Cugia, a few words must be said touching an incident that occurred in this part of the day's fighting, which strikes the ordinary reader with astonishment. General Lamarmora, in his second report "on the military operations of the 23d and 24th of June," after describing the hard fighting which resulted in the retirement of the 3d division (Brignone), and before describing the successful counter-attack of the 8th and 9th divisions (Cugia and Govone), says: " I went *in person* to *Goito* to secure that position in case of retreat, and to prepare

to bring up the troops of the 2d *corps d'armée;*" ....
that is, the divisions of Generals Angioletti and Longoni, who, however, never did come up. Now, Goito lies some six or seven miles to the rear of Custoza. The battle, it must be remembered, was raging along the whole line. On the Italian left, at Oliosi, the success of the Austrians was being effectually checked by the admirable movements of General Pianell; on the right at Villafranca they had wholly failed in their attacks upon the divisions of Prince Humbert and General Bixio, in front of whom it is important to remark, as will presently be seen, General Lamarmora says the enemy had left but "insignificant forces;" at the centre a deadly struggle was being carried on between the Archduke, who was making every effort to possess himself of the hills around Custoza, and the division of General Brignone, who was straining every nerve to prevent the enemy gaining such an advantage. At length, after much hard fighting, General Brignone was forced back. Generals Govone and Cugia were coming up, according to the commander-in-chief's orders, but had not yet arrived. And it is about this time that General Lamarmora says that he went off *in person* to Goito, some six or seven miles to the rear. For what purpose? To see that all was right in case of retreat, and to prepare to bring up the two divisions of the 2d *corps d'armée*, which, however, never took any part in the battle, although it lasted some twelve hours. Surely what the commander-in-chief went to do at Goito could have been as well and much more appro-

priately done by an officer of his staff. Surely it was of the utmost importance that the commanding general should have been at Custoza, directing operations at that vital central point against which his adversary was making repeated and desperate attacks. If aides-de-camp and staff-officers are not used under such circumstances to see that all is right in the rear and to order up fresh troops, thus enabling the commander-in-chief to direct the movements of his subordinates on the actual field of action, it is hard to see for what purpose aides-de-camp and staff-officers exist at all.

But to return to the counter-attack of the 9th division, under General Govone, sustained by the 8th, under General Cugia. Their task was a difficult one. They, however, succeeded in establishing themselves on Monte Torre and Monte Croce. Some companies of grenadiers continued to hold the eastern slopes of the hill of Custoza. The Austrians were in possession of Custoza itself, of Monte Belvedere, which lies close to it, and commands the whole position, of Monte Godio and Monte Staffalo. General Govone, seeing the necessity of re-taking Custoza, opened fire upon the Austrians who occupied it, and at length carried it at the point of the bayonet. This success was gained by the intrepid attack of the 34th Bersaglieri, united to the grenadiers, who had been disputing inch by inch the possession of Custoza. The enemy attacked in return, but were repulsed. The 51st regiment was sent forward to aid in maintaining the conquered position. But the adjacent Monte Belvedere was still in the hands of the enemy. General Govone, fully alive to the vital importance of occupying that commanding position directed against the enemy's forces which held it, a sustained and heavy fire, which inflicted upon them severe losses, and Monte Belvedere was finally carried by assault about 3 P.M., by the 34th Bersaglieri, the 51st, and a battalion of the 35th. But the Archduke was as well aware as his opponents of the vital importance of the position he had thus lost. The Austrian commander, therefore, returned to the attack as soon as he was in force to do so. Then commenced one of the fiercest struggles on record. The steady valour of the old Austrian legions, and the devoted courage of the soldiers of the young Italian army, met in fair and deadly strife. The result of the contest, sustained on both sides with the greatest courage and endurance, was for some time doubtful, but the remainder of the 35th regiment having come up, it was at length decided in favour of the Italians. The Austrians were driven back to a considerable distance in disorder. "At 3.30 P.M.," writes General Lamarmora, in his report, "the day seemed gained, at least at this important point." The Archduke Albert says:—

"Despite all the efforts of the 7th and 9th *corps d'armée*, up to 3 P.M. we had not succeeded in taking Custoza. I therefore accorded to my troops, worn out by the burning heat and by the efforts made in the struggle, a moment's repose, and then ordered the 7th corps, sustained by a brigade of the 5th corps, to make a *last* effort to take Custoza, defended by the enemy with obstinacy and great valour."

It was, in truth, the critical moment of the day, for whoever held final possession of Custoza and the adjacent Monte Belvedere, compelled his adversary to retreat. General Govone knew it well, and saw that the Austrians were as well aware of it as he was. He had therefore sent several times to his superior, the commander of the 3d corps, General Della Rocca, to urge him to send with all promptitude reinforcements, as he, General Govone, could not hold his own without; for the Austrians were bringing up every available man to carry the all-important position, for the possession of which so deadly a struggle was raging. General Della Rocca replied that he could not do so, as he had orders to hold Villafranca. The general had, however, at his immediate command, the two divisions of General Bixio and Prince Humbert, with but a very inconsiderable force of the enemy to his front, as General Lamarmora states. How inconsiderable, a reconnaissance of the cavalry attached to the 3d *corps d'armée* would have let its commander know.

General Della Rocca had at his disposal for this purpose a brigade of cavalry, consisting of fifteen squadrons, and the reserve under General Sonnaz of 2000 men. This body of troops, with the exception of three squadrons of the Alessandrian light horse, were kept completely inactive the whole day. Twice Prince Humbert sent to his superior, General

Della Rocca, to know if he might not lead his division to aid Generals Govone and Cugia, who were maintaining so gallant a fight on the hills of Custoza and Monte Belvedere, and twice he received orders to remain where he was. Indeed, General Lamarmora says in his report that the two divisions of General Bixio and Prince Humbert remained all day in the same position. There were, besides, near Roverbella, the two divisions of Generals Angioletti and Longoni, of the 2d *corps d'armée*, who were never brought up to take part in the action. General Lamarmora's report affirms that the commander of the 3d corps, General Della Rocca, "*thought of*" bringing up the two last-named divisions. It would have been better if he had done so instead of only thinking about it. Happily for the 1st corps of the Italian army, General Pianell not only *thought of* crossing the Mincio, but actually did so; and what is more, took that bold initiative on his own responsibility.

It was well, indeed, for the Austrians that the commander of the 3d corps of the Italian army was not a man of the stamp of General Pianell. Had that corps been under the orders of a general of his quickness of perception, and of his resolution in action, General Govone would assuredly not have had to reiterate his demands for reinforcements. A well-directed reconnaissance made by the cavalry attached to the 3d corps at Villafranca, would have soon let its commander know that he had but "insignificant forces" of the enemy to his front, and the obvious conclusion would have been, that the Austrians were bringing their main strength to bear against the central position of Custoza. General Bixio's division, and a brigade of Prince Humbert's, would have been well up in time to maintain the all-important positions of Custoza and Monte Belvedere, so gallantly won by the divisions of Generals Govone and Cugia. Nor would the divisions of Generals Angioletti and Longoni have been left idle the livelong day in the plain between Roverbella and Goito.

As it was, the Archduke Albert, about 4 P.M., gathered all his available forces well in hand in order to make "a *last* effort," and then launched them against Monte Belvedere and Custoza. General Govone did all that lay within his power to repel the overwhelming attack, to aid him in which no reinforcements arrived. At length his division, which had been engaged for some four hours in severe and continuous fighting, was forced to yield the positions it had so bravely won, and the Austrians regained possession of them. General Cugia retired from Monte Torre and Monte Croce, no longer tenable after the loss of Monte Belvedere. The Italians retreated, fighting as they fell back; nor was it until towards 7 P.M., as the Archduke says in his report, that he obtained final possession of Custoza.

The hills all around this latter village, which formed the commanding positions of the field of battle, being thus in the enemy's hands, General Lamarmora deemed it wise, if not necessary, to abandon Villafranca. The whole Italian army thus fell back upon the Mincio;

the divisions of the 1st *corps d'armeé* towards Valeggio, and those of the 3d corps towards Goito. The Austrians made little or no effort to pursue their retiring foe. Themselves worn out with the hard struggle, which had continued throughout the long summer's day beneath a burning sun, they were in no condition to pursue or harass their retreating enemy; and, fearing to see the attack renewed, they flung up earthworks in the neighbourhood of Custoza. The Italian retreat was covered towards Valeggio by a portion of the 1st corps, and especially by the flank position taken up by General Pianell, who did not quit it until seven in the evening. The 3d *corps d'armeé*, in withdrawing from Custoza and Villafranca to Goito, was covered in its retreat by the cavalry, and by the division of General Bixio. The latter repelled without difficulty such efforts as the enemy's cavalry attempted to make in order to disturb the retreating Italian columns. The recrossing of the Mincio was effected unharassed by the Austrians. On the 25th of June the whole Italian army was again on the right bank of that river. The 1st corps of General Durando was at Volta and Cavriana;* the 3d corps of General Della Rocca and the cavalry at Cerlungo; the two divisions of Generals Angioletti and Longoni of the 2d corps were at Goito.

Such was the battle of Custoza of the 24th June 1866, gallantly disputed for twelve hours by the soldiers of the two contending armies. The ultimate success on that hard-fought field rested with the

* Cavriana is about 5 miles north-west of Volta.

Austrians, whose disciplined legions and better generalship succeeded at last in overmatching the devotion and courage of the young Italian army, whose honest and upright chief had done so much in the work of its organisation, but who displayed so little capacity either for conducting a campaign, or for handling effectively the various divisions of a large army during an arduous and protracted battle. The numbers of each army on the field actually engaged amounted to about 75,000 men. The Italians lost in killed, wounded, and prisoners 8175 men, according to the detailed account of the losses incurred by the various divisions; they also left behind them a few pieces of artillery which had been damaged during the engagement. A statement in the *Oesterreichische Zeitschrift* of Vienna gives the Austrian loss at 7100, including more than 1300 prisoners, the greater part of whom fell into the hands of General Pianell.

The Archduke Albert and the generals under him deserve praise for the rapidity with which they issued out of Verona when assured that General Lamarmora had crossed the Mincio. By this prompt movement they surprised the Italian general on the march when he fancied that he was not going to be attacked. During the actual battle, also, the Archduke displayed more capacity than his opponent. Neither the Austrian success against the Italian left at Oliosi, nor the failure to make any impression against the Italian right at Villafranca, diverted the Archduke's attention from the vital points of Monte Belvedere .

and Custoza. Against them he directed his utmost efforts: to win them he strained every nerve. He seems to have perceived at once that they must be won, or he must retire; and that, if he won them, then his adversary must retire. He did, therefore, all that lay in his power to gain possession of those vital positions, and his persevering energy was, after a long and desperate struggle, crowned with success.

In examining the unprecedentedly short campaign of the summer of 1866, several matters of much interest come out as regards the Italian army so recently formed. The soldiers who composed it did their duty well, and fought with courage and endurance. It was also shown that the fusion of its different elements, composed of the inhabitants of all the various provinces of the newly-formed kingdom, had been thoroughly effected—a result due in no slight degree to General Lamarmora, who with others has laboured so earnestly and so successfully during the last six years at the organisation of the Italian army. Every incident of the protracted battle of the 24th of June showed that between the soldiers of one part of Italy and of another there was no greater difference to be found than that which exists in all armies—French, Austrian, or English. The officers bear unanimous testimony to the discipline and courage of their men, and their desire to measure themselves again against the enemy after the unsuccessful battle of Custoza. To this testimony must be added that of the Austrians themselves, who rendered a just tribute to the fighting qualities of their opponents.

This appears not only from the Archduke's report, but also from the language held by the Austrian officers to those of the Italians who were made prisoners during the campaign. Speaking of the military qualities of the soldiers, an Italian officer said to the writer of these pages:—" If all our generals had understood and done *their* work as well as all our men did theirs, the battle of the 24th would have been an Italian, and not an Austrian success."

As to the mistakes made in the planning and execution of the Italian campaign, it may be said that such errors occur in all wars, and that the military men of all nations have their share of blunders to answer for. It is true, also, that the generals of Italy had an arduous task before them, namely, that of attacking an army composed of the troops of one of the oldest of European military powers in possession of the strongest military position in Europe, which since 1859 had been further strengthened by every means which modern art could devise. In fact, Austria had expended, and was expending, millions in adding to the strength of the already mighty Quadrilateral. It is, however, good for the Italians themselves to consider the mistakes they committed, and to study the various criticisms which have been made upon their military operations of the past year.

Having, as they had, rather more than 200,000 men available for attacking Venetia, it was surely a mistake to divide that force into two armies of equal strength, completely separated from each other, one of which, attacking the Quadrilateral in front on the line of the Mincio, was necessarily obliged to leave whole divisions to watch the fortresses of Mantua and Peschiera. The Italian commanders thus offered to the Austrians, who had never more than 80,000 men to bring into the field, the opportunity of giving battle on their own ground within the Quadrilateral, with numbers equal to that of the Italian army on the actual field of battle—an opportunity which the Archduke hastened to profit by. The reverse of Custoza must have brought to the minds of the Italian generals the words of one of the ablest of their number, General Fanti, who died in 1865, and who, feeling his health beginning to fail, used to say, " God grant I may live long enough to persuade my brother generals not to attack the Quadrilateral in front, but to turn it."

Admitting, however, the plan of campaign actually adopted, it was surely most hazardous of General Lamarmora to attempt taking up so extended a line as that reaching from Castelnovo to Santa Giustina, Sona, Sommacampagna, Ganfardine, Villafranca, and Roverbella, without a second line, without a large reserve, with the Mincio in his rear, and a hostile fortress on each flank. The French, in 1859, with a much larger force, deemed it prudent to hold a much less extended line upon this very ground. In order to take up the position selected by General Lamarmora, his army had to traverse a broken undulating country, within sight of the great entrenched camp of Verona, out of which the Austrians could come at a moment's notice—as they did—or wait until he had taken up his too extended position, and then throw their whole weight on some one given point, to oppose which movement General Lamarmora had kept no reserve force at hand. That he had grounds for supposing that the Archduke was not in a position to attack on the 24th, may, no doubt, have been the case; but how General Lamarmora could have persuaded himself of the certainty, or almost certainty, that he would not be attacked, it is difficult to understand. There is no trace of his having concerted a plan of action with the generals under him in case of their being attacked while marching to take up the positions assigned to them; no strong reconnaissance was made in advance which would have given timely warning of impending danger. The divisions of the army marched into the Quadrilateral with considerable distances separating several of them, with baggage and auxiliary trains, with almost as little precaution as if they were going to change garrison, instead of entering the strongest military position in Europe, within sight of Verona itself! More than once General Lamarmora speaks in his report of carts and baggage obstructing the movements of his troops. But did not such untoward circumstances arise from the manner in which the advance was made, in the full conviction that the Austrians were not going to attack, but were obliging enough to wait until the Italians had taken full possession of the whole semi-circle of hills from Castelnovo to Sommacampagna and Custoza, as well as of Villafranca, in the plain below?

Surprised on his march—as General Lamarmora admits being—he fails to display that quickness of perception and sure *coup d'œil*, which sees at a glance what must be done under the unexpected circumstances, discerns instantly the vital point to be won or maintained, and brings to bear upon it every available resource. He seems to have had but a partial idea of the importance of Custoza and Monte Belvedere; true, he brings up the Brignone division to the hills of Monte Torre and Monte Croce, close to Custoza, and orders up reinforcements to support it; but instead of waiting to see them come up, and directing in person the great central struggle, bringing every available man to bear upon this key of the whole battle-field, he rides off to Goito, some six or seven miles to the rear, to do work which he should have sent his aides-de-camp to perform.

General Della Rocca also showed himself incapable of dealing with an unexpected emergency, even when the course to be taken was pointed out to him. In vain General Govone, fully alive to the greatness of the occasion, reiterates his demands to General Della Rocca for further support; in vain Prince Humbert begs to be allowed to aid the divisions of Generals Cugia and Govone. General Della Rocca replies, that he has orders to hold Villafranca, and keeps the divisions of General Bixio and Prince Humbert there the entire day, although they had before them a most inconsiderable force of the enemy ever after the attack made upon them in the early morning, as General Lamarmora says in his report, and as

General Della Rocca might have ascertained had he ordered his cavalry to make a reconnaissance to his front. As it was, he satisfied himself with holding Villafranca; kept two divisions of infantry and 15 squadrons of cavalry, with 42 guns, in the same positions they had held in the morning, doing nothing all the remainder of the day, and contented himself with *thinking about* ordering up the divisions of Generals Angioletti and Longoni, who, however, never appeared. In consequence, Generals Govone and Cugia did not receive the reinforcements so urgently needed and demanded; they were, therefore, obliged to give up Monte Belvedere and Custoza, which they had won. The Austrians thus regained possession of them, and the Italian army had to retreat; it is ordered to recross the Mincio, which it does without difficulty, the enemy making no attempt to harass it during that operation.

But if there were blunders committed by some of the Italian generals, there was considerable ability displayed by others. Generals Govone and Cugia directed with great skill and energy their successful counter-attack upon Custoza and Monte Belvedere, of whose importance they were fully aware. General Bixio was deservedly praised for the manner in which he covered the retreat of the 3d *corps d'armée*. Colonel Bonelli commanded with great ability and effect the batteries which, in the neighbourhood of Monte Vento and Monte Magrino, were brought up to check the advance of the Austrians, after the severe repulse of General Cerale's division. Colonel Boni displayed no little skill and great tenacity in maintaining throughout the day, with two battalions of grenadiers, his hold on the slopes of the hill of Custoza. Colonel Strada, with three squadrons of the Alessandrian light horse, drove back a larger force of the celebrated Hungarian hussars during the attack upon Prince Humbert's division, near Villafranca, in the early morning of the 24th.

But the Italian general whose conduct on that day deserves special praise, and who gave proof of a high order of military capacity, was General Count Pianell. Placed with his division on the right bank of the Mincio, he no sooner perceived that, contrary to the commander-in-chief's expectations, a great battle had begun, than he moved his forces towards the river, and when aware of the repulse of the 1st division he crossed over to the left bank on his own responsibility. By this bold initiative, promptly taken and ably executed, he effectually checked the advance of the Austrians, and inflicted upon them severe loss by this flank attack. Nor could any efforts of which the enemy were capable succeed in driving him from his menacing position, which he held until seven P.M., thus covering the retreat of the 1st and 5th divisions upon Valeggio.

General Pianell displayed in the very trying circumstances in which he was placed not only the quickness of perception which sees in a moment what is best to be done, and then proceeds to do it with promptitude and ability, but also that high moral courage which does not hesitate to take upon itself heavy responsibility in the performance of an arduous duty suddenly rendered necessary by unlooked-for danger. It is an interesting fact, that the gallant commander who thus distinguished himself was a Neapolitan never before engaged in actual war, but who had diligently employed his time, unknown to the world at large, in the close and careful study of military science. General Pianell now commands the important military department whose headquarters are at Verona. He will doubtless continue to hold a high place amongst those who have to regulate the military affairs of his country, or who may have hereafter to plan and execute the future operations of her army.

The necessity of being thoroughly and scientifically acquainted with the art of war in all its varied branches and details cannot be too much impressed upon the officers of the young Italian army. It is not simply by mere personal courage on the field of battle that military operations are well carried out and victories won. If such results are to be gained, courage and devotion must be supplemented by that scientific knowledge which persevering study alone can give. What brilliant results may be obtained by generals and officers who have thus studied, even when having had but little practical experience of war, is exemplified in the case of Prussia, who overthrew in a moment her powerful antagonists, and in a brief campaign of three or four weeks crushed their armies, broke up the old German Confederation, and dictated peace to the great military empire of Austria within sight of its capital.

The errors committed by General Lamarmora in conducting the operations of the army of the Mincio, which have been sharply criticised by military authorities, have been recalled in these pages because truth demanded the performance of that unpleasant duty when dealing with the subject of "Italy and the War of 1866." But the reader would be far indeed from the truth if he supposed that the enumeration of such alleged errors arose from a desire to lessen the real merits of the gallant general, or from any wish to diminish the many claims he has upon the gratitude of his countrymen. It is not too much to say that Italians and all the friends of Italy would be guilty of deep ingratitude, if the loss of a single battle, or the commission of errors which but prove the absence of great military capacity, led them to forget the immense services which, during a life devoted to the faithful discharge of public duties, General Lamarmora has rendered to his sovereign and to his country. It was he who reorganised the Piedmontese army after the unsuccessful campaigns of 1848 and 1849. It was he who led some 18,000 of those troops to victory in the Crimea, where their discipline and valour excited general and deserved admiration. It is to him, in a large measure, that praise is due for successfully forming around the nucleus of that brave army, the army of Italy, which throughout the protracted twelve hours' struggle of Custoza proved how well the work of its organisation and the fusion of its various elements had been performed. It was he whose administrative firmness and justice first succeeded in substituting something like order and good government for the chaos of corruption and vice to which the people of Naples had been accustomed by the Bourbon dynasty, whose steady aim it was to render the people they misruled ignorant, superstitious, and brutal. It was he who, in the difficulties which arose out of the transfer of the seat of government from Turin to Florence, was called to the helm of the state; and by his firm and upright conduct of affairs appeased the troubles of the hour, and carried through the celebrated convention of September 1864, which had been made with the French government, and which resulted in the withdrawal of the French troops from Rome. It was he who successfully conducted the negotiations which led to the Prussian alliance, so fruitful in its results to Italy. And if to-day (March 1867) the aspiration of centuries is accomplished, and the soil of Italy from the Alps to Sicily, and from Mount Cenis to the lagoons of Venice, is freed from all foreign rule, among those to whom that great deliverance is due he will ever hold an honoured place in the annals of emancipated Italy. Great have been the services which he has rendered to her cause; nor does it require the gift of prophecy to affirm that, if life and health are spared to him, the list of those services is not yet completed. It may be clear enough that he does not possess the highest order of military talent, such as is capable of planning and directing with success the movements of large armies against the most formidable military position in Europe, but that fact by no means proves that he is incapable of rendering in the future, as in the past, most valuable service in the conduct of political and also of military affairs. If uprightness and true patriotism—if the keenest sense of honour ever preserved unsullied—if chivalrous loyalty to his king—if constant and often self-sacrificing devotion to his country's welfare—if the assiduous and conscientious discharge of public duties are virtues which excite admiration and esteem, assuredly to no living man is such admiration and esteem more due than to Alfonso Lamarmora.

But it is time to return to the main subject, and give an account of what occurred after the battle of Custoza. The conclusion come to at the headquarters of the Italian army, after the retreat across the Mincio, is thus stated:—" Our attempt to establish ourselves between the Mincio and the Adige, in order to separate the fortresses (of the Quadrilateral) from one another, not having been successful, the position we had taken up along the Mincio had no longer any object." It was therefore determined not to renew the attack. The feeling throughout the army was of an exactly opposite kind; officers and men desired, on the contrary, to renew the attack as soon as possible, nor would there have been any difficulty in doing so a day or two later. The divisions of Generals Angioletti and Longoni had taken no part whatever in the action; to them might have been added at least a brigade of General Cosenz's division, which, with that of General Nunziante, was watching Mantua. The divisions of Prince Humbert and General Bixio were almost intact; that of General Pianell had suffered but slight losses. These various divisions made up a force of nearly 50,000 men. The three divisions of Generals Cugia, Govone, and Sirtori, which had suffered heavy losses, would certainly have been able to muster from 6000 to 7000 men each, thus making up a force of about 70,000 men. The remains of the divisions of General Cerale and General Brignone, which had been terribly cut up, could have watched Peschiera. Such a course, which the army would have gladly seen adopted, was, however, not pursued. All further attacks in the direction of Custoza and Sommacampagna were abandoned, and the army was withdrawn behind the river Oglio. The generals set about devising a fresh plan of campaign, concerning which it seems that opinions differed not a little. More than a week was consumed in these movements and discussions, accompanied, as usual in the case of failure, by a good deal of unpleasant criticism as to whom most blame was due for the want of success. This loss of time greatly displeased the nation and the army, both desirous of again measuring themselves with the hereditary foe of Italy. In the meanwhile the Prussians had been gaining continual successes, and had at length inflicted upon the Austrians the overwhelming defeat of Königgrätz on the 3d of July. The tidings of that great victory were speedily followed by an announcement which nowhere produced a greater sensation than in Italy. On the 5th appeared the following official paragraph in the French *Moniteur*:—

"A very important event has just taken place. The Emperor of Austria, having maintained intact the honour of his arms in Italy, accepts the ideas set forth by the Emperor Napoleon in his letter of the 11th June, addressed to his Minister of Foreign Affairs, and cedes in consequence Venetia to the Emperor of the French, whose mediation he accepts in order to re-establish peace between the contending parties. The Emperor Napoleon has hastened to reply to this appeal, and has immediately addressed himself to their majesties the Kings of Prussia and of Italy, in order to bring about an armistice."

On the same day the Emperor of the French wrote the following note to the King of Italy:—

"PARIS, 5*th July* 1866.

"SIRE,—The Emperor of Austria, acceding to the ideas set forth in my letter to M. Drouyn de Lhuys, cedes to me Venetia, and declares himself ready to accept a mediation in order to bring about peace between the belligerents.

"The Italian army has had an opportunity of showing its valour. A greater effusion of blood is therefore unnecessary, and Italy can obtain honourably the object of her aspirations by an arrangement with me, concerning which it will be easy to come to an understanding. I am writing to the King of Prussia, in order to make him acquainted with the position of affairs, and to propose to him as regards Germany, as I do to your majesty as regards Italy, the conclusion of an armistice, as preliminary to negotiations for peace.

(Signed) "NAPOLEON."

The King of Italy replied, thanking the Emperor for the interest he took in the Italian cause, and reserving to himself to consult his government, and to learn the views of his ally the King of Prussia concerning this most important proposal :—

"As regards the armistice or the suspension of hostilities," writes on this same 5th of July Signor Visconti-Venosta, the Italian Minister of Foreign Affairs, to M. Nigra, the Italian Minister at Paris, "the King's government has a double duty to perform; towards Prussia, who, not having notified to us her acceptation of the proposal, has a right to expect that we continue to prosecute our military operations; towards the Italian populations subject to Austria, not comprised within the administrative limits of Venetia, whose liberation ought to be the object of our utmost efforts."

On the same day, Signor Visconti-Venosta wrote to the Count de Barral, the Italian Minister at Berlin, as follows :—

"FLORENCE, *5th July.*

"SIGR. MINISTRO,—Be good enough to inform yourself with the utmost possible solicitude of the feeling of the Prussian government concerning the proposition of mediation and armistice made by the Emperor of the French. I have sent by telegram to your lordship the sense of the reply made to the same by the King. Our loyalty, and the unanimous desire of the Italian nation, secure to the Prussian government the continuance of our co-operation in so far as it has a right to ask it. We desire, under all circumstances, to come to an understanding with it (the Prussian government) as to the conditions to be established in common between Italy and Prussia, in order that we may be in a position to reply to the proposal of the Emperor of the French.

(Signed) "VISCONTI-VENOSTA."

This firm determination of the Italian government

to remain faithful to its Prussian ally, and not to conclude a peace, (even though it offered Venetia to Italy,) without having first come to an understanding with Prussia, was in full accordance with the universal feeling of the Italians. Indeed, such a course was the only one that could be for a moment entertained under the circumstances by a nation which had any regard for its honour, or the slightest feeling of self-respect. If a moment's doubt could have been entertained upon such a point, it would have been dissipated by the language of the Vienna papers, which openly avowed that peace must be made with Italy, in order to give Austria the full use of all her resources against Prussia.

The Italian government and people further determined, most rightly, that deeds as well as words must prove their unswerving fidelity to the engagements they had entered upon with Prussia before the war. Therefore it was that, on the 7th of July, the troops of General Cialdini began their movements in order to cross the Po, and by the 14th of the month they had occupied Padua. General Nunziante attacked the forts of Borgoforte on the 17th, and on the night of the 18th the Austrians were compelled to evacuate that place and retire to Mantua. General Cialdini continued his onward march, occupied Vicenza and Treviso, and pushed on beyond the Tagliamento towards the Isonzo. In the meanwhile Garibaldi attacked the Trentine district on the side of the Guidicaria and Val d'Ampola, while one of the divisions of General Cialdini's army, that of General Medici, pushed up the Val Sugana towards the town of Trent, advancing to within five miles of it, when the armistice between Italy and Austria having at length been signed, further hostilities were put an end to.

This little campaign of General Medici was very well executed, but the inferior numbers which the Austrians were able to oppose to him, owing to the withdrawal of the greater part of their army from Venetia, deprive it of value as a military success. The instant the Austrian government had handed over Venetia to France it recalled in the utmost haste its troops from that province in order to protect Vienna, which was in the most imminent possible danger after the crushing defeat of Königgrätz. The Austrians left only the necessary garrisons in the fortresses of the Quadrilateral and in those of Venice. The defence of the Trentine district was left to a body of troops much inferior to those under the command of General Medici, and the volunteers of Garibaldi. Some of the enemies of Italy have therefore represented the advance of General Cialdini as a vain-glorious affair, undertaken at a time when the Austrians, on account of the Prussian victories, were obliged to evacuate Venetia. Such a statement is an utter misrepresentation of the case. No Italian ever speaks of General Cialdini's advance, or of whatever advantages General Medici may have gained, as if they were occasioned by Italian successes. That advance was made as an assurance to Prussia that the Italians did not consider the handing over of Venetia to France by Austria as in any degree freeing them from their engagements with their German ally; those engagements being binding until Prussia herself was satisfied, in common with Italy, as to the terms of peace granted to the allies by Austria. They further desired, by taking possession of whatever portion they could of Venetia, and by pushing on to the Austrian frontier, to hold such a position as would enable them effectually to aid Prussia in the case of Austria not accepting the conditions demanded, and the war in consequence being resumed ; a possibility which might easily have occurred, as the Prussian demands included the ejection of Austria from the German Confederation, to which the house of Hapsburg was not likely to assent, unless from the belief of being wholly unable to continue the war against the allies. The conduct of Italy was therefore not only justifiable, but was the only course which could have been pursued with honour. That she did pursue it without hesitation, and without allowing herself to be hindered by the cession of Venetia to France, only proved that Italy possessed a proper sense of the binding nature of the engagements entered into with Prussia, which she rightly deemed must be faithfully and fully maintained at all costs. This conduct of Italy was spoken of in the highest terms, as it well deserved, by Count Bismark, in a speech delivered on the 20th December, in the Prussian Chambers, on the subject of the war and the negotiations which followed it.

"We had," he said, "a powerful support in the unshakeable fidelity of Italy—fidelity which I cannot sufficiently praise, and whose value I cannot too highly appreciate.

The Italian government resisted with great energy the temptation of abandoning the alliance on account of Austria's gift (that of the cession of Venetia) who was our common enemy; from this fact we can draw legitimate hopes in favour of the friendly and natural relations which in future ought to unite together Germany and Italy."

The Emperor of the French has been blamed for the manner in which he stepped in, as tending to arrest the action of Italy in a way which it was wholly impossible for her to agree to with honour. Indeed the Italians felt not a little irritated by the position in which the intervention of the Emperor placed them. That irritation gradually subsided as circumstances enabled them to form a juster idea of the course pursued by the French government, which in the first instance, it must be owned, seemed to take too little into account the just susceptibilities of a people smarting under a defeat, which only made them more anxious to keep scrupulously their engagements, and show that they were ready to strike another, and, as they hoped, a more successful blow against the common enemy. Such feelings were natural and even praiseworthy, in so far as they showed a keen sense of national honour; nor is there any other people possessed of a proper sense of what is due to itself and to others, who would not in like circumstances have felt as did the Italians.

The intervention of the Emperor Napoleon had too much the appearance of wishing to separate Italy from Prussia, thereby enabling Austria to direct all her forces against the latter. Such was the impression produced by the announcement of the cession of Venetia at the headquarters of the Prussian army, where, as generally throughout Germany, much irritation was felt against Austria for having called in French intervention to put an end to the quarrel between the German powers. The Vienna papers openly declared that Italy was to be appeased in order that Austria might have at her disposal her whole available forces against her rival in Germany. Such statements only made the Italians fear the more that their Prussian allies might suspect them— as they seem for a moment to have done—of being faithless to the engagements entered into before the war. The possibility of such a suspicion naturally irritated the Italians, who complained much of the position in which they were placed. Nor was such irritation lessened by the fact, that while the important announcement in the *Moniteur* spoke of the Emperor of Austria "having maintained the honour of his arms intact in Italy," it uttered no word tending to smooth the *amour propre* of the Italian army, nettled by a defeat in which the capacity of one or two of its generals, but not the courage of its soldiers had been found wanting. It has been said that such a feeling of *amour propre* was out of place. To which it may be replied, that such a feeling was an inevitable consequence of what had occurred; that to have repressed it was impossible; that no other people would have been without it under similar circumstances.

The truth is, that the victory of Königgrätz made

the French government forget for the moment every other consideration excepting that of saving Austria. Nor is such a consequence to be wondered at. France had every possible reason for preserving Austria from what threatened to be simple annihilation. It would be unjust to the Emperor Napoleon to forget the difficulties and dangers of every kind which would have come upon him had he allowed Austria to have succumbed completely to her rival. The danger was imminent, and he is scarcely to be blamed, if, when it first arose with a suddenness that baffled all previous calculation, he somewhat forgot what was due to others in his efforts to ward off a catastrophe fatal to Austria, and fraught with no little danger to himself. But Austria once saved, though at a heavy cost to herself, the Emperor of the French gave abundant proof that his feelings of friendship and goodwill towards Italy were as strong as ever. It is easy to point out the shortcomings which have marked on more than one occasion his Italian policy; but whoever bears in mind the innumerable difficulties of his position cannot but allow that the Emperor Napoleon has after all been a faithful friend to Italy, and that her freedom would assuredly not be to-day an accomplished fact but for the great policy which, in spite of the utmost opposition both at home and abroad, he inaugurated in 1859. The consequences which have flowed from it have surpassed the good which the Emperor intended to effect, namely, the exclusion of Austria from the peninsula by the establishment of a kingdom of North Italy; but those greater consequences do not diminish the merit of Napoleon's original intention—they only redound to the wisdom and courage of the Italians, who thus proved how capable they were of turning to the utmost account the occasion offered them by the enlightened policy and sincere friendship of Napoleon III.

If, however, the Italian government deserves real praise for the determination and fidelity which it showed towards its ally at the moment of the Austrian cession of Venetia to France, it clearly erred in not at once accepting and signing an armistice when Prussia agreed to do so at Nikolsburg on the 26th July. The true course of Italy was to have gone completely hand-in-hand with Prussia under all circumstances which came within the engagements made before the war. It may be that all the causes are not yet known to the world at large which led to the delay in signing the armistice between Austria and Italy, which did not take place until the 12th August; but from what is actually known, it appears that the delay occurred from Italy's endeavour to conclude the armistice on the basis of the *uti possidetis* with a view of making good her claims to the Trentine district, her forces being in possession of a large portion of that province. She sought to reserve to herself expressly the power of raising the question of the Trentino during the negotiations for a final peace, in order to obtain a rectification of frontiers which would unite to her the Trentine province, and make the river Isonzo itself her eastern frontier. But inasmuch as Prussia had only engaged before the war to obtain the liberation of Venetia, the cabinet of Berlin was in no degree bound upon the subject of the Trentino nor upon the question of the *uti possidetis*. Prussia had indeed obtained her armistice upon the basis of the *uti possidetis*, but then there was this great difference between the position of the two belligerents—the one, Prussia, had been victorious; the other, Italy, had been beaten. It is true that France had agreed to use her best efforts, as she did, to obtain an armistice for Italy on the basis of the *uti possidetis*, and that the Emperor was favourable to such a frontier between Italy and Austria as was desired by the former of these two powers, wisely deeming such a frontier to be really in the interest of both, and as being more conducive to a lasting peace between them. But it surely required no extraordinary foresight to perceive that if Austria refused such terms, France would not enforce them by arms. When, then, Italy found that Prussia was not only agreeing to an armistice, but was even hurrying on negotiations for peace, as well she might, considering that her supremacy in Germany was secured by the ejection of Austria from every German confederation, the Italian statesmen should at once have agreed to an armistice and negotiations for the re-establishment of peace conjointly with Prussia. Had they taken that clear and penetrating view of the case which is rarely wanting to Italians when the question to be solved is one of diplomatic tact and skill, they would have perceived that this hanging back upon the questions of the *uti possidetis* and the rectification of frontiers, when Prussia was pressing on, and when France had no intention of going beyond a diplomatic support of Italian claims, could only result in the isolation of Italy, and would oblige her finally either to accept the armistice and subsequent negotiations upon the Austrian terms, or to recommence hostilities single-handed against Austria, thereby putting in peril the acquisition of Venetia itself. And this was precisely what occurred, the end being, that Italy had to accept the terms offered by Austria, thus bringing upon herself a diplomatic defeat in addition to the material ones she had already suffered by land and sea.

But the fault thus committed was quite as much due to the condition of public feeling as to the mistakes of the Italian government. Bitterly disappointed at the result of the war, smarting under unexpected defeats, justly angry with more than one of their military and naval commanders, the Italians were unable at the moment to take a calm and just view of the circumstances in which they were placed, and failed to see the absolute necessity of yielding to the inevitable conditions which those circumstances had created. It is rare indeed that they fall into such errors, but so it was in this instance, as the Italians now admit; one of whose excellent qualities it is, that they never seek to blind themselves as to their mistakes, faults, and failures. At present they are much inclined to exaggerate them, a wholesome fault, which their sincere friends will be in no hurry to check. Many of them, indeed, grumble and find fault with everything and everybody, in a manner worthy of old John Bull himself, with whom grumbling is a cherished and oft-exercised privilege. The symptom is by no means a bad one; and even though it may sometimes run into exaggeration, its effects are much more likely to be beneficial than hurtful.

Those, however, who have known what it is to see expectations falsified and failure incurred where success was justly anticipated, (and there are no nations who have not gone through that unpleasant experience at some moment of their history,) will find perhaps some excuse for that ill-humour of the Italians, which prevented them seeing the best course to be pursued on the question of the armistice, if it be remembered that it was just in the midst of the delicate negotiations consequent on the cession of Venetia to France that the defeat of the Italian fleet at Lissa occurred. True, such disasters ought to make the sufferers more reasonable, ready to lower their demands, and inclined to yield; but in almost all cases they only irritate a people, particularly if high-spirited and sensitive, so as to blind them even to their own real interests under the circumstances. If ever irritation were excusable, it assuredly was so in the case of the Italians when they learned of the defeat sustained by Admiral Persano. They had spent ungrudgingly their money in order to create a navy in accordance with the wants of Italy's maritime character and position. The Peninsula possesses a considerable population along its extended coasts, fond of the sea, and composed of brave and skilful sailors. The Italians possessed a fleet much more numerous than the Austrian, more heavily armed, and composed of a larger number of ironclads, more than one of which was superior to any similar vessel in the Austrian navy. It was therefore natural that they should anticipate decided success at sea; instead of which Admiral Persano, whose fleet included twelve ironclads, was beaten by Admiral Tegethoff, who had at his command but seven of that class of ships.

Admiral Persano first directed an attack against the island and forts of Lissa, which he failed to take. When the Austrian fleet arrived, with the object of obliging him to cease his attack on Lissa, Admiral Persano, although he had obtained information beforehand of the approach of his adversary, not only failed to beat or drive off the enemy's fleet, but was himself driven off, with the loss of two vessels. Admiral Tegethoff thus succeeded in relieving Lissa, into whose port he entered without the loss of a single vessel, after a fight of from three to four hours, which Admiral Persano, although still in greater force than his adversary, did not attempt to renew; on the contrary, he drew off and made for Ancona, after having wholly failed to effect any one of the objects for which the expedition was undertaken. This failure was greatly aggravated by the fact that the ship on board of which Admiral Persano placed himself during the action, inflicted no loss whatever upon the enemy, although belonging to a most formidable class of the newest kind of war-ships. Her name was the *Affondatore;* she was a powerful ironclad monitor, furnished with an immense spur, for the purpose of charging and running down her antagonists; she had a couple of 300 lb. Armstrong guns on board, measured 4000 tons, and had engines of 700-horse power. The admiral left his own ship, the *Re d'Italia*, only just before the battle commenced, to go on board the *Affondatore*, placed her "out of the line of attack," in order, as he says, "to take a part according to circumstances in the combat at the most opportune moment, and to convey orders more promptly to the various parts of the fleet." In fact, it appears that the *Affondatore* took up her position behind the other ironclads. The admiral relates a series of manœuvres executed by this vessel, which may have been very masterpieces of nautical skill, but which, as a matter of fact, failed to inflict the slightest loss upon the enemy, and "the whole of which history," as Colonel Rustow justly observes, "is singularly obscure." Indeed, to the ordinary reader, with nothing but common-sense to guide him, it seems little else than a miserable attempt to conceal a miserable failure. The only part of the account which is clearly corroborated by facts is, that the *Affondatore* took up her position "out of the line of attack;" and that, after a fight in which Admiral Persano losses two vessels and some 900 men, he withdraws from the scene of conflict, so as to be completely out of sight of Lissa by the following morning. Yet it is in the face of such facts that a despatch, dated "the channel of Lissa, 20th July," contains these words: "The Italian fleet remained master of the waters in which the combat took place," —a phrase which will ever rank as one of the most absurd and impudent attempts to conceal the truth which was ever penned. In truth, the only success which Admiral Persano gained in all this wretched business of Lissa, was that of deluding, for a day or two, the Italian public into the belief that his disgraceful failure had been a victory. But the truth soon came out, and naturally produced a feeling of just and general indignation. It was determined that a strict investigation should take place as to the facts of the case and the conduct of the admiral. A sincere and searching examination was imperatively demanded; and the Senate, to which body Admiral Persano belonged, was finally called upon to exercise its constitutional function of investigating and judging the conduct of its member, who had given his country good reason to suppose that he was himself the chief cause of the disaster of Lissa. Such a course was not only justifiable but right; for by it alone could be determined the measure of blame due to Admiral Persano, and what amount, if any, fell to the share of others.

The conduct of Admiral Tegethoff was that of a brave and able man, who, though possessed of means very inadequate to the task assigned him, yet knew how to make them sufficient for the purpose by the boldness with which he used them, and by the confidence which his courage and determination inspired.

As soon as he found that Admiral Persano was attacking Lissa, the Austrian commander made at once for that place. He knew that he was about to meet an enemy superior to him in force; but, nothing daunted, he determined to drive his adversary away from Lissa, or perish in the attempt. Instead of placing the vessel he commanded "out of the line of attack," and making her take up a position behind the other ironclads, Admiral Tegethoff gallantly led them on. Nor does that course appear to have at all prevented him "from conveying promptly his orders to the different parts of his fleet." As regards that "opportune moment" for attacking and damaging the enemy, which Admiral Persano was never fortunate enough to hit upon, Admiral Tegethoff discovers it instantly, and uses it to such good purpose, that with his own vessel, the *Archduke Ferdinand Maximilian*, he sinks the *Re d'Italia*. The general result of his courageous onslaught being, that he destroys two of the enemy's ships, breaks through his fleet, which sought to prevent the Austrians from reaching Lissa, and takes up a position in front of that port, so as to protect it from further attack: after which Admiral Persano drew off, and by the next morning was out of sight, making for Ancona.

If Admiral Tegethoff had had to measure himself with a man of his own pluck, he must have been beaten, being, as he was, so inferior in ironclads to his adversary. That he would, even in that case, have inflicted some loss upon the Italian fleet is quite possible, because he is one of those com-

L

manders who know how to lead gallantly gallant men. He would therefore very probably have made his enemies pay dearly for their victory. As it was, he won without the loss of a single vessel, and if his adversary rejoiced in being "master of the waters," the Austrian admiral no doubt found sufficient consolation in the fact that he was "master of Lissa." Such having been the result of the naval operations commanded by Admiral Persano, it was both just and natural, under the circumstances, that the whole affair should be carefully examined, and an authoritative decision be arrived at. At the end of January 1867, the Senate decided by 71 votes against 60, that there was not sufficient ground for bringing the admiral to trial on the charge of cowardice; but a majority of 116 to 15 decided that there was ground for proceeding to try him on the charges of incapacity and negligence, as also upon that of disobedience, this last accusation being sustained by 83 votes against 48. If the three charges of incapacity, negligence, and disobedience be proved, Admiral Persano will no doubt be deprived of all further opportunity of winning victories which leave his adversary master of the place attacked, and himself "master of the waters." *

The armistice which was signed between Italy

* On 15th April 1867 the Senate pronounced Admiral Persano guilty on the charges of incapacity, negligence, and disobedience; it sentenced him to retire from the service, to be degraded from the rank of admiral, and to pay the costs of the trial. It has been well said that at the battle of Lissa "every man in the Italian fleet—but one—did his duty." Upon that one man the Italian Senate justly inflicted signal punishment, after full and fair investigation.

and Austria on the 12th August, was followed by negotiations which led to the conclusion of a treaty of peace between the two powers on the 3d October 1866, at Vienna. The Emperor of Austria renounced his title to the Lombardo-Venetian kingdom, and consented to its union with the kingdom of Italy, which he at length recognised, and with which he agreed to establish diplomatic relations. The debt that Italy took upon herself in consequence of receiving Venetia, was not regulated upon the basis of the proportion of the debt of that province to the general debt of the Austrian empire, but upon the principle of its being a portion of the debt of the Lombardo-Venetian kingdom only, as was done in the case of the cession of Lombardy by the treaty of Zurich in 1860. In maintaining that basis for the settlement of the debt, much more advantageous to Italian interests than the other, Italy was warmly supported by France and Prussia. It was further agreed that the frontier of the ceded territory should be that of "the actual administrative confines of the Lombardo-Venetian kingdom."

The Trentine district was thus left to Austria, while the eastern limit between the two States, instead of being the river Isonzo, is a line presenting a mere arbitrary and imaginary frontier, running just to the west of that river. General Menabrea, the Italian plenipotentiary at Vienna, in a remarkably able and temperate despatch of the 2d of October, shows the great inconvenience of such a limit between Italy and Austria. He points out that the Isonzo itself formed the frontier between the Italian kingdom, under Eugène Beauharnais, and the Austrian empire, adding, "it was under these conditions that Venetia fell again to Austria during the events of 1814–1815." That the Isonzo offers a far more suitable frontier than the present arbitrary line, both as regards custom-houses, and for all other purposes which render a frontier useful and necessary, is obvious to any one who judges the question impartially, and that in the interest both of Austria and of Italy. In touching upon the question of the Trentine district, the general dwells upon the fact, that so great is the difference of ideas and interests which exist between the Italian people of the Trentino and the German populations of the Tyrol, that the Austrian government itself separated the two peoples, and gave to the former a distinct administration of its own. Nor did the government of Vienna stop there; but "recognising the constant aversion of the Trentino to organise the defence of their country after the model of the Tyrol, it adopted for the district of Trent a different system, similar to that established in its ancient Italian provinces," viz., Lombardy and Venetia. He recalls, also, the well-known fact, that in 1863 the deputies elected by the Trentine province drew up a memorial to the Emperor, in which they stated their reasons, founded upon considerations of race, language, history, and interest, which led them to refuse to take part in the Diet of Innspruck. So, again, in 1866, after the re-establishment of peace, the great majority, if not all, of those elected as deputies, refused to present themselves in that assembly. It was known beforehand that such was their intention if elected, and they were therefore chosen as representing the feelings of the province in the matter. Since then the government of Vienna have asked the municipalities of Trent and Riva to state how the frontier could be so drawn as to be most in accordance with the interests of the province? The reply was very detailed and very respectful in form, but in substance it amounted simply to this: the frontier line which would leave us united to Italy, is that which most accords with our wishes, wants, and interests.

It has been said that when, during the late war, the Italians entered the Trentine district, the peasants, instead of taking up arms against the Austrians, showed themselves very indifferent on the subject of being united to Italy. Admitting such to have been the case, it is a fact of little weight as compared with the repeatedly-expressed will of the more intelligent classes of the community, manifested by the election of representatives who always refused to take part in the proceedings of the Diet of Innspruck, the seat of the Tyrol government. Nor must it be forgotten that such has been the course deliberately and constantly adopted under Austria's own rule, who did her utmost to induce the electors of the Trentino to pursue exactly the opposite course, and to allow themselves to be represented in the Tyrolean Diet.

General Menabrea shows further, with great clearness, that the actual frontier renders the economical condition of the Trentine province such as to make its possession a burden rather than a resource to the empire. Nothing, in fact, can be much worse than its present position. It is a small district, of very limited resources, containing a population of 350,000 inhabitants, cut off from the Tyrol and the rest of the Austrian empire by the immense barrier of the Alps, and therefore naturally drawing its supplies from the Italian provinces to the south, from which it is now separated by a frontier line of custom-houses. This line, open on all sides, will necessitate a perfect army of employés to prevent smuggling, which will assuredly be attempted on no small scale—a natural consequence of cutting off the Trentino from that natural source of its supplies, the fertile Italian provinces to the south. Besides this, Austria will have to fortify this outlying dependency, thereby further increasing the cost it entails. Now, as the sum of 400,000 francs (£16,000) represents the net annual revenue which Austria has hitherto obtained from this little district, it is not difficult to see that, what with fortifications, soldiers, and employés for custom-house purposes, and for putting down smuggling, the Trentino will be a dead loss to the Austrian exchequer. It is, then, in the interest of this latter power, as well as in that of Italy, to put an end to such a state of things, bad for all concerned, a last though small cause of difference between the governments of Florence and Vienna. The true frontier is that of the mountains between the towns of Trent and Bolzano, as wisely suggested by Lord Palmerston in one of his far-sighted despatches written in 1848.

What incalculable losses, what terrible defeats, has Austria not brought upon herself by refusing to follow the wise suggestions of that English statesman, given in the memorable year referred to! It surely may be hoped that a man of M. Von Beust's ability will not fail to apply to this Trentine question a solution in conformity with Lord Palmerston's views expressed nearly twenty years ago, which events have so completely ratified, and in conformity also with the real interests of Austria. If the frontier were placed, then, between Trent and Bolzano, and if the river Isonzo itself were taken as the eastern limit between the two powers, every just cause of future difficulty between them would be removed. Such a course would completely heal the wounds caused by the past errors of a diplomacy which cared only for dynastic interests, built too often on an arbitrary and artificial basis, without paying any attention to the rights or wishes of the people. It would consolidate the good feeling already fast springing up between Italy and Austria, who have need of one another, and whose common interests are best served by a common regard for each other's just claims and necessities. Nor are such ties of goodwill and interest desirable only for Austria and Italy, but for the whole of Europe, whose statesmen, by putting an end to every future source of discord between these neighbouring countries, would thereby obtain an additional guarantee for the general peace of Europe, and an additional means of developing its moral and material resources. Incalculable as have been the woes inflicted by the past antagonism of Italy and Austria, they will assuredly be surpassed by the benefits which shall spring from their future harmony and goodwill; because, immense as are the evils arising from injustice, oppression, and wrong, still greater are the blessings which have their eternal source in justice, liberty, and right.

Great was the joy throughout Venetia when the official announcement was published that peace had been finally signed between Italy and Austria; for the people were weary of the delays which diplomacy interposed between them and their deliverance from foreign rule. In Venice itself there had been various signs of a growing impatience; but the tact and good sense of General Alemann, the Austrian governor, united to the moderation and good conduct of the Venetian people, happily averted all unpleasant consequences. It was, indeed, a spectacle almost unique in the world's history which Venice thus presented during the last moments of Austrian rule, as she awaited its final disappearance, impatient to welcome her own and Italy's chosen king. As time passed on, and the sway of the foreigner drew surely and gradually towards its close, General Alemann wisely permitted certain measures to be adopted and certain demonstrations to take place, which indicated the near approach of Venetian independence. Thus it was that he allowed the organisation of the National Guard, and ultimately made use of it in maintaining public order. Its band, in preparation of the approaching national *fêtes*, was allowed to practise well-known Italian airs in one of the large Venetian palaces.

When it had attained a certain perfection, it played in the presence of a Venetian audience assembled in the theatre of St Samuel, which was decked out with tricoloured flags, and resounded with the repeated acclamations of those present to the memory of the illustrious Daniel Manin, as well as in favour of Italian unity, Venetian independence, Victor Emmanuel, and Garibaldi. The portraits of the royal and popular hero, the representatives of the principle of order and the principle of liberty, happily and inseparably united in the just cause of national independence, began to show themselves; and soon shop windows were adorned, not only with them, but with various other well-known Italian statesmen aud generals, among whom naturally figured the special patriot and hero of Venice, Daniel Manin. Groups of people crowded to behold with eager gaze and joyful hearts. As they discussed the news of the hour, and refreshed their eyes with the sight of portraits so long forbidden to public view, they questioned among themselves as to the day, so ardently desired, when *I nostri* would at length enter Venice, and as to the fetes which were to celebrate their arrival and that of "Vittorio," as soldiers and people ever call the king. In truth, preparations of various kinds, some visible and some invisible, were quietly beginning. The fronts of houses and shops were cleaned and painted white; green was selected as best suited to shutters, doors, and window-frames, to which was added a red line in some conspicuous place, or the owner's name in that colour; so that, when the painting and cleaning was finished, the eyes of all good patriots—that is, of the entire population—were gratified with the sight of the national colours—red, white, and green. On Sunday, the 1st October, as if in anticipation of the news which arrived three days later of the conclusion of peace, the whole population bedecked itself with the national Italian colours. The organs in the street took courage, and regaled the passers-by with "Garibaldi's Hymn," the Royal March, or that of the Bersaglieri. The Austrian authorities meanwhile took no notice, rightly believing that such harmless demonstrations tended to prevent difficulties by giving a vent to the popular feelings. Whenever, during the last few weeks of Austrian rule, any symptom indicative of disorder occurred, General Alemann issued some temperate proclamation to the effect that the simplest means had hitherto sufficed, to his great satisfaction, for the maintenance of public order, and that he trusted that such would continue to be the case so long as he remained in Venice. The municipal authorities spoke in the same strain, and the National Guard used its influence to persuade the people to indulge in no demonstration prohibited by the Austrians, whose dominion was so rapidly drawing to a close. The Venetian people, naturally gentle and easily governed, were thus induced to be patient, and to content themselves with giving only such expression to their patriotic feelings as was wisely permitted by those still in power. At length, on the 4th October, the walls of the city were placarded with the official news of the signature of peace, and the congratulations of the Italian government upon the auspicious event which at length restored Venice to freedom. The news ran like lightning through the city, and crowds formed in a moment round the placards announcing the joyful intelligence. As the writer was standing in one of these groups some Austrian soldiers passed by, upon which a woman cried out to them, "You can stay or go now, as you please, because you are no longer our masters, but only our guests." "Well said," cried another bystander, "for we are the masters now." Such was the bearing of the Venetian people in the hour of their liberation, in the day of their returning power, after years of long and cruel oppression, during which many of their countrymen had suffered exile, imprisonment, and death, because guilty of labouring to effect their country's freedom, and of seeking to break the chains forged at Campo-Formio and riveted at Vienna.

Now followed in hot haste the preparations for welcoming the Italian troops and the Italian king —preparations in which all classes busied themselves to the utmost. The cleaning and painting went on with redoubled ardour; poles, flags, flagstaffs, crowns, crosses of Savoy, hangings for windows and balconies, tricoloured rosettes, lanterns for illuminations, were fabricated by the thousand. Hundreds were at work on the scores of gondolas, public and private, which formed so striking a feature in the public *fêtes*. St Mark's Square re-echoed with the unaccustomed sound of shrill voices shrieking out the names and prices of innumerable papers, which came in like a flood from all quarters of the Italian kingdom upon Venice, or sprung into life within her sea-girt limits. Thus matters proceeded up to the 19th October, when the Austrian authorities finally quitted the city. As General Alemann went on board the steamer which was to take him to Trieste, the people saluted him with a quiet and friendly adieu, in testimony of the goodwill he had manifested in the performance of his duties during the last days of Austrian rule. An hour or two later the national colours were hoisted on the great flag-staffs in front of St Mark's Cathedral; and then, amidst the pealing of bells and the booming of cannon, accompanied with warm greetings and tearful eyes, burst forth that heartfelt and boundless joy with which Venetians of every age and rank hailed the longed-for hour of their deliverance. How deep and universal was the feeling, how striking and multiplied its outward tokens, have been so thoroughly described by many an eye-witness, that there is no need nor room for dwelling upon them in these pages. Suffice it to say, that nothing which the Venetians could do was left undone to celebrate worthily their union to Italy, and give a fitting welcome to the brave and honest sovereign who has borne so large a part in accomplishing that mighty work of national independence which has given to Italy her rightful place among the nations of the earth.

When the Italian Parliament met on the 15th December, at Florence, the king was able to announce in his speech from the throne that the aspirations of centuries had been accomplished, and that Italy was "freed from all stranger rule." The troops of Austria had ceased to occupy Venetia and the Quadrilateral; those of France no longer kept guard in Rome. Italy has thus entered upon a new era after centuries of discord and oppression. The stranger has at length quitted the land; its people and government are free; and the first duty that their freedom imposes upon them is the homely one of setting their house in order. It calls for earnest exertions, which, if well directed, and perseveringly maintained, will bear rich fruit to the present generation, and far richer to those who shall come after. Not that Italy has done nothing towards improving her internal condition since 1861, when its new-born monarchy first demanded and obtained recognition at the hands of other nations. On the contrary, both morally and materially, much has been done; but owing to the peculiar circumstances of its condition, arising chiefly from the possession of Venetia and the Quadrilateral by Austria, the position of Italy prevented her devoting herself to the single work of internal improvement, and obliged her to form and maintain armaments whose huge proportions overburdened her with taxation, and checked the development of her resources. It is a most healthy sign, that the government and nation (now that Austria no longer menaces their very existence from the banks of the Adige and Mincio) are directing their special attention to the questions of finance and the diminution of their armaments, with the wise resolve to apply an efficacious remedy to the financial difficulties of the country. That the army should be diminished and reduced to the lowest point consistent with Italy's imperative needs both at home and abroad is agreed upon all hands; but what that point is must necessarily be a matter for consideration and discussion, which cannot be too thorough and searching. Upon such a subject it would be presumptuous of foreigners to pronounce an opinion, for even the best-informed amongst them cannot pretend to have that thorough and intimate knowledge of the country and its wants which is necessary to determine such a question; it must, therefore, be left to the decision of the government, parliament, and people of Italy. It is, at any rate, satisfactory to see, that while other nations seem only bent upon increasing their already overgrown and unwieldy armaments, free Italy is reducing hers, that she may lighten the burdens of taxation, give freer scope to the development of her resources, and establish a permanent equilibrium between her income and expenditure.

But it is not only by reduction of military expenditure that Italians can improve their financial condition. A better system of taxation and improved administration will do much towards that end. It is not rare to hear it said that the form in which the taxes are laid on aggravates their burden. They are often unnecessarily vexatious and troublesome, press unequally and illogically upon the persons who pay and upon the objects taxed, so that the public would contribute more readily and easily a larger sum under a better and simpler system than the actual amounts to which it is liable under the system at present in operation. It is not so very long since, that similar complaints were heard in England, the causes of which have been removed by various changes made in the mode and manner of taxation, which have been amongst the most useful reforms introduced of late years into England's financial system. Italian financiers cannot do better than follow such an example, thereby relieving the tax-payer and benefiting the treasury. Administration is still the weak point of Italian statesmen. No matter of surprise, as good administrators are very rarely improvised; they must be formed by experience and practice, which is exactly what the public men of Italy have hitherto had no opportunity of acquiring ; for up to the formation of the present kingdom the country was divided into a number of small governments, which, even when well administered, like that of Piedmont from 1849-1859, offered far too limited a sphere of action for the formation of a class of administrators capable of dealing with the wants and circumstances of a large kingdom numbering 25,000,000 of inhabitants. Already several mistakes have been made, and consequent injury inflicted, from the error of supposing that what was applicable to the small community was equally so to the larger one, and *that* despite of the latter's widely differing circumstances and condition. Nor must it be forgotten that those circumstances and conditions are specially varied and difficult to deal with in the case of Italy ; the result of many causes, and amongst others of the ceaseless efforts of the fallen governments to keep the people of Italy as much divided as possible, and to foster among them every difference of custom, every local jealousy, prejudice, and animosity for the furtherance of the selfish and unworthy ends of their petty rulers. To financial and administrative improvement must be added increasing efforts in the vital work of popular instruction, and the scarcely less important one of the construction of common roads, the want of which in the southern provinces is immense, a century of Bourbon rule having left them almost wholly unprovided with those two essential instruments of a people's welfare, public roads and public schools. The present constitutional government is fully aware of their importance, and is earnestly at work in creating them; it cannot labour too assiduously in the matter, for roads and schools will do more than all else to diminish and get rid of ignorance and superstition, mendicity and brigandage, with all their attendant ills and crimes.

But if the ministers and administrators of Italy have much to learn and to do, there is also room for improvement in the parliament itself. That body has without doubt rendered good service to the country, but it might render greater still were it to give a working majority to an intelligent and upright administration, which although by no means perfect and producing perfect measures, would with no great difficulty lay down a good line of policy and act steadily upon it. Instead of that, the Italian deputies are too apt to form themselves into various and ill-defined groups, giving an uncertain support to a cabinet, and then tripping it up upon some minor point or question of detail. Now what Italy wants at the present time is not so much some statesman of immense genius, furnished with some marvellous plan capable of setting everything right in a moment, but a government of clear-headed and patriotic ministers, by no means hard to find, supported by a manageable majority, whose members, instead of being each bent upon his own pet scheme, should support the government in the continued application of a well-considered policy. Constant changes of government and government plans are injurious to the public interest and to the credit of the parliament; whereas the adoption and steady application of a moderately good financial and administrative system would in a few years, if but patiently persevered in, go very far indeed towards restoring the financial condition of the country and developing its resources. Italian deputies will do well to take this plain and practical view of Italy's political necessities, and so avoid those useless and too frequent changes of administration which become both ridiculous and hurtful. Such, then, are the principal difficulties and defects which Italy has to surmount and correct, such the work she has to accomplish. Her statesmen and people are alive to the necessities of their country and to the greatness of the task before them. As to the means, the will, and the power which they possess for accomplishing that work, they shall be for the present left untouched, because time and space are wanting to deal fully with them, and also because it is better, at the present juncture, that Italians and all the friends of Italy should direct their undivided attention to the dangers to be overcome, and the faults to be corrected, rather than enumerate successes already obtained, or dwell complacently upon Italian merits and capacity. Suffice it here to express the firm belief that Italy's government and people possess alike the means of triumphing over present difficulties, and the qualities necessary to the successful application of those means. Though many obstacles and dangers still encumber the path of the Italian nation, yet theirs shall be the final victory—a victory precious not to Italy alone, but to the world at large, because it establishes national order, liberty, and progress in the place of foreign domination, that fruitful source both of tyranny and revolution; because it is the consecration of the rights and liberties of a whole people hitherto down-trodden and oppressed, but now recognised by all the powers of the earth; because, in a word, it is the victory of justice, liberty, and right.

To the house of Savoy is given the noble task of heading this great national uprising. It is not a little interesting thus to see the chief and the members of one of the very oldest royal families in Europe leading the great popular movement in Italy. Instead of throwing themselves blindly into the arms of the reactionary party, as has been done by so many of their compeers, they wisely embraced the national cause which the other Italian rulers hated and betrayed; they recognised Italy's demands for freedom and independence, and sustained them with honesty and courage in the name of constitutional liberty; they have had the wisdom to understand and in some degree to direct the onward movement of their age and country, lending to it their willing aid instead of repressing it by violence or treachery. Brave and honest, faithful to the rights and liberties of their people, they have been rewarded by that people's gratitude and love, thus winning for themselves the leadership of one of the noblest works of national regeneration that the world has ever seen. This they have done, not by the possession of great genius, but by a certain tact and instinctive knowledge of the times they live in and the people whom they rule, united to unswerving honesty of purpose and hereditary courage. Yet the princes of the house of Savoy will do well to remember that such good qualities are much enhanced when united to the virtues of private life, and also that they may be further improved and turned to ever better account by continued study and self-instruction. No slight benefit is conferred on a country when those in high places set a good example to the nation not only in the discharge of public duties, but also in those of a more private character, in a well-ordered court and household. Whereas the contrary is hurtful alike to the ruler and the people, injures the family which occupies the highest position in the realm and society at large, gives their enemies a handle against them, and discourages their friends.

It is important also, in Italy's position, that her princes should make themselves thoroughly acquainted with the principles of military science and of constitutional law, subjects which demand close and persevering application. Assuredly courage on the battle-field is admirable, and seems an hereditary appanage of Savoy's royal house, but the possession of that quality alone is not sufficient for conducting a campaign skilfully, or even for winning a victory; such success is the result, in no slight degree of a thorough knowledge of the art of war, which must be acquired by careful and accurate study. Without it Prussian generals would not have planned, nor would Prussian princes have executed, their brilliant campaign of 1866. The generals and princes of Italy cannot do better than imitate such an example, and in this matter the house of Savoy would do well to follow in the steps of the house of Hohenzollern.

Fidelity to the rights and liberties of the nation, and an ever honest support given to them, cannot be too highly praised; but princes who desire really to understand the principles of constitutional rule, and practise them well, should study carefully the history of those countries which have grown and prospered under the *régime* of limited monarchy. Such study, united to the daily acquisition of knowledge concerning the condition of their own land and people, is a sure means of becoming thoroughly acquainted with the varied duties of constitutional rule, and the best means of fulfilling them. There is no greater mistake than that of supposing that the chief of a constitutional government is a mere *roi fainéant*—that any puppet will do for such a place. On the contrary, he has, within the limits of his power, an ample field for the exercise of the highest intelligence. Of this it would be difficult to find a better proof, both as regards its results to the country governed as well as to the royal family itself, than that offered by Leopold I., king of the Belgians, one of the ablest and most enlightened men of the present century. On the other hand, Spain is a terrible example into how pitiable a condition a fine country, and a people by no means destitute of good qualities, may be brought, when the sovereign is ignorant of the real principles of constitutional rule, or untrue to them ; when a willing ear is or has been too often lent to unworthy favourites; when the court, instead of setting a good example to the nation, is immoral and corrupt, containing within it those who pander to royal passions, and whose evil influence outweighs that of faithful and upright counsellors, who alone are alike loyal and patriotic ; when the difficulties arising from party contests, instead of being overcome by the healthy action of public opinion, operating through constitutional channels, are aggravated a hundredfold by military pronunciamentos, which place the country at the mercy first of one and then of another military adventurer, whose pompous titles are too often won upon the sorry field of civil discord ; when the ruler falls under the influence of priests, ever (in all ages and countries) striving after temporal supremacy—ever opposed to perfect religious freedom—ever seeking to impose or maintain some burden upon the members of other communions—ever disfiguring by ecclesiastical fancies and systems the divine and simple precepts of holiness and love which appeal in the name of God to the conscience of man.

How immense, on the contrary, are the benefits resulting to a nation constitutionally governed—when its ruler and royal family rightly understand and practise constitutional principles ; when its sovereign unites to the faithful discharge of public duties the example of a pure and consistent private life ; when favouritism and bigotry find no favour near the throne ; when every effort is made to offer in the highest quarters a good example to the nation—may be seen to-day, not only in the general condition of England, despite all her faults, but also in the merited respect and love with which the nation looks up to its Queen, in its deep-rooted attachment to the national laws and liberties, in the feeling of loyalty and the love of freedom which are blended together in the hearts of its people.

It is well, then, for Italy and her princes that they should meditate upon these things—well that they should study the examples of England and of Belgium—well, also, that they should take warning by that of Spain—for it is the high privilege of Italy's royal family to head a work of national regeneration rarely, if ever, surpassed in the loftiness of its aim—a work which fixes on the members of that family, and on their country, the eyes of all men—of enemies gloating over every defect and error, of friends rejoicing in every progress made, and in every virtue called into life and action. Those, then, to whom so glorious a mission has been given should ever bear in mind how much their personal influence and example can do in its fulfilment—how much they can help forward, even by their daily life and conduct, that great cause of which they are the acknowledged chiefs. Influenced by such truths, may all the members of the house of Savoy seek faithfully to fulfil even the least of the many duties, private as well as public, which belong to their high station: thus shall they win ever more and more the love and esteem of their country, in whose triumph their honesty and courage have had so large a share. So shall Italy's new-born freedom be consolidated and secured, its roots strike deep into her soil, its blessings spread to every class of her gifted, but hitherto misgoverned and neglected people; so shall the structure of her laws and liberties bind in ever close union the nation's freedom and the sovereign's rights, establish order and liberty in the place of mingled despotism and anarchy, thereby bearing rich fruit to those of our own day, and richer still to generations yet unborn.

TWO TEMPORAL POWERS.

Reprinted from the "Westminster Review" of 1st January 1868.

1. *Ireland and her Churches.* By JAMES GODKIN. London: Chapman and Hall. 1867.
2. *Histoire du Canada depuis sa découverte jusqu'à nos jours.* Par F. X. GARNEAU. 3me édition, revue et corrigée; imprimée par P. Lamoureux, No. 1 Rue Buade, Quebec: 1859.
3. *La Convention entre la France et l'Italie, signée le 15 Septembre* 1864.
4. *Lettre adressée par le Maréchal Niel, Ministre de la Guerre, au Colonel commandant la Légion d'Antibes.* Paris: le 21 Juin 1867.

WHENEVER the expression "Temporal Power" is used, the thoughts of Englishmen revert to Rome. They too often forget that it is not in other lands only that a church exists whose temporal status is opposed to the wishes and liberties of the great majority of the people in whose country that church is established. The temporal power of an ecclesiastical body imposed upon an unwilling nation by force excites the warm disapprobation of Englishmen; they see and condemn such a system in the case of others with that clearness and force which usually characterises persons when judging, not their own defects, but those of their neighbours. Far be it from the writer to deny the justness of such a judgment. But would not Englishmen do well, while condemning the temporal power of the Roman Church in Italy, not to forget the temporal power accorded to the Anglican Church in Ireland? When we ourselves cease to impose by force of law a Protestant Establishment upon a Roman Catholic country, we shall prove by the most effectual of all means—that of example— our sincerity in condemning others who are maintaining by force the temporal power of *their* church in opposition to the will and liberties of an entire people. When we have cast first the beam out of our own eye, we shall see clearly to pull out that which is in our brother's eye. Beginning then at home, let this subject of the "Temporal Power" be first considered as it exists in connexion with the Church Establishment in Ireland, and afterwards as maintained in Rome. Such is the twofold aspect presented by this important question which it is now proposed to examine, so far at least as can be done within the limits accorded to a review article.

It is a noteworthy fact that tithes were first introduced into Ireland, or at least first enforced, by the secular arm, at the time of the conquest of that island by Henry II. in 1156—a conquest made with the approbation of the reigning Roman Pontiff, Pope

Adrian IV. The present Lord Primate of Ireland, in a charge delivered to his clergy in 1864, said :—

"To the clergy of the early Irish Church tithes were *not* paid, though it appears by some ancient canons attempts were made to establish them. In the year 1127 St Bernard complains of the Irish, 'they pay no tithes;' and in the year 1172 Pope Alexander III., in a letter dated 20th September, states, among other abuses of the Irish Church, 'the people in general pay no tithes.' English influence, however, in that year sufficed to introduce them at the Council of Cashel. They formed part of the splendid bribes which Henry II. gave to the Irish clergy to induce them to conform to the usages of the English Church and acknowledge the Papal supremacy."

However, then, ecclesiastics may dispute about the condition of the early Irish Church as regards its dogmas or its relationship to the See of Rome previous to the English conquest by Henry II., it becomes quite clear that by that conquest the tithe system and the Roman Catholic Church were established together; and further, that the tithe system was so established for the benefit of the Roman Catholic clergy.

The great religious revolution of the sixteenth century, known as the Reformation, separated both England and Scotland from the Church of Rome. The result of their conversion to the Protestant faith was the establishment in the former country of the Episcopal Church, and in the latter of the Presbyterian.

This change, however, was not effected in Scotland without a bitter struggle, on account of the wicked attempt made by the English government to force upon the Scotch an Episcopal Establishment. The attempt was successfully resisted, to the lasting benefit both of England and of Scotland. For had an established church distasteful to the great mass of the Scotch people been forced upon them, it would assuredly have created and perpetuated all the innumerable evils necessarily arising from so execrable and anti-Christian a policy.

The reformed doctrines were not accepted by Ireland; her people remained faithful to the Church of Rome. Then it was that the English government established by force in Ireland a Protestant State Church, handing over to it, without demur, the tithes which had belonged for 400 years to the Roman Catholic Church. Then it was that to old feuds springing out of conquest and antipathies of race were superadded those arising from religious differences, of all roots of bitterness the bitterest. Then it was that England's government, in their endeavours to force Protestantism upon Roman Catholic Ireland, set (during two centuries) its hand to a work as full of oppression and injustice as ever darkened the world's history, or disgraced the Christian faith. Yet, despite all the efforts made, nothing resulted but ignominious failure. Of this no better proof can be given than the fact that, whereas, according to Sir W. Petty, the Protestants in Ireland numbered, in 1672, 300,000, and the Catholics 800,000, in 1861 the Protestants were 1,293,702, and the Catholics 4,505,265. Thus there had been a relative decrease of Protestants during that period of nearly 200 years. It must be further borne in mind that of these Protestants rather less than 700,000 belong to the Established Church, which possesses an income of half-a-million sterling, while the Roman Catholic clergy depend for their daily subsistence upon the voluntary contributions of their flocks.

The history of Ireland from the Reformation until towards the close of the last century is, speaking generally, that of oppression on the one side and resistance on the other. It would, however, be an exaggeration to say, either that there was no good attempted or performed by the English government in Ireland during that period, or that the Irish were wholly blameless as regards the ills which came upon their island in the shape of conflicts, rebellions, confiscations, and slaughters, which desolated the land and its inhabitants with the sword, the famine, and the pestilence. Still the great general characteristic of that sad and lengthened period was the misery arising from the wrongful and persevering attempt to force upon Roman Catholic Ireland the church and the rule of the Protestant minority. At length, towards the close of the last century, the cruel penal code which had long been in operation was relaxed in various ways, and the suffrage was accorded to the Irish Roman Catholics, in whose Parliament, however, Protestants alone could sit.

It was after the suppression of the rebellion of 1798 that Mr Pitt determined upon a policy whose large and liberal scope would have cut at the root of

Irish grievances, had he been allowed to carry it out. He proposed to abolish the Irish Parliament as a separate body, and by uniting the Irish, Scotch, and English representatives in one assembly, to be called the Parliament of the " United Kingdom," so to effect a complete legislative union between Great Britain and Ireland. He desired also to emancipate at the same time the Roman Catholics from civil disabilities, and to make a State provision for the Irish Roman Catholic clergy. Unhappily the policy of the great minister was stultified by the narrow bigotry of George III. The union with England, the least popular part of the scheme in Ireland, was carried out. To the rest the king and his friends absolutely refused to agree. In consequence Mr Pitt resigned. It is sad, indeed, to read this page of our history, which exhibits the melancholy spectacle of the just and liberal designs planned by such an intellect as that of Pitt, brought to nought by an intelligence so petty and so poor as that of George III. The emancipation was not granted for nearly thirty years, and then only on compulsion, the Duke of Wellington declaring that if it were refused he could no longer answer for the tranquillity of Ireland. Thus this great act of justice lost nearly all the benefit that might have been reaped from it, on account of the tardy and ungracious manner in which it was bestowed. The College of Maynooth, for the education of students designed for the Roman priesthood, was established by Mr Pitt in 1795. The Protestant Dissenting ministers continued to enjoy the Regium

Donum, a grant the origin of which appears to have come from sums given by Charles II. out of the "secret service money." It was not, however, until the reign of William III. that the grant was publicly conferred and enlarged. It has been continued ever since, and increased from time to time; its present amount being about £40,000.

But the tithes, and a part of the ecclesiastical property,* were, from the Reformation downwards, appropriated to the exclusive use of the small Protestant Episcopal minority and their State Church. Mr Pitt's scheme of paying the clergy of both churches may doubtless be considered less good, and certainly less suitable to our own days than that of paying no church. Still it was a just and liberal policy, which, if adopted, as it might have been in his day, would have been an immense improvement upon the injustice of forcing Roman Catholic Ireland to maintain a Protestant Establishment for the benefit of a wretchedly small minority.

But this injustice was greatly increased by the way in which the tithes were collected, even up to so recent a date as the year 1832, when the Irish Tithe Commutation Act was passed. That Act was only at length wrung from the Legislature, when the aggravating and oppressive mode of collecting the tithes in Ireland had produced such violence and such resistance, such bitter hatred and such fearful outrages,

* Some of the ecclesiastical property was secularised, portions being bought by laymen, and not a little of it being handed over to courtiers and favourites.

that it had brought about a state of things so nearly bordering on general insurrection as to be called the "Tithe War."

It will, perhaps, be asked, why refer to these circumstances which no longer exist? Firstly, because it is well that we Englishmen should remember that such a system, so fraught with evil, was in actual operation only thirty-five years ago; its memory therefore rankles still, it may be, among other past wrongs, in the hearts of the Irish (as it would in our own had we been subjected to it), and therefore, in some degree, accounts for the ill-feeling still only too prevalent in Ireland. Secondly, because we should never forget that although the oppressive mode of collecting tithes alluded to has been abolished, the injustice itself of compelling Roman Catholic Ireland to pay tithes in support of a Protestant Establishment still exists; tithes whose history is inseparably connected with the recollection of conquest, and which, when first imposed, were imposed for the maintenance of the Roman Catholic Church. To that Church they continued to be paid for 400 years; after which lapse of time it seemed good to Englishmen who had become Protestants, to oblige Irishmen who remained Roman Catholics to pay those tithes, and to hand over much of the ecclesiastical property to the Protestant Anglican Church, thus by force established and maintained even to this day. Therefore is it that we Englishmen should be reminded of these things,—we who boast so often of equal laws, of ancient liberties, of the rights of conscience; we whose Protestant faith proclaims the freedom of private judgment.

But it has been said that after all the Irish State Church is only a "sentimental grievance." A very few questions will dispose of that assertion. If at the time of the Reformation Ireland had been the strong country and England the weak one; if England having become, as she did, Protestant, Ireland had imposed by force a Roman Establishment upon England; if at this hour to such an establishment, hateful to the great mass of Englishmen, they were yet obliged to pay tithes; if our English bishops and clergy (ignored by the State) depended on voluntary contributions, while Archbishop Manning and his brother prelates inhabited palaces, enjoyed large or comfortable revenues, and graced with their presence the House of Lords—would Englishmen describe the existence of that Papal Church Establishment in Protestant England as merely a "sentimental grievance?" Some object to the abolition of the Irish Protestant Establishment, on the ground that it would do little or nothing to pacify Ireland. Even if this could be proved before the event, which it cannot be, it would be no sound argument against abolishing the grievance in question. "Be just, and fear not," is a good moral maxim, and not a less good political one. To do right without being deterred by a consideration of consequences is as wise and Christian in public as in private life. There is, however, no occasion to take up time with mere argument, because there lies at our doors a *fact* which throws no little light upon this matter. There exists a province subject to England, the great majority of whose population is neither English nor Protestant, yet there is no county in Great Britain more loyal or more attached to England's crown than that province of Lower Canada, Roman Catholic though it be by religion, and French by origin. It was the writer's good fortune, while in America' ten years ago, to make an expedition from Quebec down the St Lawrence and up the Saguenay river in company with several Canadian Roman priests. The conversation turned chiefly upon Canada, its condition and politics, a subject which led the priests to speak in the highest praise of the English government, while bearing testimony at the same time to the good feeling prevalent throughout Canada towards England. Yet but some twenty years before, Lower Canada was, and had been for a lengthened period, discontented with the manner in which it was governed. This discontent more than once broke out into open violence, and even actual rebellion. Now, no one who has sought impartially to investigate that unhappy condition of things can rise from such investigation without being convinced that its chief cause lay in the attempt to maintain, more or less, the ascendancy of the British Protestant element over the French Roman Catholic element. Nor is it less evident that the Clergy Reserves were also a great source of discord. These Clergy Reserves were created by an Act of the English Parliament in 1791, which directed that in respect of all grants made by the Crown, a quantity equal to one-seventh of the land so granted should be reserved for the clergy. This apple of discord did not fail to produce its natural effects, by giving rise throughout Canada to dissensions between Protestants and Romanists, Churchmen and Dissenters. Not until after many years of dangers and conflicts of every kind between the colonies and the mother-country, as well as between the various national, political, and religious sections of the colonists themselves, was the system changed. At length the attempt to override one class or section by another was abandoned, the Clergy Reserves were swept away, and a system of perfect religious equality was inaugurated. From that time discontent died out, peace and order flourished. And so it has come about that loyal attachment to England pervades the whole of our North American colonies; nor are those feelings anywhere stronger than in Roman Catholic Lower Canada, the language and customs of whose people still denote their French origin. Let English statesmen profit by the lesson, and do without more delay in Ireland that which has borne such good fruit in America.

The question of what is to be done with the tithes when the Irish Establishment ceases to exist, though a question requiring serious consideration, is not one presenting insuperable difficulties. If nothing were left but the choice of either continuing the present system, or of simply abolishing the legal obligation to pay tithes upon the death of the incumbent of each parish, the second alternative would certainly be by far the least of the two evils. There are, however, other modes of dealing with the moneys derived from the tithes. That of handing over a certain portion of them to the Catholic priests can no longer be entertained, both as being repugnant to the principles of many Protestants, (especially to those of the Protestant Dissenters,) and, above all, because the Roman Catholic clergy refuse such aid. These ideas are set forth in a resolution of the "National Association," of which most of the Roman Catholic prelates in Ireland are members. The resolution, adopted in December 1864, was as follows:—

"That we demand the disendowment of the Established Church in Ireland, as the sole condition upon which peace and stability, general respect for the laws, unity of sentiment and action for national objects, can ever prevail in Ireland. And in making this demand we emphatically disavow any intention to interfere in the vested rights, or to injure or offend any portion of our fellow-countrymen, our desire being rather to remove a most prolific source of civil discord, by placing all religious denominations on a footing of perfect equality, and leaving each Church to be maintained by the voluntary contributions of its members."

These principles have been very recently affirmed afresh by the Irish Roman Catholic hierarchy. By thus abolishing the Establishment, the incomes arising from tithes would lapse to the State, as benefices became vacant. It would be for Parliament to decide to what purposes such revenues should be applied. It is pretty clear that no better use could be made of them than by applying them, in great part at any rate, to educational purposes.

The recent refusal of the Roman prelates to receive State aid was no doubt wise. It is also a course that deserves the approbation of all the friends of perfect religious liberty. Thus the Irish Roman Catholic clergy renounce all support of a temporal character, conferred by a temporal power. Having taken up this position, they may still (from their point of view) say to their people: We possess no legal means of enforcing your support, much less of wringing support from those who are not of us; we have no temporal arm to call to our aid, neither do we possess temporal power, for "the weapons of our warfare are not carnal;" we stand before you as the ministers of Christ's Church, not as the paid agents of the State; we serve the Altar, and we are content to live only by the Altar; we ask nothing of Cæsar, and we receive nothing from Cæsar; we have neither rich revenues nor sumptuous palaces; we have no other blessings to offer but the ministrations and consolations of the Church—her teachings and those of her Lord; these gifts, and these alone, have we to bestow—"silver and gold have we none."

Surely such a position and such language are those most really in keeping with the character of the ministers of Christ, who refused all temporal power, who said "My kingdom is not of this world," who used no other means of propagating or maintaining His teaching save those of awakening the conscience, convincing the judgment, and converting the heart. Can similar language be used by the bishops and clergy of the Anglican State Church, whose temporal power and position is established and maintained by the strong arm of the law, in opposition to the wishes and religious liberties of Roman Catholic Ireland? That Church Establishment contains numbers of benefices whose populations, varying from 500 up to 7000, very rarely include 100 churchmen, and often the number is far less. The incomes of those benefices run from £100 up to £500, £600, and even £900 per annum. Only a very few examples can be given here, as both our space and time are limited :—

Benefice.	Population.	Church Members	Income or Value of Benefice.
Garrycloyne	3427	38	£866
Donoughmore	3999	84	662
Clonmu t	621	9	174
Kilworth	5000	144	516
Inchigeelagh	4020	55	297
Knockavilly	1155	64	438
Fethard, (7 parishes)	5972	192	985
Kilbehenny	2348	16	299
Aney, (7 parishes)	7076	30	398
Prebend of Killandry	963	7	291
Kilma-tulla, (2 parishes)	2611	53	554
Moyne, (2 parishes)	1451	41	364

The actual number of those who are members of the Irish Church Establishment is only 693,357, while its annual revenues amount to £559,763. Parliamentary returns give the public grants of money made to the Irish Church from the Union in 1801 to the year 1844 as follows :—

> For building churches . . . £525,371
>   ,,   glebe-houses . . . 336,889
>   ,,   Protestant charity-schools . 1,105,588

In 1842, during a debate in the House of Commons, statistics were produced, extracted from the probates of wills in the registry office, Dublin, from which it appears that—

Archbishop Fowler, of Dublin, left	.	£150,000
,, Beresford, of Tuam ,,	.	250,000
,, Agar, of Cashel ,,	.	400,000
Bishop Stopford, of Cork ,,	.	25,000
,, Percy, of Dromore ,,	.	40,000
,, Cleaver, of Ferns ,,	.	50,000
,, Bernard, of Limerick ,,	.	60,000
,, Porter, of Clogher ,,	.	250,000
,, Hawkins, of Raphoe ,,	.	250,000
,, Knox, of Killaloe ,,	.	100,000

Making in all the goodly sum of £1,575,000. These prelates died at various dates between 1800 and 1833, in which latter year the Church Temporalities Act was passed, limiting episcopal revenues, reducing the Irish archbishoprics from four to two, and the bishoprics from eighteen to ten. Such accumulations of wealth are assuredly not in harmony with the apostolic saying, " Silver and gold have I none." Neither are rich benefices united to immense poverty of church members in keeping with apostolic precedents. It is true, indeed, as regards the wealth left by the prelates mentioned, that those golden days belong rather to the recent past than to the actual present. The wealth so left arose in some cases from the possession of private property as well as from ecclesiastical revenues ; but it is not the less true that while bishops of the Establishment were thus heaping to themselves riches, Roman Catholic prelates and clergy had no other means of subsistence save the voluntary contributions of their flocks. Some of the worst and most scandalous grievances connected with the Irish Establishment have been done away ; but the injustice of forcing a Protestant State Church upon Roman Catholic Ireland still exists, producing the evil fruit naturally springing from such a root of bitterness. Doubtless many of the bishops and clergy of the Irish Establishment are excellent men, but that by no means proves the excellence of the system by which they live ; for unfortunately history furnishes only too many instances of excellent individuals supporting, and being supported by, unjust systems. No abundance of such precedents can, however, prove the goodness of a given system, change injustice into justice, or convert wrong into right.*

As in Great Britain, so throughout her numerous colonies, peopled by English, Scotch, and Irish, by Churchmen, Dissenters, and Roman Catholics, there is nowhere to be seen in operation this evil principle of imposing by force the Church Establishment of the small minority upon a large and unwilling majority. In Ireland alone is such injustice perpetrated, and in Ireland alone is discontent chronic. In England and Scotland the Establishment is at any rate that of the most numerous Church ; and in both countries much

* Mr Godkin, in is able and interesting work, entitled " Ireland and her Churches," published in 1867, says : " I have, with the kind permission of the registrar, extracted from the registry in the Court of Probate the amount of assets left by every bishop who died since 1822, with the exception of a few who were but a short time in their sees. The assets were sworn to be under a certain sum, on which duty is paid. But this sum does not include any real property the deceased may have purchased, nor any settlements he may have made on members of his family, nor any stock he may have transferred to avoid of the spiritual teaching of the State Church is in harmony with that of those Protestant Dissenters who, with the members of the two Establishments, form nine-tenths of the whole population of Great Britain, in none of England's colonies does an Established Church exist. That which the Roman Catholics of Ireland demand at the hands of the Parliament of the United Kingdom is not even, as in Great Britain, the establishment of the church of the majority, but the yet fairer system of being burdened with no establishment whatever, as in the case of all our English colonies. Were Parliament wisely to adopt that system by abolishing the payment of tithes

legacy-duty, or possibly to avoid the fame of having died too rich for the bishop of a poor Church."—Pp. 18, 19 of "Ireland and her Churches."

Name.	See.	
Broderick	Cashel	£80,000
Trench	Tuam	73,846
Alexander	Meath	73,000
J. G. Beresford	Armagh	70,000
Tottenham Loftus	Clogher	60,000
Lawrence	Cashel	55,000
Bisset	Raphoe	46,000
Magee	Dublin	45,000
Griffin	Limerick	45,000
Whateley	Dublin	40,000
Leslie	Kilmore	40,000
Ritson	Killaloe	40,000
Beresford	Kilmore	36,000
Knox	Derry	27,692
Plunket	Tuam	26,331
Stewart	Armagh	25,000
Singer	Meath	25,000
O'Beirne	Meath	20,000
Kyle	Cork	20,000
Stopford	Meath	14,000

to the Irish Episcopal Church as its living ministers died out, by a gradual (if not immediate) withdrawal of the Regium Donum given to Dissenters, and also of the grant to Maynooth, there would within a comparatively small number of years be inaugurated in Ireland that just system described by the Irish "National Association" as "placing all religious denominations on a footing of perfect equality, leaving each church to be maintained by the voluntary contributions of its members." If such a course were adopted in the sister island, one source of discord at least would be put an end to, and thus a hope might dawn of seeing commenced in Roman Catholic Ireland some such happy change as that which has occurred in Roman Catholic Lower Canada. It is said, however, by some that it will never do to abandon the Irish Establishment, because if that be done the English Establishment must fall also. These persons hope that by uniting the fortunes of the two they will save both. Are they quite sure that that will be the result? May it not happen that instead of the English Establishment saving the Irish, the Irish will be the means of dragging down the English? A good swimmer has ere now saved a bad one; but, on the other hand, often has the former not only failed to do so, but has himself been drowned in the attempt, and so both have perished together. It is often wise to lighten an overladen vessel before the storm is at its height; nay, more, it is often the only hope left of saving the ship. Some may think an all-or-nothing policy wise, and even heroic; they will, however, do well to remember that it may prove most disastrous to their cause. Very recent events have shown that those who are loudest in refusing comparatively small concessions one year, may find themselves forced to give large ones the next.

Happily, to England's people has just been accorded a great extension of the suffrage. This affords much hope as regards Ireland, for the English people are bent upon doing justice to their Irish brethren. There are no doubt, besides the ecclesiastical question, others of the very utmost importance to Ireland, which urgently require speedy and fair adjustment. Englishmen desire earnestly to co-operate with their Irish fellow-countrymen in settling them satisfactorily. They cannot, however, be entered upon here, as space does not permit of it, neither do they fall within the scope of this article.

It is indeed unhappily true that in all probability no abolition of wrong systems, no wise reforms, will conciliate those extreme members of the Fenian plotters in Ireland, who seem bent upon the hopeless and criminal attempt to separate her altogether from Great Britain by revolution and armed violence. Yet that sad probability is by no means a reason for not sweeping away institutions founded on injustice, or for neglecting to carry out wise reforms. On the contrary, it is a strong argument for so doing. Because by thus acting, the government of the United Kingdom would commend itself to the consciences of its own people, as well as to those of the enlightened men of all civilised nations. It would render its moral and legal position impregnable if, while firmly putting down every attempt to overthrow its just rule and authority by armed violence, it at the same time carried out a vigorous policy of reform as regards every wrong, great and small, of which Ireland can still complain. It is not too much to expect that such a policy, inaugurated without delay and steadfastly maintained, would ere long rally round it a large public opinion in Ireland itself, and detach from the ultra-leaders of Fenianism many of the Irish who now have more or less sympathy with it, owing to the recollection of past injustice, or to the existence of such as still continues to afflict their country. Justice demands that all those evil relics of evil times be swept away, and wisdom counsels prompt and wise legislation upon such important matters as education and the tenure of land. As regards these last two questions, our legislators will do well to consider, not so much what is done in England, and what works well *there*, but what is best for Ireland, what is most likely to work good *there*, and what is most suited to her wants and to the character of her people. Differences of law and custom are often good, because, though incompatible with a hard outward uniformity, they very frequently strengthen that which is really essential—namely, a sound and living unity. Thus there are great differences in the customs and legal procedures, as well as in the ecclesiastical state systems, of England and Scotland, yet nothing can be more perfect than their cordial union, so beneficial to both. Indeed, it may be said that any attempt to make the two countries absolutely uniform in the matters referred to would only impair their living unity. In legislating for Ireland this principle should be borne in mind and practically applied.

It may here be permitted to say a few words touching the criminal attempts of the Fenian leaders to bring about the secession of Ireland by an appeal to arms and violence. From the constitutional point of view the case is clear. No portion of the United Kingdom, whether it be Ireland, Wales, Scotland, or England, has any power or right to make any law for itself, much less to secede from our Union, except with the consent and concert of the people of the United Kingdom, to be given through its national representatives in the two Houses of Parliament, and sanctioned by the Crown, in conformity with the provisions of the constitution of this realm. The Fenians may indeed use those, but only those, lawful means which our free constitution gives, to work upon the public opinion of the whole nation, so as to try and persuade its majority, and thereby the majority of its representatives, to sanction the secession of Ireland, and its erection into an independent republic. If they kept thus strictly within constitutional bounds they would be wholly blameless, and as legal in their course of action as any political association which has ever aimed at effecting political changes by constitutional means. The Anti-Corn-Law League is a notable example of such a mode of action crowned with splendid success.

But if because the Fenian leaders cannot persuade

the majority of the people of the United Kingdom and their lawful representatives to agree to the secession of Ireland, or because they feel it to be hopeless even to attempt such lawful persuasion, they therefore seek to compass their object by armed violence or war, then they must be firmly put down by that executive power whose duty it is to protect, by force if necessary, the rights, laws, and liberties of the United Kingdom. The principles thus laid down are essential not only to order but to freedom. For if it be once admitted that a minority has a right to appeal to force because it cannot persuade the majority to adopt a given line of policy, then all free government is at an end, and liberty (whether it take the form of a united constitutional monarchy, or a united federal republic) is simply rendered impossible, and must give place to anarchy. Popular and democratic politicians of all countries must be reminded that this very line of argument was used and enforced by the government of the United States when the Southern Secessionists sought to secede by force of arms from the Federal Union. Most memorable are those words addressed, at Mr President Lincoln's bidding, by Mr Seward to certain Secessionist leaders, in March 1861, that no State could withdraw from the Federal Union "in any other manner than with the consent and concert of the people of the United States, to be given through a national convention, to be assembled in conformity with the provisions of the constitution of the United States." Let all politicians ponder well those words, and remember how they were enforced, and justly enforced, by one of the very freest governments that has ever existed. Now the great majority of the people of the United Kingdom, (not, alas! of its upper classes,) especially the intelligent artisans of our great cities, cordially sympathised with the government and people of the United States during the Secessionist war. They can therefore have no hesitation with regard to any attempts at bringing about secession at home by armed violence, unless, indeed, they would fly in the face of the very principles they supported, and which many well-known men amongst them vindicated with great force of argument throughout the late American war. As to those who in England espoused, more or less, the cause of the Southern Secessionists, it is to be hoped that they see by this time, at any rate, the error of their ways. In this matter our conscience is clear; for as, from first to last, we blamed and abhorred the armed Secessionist movement in the United States, so assuredly not less do we hate the like criminal movement in the United Kingdom. For whatever may be their national faults or the defects of their constitutions, (which while different in form are yet both based on the principle of free self-government,) these two great nations are respectively, in the new world and the old, the depositaries and guardians of well-ordered yet free systems of the utmost value to mankind as well as to their own people. Therefore any design on the part of any section of their subjects to change those systems by other than constitutional means is blameable; while any attempt to break them down by armed violence cannot be too strongly condemned, and should ever be promptly and firmly repressed. The great majority of the people of the United States supported their government in so doing, and such in similar circumstances will ever be the course adopted by the great majority of the people of the United Kingdom.

But to return, though only for a moment, to the Irish State Church, which forms the subject of the first part of this article. It seems clear that in Great Britain the conviction is ever increasing that the wrong of an ecclesiastical establishment, hateful to the great majority in Ireland, yet forced upon her, and maintained by force, can no longer be allowed to exist. Nor should it be forgotten that this injustice is one which lowers our country in the eyes of foreign nations, who justly reproach us with it, being, as it is, in flagrant contradiction with our principles of civil and religious liberty, and with that freedom of private judgment proclaimed by Protestants. It produces evils which affect all parties alike, both those who perpetrate the injustice and those who are compelled to endure it. It is a wrong to Ireland, a disgrace to England, and a dishonour to her Protestant faith. So long as it shall exist, so long will it continue to produce, as in the past, those evils which naturally spring from it. Only when overthrown will there be some hope of substituting for those evils the blessings of concord, peace, and contentment. May the first use which England's people make of their newly-acquired liberties be that of applying efficacious remedies to the ills of Ireland. And who can deny that one of those ills which *must* be put an end to, is that great ecclesiastical injustice which in the sister island still tramples down the sacred rights of conscience, and makes the term "religious liberty" a cruel mockery when applied to Ireland? When that wrong shall be undone, and not till then, can the hope arise, that these Islands, (whose ancient sceptre is swayed so gently and so well by England's Queen,) may become of a truth, and not be by legal title only, a "*United* Kingdom."

The same frankness which has been used in dealing with the temporal power and position of the Protestant State Church in Ireland must now be applied to the temporal power of the Roman Church as exercised by the Pope, who is also its spiritual head. That spiritual headship is willingly acknowledged by all Roman Catholics, however much they may differ upon the question whether the temporal power of the Roman Pontiff should be restored to the position it held previous to the formation of the Italian kingdom, or be limited to a far narrower compass, or be completely abolished. That such differences of opinion do exist amongst Roman Catholics upon this subject is a simple fact. To deny it is as futile as to deny that different views are taken by English Churchmen upon the question of inspiration, and by English statesmen upon that of the Irish Church Establishment. Yet, inasmuch as this temporal power touches matters more or less connected with the religious convictions of devout Romanists, care should be taken in discussing it to avoid giving any unnecessary pain to their feelings. The discussion should be earnest and serious, as well as free and searching. It is in such a spirit that the writer desires to treat (with all due respect to the convictions of others, yet with freedom and sincerity) this question of the Papal "Temporal Power," which is now exciting such deep interest throughout the world.

No one can have investigated what has been going on in Italy for many years past, without seeing how hopeless a task has been that of France in endeavouring to awaken the Papal Government to the necessity of ruling in accordance with the feelings, the progress, and the necessities of the times. Thus, in 1849, M. Drouyn de Lhuys, the French Minister for Foreign Affairs, in a despatch dated Paris, 9th May 1849, urges the Pontifical Court, then at Gaeta, to proclaim some clear and tangible concessions in order to prepare the way for its return to Rome, and so give some security to its future government by awakening well-grounded hopes in the minds of the Romans. In one place the minister writes:—

"Besides, can it be thought a matter of indifference to reassure that numerous portion of the Roman population whose moderation, while detesting a régime of anarchy, fears almost equally the return of that which marked with so sad a character the reign of Gregory XVI.—of that

O

régime which, on the death of that pontiff, rendered a change of system absolutely necessary?"

It is worthy of special remark that this minister, who is considered one of the French statesmen the most favourably disposed to the Papal power, should thus pass a distinct condemnation on the reign of the preceding pontiff, thereby showing that the ill adaptation of the Papal temporal rule to present times is nothing new. He further warns those who were about to resume the direction of that rule in Rome, against following so fatal an example. Again, on the 6th June 1849, M. de Tocqueville, who had succeeded to the Ministry of Foreign Affairs in France, wrote a despatch to the French Minister at the Papal Court, in which he insisted on the necessity of " not re-establishing those institutions and forms of the past which have given rise to complaints;" declares the earnest wish of his government " to assure to the States of the Church institutions really liberal;" and says that " France, in return for the sacrifices already made, has a right to expect that the conditions necessary to the existence of a government liberal and worthy of the enlightenment of the age should not be refused." On the 18th August 1849, followed the celebrated letter of the Prince-President, now Napoleon III., to Colonel Ney, dwelling upon the same theme. "I resume thus," says the writer of that letter; "the re-establishment of the temporal power of the Pope, a general amnesty, secularization of the administration, Code Napoleon, and a liberal government."

Thus every attempt was made, but unhappily in vain, to pave the way for a better state of things upon the restoration of the Papal temporal power by French arms. During the years which elapsed from the time of that restoration to the year 1859, the Imperial Government of France constantly warned and expostulated with the Pontifical Government; still, throughout the period mentioned, little or nothing was done in the way of necessary improvement. The administrators of the temporal power remained deaf to all advice, and persisted in a policy of the most reactionary and retrograde character; maintaining, at the same time, their rule in Rome by the aid of French soldiers, and in Bologna by that of Austrian. In *those* days Austria was the perfection of absolutism and so-called divine right in church and state; nor did she fail to use all her influence in sustaining those principles in Rome, whose government was only too happy to follow such advice. What terrible disasters the Viennese statesmen who pursued this wretched policy brought upon their unfortunate country, as well as upon the Papal temporal power, has been made manifest to the eyes of all men. But while touching upon that dark and melancholy period, we cannot but for a moment refer to the brighter present, in which an absolutely opposite policy gives the hope of seeing the whole Austrian empire regenerated by the operation of constitutional liberty and progress. Cordially do all the friends of freedom hail the change which has been thus inaugurated in Austria by men so eminent as M. von Beust, Count d'Andrassy, and last, but not least, the patriot statesman of Hungary, Francis Deak. Englishmen of all parties and classes watch the progress of this noble work with joyful hope, and give to the constitutional Austro-Hungarian State of to-day their warmest sympathy and heartiest God-speed.

But to return to the subject in hand. When the great events of 1859 overtook the Papal Government, its weakness became manifest. The moment the Austrians withdrew from Bologna, and so liberated the populations of the Romagna provinces from foreign occupation, they at once declared against the Papal temporal rule, and overthrew it. Nothing occurred at the time in those provinces to bring about this change, save the withdrawal of the Austrian troops. Neither French nor Piedmontese appeared upon that scene. Garibaldi was away in the mountains of North Lombardy. Such was the effect in the Romagna of the cessation of that foreign aid which had there been for years the sole support of the temporal power of the Holy See. Besides, it must not be forgotten that this proceeding, and the annexation it led to, like that of Parma, Modena, and Tuscany, took place in spite of French diplomacy: the Emperor Napoleon, at the peace of Villafranca, having expressed his desire to see the old authorities restored in all those provinces—a desire which he, however, refused to realise by force, and which he forbade others to attempt by that evil means.

When the marvellous exploits of Garibaldi in Sicily and Naples had made it clear to Italy that the establishment of a united Italian State had been changed from an idea into a possibility, the provinces of Umbria and the Marches showed manifest symptoms of desiring to share in the great national movement, despite the presence of a papal army, composed chiefly, then as now, of French, Swiss, German, Belgian, and other foreigners, commanded at that time by the late French General Lamoricière. As soon as the provinces just named were freed from the foreign soldiery who maintained the temporal power, they declared, like their brethren of the Romagna, for annexation to the new Italian kingdom. Indeed the fact that the Pontifical Government has long been unable to exist save by foreign support in one form or another, is an overwhelming proof that its temporal power rests only upon mere force—the force of foreign bayonets, ever destructive in the end of the very power they support, because rendering it unspeakably odious to its own subjects. This odium only increases in proportion to the number of bayonets, and to the length of time during which their detestable agency is employed. No more striking proof of this truth exists than the case of the Bourbons, restored in 1814–1815 to the throne of France by the allied armies of Europe. It may truly be said that the unfortunate princes of the Bourbon line have never got over the fact of having been restored to power by such means. Again, in 1852, the election of the present French Emperor to the imperial throne was probably in some degree due to the fact that such a choice by no means harmonised with the general views of the foreign powers who had made the treaties of Vienna, one of whose most special objects was the overthrow of the first Napoleon and the restoration of the Bourbons. Indeed, it appears that some of those powers determined at the time (1815) that *no* Bonaparte should ever again be recognised as ruler of France. The French profited by the occasion offered in the year referred to (1852), to settle the point once for all by electing the present Emperor and calling upon Europe to recognise him. More than this, the Emperor purposely took the title of Napoleon III., thereby maintaining in the face of the world the principle of the continuity of the Bonaparte dynasty; thus vindicating at the same time what he considered to be his family claims, as well as the incontestable right of the French people to choose whatever temporal rule seemed good to them. The result was, that Europe bowed its head to the will of France and of her Emperor, to the immense satisfaction of both.

In the name, then, of what principle does this same France impose or maintain by force, upon Italians or any other people, a temporal power of any kind which they desire to get rid of, or greatly to curtail and modify? Is it because that people are comparatively weak? Is it from a selfish fear, the offspring of a despicable jealousy, which dreads to see in the future a united Italy growing in strength and prosperity, and so emancipating itself from what a powerful neighbour is pleased to call his *just* influence? Can it be that such unworthy motives, such unjust pretensions, are really in harmony with the feelings of the French people, who, whatever may be their faults, have often deserved to be called great and generous, and often done much for the liberties and progress of mankind? To the conscience of France these questions are addressed; from her conscience let the answer come.

But there are those who say that it is for the sake of religion—the religion of Christ—that the temporal power of the Roman See must be maintained at all costs, even by absolute force, and the aid of foreign soldiers, other means failing. The employment of these violent methods, (in opposition to the national will and aspirations of the people upon whom this temporal power is thus by force imposed,) is justified on the ground that the conservation of that power is necessary to the independence and due exercise of the spiritual authority of him who claims to be on earth the Vicar and representative of Christ. When these or similar assertions are heard or read, the minds of reflecting men instinctively recur to the evangelical writings which narrate the life and death of the holy Jesus. There it is told how full of love and gentleness He was, how meekly He bore all injuries, how He repelled not violence by violence, how He rebuked His disciples for wishing to call down fire from heaven upon those who would not receive Him, saying: "Ye know not what manner of spirit ye are of;" how He refused all temporal power, departing when He "perceived that they would come and take Him by force to make Him a king;" how He declared "My kingdom is not of this world; if my kingdom were of this world then would my servants fight." In propagating and maintaining His spiritual teaching and authority, He used no other means save those of awakening the conscience, convincing the judgment, and converting the heart.

Yet to-day we are told that foreign aid, foreign soldiery, the newest and most improved weapons for destroying human life, war with all its bloodshed and horrors, not only may, but ought to be employed in order to impose upon an unwilling people the *temporal* power of him who proclaims himself to be the Vicar and representative of that very Christ. In all seriousness we ask those Roman Catholics who hold such opinions, is it by such signs that we Protestants are expected to recognise the true head of the Christian Church on earth, the chief pastor of that faith which proclaims "peace on earth and good-will towards men;" whose golden rule bids us "to do unto others as we would they should do unto us?" Is the spectacle of Roman Catholic France forcing Roman Catholic Italy to accept the temporal power of the Pope calculated to give Protestants a pleasing idea of that unity and brotherly love which is so often boasted of by members of the Church of Rome? Is it not more likely to make us heretics thank the Reformation for having freed England from connexion with Rome, and so having preserved us from those quarrels about the papal temporal power which set Romanist against Romanist even to the shedding of their brother's blood? Can those who enjoy and maintain that temporal power by means of foreign aid and foreign soldiers, duly armed with a Chassepot rifle, which "does wonders" in its bloody work of death and slaughter, say—"We serve the altar, and we are content to live only by the altar; we ask nothing of Cæsar, and we receive nothing from Cæsar; our kingdom is not of this world;" "the weapons of our warfare are not carnal?" If such things continue to be done, there will be no difference between the manner of upholding the temporal power which exists in Rome and the temporal power which exists in Warsaw; between the means employed to maintain the earthly crown of the Pope in Italy and the earthly crown of the Czar in Poland; unless it be that the former is obliged to have recourse to foreign aid, while the latter is able to do without that degrading expedient.

Do not Roman Catholics perceive the immense danger which such a policy creates of alienating the Italian nation from the spiritual authority of the Roman Catholic Church, as well as from its temporal power? This latter power, indeed, is already odious to the great majority of Italy's people, nor are all the bayonets of France able to restore it; nay, they but increase that odium in proportion to the number employed against Italy, and to the duration of their stay within her limits. When then Italians, finding the temporal power the one remaining obstacle to the realization of their country's perfect union and freedom under a constitutional sovereign of the nation's choice, are at the same time told that such temporal power is absolutely necessary to the due maintenance of the spiritual authority, there is no little danger of their confounding both in one common hatred. Where to-day would be the religious influence of England's clergy if they favoured the maintenance of a Prussian garrison in London for the sake of maintaining the temporal power and position of their Church? Where would be that of the French priests if they openly advocated the maintenance of an Austrian or Spanish garrison in Avignon for the sake of maintaining there the Papal temporal power which actually existed in that city for centuries, and was only finally swept away by the great Revolution in 1791? What would France have said, at this or any other period of her history, if her bishops and clergy had opposed her formation into one national kingdom because they affirmed it to be incompatible with the interests or necessities of the Church? Such a course would have caused irreparable damage to her in France, and no other result can be expected in Italy. Surely, then, this maintaining of the "temporal power" of the Pope at all costs, and by every means, even the most violent, endangers his spiritual authority, and brings not only dishonour, but even peril on the Church herself. Such, or at least very similar, appears to have been the opinion of one who was no Protestant, but a devout Roman Catholic in all religious matters — of one who ranks amongst the mightiest geniuses of the world, whose name sheds imperishable lustre upon his age, his Church, and his country; for it was the illustrious Dante, who, nearly 600 years ago, seeing how fatal an adjunct to the spiritual authority of the Roman Church was the temporal power, how hurtful to her the union of the two within herself, wrote those lines, never more true than to-day:—

> "Di' oggimai che la chiesa di Roma,
> Per confondere in sè duo reggimenti,
> Cade nel fango e sè bruta e la soma."
> *Purgatorio*, xvi. 127-129.

Say henceforth that the Church of Rome,
By confounding within herself two régimes,
Falls in the mire, defiles both herself and the burden (she bears).

And again,—

> "Ahi, Costantin, di quanto mal fu matre,
> Non la tua conversion, ma quella dote,*
> Che da te prese il primo ricco patre!"
> *Inferno*, xix. 115-117.

Alas! Constantine, of how great ill was the mother,
Not thy conversion, but that dowery,*
Which from thee accepted the first rich father.

Who, indeed, can look to-day on Italy or Ireland without seeing what fearful wrongs and evils the Christian Church has inflicted both on herself and others by accepting temporal aid and temporal power, so calling in the secular arm to help her, as she vainly imagined, in her spiritual work?

Perhaps some such feelings and ideas were mingled

---

* Dante here alludes to what was believed in his days, viz., that Rome and the territory around it, called the Patrimony of St Peter, were given by Constantine to Pope Sylvester.

with those of a more worldly character which made Napoleon III. desirous of withdrawing his troops from Rome. For he well knows, that being, as his soldiers now are, the only foreigners in forcible possession of Italian soil, a cause of perpetual irritation is thereby kept alive in Italy against France, which is destructive of the natural ties that would otherwise unite them together. He appears to have hoped to put an end to his occupation of Rome by the Convention made in September 1864, with the Italian Government. That hope he has not, however, realized—a result by no means surprising, when the discussions (about the instrument itself) which occurred between the two governments, and the general circumstances of the case, are fully considered. The Convention stipulated that Italy should promise not to attack the present territory of the Pope, and "even prevent by force" any attack proceeding from the exterior; that France "should withdraw her troops" from the Papal States within two years; that the Italian Government should make no protest against the organization of a " Papal army even composed of foreign Roman Catholic volunteers," provided such a force did not degenerate into a means of attack against the Italian government. Italy further declared herself ready to enter into an arrangement for assuming a proportional part of the debt of the former States of the Church. A protocol regulated the transfer of the Italian capital from Turin to Florence. Such were the leading features of the Convention. No sooner had it been signed than a good deal of discussion ensued between the French and Italian governments as to what would or ought to be the line of action pursued respectively by the contracting parties in case eventualities arose which were not provided for in the Convention itself. That such eventualities might arise was clear enough ; thus, there might be an internal revolution in Rome, or the Italian government might fail in its endeavours "to prevent by force" a hostile incursion into the Papal States. The Cabinet of General Lamarmora (then in power) pointed out, amongst other things, the immense difficulty of successfully and completely "preventing by force" such attack, even when employing for that purpose a large army; because it was almost impossible really to cover such a frontier as that of the Papal States, which is but a mere line, and is open in all directions to the incursion of hostile bands. In case, then, these or similar circumstances arose, what was to be done? After no little discussion, it was finally determined that as it was impossible to foretell and therefore provide for all future eventualities, it would be better for both the contracting parties to reserve their liberty of action as regarded any future circumstances not positively provided for in the Convention itself. Thus there was left, unfortunately, as it has turned out for all concerned, no slight danger of future complications.

The Papal government received volunteers chiefly from France, Germany, Switzerland, and Belgium. Amongst its defenders, however, was a corps named "The Antibes Legion," whose formation calls for special remark. A French writer of position and ability refers to it in these words :—

"France furnished to the Pope, under the form of volunteers freely enrolled from the ranks of the religious party, the corps of Pontifical Zouaves; the Zouaves were the contingent of the clerical party in France. Apart from this spontaneous movement the French government took the initiative of a more important combination. It favoured the creation, for the military service of the Holy Father, of a corps which was called the Antibes Legion. The manner of recruiting this Legion was peculiar. We do not know how it could be justified as being in conformity with our military laws. In any case it cannot be disputed that it bore an irregular appearance. The soldiers of the Antibes Legion are soldiers of our army; they are commanded by French officers, who, during the time of their service in the Legion, preserve their rights of promotion. Our military contingents are determined by the laws voted by the national representation, and affected exclusively to the service of the country. It is difficult to understand how any fraction of those contingents can be legitimately detached from the service, and authorised to pass into the pay and under the flag of a foreign state."

A little further on the same writer remarks :—"The journey of General Dumont to Rome, and above all a letter of our Minister of War (Marshal Niel), gave to the Antibes Legion a meaning more marked and more disquieting to Italian susceptibilities." The French General mentioned went to Rome and inspected the Antibes Legion in July 1867. It was affirmed that he went officially; then it was said by the *Moniteur* of 1st August 1867, that his mission was of quite a private character. The French blue-book, however, published at the end of November, under a paragraph headed "Mission of General Dumont to Rome," says he was *sent* to ascertain the causes of discouragement in the Legion, and to reanimate the spirit of the corps. In the speech he made to the soldiers of that corps he is reported to have told them in so many words that they were "French soldiers;" then it was said that the reports given of the General's speech were not accurate. It is difficult to arrive at the exact truth in the matter; but at any rate, the General certainly saw those in high official position before being *sent* from Paris to Rome. That fact, connected with what he did say to the soldiers of the Antibes Legion (whatever may have been the exact words used), roused—as well such circumstances might—the susceptibilities of the Italian government, which in consequence asked for explanations from the French government touching General Dumont and his inspection of the Antibes Legion. Throughout Italy generally this matter produced much irritation, which certainly was not to be wondered at, for it looked only too like a breach, of the spirit at any rate, of the September Convention, which stipulated that the imperial government should withdraw its troops from Rome. But whatever Italian susceptibilities General Dumont's mission naturally roused, it was, "above all," the letter of Marshal Niel, the French Minister of War, to Colonel D'Argy, the commander of the Antibes Legion, which gave Italy just cause of complaint. This letter ran as follows:—

"PARIS, 21st June 1867.

"MY DEAR COLONEL,—My attention is too seriously fixed on the Roman Legion to allow of my ignoring the grave facts which for some time past have taken place in reference to it. How can this desertion, not individual, but collective, which threatens to reduce your effective force to nothing, be explained? The soldier has no reason to envy the troops of the mother country; he is commanded by French officers who hold suitable positions (*convenablement posés*) in our army; he serves a respectable cause which he has asked to serve; he has before him that which has always inflamed the French soldier, an enemy to combat, a danger to face; and yet he shamefully deserts the flag which he has freely chosen, and, yielding to culpable enticements, he abandons his chiefs in order to follow despicable foreign seducers, (*de misérables embaucheurs étrangers*.)

"It is not the desire of again seeing his country which is an excuse; for he knows well that so soon as he has entered France he is sent into a disciplinary African corps, (*un corps disciplinaire d'Afrique*,) where he remains until the expiration of his time of military service. I deplore this state of things, my dear Colonel, because it is a stain on our army which, wherever it is represented, ought to preserve its prestige of honour and courageous abnegation. Notwithstanding these sad incidents, my dear Colonel, I do not lose the hope of seeing the good elements which your Legion still includes efface, by dint of devotion and perseverance, the memory of these last times. Your energy is well known to me; the government of the Emperor and that of the Holy Father know that it will not fail. It is of importance that your officers, upon whom you firmly count with just reason, give confidence to the troops by their bearing, by their language, by that military spirit which is, amongst us, the source of such great things. Amongst men of all ranks in your Legion, I shall be happy to signal to the Emperor all those who make themselves remarked by their conduct. I know that you are to present to me

Serjeant Doussin and two of his soldiers. I shall examine their claims with great interest.

"Tell your Legion plainly, my dear Colonel, that we have our eyes upon it, and that I suffer deeply as regards everything which is an affront to its flag, so justly venerated. I confound it with the corps (*les corps*) of our army in everything which touches its military honour and the necessities of its organisation.

"Receive, my dear Colonel, the assurance of my most affectionate sentiments.

(Signed) "Le Maréchal de France, NIEL."

Such is the letter of the French Minister of War to the Colonel, himself a Frenchman, of the Antibes Legion. Let the facts thus gathered from these various French sources be now summed up. They clearly show that this Antibes Legion was composed of the soldiers of the French army, who were permitted, if not induced, to enlist forthwith into the Legion. Their officers are French officers, "who, during the time of their service in the Legion, preserve their rights of promotion." No wonder the French writer, when commenting upon these most unprecedented arrangements, calls such a mode of recruiting "peculiar," doubts much its "being in conformity with our military laws," and describes the whole affair as "disquieting to Italian susceptibilities." But what says Marshal Niel, the Minister of War? What light does his letter throw upon the subject? After lamenting over the desertions which had taken place among the soldiers of the Legion, he says distinctly that they are commanded by *French officers* who hold suitable positions in *our* army;"

P

that is, who as such continue to preserve their rights of promotion in the French army. Soldiers who so desert, adds the Marshal, cannot be led to commit that grave offence from wishing to return to France, because when found there they will be sent off into a disciplinary African corps; that is, punished by the French military authorities for such desertion. The Minister of War deplores this state of things in the Antibes Legion as "a stain upon *our* army." He expresses his willingness to point out to the Emperor any soldiers of the Legion who may duly distinguish themselves; and as a proof that he really means what he says, he mentions by name a worthy serjeant, whose claims, with those of two of his men, he will "examine with great interest." Once again the Marshal declares how deeply he suffers for every dishonour inflicted on this much-loved Legion, and then concludes with these astounding words:—" I confound *it* (the Legion) with the corps (*les corps*) of *our army* in *everything* which touches its military honour and the *necessities of its organisation*."

Let those who are versed in the military code of France decide whether such arrangements infringe it or not. But it is in the name of common sense and common honesty that the question must be asked: How is it possible to justify such proceedings and such language in the face of the distinct stipulation contained in the September Convention, that "French troops" were to be withdrawn from Rome? Let quibblers split what hairs they will, but upright and impartial men will not fail to say that all such doings assuredly broke the spirit, if not the very letter, of that stipulation. Now, when a strong power makes a compact with a weak one, the former is specially bound, by every honourable feeling, not to permit anything to be done on its part which appears even like tampering with that compact to the disadvantage of its weaker partner. The French government has not acted in conformity with this principle in the case of the Antibes Legion, and the various circumstances connected with it. Imperial France has thereby laid herself open to just and severe censure. None can help contrasting the complete and absolute manner in which French troops were, according to promise, withdrawn from Mexico, and the very incomplete and questionable manner in which the like promise of withdrawal was kept as regards Rome. Nor will the imperial government do well to say that the two cases are different, because its enemies will quickly reply: Assuredly, all the difference of the distance between Toulon and Civitia Vecchia, as compared with that between Brest and Vera Cruz; all the difference between Italy, alone and weak, and Mexico, *not* alone, but warmly befriended by the great republic of the United States, with victorious generals, tried armies, and well-equipped fleets at its command. Be all that as it may, one thing at least is certain, that with these matters of the Antibes Legion, Marshal Niel's letter, and General Dumont's mission, known to the whole world, the French government will do wisely to make no allusion to Italy not having been successful in its attempts to prevent by force, last autumn, an attack upon the Papal States. A very common proverb bids people who live in glass houses not to throw stones. What share all these proceedings of the Imperial Government had in rousing Garibaldi to direct an armed attack against Rome, thus re-opening violently that question, and defying the September Convention which French authorities had so flagrantly tampered with, we have no means of knowing; but that those proceedings did influence the course taken by Garibaldi, and those who acted with him, can scarcely be doubted, and is not to be wondered at. The following facts are, at any rate, indisputable:—That immediately after the Convention was concluded, the Antibes Legion was formed in the manner described; in the summer of 1867 came, first, Marshal Niel's letter; then General Dumont's mission; and in the autumn of that year followed the Garibaldian attack directed against Rome.

It was about the middle of September that Garibaldi, taking counsel only of his own patriotic aspirations, put himself at the head of the volunteers who were assembling at his bidding to attack the Papal States. The Italian Government had forbidden all such proceedings, and placed troops to guard the frontier. Before the month closed, Garibaldi was arrested and sent to Caprera. There he was closely watched by the vessels of the royal navy, who at first succeeded in preventing his return to the mainland; but at length he eluded their vigilance, and made at once for the Papal frontier. Despite the efforts of the Italian government, the volunteers continued to get into the Papal territory, and were continually reinforced: among them were Garibaldi's two sons. The General himself now joined them, and led them against the Papal forces, whom they beat at Monte Rotondo: this place, occupying a strong position, was taken by the Garibaldians. Rome itself was in much danger. Already one or two collisions had taken place between the garrison and some of those within the walls. It was at this critical moment that the French government intervened by sending a considerable force to occupy Civita Vecchia and Rome. Upon hearing of this, the Italians urged their government to intervene. Those at the head of affairs appear to have vacillated much upon this momentous subject, involving, as it did, hopes and aspirations, dangers and risks, the magnitude of which language can scarcely exaggerate. Vacillation is always a mistaken policy; but in this case it is scarcely to be wondered at, though it must be censured; for rarely, if ever, has any government been surrounded by difficulties and dangers of a greater, and at the same time of a more opposite kind, than was that of Italy on this occasion. Postponing for a few moments further observations upon such and other kindred matters, this question only shall *here* be asked: Who, after all, are most to blame—those whose rash patriotism creates a crisis necessarily fraught with the utmost danger to their country and her cause, or those at the head of affairs, who, after wisely endeavouring, at the outset, to dissuade the leader of that rash patriotism from entering on a course so full of peril to his country, fall at last themselves into the error of vacillation, or commit other mistakes, while doing their best to steer the ship of state safely through the fearful perils which Garibaldi's rashness had created?

The Ratazzi Cabinet resigned, and after some delay, owing to General Cialdini failing to form a government, the arduous task was finally undertaken and performed by General Menabrea. Not until after the French had landed in Italy, did the Italian troops cross the frontier, taking, at the same time, every precaution to guard against a collision with the French, while pressing messages were sent to Garibaldi to try to persuade him to abandon his now hopeless enterprise. As soon as Rome had been secured by the soldiers of Imperial France, 2000 of them, armed with the new Chassepot rifle, together with 3000 Pontifical troops, well equipped and accompanied by artillery, marched out against the Garibaldians. The two hostile corps, each numbering, as it seems, 5000 men, met at Mentana. Garibaldi and his men, generally badly armed and poorly clothed, fought with such determination and courage, that the conflict continued to rage fiercely from one in the afternoon until dark, and though the French and Papal troops had gained decided successes by nightfall, they were not able to complete their success before it was actually night, but had to wait until the next morning. Such a defeat reflects, indeed, the highest honour upon Garibaldi and his brave men; for opposed to them were 2000 regular French troops, who, armed with the Chassepot rifle, which "did wonders," evidently turned the fortune of the day. But despite the courage and devotion displayed by the Garibaldians, ultimate success against such forces as those opposed to them was hopeless. Gradually driven back, after much hard fighting, they retreated under cover of night, having suffered heavy losses, and leaving many prisoners in the hands of the enemy, When within the limits of the Italian kingdom, Garibaldi was taken by its authorities, and sent to the fortress of Varignano, in the Gulf of Spezia. He might have resisted; but, to his honour be it ever said, he would permit of no resistance, because he never will allow his own person to be the cause of armed conflict between Italians. Such a conflict, willingly and intentionally brought about, would be not an error, but a crime. For whatever differences may exist among them as to the best means of attaining the great object all have in view, the whole nation is *one* in its firm determination to attain that object, which is but that of freeing for ever their native land from the presence of foreign soldiery, and the wrong of foreign interference. Their neighbours, French, Swiss, and German, have attained that result, and Italians are steadfastly determined to do likewise.

After the French had landed in Italy, the Italian troops had, as just mentioned, crossed into the Papal territory. This passage of the frontier gave great offence to the French government. For what reason it is hard to say, except that the French are inclined to be much too easily offended if any one, except themselves, ventures to do anything. This same kind of touchiness some of them have lately shown most unwarrantably towards Germany, with whose work of internal reorganisation no other nation whatever has the slightest right to interfere. But happily the Germans are very numerous and very strong. It is to be hoped that that fact, coupled with their absolute right to do what they please in their own country, will ever be sufficient to protect them from the wrong of foreign interference while engaged in reconstructing the government of their great fatherland.

The circumstances connected with the crossing of the frontier by the Italian army fully warranted such a step on the part of the Italian government, for they clearly belonged to those future eventualities not expressly provided for in the September Convention—eventualities concerning which each government had reserved its "freedom of action." When, then, the imperial government made use of that freedom of action (as it had a right to do) to enter the Papal territory, the Italian government was perfectly justified in doing the same. Not only would Italy have had good ground for occupying Rome jointly with France, but that would have been by far the most politic and equitable arrangement. Instead of that, the imperial government became very indignant with the Italian for having ordered its army to cross the frontier at all, and appeared (though it seems almost incredible) inclined to pick a wolf-and-lamb quarrel with its weaker partner. In all this the French government acted most unfairly. Nor has it a right to utter a syllable about the Italian government having been unsuccessful in its attempts to prevent the Garibaldians from entering the Papal territory, because success neither had nor could be stipulated for; on the contrary, the Italian government had pointed out from the first (in 1864) the immense difficulty of successfully doing so. But there was another and far more powerful reason which should have made the French government hold altogether a different tone to the one it affected—namely, that scarcely had the Convention been signed when the imperial government began to tamper with its spirit, if not its letter, in the matter of the formation of the Antibes Legion, as has already been plainly shown. No wonder, under these circumstances, that this high-handed conduct of Imperial France to a weaker neighbour caused her enemies to draw many a biting comparison between her bearing towards Italy on the Roman question and her bearing towards the United states in the Mexican; nor did they forget to remark sarcastically on the quiet and proper manner in which the imperial government accepted the perfectly just, but most decided refusal given by Germany to listen to any proposal for the rectification of the Rhine frontier. As to the acclamations with which French telegrams announced the reception of French troops in Italian towns, not only were they at variance with the testimony of independent witnesses of the receptions given, but they were at the same time in complete harmony with the official announcements (made during some two or three years) of the rapturous reception given to French troops in Mexico. Yet no sooner did French bayonets cease to uphold that Mexican State which they had temporarily called into existence, than it fell hopelessly and utterly within a few weeks. Not only have Mexicans given no signs of love to France since, but they have, by the cruel execution of the poor Archduke Maximilian, flung in her face the most terrible insult that ever one nation offered to another. The French Emperor will do well to bear in mind that these things are remembered and freely discussed, if not in France, at least in other countries. Nor can the truth be concealed that, though the citizens of free nations may deem Garibaldi's course unwise or inexpedient, yet assuredly their sympathies were *not* with those who, on Mentana's field, handled the "wonder-working" Chassepot, but with those who faced it with heroic courage, animated by the "wonder-working" love of freedom and of country.

As soon as the Papal territory had been evacuated by the Garibaldians, the Italian troops withdrew from it also. This step was taken by the king's government of its own accord, though it would be folly to deny that in taking it they were uninfluenced by the hostile attitude unjustly assumed by France. At the same time, it would be unfair to the rulers of Italy not to admit that if they were greatly influenced by prudence in avoiding all risk of war with a neighbour so immensely powerful, they were also influenced by gratitude from a recollection of the generous aid afforded by France in 1859. Yet this latter power should remember that generosity at one time is no excuse for injustice and overbearing conduct at another. It is sad, indeed, to see the noble work commenced in that memorable year, endangered and delayed by an uncertain and changeable policy, creating general distrust, because its author will persist in the vain attempt to support at the same time two hostile systems and serve two hostile masters.

When the immense dangers and difficulties of every kind which surrounded the Italian government are taken fairly into account, its conduct in thus giving way to France, and so avoiding all present danger of a conflict with a neighbour so immeasurably stronger than Italy, is, to say the least of it, excusable. Certainly, her rulers took in this matter the prudent rather than the heroic line. In consequence, there have been some English writers who have, when commenting upon this subject, spoken of the Italian king and government in the harshest terms. Surely such critics will do well to be more considerate, if not for the sake of Italy, at least for that of England. For when foreigners read such very severe criticism, coming from such a quarter, they will be tempted to ask, Did not England, despite all her vast power and resources, finally take, in the Danish question, the *prudent* rather than the *heroic* line? Can we English deny that that prudence was preceded by a great deal of what our American cousins amusingly term "tall talk?" That having been the case, Englishmen will be wise not to judge over harshly a young country, infinitely less powerful than their own, which, in circumstances of far greater danger, followed, like England, the counsels of prudence rather than those of heroism. As to Italians, however bitterly they may feel just now at having been forced to give way to Imperial France; however much the rash amongst them may have wished that their sovereign had defied her to the uttermost, at whatever risk; they will not allow themselves to be so blinded by such feelings as to listen to designing persons, who, in their folly or their wickedness, seek to turn the hearts of their countrymen from their honest king. Italians will not forget that for eighteen eventful years Victor Emmanuel, whether as King of Piedmont or of Italy, has ever been true to his country's rights and liberties, has ever faithfully preserved them when the rulers of neighbouring nations were trampling those of their people in the dust. They will remember that, in the cause of Italy, he has more than once risked life and crown. Under his honest rule their native land, (which scarcely ten years ago was but a downtrodden slave,) has not only broken the old yoke, but has made greater strides towards becoming a free and united nation than was ever effected in the same brief time by any people in the world's history. It is not too much to say, that the unswerving devotion of Victor Emmanuel to Italy's righteous cause, and his honest faithfulness to his people's liberties, have been as efficacious in bringing Italy so far forward on her way, as the genius of the great Cavour, or the burning patriotism of Garibaldi; for without such a king, the illustrious statesman would never have risen to power, and the great patriot would, in all probability, have passed his life, from 1849 to the present day, as a comparatively unknown exile. Italians cannot but feel sure that what their sovereign has done at this time he has only done because he honestly believed (rightly or wrongly) that it was, on the whole, the best that was possible amidst the unspeakable dangers of a crisis brought on by Garibaldi's movements. Well are they aware that none regret more than the king himself, his country's not yet being equal to the great military monarchies of Europe, which have grown to their present strength in the course of centuries. It would indeed be a miracle if Italy were so, considering she numbers scarce seven years of national existence. And none but wild fanatics can suppose that such a miracle could have been wrought by Italy's adopting any other form of government, or by selecting as her rulers any other class of men whatever. Granting, then, that the statesmen of Italy have, in the last terrible crisis, made mistakes, failed to take the best course, or preferred prudence to heroism, who shall on that account fling at them the first stone? Shall England? Thoughts of Denmark, if nothing else, will stay her hand. Shall France? Is Mexico so soon forgotten? If, then, in circumstances far less difficult, two of the greatest nations in the world must own to a policy whose results were anything but flattering to their pride and self-esteem, Italians may well pardon (while freely, within the limits of their constitutional liberties, pointing out) the mistakes of their government. This is the course they will pursue. At the same time, they will rally closely around their king and parliament, and so by firm union, and careful preparations of every kind, become better able in the future to enforce, if necessary, their just rights and claims; for, acting otherwise, they would but play into the hands of their country's bitterest enemies. Nor will Italians forget that some of those amongst them who have been loudest in demanding that Italy should plunge headlong into an unequal contest with France, have been but lately the loudest to cry out for the reduction of their army to the lowest possible point, and *that* just when the French Emperor (without any sufficient cause) was devising fresh plans with the object of strengthening his military system. The inconsistency of such men needs only to be mentioned to be exposed. Of two things, one—either Italy may ease her finances by cutting down her army to the utmost, and then she must abandon all idea of resisting an overbearing neighbour of ten times her strength, who persists in doing the contrary; or else her soldiers must be very numerous, thoroughly well-armed and equipped, and then Italians must consent to a taxation in proportion to the expenditure necessitated by maintaining so large a force. The fault of such a state of things must not, however, be laid at Italy's door, who, like her German neighbours, simply asks to be let alone, and left to regulate her own internal affairs as she pleases, just as Germany does and has a right to do.

Happily this latter country is strong enough to keep meddling neighbours from interfering with that right. The fact is, that the huge standing armies which disgrace our age and civilization, are caused chiefly, if not wholly, by the imperial government of France. For by maintaining and strengthening the enormous military establishments which it persists in keeping up, it compels its neighbours to be well, if not equally, prepared. Yet France has no need for such an overgrown army as that which weighs down her people with an ever-increasing taxation; while the capricious foreign policy of her government entails the burden first of one, and then of another military expedition, abundant in cost, but certainly not in glory. Such a policy keeps all the world in perpetual alarm, to the detriment alike of France and other nations, from the uncertainty and misgiving to which it naturally gives rise. This conduct of the imperial government is without excuse, for no one menaces France, none do her dishonour (unless it be Mexican Juarez,) none seek or wish to deprive her of any fraction of that which is hers, neither do any of her neighbours possess so much as a single village which has the least desire to belong to Imperial France. Were her government to prove its love of peace by a policy of strict non-intervention in the concerns of other countries, instituting at the same time large and obvious reductions in its huge military establishments, instead of merely protesting in words its peaceful aspirations, the present state of uncertainty would soon pass away, and there would be some hope that over-taxed Europe would see a diminution, at least, of the standing curse of standing armies.

The actual crisis through which Italy, not to say Europe, is passing, cannot be considered without making a few observations upon the course pursued by Garibaldi. Burning with a devoted patriotism that knows no bounds, ever exposing himself to all the dangers incurred in the carrying out of his rash plans, Garibaldi will ever command the sympathy of all those who believe that every people have a right to struggle against foreign interference, whether it take the form of threats or of force backed up by bayonets. But it does not by any means necessarily follow that the mode of proceeding adopted by him is therefore the wisest or the best. That must depend upon quite other considerations, themselves depending upon a variety of circumstances well worth a few moments' serious attention.

Garibaldi is to-day the subject, indeed one of the representatives, of the Italian kingdom, not yet completed, but assuredly deserving the title of free within its actual limits. At its head is a sovereign faithfully carrying out constitutional principles; under him are really responsible ministers, answerable to the freely-elected Parliament of a people who possess the most substantial liberties,—amongst others, those of the press and of public meetings. Now the question arises, which is best for Italy, that Garibaldi, keeping himself within the limits of action which a free state necessarily (as in the case of England or Belgium) prescribes to all its citizens, should unite himself with the governing powers of his country in the arduous task of solving the last great question which still impedes the completion of Italy's union and independence? or whether he should take a course which almost of necessity brings him into collision with those at the head of affairs, nay, what is far worse, brings his country into only too possible collision with imperial France, for whose power he must know that Italy is, and can be, no match? for no political machinery can even be conceived which could possibly in six or seven years make a people who have long been downtrodden and divided equal in arms to a military nation whose strength is the growth of centuries. Surely, if Garibaldi were as wise as he is patriotic in heart and courageous in deed, he would, in the altered condition of Italy, (being as it is so widely different from what it was in the days of his earlier career,) see the expediency and wisdom of altering his own course according to the altered circumstances of his country. For her sake he would do well to curb his too daring ardour, and help her honest King and free Parliament in their endeavours to solve the Roman difficulty, instead of causing embarrassment and danger, not only to them, but even to that noble Italian cause which, since 1859, has made such gigantic strides towards its destined goal— that great consummation of Italy's complete union and independence, which is the earnest desire not only of her own children, but of all who love national freedom, and hate foreign interference in whatever garb it clothes its odious form. Again, Garibaldi seems to believe that the French Emperor is the worst of men, and in his heart a hater of Italian freedom. Assuming, for the sake of argument, this to be true, does not the General perceive that his own conduct gives that very Emperor a handle for employing the worst kind of interference, that of bayonets and Chassepots? To say that France has no more right to maintain by force of arms in Italy any temporal rule whatever, than Italians have to do the like in France, is unquestionably true; but unfortunately (not only for Italy and Europe, but for France herself) she has the *power* to do so, and is only too much inclined to exercise it. This fact is incontestable, and when Garibaldi, choosing to disregard it, gives by the course he pursues an excuse to Napoleon for interfering in Italy, the imprudent patriot only plays the game of the very man whom he declares to be Italy's worst, because most insidious, enemy.

Moreover, the citizen of a free country is not justified in endeavouring to force his government by *extra*-legal means to pursue a given line of policy or conduct, instead of employing only the many legal means of doing so which are at his command, thanks to the constitutional liberties such a country bestows on its people. When, then, any citizen pursues such an erroneous course, he endangers the liberty he loves, because he breaks down those proper and legal bounds which in all free lands must and ought to be preserved, as being absolutely necessary to their freedom. Thus acting, such a citizen (whatever may be his past services or intrinsic merits) does wrong, imperils his country and her cause; therefore he must be blamed. To say that Garibaldi's character and services are such that the above rule is inapplicable, cannot be admitted. That character is noble, those services immense; they may be pleaded in extenuation of the course he took last autumn; but considering the actual point at which Italy has arrived in the establishment of a national and constitutional system of freedom, Garibaldi's proceedings were not, under the circumstances, really wise or justifiable, for that system offered him other, better, and safer ways of devoting himself to his country's service. It will perhaps be said, that what he has just done will, after all, help on in the end the cause of Italy. Very possibly; but that does not therefore make the particular way in which he acted necessarily commendable. Yet whatever Garibaldi's faults and errors—for neither popular nor royal heroes are exempt from them—his name is, and ever will be, loved wherever freemen dwell, as expressing in a single word life-long, undying devotion to the sacred cause of his country's rights and independence.

Among the thousand arguments and reflections to which the mighty work of Italy's union and regeneration gave rise, but few indeed can here be even touched upon. There is one assertion, however, which must not be forgotten. It is sometimes said that the Papal government only desires to be left quietly in Rome. This is wholly contrary to the fact. What it has ever, hitherto at least, demanded, is that all its former provinces be restored to it; in other words, that the Italian kingdom be broken up. It says to Italy: Your existence as a free and united nation is incompatible with my temporal rule; I therefore demand your destruction. What would be the reply of France, England, or any other nation, if, being in the position of Italy, such language were addressed to them? Again, the chief of the Papal government hurls his anathemas at Italy for adopting a variety of laws which are not only demanded by modern progress and civilisation, but which Roman Catholic France and Belgium have already adopted, and which the free Austria of to-day is hastening to adopt. Who amongst enlightened men does not sympathise with the work which is now being carried on by the Austro-Hungarian diets and statesmen? With what disgust would not every friend of justice and freedom see to-day Vienna or Pesth in the hands of a temporal power maintained by foreign bayonets, anathematising and impeding at every turn the great work of national regeneration, liberty, and progress now being carried on in the Austro-Hungarian state? Assuredly such a spectacle would be hateful in Vienna or Pesth, and assuredly it is not less hateful in Rome.

There is a desire often expressed by many of the most inveterate enemies of the Roman Church, which Roman Catholics will do well to consider. It is this: that the temporal power of the Pope may continue to be prolonged by forcible means, because thereby the greatest possible damage will be inflicted upon his spiritual power. These bitter foes of the Holy See will certainly read with joy of the Roman Pontiff blessing and decorating the foreign soldiers who have fought for the shred of territory still left him—soldiers whose Chassepot rifle "did wonders" in its murderous work of death and slaughter. But what answer can be given to those inveterate enemies when they ask, pointing to the hecatomb of mangled corpses which strewed Mentana's field: Are these the bloody tokens by which the Papal king would have mankind believe that he is indeed the true representative on earth of the gentle and loving Jesus who refused to be made king—who was named the Prince of Peace; who "came not to destroy men's lives, but to save them?"

Those who, in examining this double question of the "temporal power" of the Roman Church in Italy, and of the Anglican Church in Ireland, look only to the vast material strength of France and England, will perhaps come to the conclusion that the "temporal power" of the two churches, which those nations respectively uphold, is in no danger of being brought to an end, or even of being greatly modified. But those who observe the direction in which the current of civilisation and progress is running, who watch the onward flow of civil and religious liberty in all directions, who mark the successful vindication of national and individual freedom, even in countries hitherto most opposed to all such principles, will come to a very different conclusion. The ruined and decaying remains of a vast armoury of weapons by which arbitrary statesmen and bigoted ecclesiastics sought to sustain and strengthen, as they imagined, the cause of religion, are to be seen lying broken and disused on all sides. Such instrumentality belongs to the past, whether its outward forms were to be seen in the stake and torture of ages long gone by, or in those civil disabilities and offensive oaths which were abolished but yesterday. The attempt to maintain by force the temporal power and position of an ecclesiastical body, in opposition to the will, the liberties, and the progress of a whole people, is but a vain endeavour to preserve the last remnants of the old system, which sought in a thousand ways to shackle the liberties and consciences of men, by compelling them to accept, or at least support, some form of religious belief which their brother men believed to be the truest and the best. Those last remnants will be as surely swept away as those around which the present generation can remember the battle raging, but which now exist no longer. More time may yet have to be lost in the struggle, that struggle may blaze forth for a moment hotter and fiercer than ever, but the ultimate result is inevitable. France may be the greatest of military powers, while Italy has not yet organised the undeveloped resources of a nation whose birth-throes we have witnessed and yet are witnessing. England possesses might and resources such as may well make the strongest shrink from rousing her to hostile action; while Ireland may be said never even to have known an existence at once independent of others and united within herself. Yet when Italy and Ireland demand the cessation of the temporal power and rule of an ecclesiastical body which weighs down their liberties, stops their progress, and poisons their whole national life, it is with them that the final victory will rest, despite all the strength of France and England, who respectively uphold in Italy and Ireland the temporal power of the Roman and Anglican hierarchies. For while the former nations have on their side, in this matter, only the material strength of Chassepot rifles and Armstrong guns, the latter have with them the whole current of modern civilisation and progress, united to the divine power of justice, liberty, and right, now, as ever, numbered amongst the best gifts which God has bestowed on man.

If, moreover, a glance be directed from the old world to the new; whether to the vast dominion of the great American republic, or to the rising communities of England's colonial empire—those free nations of a no distant future—the system of absolute religious freedom and equality will there be seen reigning unquestioned, none having the least desire to disturb, in those countries, that universal settlement which, to the benefit of State and Church, leaves both unhampered, thus realising the idea of a free church in a free state—"Libera chiesa in libero stato," as said Cavour.

Such facts, when connected with the manifestly increasing tendency of the more enlightened and powerful European nations to put in practice the principle of complete religious freedom, reveal clearly to every thoughtful observer what must be the final result. Is such a result to be dreaded? Is it indeed to be lamented that the prospect opens of a time when no temporal power of any church whatever shall thwart the independence and progress of a whole nation; when no country shall be compelled to support a church hateful to the great majority of its people? Surely the fall of such systems, not less unworthy of an enlightened age than of the Christian faith, should be hailed with thankfulness; while at the same time due preparation should be made so to meet that salutary change as to turn it to the best possible account, for if well and wisely profited by, it will usher in the full reign of absolute religious freedom and equality. Then shall all those who share a common faith, and "reverence their conscience as their king," follow its dictates without let or hindrance, without paying tax or tithe to any other creed save that which reigns in their own hearts. Thus shall religion rest upon conviction, its only sure foundation, and so the sacred claims of man's spiritual life be brought into harmony with the no less sacred rights of freedom, truth, and conscience.

The debates which have occurred in the French Chambers since our article on the Two Temporal Powers has been put in type, lead us to add the following remarks:—M. Rouher has declared that Italy shall not be allowed to seize upon (*s'emparer de*) Rome. If he means that France will under no circumstances allow that city to become the capital of Italy, the conference proposed by the French government cannot take place. For it is doubtful if any of the great powers will endorse such a doctrine; certainly England will not. If the French minister only means that Italy will not be allowed to seize on Rome by violence, because a European conference is going to take in hand the Roman question, there is still room for negotiations, however slight the hope of their leading to a satisfactory result. M. Rouher has delivered himself of one of those phrases, so dear to the second empire, which may be explained according to circumstances. Such phrases often give at first alternating hopes to the various political sections of France, and not unfrequently end in displeasing them all. The French minister also informed the Chambers that the Holy Father raised in Rome his venerable hands in prayer for the good of Christendom; be it so, but it must not be forgotten that he raises his voice there also to anathematise the just and equal laws passed by the Italian government for the good of its own people; laws not only in consonance with the civilisation of the age, but which France has herself long since adopted.

M. Moustier, the French Minister of Foreign Affairs, in his speech (4th December 1867) said that M. Nigra, the Italian minister accredited to the French court, in proposing to France a joint French and Italian occupation of Rome, asked the French to become "not only dupes but traitors;" adding, "Our honour, our uprightness, all the sentiments that exist in the hearts of Frenchmen, as in their national soil, revolted against it." This proposition was therefore "rejected with indignation." Now, only a few weeks before (17th October) M. Nigra, writing to his government at Florence, says, "M. Rouher proposes that the *double* intervention may be regulated by a common agreement and contemporaneously effected." This idea of M. Rouher's was, as facts show, not acted on by the French government; it preferred going to Rome alone, and M. Rouher finally agreed to that plan. But what will the world think of M. Moustier officially declaring his own colleague's proposal of a joint occupation of Rome to be one which made them "dupes and traitors," which Frenchmen "revolted against," and which France "rejected with indignation?" These two French ministers have thus brought the utmost discredit upon their own government, unless indeed they have some very clear and straightforward statement to make, which shall explain this extraordinary conduct and language of theirs, touching the proposal of a joint occupation of Rome. Such a specimen of the way in which the imperial government carries on negotiations upon vital questions with another government, of whom it professes to be the friend and even ally, will make most people think that the fewer negotiations foreign countries have with such directors of statecraft the better. But the recollection of how much weaker Italy is than France throws into the background the absurdity of these proceedings of the French government, only to bring out more forcibly the disgrace which of necessity attaches to them.

Besides M. Rouher and M. Moustier, another high

authority, M. Thiers, has spoken. If what *he* says means anything, it means that, arms in hand, France ought to have opposed, if not even now break up by force, German and Italian unity. He advocates unblushingly the most selfish and narrow of policies. The neighbours of France are to be kept weak and divided that she may be strong. According to this doctrine, the French may be united, may change their dynasties and governments as often as they please, may be absolute masters of their own destinies and country; but woe to Germans and Italians if they do likewise. That the neighbours of France have no right to interfere with Frenchmen as regards the management of French affairs in their own land, is assuredly true; but no eloquence of M. Thiers will prove that those neighbours have not the same absolute right in their respective countries, as against French interference. It is now clear to the world that all those fine phrases about protecting the independence and spiritual authority of the Pope are but hypocritical devices which attempt to conceal beneath the garb of religion a policy of interference as petty, as selfish, as opposed to the Christian precept of not doing to others what we would not have them do to us, as ever disgraced the worst times of purely selfish and autocratic misgovernment. Melancholy indeed is it to see the professed advocate of free constitutional principles thwarting their progress in other lands instead of aiding them in their glorious work. Such men do but bring dishonour upon themselves, as well as on the party to which they are attached.

If, as the words of the statesmen referred to seem to imply, France has determined to prevent, under all circumstances, Rome becoming the capital of Italy, France will assuredly find herself occupying a very isolated position. Such a policy, based on dislike to the unity and independence of her neighbours, will create uneasiness and suspicion throughout Germany, hatred in Italy, and decided disapprobation among the free people of England and the United States. Russia holding down Poland will smile grimly at imperial France holding down Rome; but as to sympathy, there will be none. Nor will Austria and Hungary have any to bestow, for they are fully occupied with the arduous and noble task of internal union, progress, and liberty, upon the success of which their future prosperity depends. Very many of the sons of France will wish that her work resembled more that of the Emperor-King (Francis Joseph), instead of bearing such an unpleasant likeness to that of the Czar. "Vive la liberté comme en Autriche!" How strange that cry, uttered but the other day in Paris by those who boast of 1789.[*] It may be that the French people, so full of generous impulses, will at length say: Enough of a policy advocated by those who bid us selfishly inflict upon our neighbours an interference we should not for a moment tolerate from them; enough of a conscription creating huge armaments which burden us with an ever-increasing taxation while depriving the land of tens of thou-

[*] On the occasion of Emperor Francis Joseph's visit to Paris in the autumn of 1867.

sands of able cultivators; enough of foreign expeditions which cost France millions of money and thousands of lives; enough of a policy which hides national selfishness beneath the garb of religion, and then dares to describe it as patriotism. No neighbour threatens us; each one but asks that we interfere not with him, even as he interferes not with us. It is but just, for there are none upon our frontiers who desire to be under our government, each one being content to be united to his own fatherland. We number 38 millions, in possession of a rich and magnificent country, whose just rights we are more than able to defend. Let us leave others in peace to do as they will with their own, while we consecrate ourselves to the work of developing the resources, rights, and liberties of our noble France. So shall we worthily fill our place among the nations, and be a blessing both to ourselves and others. Pursuing steadily such a course, we cannot fail in time to reap all the rich blessings bestowed by those mighty principles of freedom and the rights of nations which we and our great forefathers have done so much to sow broadcast throughout the world.

THE CHURCH SYSTEM OF IRELAND AND CANADA.

Reprinted from the " Westminster Review" of the 1st April 1868.

SO paramount is the importance of the Irish question that no apology is needed for keeping it constantly before the public mind; rather is it a positive duty to do so until a satisfactory solution has been obtained; for the welfare alike of Ireland and of England is involved in the issue. The question itself embraces two subjects closely connected with each other—the land and the Church. It is the latter which will be specially dealt with in this paper.

When the justice and expediency of maintaining intact the Protestant State Church in Ireland are called in question, its supporters are fond of reminding their opponents that the great majority of Irish landlords are members of the Established Church. This fact at once provokes the question, How is it that, while the great mass of Ireland's people are Roman Catholic, the great majority of her landed proprietors are Protestant? In no other country is to be seen a like strange phenomenon. Presbyterian Scotland, Roman Catholic France, Lutheran Prussia, Protestant England, present no such abnormal condition of things. Whence, then, does it spring in Ireland? One word, pregnant with innumerable ills, goes far to solve the problem—Confiscation. Lord Clare, the Irish Lord Chancellor at the time of the Union in 1801, said: " So the whole island has been confiscated, with the exception of the estates of five or six families of English blood, some of whom had been attainted in the reign of Henry VIII., but recovered their possessions before Tyrone's rebellion, and had the good fortune to escape the pillage of the English republic inflicted by Cromwell; and no inconsiderable portion of the island has been confiscated twice, or perhaps thrice, in the course of a century." So again, a very different authority, Mr J. S. Mill, writes :—" According to a well-known computation, the whole land of the island has been confiscated three times over. Part had been taken to enrich Englishmen and their Irish adherents ; part to form the endowment of a hostile hierarchy; the rest had been given away to English and Scotch colonists, who held, and were intended to hold it, as a garrison against Ireland." This evil work was further aided by that penal code which oppressed Irish Roman Catholics up to nearly the close of the eighteenth century. It enacted, amongst other things, that no member of the Church of Rome could take or transfer lands by devise, descent, or purchase; that he could not dispose of his estate by will, or lend money on the security of land. A child, conforming to the established religion, might force his parent to surrender his estate, under a fair allowance. A younger brother might deprive the elder brother of the legal rights conferred by primogeniture.

With such causes to account for the fact, (without parallel in Europe), that while the great majority of landed proprietors in Ireland are of one faith, the great majority of her people are of another, common prudence (if no higher principle) would have suggested the wisdom of not adducing that anomalous condition, in order to justify the maintenance of the Church of the small minority as the State Establishment of the whole country. One would have thought that the defenders of the Anglican hierarchy in the sister island would have avoided using an argument which, when examined, is proved to rest upon a fact originating in the cruel wrongs of past times—wrongs which now meet with universal condemnation. To right them completely and fully to-day is unhappily impossible; but assuredly that is no reason for bringing them forward in order to prop up an unequal system which it lies within our power to abolish. The merest expediency and the highest principle alike forbid the folly which vainly seeks to justify the crying anomalies of the present by appealing to the yet more crying wrongs of the past.

But without dwelling further upon this aspect of the subject, let the Irish State Church, as it actually exists, be now briefly yet carefully examined. Since the Commutation Act was passed, (1832,) the taking a tenth of the cultivator's produce, the seizing for payment his only cow or pig, by way of collecting tithe dues, has been done away. The ills produced by such a mode of proceeding became too aggravated to allow of its continuance. The tithes are now only recoverable from the head landlord. He pays them out of the rent he receives from his land, upon which they are a first charge. Inasmuch, however, as the rent is derived from the labour of the occupier who cultivates the soil, that labour evidently contributes largely and directly to the payment of the tithes. This mode of collecting them, under the Commutation Act, is certainly better than the old system of levying them by the seizure of the cultivator's produce or stock: but, however ameliorated the form, the cultivator of the soil still bears his full share of the payment. Nothing can alter the fact that all charges upon land press upon both tenant and landlord. Now, in Ireland the great majority of actual cultivators or tenants are Roman Catholics, who are thus obliged to contribute directly to the support of the Protestant establishment; so that the injustice remains of obliging by law the members of the Roman Communion to pay for the Anglican Church. Again, it is urged that as both he who owns the land and he who cultivates it knew of this tithe-charge when they became owners or cultivators, neither of them have a right to complain. Such an assertion is a very exaggerated statement of the case. What may fairly be said is, that being aware of the existence of such a charge on land, they have no right to refuse its payment as long as the law demands it of them; but they have a perfect right, if they think such an arrangement tainted with injustice, to use every constitutional means for obtaining a change of the law. That persons buy or lease under such conditions does not by any means necessarily prove that they think such conditions exactly what they ought to be; all it really proves is, that such persons are so desirous of becoming owners and cultivators that even those amongst them who contend that the obligation to pay tithes is unjust, prefer doing so rather than cut themselves off from the land. But such compliance with the existing law by no means invalidates their right to get rid, by constitutional means, of the obligation which they deem unjust. This becomes clearer still if a similar case, though under different circumstances, be imagined. Suppose the legislature, having imposed a five per cent income tax on its subjects, further enacted that all persons with blue eyes should pay an additional one per cent, thus making the tax in their case six per cent. Doubtless every blue-eyed person who, after the enactment, continued to reside in the country and derive his income from it, would be legally and morally bound to pay the extra one per cent; but that would by no means deprive him of his right of using all legitimate means for the repeal of the enactment in question. A blue-eyed person would not, by continuing to reside in the country, prove that he thought the extra tax reasonable; the fact of continued residence would prove nothing more than that he thought such extra tax a less evil than that of leaving the country, with all his possessions; nor would he by thus continuing to live in his native land weaken in any degree his right to agitate for the repeal of the tax. Such a foolish and oppressive measure would offend against justice, not against religious convictions. But inasmuch as these latter feelings are very generally as deep-rooted in the human breast as the sense of justice, such an enactment as the one supposed would not be more oppressive than that which says to a whole people: None amongst you shall possess, nor even cultivate, any portion of the soil of your own country, except upon the condition of paying tithe in support of a religion which the great majority of your people deem wrong and schismatical. Yet such has been the treatment inflicted for 300 years by England upon Ireland. In the 16th century England became Protestant, Ireland remained Roman Catholic. Upon which England, being the stronger, compelled all Irish proprietors and occupiers of land to support, from that time forward, a Protestant State Church in Ireland.

There are some who fancy that they successfully apologise for this by asserting that the whole change (the cruel penal code of the last century included) was effected by the Irish parliament. Irish indeed; for although three-fourths of the Irish were Roman Catholics, no Roman Catholic was allowed to have a seat in Ireland's legislature, nor even to possess the suffrage. Have those who make use of this argument about the Irish parliament ever asked themselves what they would think of an English parliament in which no Protestant could sit, and in the election of whose members no Protestant could vote? Thus is it that men wedded by habit to a long-standing wrong, blindly endeavour to prop it up by means of another and yet greater wrong. Those who thus argue are about as wise as persons who should seek to extinguish a conflagration by turning upon it an abundant supply of oil. Such arguments (and there are many of a similar character brought to bear) really tempt the writer, despite his English birth and Protestant faith, to wish that by some miracle Ireland would suddenly become far stronger than England, and then treat her for a year or two to a Roman Church establishment on *this* side of St George's Channel. It would then be seen how Englishmen would deal with arguments in favour of a church establishment of the small Roman Catholic minority forced upon the unwilling majority of Protestant England. Eighteen months of such a *régime* would clear away many a sophism by which Anglican Churchmen seek now to justify such a system when applied to Ireland. It would be edifying to see the new light which would break upon their minds. Our public halls would ring with many an eloquent speech proclaiming the freedom of private judgment and defending the rights of conscience. The occasion would, no doubt, be further improved by reminding Roman Catholics that, as professed Christians, they were bound to do unto others as they would be done by. Many and powerful discourses would be preached setting forth the apostolic maxim, that the weapons of the Christian warfare are not carnal. Others would dwell with great force of argument upon the truth that the Christian kingdom is not one of temporal but of spiritual rule, even as Christ himself declared when He said, "My kingdom is not of this world." In vain would our Irish fellow-countrymen seek to improve their position by passing an Ecclesiastical Titles Bill forbidding our Protestant bishops to assume, for the future, territorial designations. Nor would content be increased by the suspension of the Habeas Corpus Act, although it might well be that such suspension was necessary to the peace of the country, thanks to the ecclesiastical *régime* thus imposed upon Protestant England by Roman Catholic Ireland. Indeed it would not be surprising if the head of the police had to call in the authorities of the Horse Guards to enable him to protect Archbishop Manning (by law transformed into His Grace Henry Edward, Lord Archbishop of Westminster, Primate of all England and Metropolitan), as he went to take his seat in England's House of Peers.

Under such circumstances, even those who are loudest in proclaiming that changes in our government are to be effected only by constitutional means, might be sorely tempted to fall away from that orthodox faith. Some might perchance give ear to evil-disposed persons who should whisper that our forefathers resisted oppression by other than merely moral force and constitutional opposition. Very fervid

Protestants, perhaps even Church dignitaries, roused by what seemed to them a grievous wrong, and hopeless of any other remedy, might cry in their despair, "Repeal the Union." One thing, at least, is certain; that no amount of oratory, no abundance of leading articles, would ever convince Englishmen that a Papal Church established by law in Protestant England was after all "only a sentimental grievance." Now, let it further be supposed that such a Roman establishment were accompanied by a wide-spread system of confiscation, which handed over three-fourths of England's soil to Irish Roman Catholics and their dependents. What would Englishmen say if such a change, brought about by such means, were adduced as an argument to prove that a Roman State Church was no real hardship to England? Would not her people condemn the whole proceeding as a monstrous iniquity, and denounce the argument as one which only added insult to injury? Such assuredly would be England's sentence in her own case, and such, if justice or manly honesty have any influence over her, must be the sentence she pronounces in the case of her neighbour. To judge otherwise is to run the risk of no slight peril, if, indeed, there be truth in those words: "With what judgment ye judge, ye shall be judged; and with what measure ye mete, it shall be measured to you again."

Many defenders of the present Irish Church Establishment affirm that it is the real representative of the early Irish Church as it existed previous to the conquest of Ireland by Henry II. (1156-1171). They say it was that sovereign who first brought the Church of the sister island to acknowledge the Papal supremacy. Elaborate arguments are adduced to prove, and not less elaborate ones to disprove, the alleged fact. The discipline, dogmas, rites, succession, condition, &c., of the early Irish Church are gone into with more or less of success, or want of success. An intricate mass of conflicting evidence is produced, revealing a most confused state of things, inextricably interwoven with ecclesiastical difficulties and theological subtleties, the general result resembling anything rather than the simplicity of truth. Let ordinary readers at least beware how they venture upon the bewildering entanglement of that theological maze.

> "Ahi quanto, a dir qual era, é cosa dura,
> Questa selva selvaggia ed aspra e forte,
> Che nel pensier rinnova la paura!"—DANTE.

> "Alas! it is in sooth a hard matter to describe it,
> That forest drear, rugged, and toilsome,
> The very thought of which rekindles terror!"

The writer, at any rate, prefers at once admitting that the existing State Church is the true successor of the early Irish Church, despite the earnest protest of Roman Catholic divines. Protestant Churchmen must, however, be reminded that tithes were unknown to the early Irish Church. They were first introduced, or at least enforced, by the secular arm—that is, made compulsory as a legal obligation—by Henry II. for the benefit of that Roman Catholic Church and Roman Catholic priesthood which it is affirmed the monarch in question established for the first time in the sister island. The matter is thus stated by the present Lord Primate of Ireland, in a charge delivered to his clergy in 1864:—

"To the clergy of the early Irish Church tithes were not paid, though it appears by some ancient canons attempts were made to establish them. In the year 1127 St Bernard complains of the Irish, 'They pay no tithes;' and in the year 1172 Pope Alexander III., in a letter dated the 20th September, states, among other abuses of the Irish Church, 'The people in general pay no tithes.' English influence, however, in that year sufficed to introduce them at the council of Cashel. They formed part of the splendid bribes which Henry II. gave to the Irish clergy to induce them to conform to the usages of the English Church and acknowledge the Papal supremacy."

Let, then, the present Irish State Church, whose members so loudly proclaim that they only are the true successors of the early Irish Church, return to its primitive practice, and no longer claim tithes by right of law under State guarantee. Is it not manifest that they are but a popish invention, nay (according to my Lord Primate), a popish bribe, employed by a popish king for the benefit of Papal supremacy? Why will the true heirs of Ireland's pure primitive Church defile themselves by touching this unclean thing? But in this matter of tithes a singular change comes over the members of the Irish State Church, for they utterly discard the pure example of the primitive Christian ministers of Ireland, and cling pertinaciously instead to the precedent established by Popery. Their conduct recalls to mind the story of an old woman who was arguing vehemently in favour of a favourite theological tenet. She quoted, to her own satisfaction at least, gospel and epistle in its support; but her opponent, skilled also in the use of such weapons, met her with a text so clearly opposed to her views that to gainsay its force was impossible. The worthy dame, however, was not to be silenced. Carried away by the heat of argument, she exclaimed, with more warmth than reverence, "Ah! that's where Paul and I differ!" So those who maintain that the Protestant Establishment in Ireland is the rightful heir of that Church which existed previous to the conquest of Henry II. in 1156, when brought face to face with the fact that that primitive Church exacted no tithes by force of law, are obliged to exclaim, if not in words, assuredly by deeds, "That's where the early Irish Church and we differ." In vain do those search who seek for precepts in apostolic writings which tell the ministers of Christ to call in the arm of the temporal power in order to force by legal enactment the payment of ecclesiastical dues. Such proceedings came into fashion under very different auspices, when the Church had changed its condition of persecuted into that of persecutor. From the fatal hour of her union to the temporal power, and to the use she made of it, dates that violence and persecution, those penal enactments and civil disabilities, which through long centuries oppressed mankind. Only too constantly have the professed ministers of Christ been foremost in this ruthless and anti-Christian work. So has it come to pass that every outward Church which has obtained temporal power, has been one of the chief causes of that hatred and ill-will, that war and bloodshed, which have set Christian so bitterly against Christian, that the infidel and the heathen who read that dire eclipse of Christianity, have but too much reason to exclaim, " See how these Christians *hate* one another."

Such have been the consequences of the union of the temporal and spiritual; of forsaking the example of the primitive Church; of not acting in accordance with the apostolic precept, " The weapons of our warfare are not carnal, but mighty through God;" of paying no heed to the Master's words: "*My* kingdom is not of this world; *if* my kingdom were of this world, *then* would my servants fight." Those who really love the name of Jesus should then aid in abolishing every form of compulsion which forces their brother men to support any creed to which their consciences object. For all such compulsion does but dishonour the Christian Church, and sets at nought that golden precept of her Lord, "*All* things, whatsoever ye would that men should do to you, do ye even so to them." As to those who say that State aid is necessary to their Church, or to the maintenance of its tenets or system, they do but proclaim how wide is the difference between it and the Church of old. Such persons, instead of trusting to the arm of flesh, will do better to rest in faith upon the promise, " Lo! I am with you alway;" they should bear in mind those who, eighteen centuries ago, went forth, not with State aid, but in opposition to all the State power of imperial Rome, went forth and conquered. Or if they need less exalted examples, let them look at those unaided members of Christ's Church called

Nonconformists, who, though paying tithe and rate to the State Church, yet flourish vigorously. But they, it is true, are free, having neither State aid nor State fetters. It is to be hoped that Christian ears may be henceforth spared the degrading complaint uttered by others who cry that their Church can no longer exist unless the legislature dole out to it so many thousands a year. Not such was the language of the mighty Apostle, whose wealth consisted in no like beggarly elements, but who was rich with all the "unsearchable riches of Christ." Not by penal laws nor civil disabilities, not by compelling support from those who were not of it, nor yet by any other wrong to the consciences of men, did Christianity win over to itself a hostile world. By the simplicity of its faith, by the purity of its holiness, by the divineness of its love, was the victory won. Nor is it by any other means that the Christian Church can retain its conquest, renew its strength, or bestow upon mankind that "liberty wherewith Christ hath made us free."

It is ever a difficult matter to remedy an injustice of long standing. Not on that account, however, must the duty of so doing be abandoned. Now, in dealing with the present ecclesiastical system of Ireland, it will be wise to look round and see if any similar question has presented itself in recent times, and been successfully solved. Such a case does exist, the examination of which will well repay those who really desire to bring about a just and permanent settlement of the religious or ecclesiastical part of what has been well termed the Irish difficulty. The case referred to is that of Canada, where, as in Ireland, a variety of races and creeds are mingled together. Its inhabitants have long been partly Protestants of English blood, and partly Roman Catholics of French blood.[1] As the colony developed, the elements which composed it became more numerous and varied. Not only English Churchmen, but Scotch Presbyterians and English Dissenters, multiplied. To the French element was added continually increasing numbers of Irish Roman Catholics.

Now, in the year 1791, an Act of the English parliament had directed that, in respect of all grants made by the Crown, a quantity equal to one-seventh of the land so granted should be reserved to the clergy. Here, then, was established the principle, if not of a State Church such as existed in the mother country, at any rate of an endowed and privileged clergy. This was avowedly done for the benefit of the Protestant Church; whether of the Scotch as well as of the English, became a matter of dispute. Nor did disputes upon this subject by any means end here. These Clergy Reserves, as they were named, set at variance Churchmen and Dissenters, Protestants and Roman Catholics; stirring up at the same time (as was natural) no little ill-will between the various races—English, French, Scotch, and Irish—who inhabited Canada. Thus were created and kept alive bitter differences, not only amongst the colonists, but also between the mother country and the colonies;

[1] Lower Canada is essentially Roman Catholic, the great majority of its inhabitants being of that religion.

until at length there was brought about as apparently hopeless a state of discord and ill-will as ever irritated any people or perplexed any government. Other difficulties there were besides this ecclesiastical one, which, however, as usual in such cases, played a prominent part in the general discontent and perplexity. The rulers of Canada in past days, (or many of them, at any rate,) by way of showing, as they thought, their skill in statecraft, hit upon the notable device of backing up the English Protestant element as against the French Roman Catholic. The former was dubbed the loyal element, the mainstay of the connexion with England. The latter was treated sometimes with injustice, and almost always with coldness and suspicion; the natural result being, that the French portion of the colonists became more and more irritated and difficult to manage. So matters went on from bad to worse, until discontent grew into turbulence, and turbulence into rebellion. Such were the fruits of this good old policy of the good old days.

Now, it is most instructive to remark how the disturbing element of the Clergy Reserves was dealt with; how it passed through two distinct phases, and was finally disposed of. First came the Act of the English Parliament, passed in 1840, which put an end to any further reservation of land for the benefit of the Church, and then proceeded to divide the funds arising from the existing reserves amongst the different religious denominations. The Churches of England and Scotland got the lion's share; the remainder was divided between Protestant Dissenters and Roman

Catholics. Something like an approach to religious equality was thus gained. In consequence, a far better state of feeling pervaded the colonies, but, as usual, these half measures proved insufficient. The great mass of the colonists craved after perfect religious liberty and equality; they wanted to abolish the connexion between the government and the churches, so that both might be free. Then it was that in 1853 the English government, that of the late Lord Aberdeen, introduced and carried through the imperial parliament a bill handing over the Clergy Reserves, and all questions connected with them, to the Canadian legislature, to be settled by it in accordance with the wishes of the Canadian people. It is not a little interesting to refer back to the debates which then took place. The late Duke of Newcastle, at that time Colonial Secretary, in introducing the bill into the House of Lords, said: "In different shapes and ways this subject has been in agitation for the last thirty years. . . . . As long as we leave the religious question to excite the people of Canada, we are in danger of disturbing and disorganising the whole foundations of government in one of the tenderest points on which it can be affected." The arguments of the opponents of the bill were such as might be expected. They opposed it in the name of Church and State, Church rights, Church property; if passed, the differences between the various denominations would become more marked and bitter, the sentiment of loyalty be undermined, the connexion with England weakened, and the funds arising from the Reserves be secularised. In a word, it was a dreadful bill, and would produce dreadful consequences. The bill, however, became law.

In the following year (1854) the Canadian legislature passed " an Act to make better provision for the appropriation of moneys arising from the lands heretofore known as the Clergy Reserves, by rendering them available for municipal purposes." The principle upon which this measure was based appears clearly from the words occurring in the third section of the Act: "Whereas it is desirable to remove all semblance of connexion between Church and State," &c. Existing life interests only were cared for, and the funds handed over to the municipalities, to be disposed of as they thought fit. It appears that they applied the funds thus obtained chiefly to educational purposes. Every vestige of a privileged Church was swept away. The endowment by the State of all Churches was got rid of, as well as the endowment of one privileged Church. The axe was laid to the root of the tree. All "semblance" even of connexion between Church and State was blotted out. Thus the true Christian principle of perfect religious liberty and equality now reigns unquestioned throughout our North American colonies. The Churches are free Churches in a free State.

And now comes the crucial question: What has been the result of this new order of things? Simply this, that while ill-will and discontent culminating in rebellion existed under the old system, there is now to be seen, under the new, contentment, peace, and loyalty. The voices of angry sects are hushed, for there is now no dominant church creating jealousy and heartburnings. In Canada has been restored the practice of primitive times, when Christians gave freely to the faith they loved, and when Christian ministers had no secular arm to aid them in the unchristian work of wringing support from those who were not of them. Thus have freedom and order, peace and loyalty, taken the place of strife, discontent, and rebellion. Nor is there to be found any exception to this happy change among those of any race or any creed. Nowhere throughout England's empire is to be seen greater attachment to the mother country, or more contentment with her easy yoke, than in that Canadian dominion peopled by English Churchmen and Dissenters, by Presbyterians of the Scotch Church and of the Free Kirk, mingled with a large population of French Roman Catholics, whose congregations are constantly increased by numerous arrivals of their co-religionists from Ireland.

Such, then, is the actual condition of our North American colonies, under a system of absolute religious freedom and equality. How widely different from that of the sister island, where (alone throughout England's empire) is to be seen the dominant Church of the small minority lording it over all Churches. There it still stands, a monument of past conquest and present injustice, which naturally creates discontent; yet when that discontent shows itself, the members of the Irish State Church say with unblushing effrontery,—See! we alone are loyal subjects, we alone are true to England!

There has lately been furnished a remarkable test of Canadian loyalty to England which must not be passed over. The Fenians in the United States have endeavoured in vain to draw away the Canadians of any race or creed from their allegiance to the mother country. Thus foiled, these lawless marauders actually attacked Canada by armed violence, thus wickedly exposing to the dangers of war a people who have done them no wrong, who suffer under no grievance, and who ask only to be left in peace to manage their own affairs and prepare their own future as seems good to them. This Fenian wickedness against Canada happily brings its own punishment with it, for it but makes Fenianism hateful to the Canadians, while drawing more closely the ties which unite them to England. It has but brought out in stronger relief than ever the loyalty and contentment of all the various peoples and creeds of the Canadian dominion, and of none more than of her Roman Catholic population, whether French or Irish.

This matter of Fenianism brings to mind the assertion that that brotherhood of ill does not object to the Church Establishment in Ireland, nor wish it done away. It would probably be more correct to say that the Fenians desire its continuance. The reason is obvious enough. They know well that the Establishment creates discontent among the Roman Catholics of Ireland. Now, the more discontent there is, the more suitable is the state of the country for Fenian plottings. To keep the Irish State Church in existence is really a help to Fenianism. Among its best allies, therefore, are those who would maintain intact the present ecclesiastical condition of Ireland. If they can succeed in upholding the dominant church, so much the better for Fenianism, and so much the worse for England. A like system of church supremacy was tried for years in Canada, with what result England knows to her cost. At length it has been changed for one of absolute religious freedom and equality. The benefits which have sprung from that change have surpassed the most sanguine expectations. Is not the lesson one which he who runs may read? With such results before their eyes, how much longer are English legislators going to stand face to face with the Irish Church difficulty, asking hopelessly what is to be done, or pitifully wrangling about the manner of procedure? Is England become so dull that she cannot even learn by experience? Or is it deemed wise to wait until an indignant people, newly enfranchised, sweep away at a single blow the crying wrong, levelling all injustices, not with over-careful hand, but rather in the fierceness of their wrath? Or will the retrograde party resist all innovation until the storm of popular opinion grow loud and menacing; then hustle through a sweeping change (which in their hearts they hate, but dare not refuse) leaving some one of their number, "faithful among the faithless," to write the story of another "Conservative surrender?"

Be all that as it may, true Liberals, at any rate, must pledge themselves to the principle of absolute religious liberty and equality, at least in Ireland. What ministry shall carry out that programme is a secondary consideration. The vital point is to do it thoroughly, and to do it quickly. Which is the best plan to adopt; that of endowing all denominations in proportion to their number, or that of endowing none? With all deference to more than one high authority, the writer unhesitatingly advocates the latter principle, that of no longer endowing any church, due regard being had to existing life interests. The example of Canada is strongly in favour of such a course. There the system of paying all was tried, and found to be but a half-measure that did not satisfy. Whereas that of paying none, leaving each church to be supported by its own members, while handing over the old ecclesiastical funds for educational and other purposes, has completely settled the vexed question, and ended in creating general contentment. Nor must it be forgotten that the Roman Catholics of Ireland demand the application of this very principle; they ask for "the disendowment of the Established Church," for the "placing of all religious denominations on a footing of perfect equality, and leaving each church to be maintained by the voluntary contributions of its members." Such is the language of the Irish National Association, of which most of the Roman Catholic prelates are members. It would be heartily endorsed by the whole body of English Nonconformists. It enunciates a principle which the Scotch, and probably the evangelical party in the Church of England, would much prefer to that of either endowing or paying all denominations according to their numbers. While those who have freed themselves from ecclesiastical fetters, and from the special dogmas of particular churches, would give a far more ready assent to a measure that endowed none, than to a measure that endowed all. Complete disunion of the spiritual from the temporal power can alone bestow the boon of freedom alike upon the Churches and upon the State. Let it, then, be applied, and applied at once, to Ireland, just as has been done in Canada. There the angry strife of religious denominations no longer troubles the State, because there the State secures full religious freedom and equality to its subjects of every race and of every creed.

Moreover, this principle of disconnecting all churches from the civil power is in harmony with the highest and truest views of Christian liberty. By it the temporal ruler treats religion as alone it should be treated, as a matter of conscience, not as an affair of State. He thereby declares himself unwilling and unable to legislate about those matters of religious faith for which a man is accountable, not to his fellow-man, but to his conscience and his God. Such sacred subjects must be dealt with by the convictions of the heart. Upon that foundation alone can man build his spiritual life. This is no question for a party debate, nor can it be decided by a majority of votes, nor be regulated by a State legislature. Far other is the tribunal which alone of right gives sentence in this deepest of man's concerns, in which the human and the divine are inseparably blended—even the tribunal where in secret the soul of man communes and pleads with the God and Father of mankind.

Those who say that their creed will not endure under a system thus bereft of all State aid, can have but little real belief in its divine origin or life. Those, on the contrary, who have no like fears, who believe that divine truth possesses divine power, will welcome such perfect freedom for the truth's own sake, as well as for themselves and for their brother men. For they at least believe that never is truth more secure, never is its purity more unalloyed, than when itself is true to the cause of freedom and is faithful to the rights of conscience.

Touching what has been justly termed the Irish difficulty, Englishmen must remember, that to ask what suits England in this matter, what is in consonance with *her* feelings and ideas, is emphatically *not* the question. That difficulty can be satisfactorily settled by the imperial legislature of the United Kingdom only when it has determined to consider above all what is good for Ireland, what is in accordance with *her* needs, what suits the character, the habits, and the genius of *her* people. The great object to be aimed at, as necessary to the welfare both of Great Britain and Ireland, is not uniformity of system as regards either land or church, but an equal, just, and cordial union. England and Scotland have attained that result to their great and common advantage. But they have attained it by sacrificing the letter of outward uniformity to the spirit of living unity. In their church systems and in their legal proceedings and customs there are marked differences, in accordance with the different characters and wishes of their respective people. So must it be with Ireland, if she is to become a contented and prosperous member of our body politic. Let then the argument, that such a course is not followed in England, and does not agree with her precedents, be heard no more. All such prejudices must be cast off for ever. The one paramount question is, What is good for Ireland? what is suited to *her* condition and needs? To these alone must England lend a willing ear, and give a helping hand. For thus only can efficacious remedies be applied to our sister's ills; thus only can be satisfied the righteous cry of "Justice for Ireland."

In dealing with the question of Ireland's State Church it is worthy of observation that extreme Conservatives and extreme Radicals not unfrequently unite in declaring that if the Irish Church be disestablished, the English and Scotch Churches must necessarily be disestablished also. Doubtless there are some principles common to all Establishments, and some arguments equally adverse to all; others, however, there are of less wide scope; there is, besides, the all-important question of the practical application of general principles—a question which must be very carefully considered when actual legislation is contemplated.

Now, as regards the *principle* of Establishments,

none can deny that it is one of human origin. The present Archbishop of Canterbury stated this very recently at a public meeting convened to oppose the disestablishment of the Irish State Church. His Grace said:—

"Now, the establishment and the union of Church and State has been created by the breath of man, because for the first three centuries we know that there was no union between Church and State. It was in the time of Constantine that the union was first effected."

Those who look closely into the present condition and tendencies of the Christian world will have good ground for believing in an approaching dissolution of this union between Church and State in all countries in which such union actually exists. Such a change, if temperately brought about, will, on the whole, be probably more fitted to meet the needs and circumstances of modern Christendom than the system of Establishments—it will be better both for State and Church. But the question of the practical adoption of that great change must be determined not only by abstract principle and logical argument, but also by a careful consideration of all the circumstances of the particular Church and State whose union is being discussed. It may well be that this important subject of Church Establishments ought not to be dealt with either in the narrow spirit of "No surrender," or after the radical fashion of instant and world-wide abolition. It is not difficult to show weighty reasons which will lead wise legislators to disestablish in one case while refusing to disestablish in another. Let the circumstances of our own country be briefly considered. In the United Kingdom there are two Church Establishments—that of the Episcopal Church in England and Ireland, and that of the Presbyterian Church in Scotland. Now, although the principle of Establishment is common to both, there are yet very wide and essential differences in the circumstances and condition of these countries, and of their Church Establishments. Thus, England and Scotland are essentially Protestant countries, their respective Establishments being the oldest and largest Protestant communion in each country, much of whose spiritual teaching is in harmony with that of the Nonconformist Churches. Ireland, on the other hand, is essentially Roman Catholic—so much so, that she remains faithful to Rome despite her union to Protestant England, and despite all the efforts (often amounting, in past times, to actual persecution) made by the English government to protestantise the sister island. Yet the Establishment maintained by law in Ireland is that of the Church of the small minority, which the great majority of the Irish consider heretical and schismatical. For England thus to force a Protestant Establishment on Ireland is as unjust as it would be for Ireland to force a Roman Catholic Establishment on England. It is the same wrong which was done in past times when England endeavoured to force upon Presbyterian Scotland an Episcopal *State* Church. That injustice brought innumerable evils upon both England and Scotland. A like injustice has brought like evils upon both England

and Ireland. At length to Presbyterian Scotland was granted what she desired, a Presbyterian Establishment: let Roman Catholic Ireland have what she desires. Happily the Irish Roman Catholics do *not* demand the establishment of their Church, or the endowment of their priests. What they do ask for is, that all Churches should, in Ireland, be placed on an equal footing, and be supported by the voluntary contributions of their respective members.

With such wide differences existing in the cases of England, Scotland, and Ireland, surely the wisest practical course is not to preach a crusade against all State Churches, but to enter into a well-considered compromise. That compromise should be, to allow the Establishments in England and Scotland to continue, but to disestablish the State Church in Ireland. In effecting such disestablishment in the latter country, the life interests of all living ministers should be preserved untouched; all vested rights should be dealt with in the spirit of the most scrupulous justice; and the grants to Maynooth and to the Irish Presbyterians be in like manner done away with. Such a compromise as the one thus indicated will not, perhaps, please the ultra-partisans of Church Establishments, who will agree to no change, nor yet the ultra-advocates of the Voluntary system, who would sweep away all Establishments at once, without regard to place, time, or circumstances; yet surely this compromise would be the wisest course, getting rid, as it would, of an obvious wrong in the case of Ireland, while leaving those who come after us to determine whether the principle of Establishment or of *non*-Establishment shall ultimately prevail in England and in Scotland. Let those who to-day refuse to surrender anything beware. Ought they not to take warning from very recent events? Have not those who only two or three years ago opposed all change upon another great question—that of parliamentary reform—found themselves (after defeating a proposition for a moderate change) obliged to consent the very next year to an immediate and sweeping alteration of the law upon that very question? Thus it was that stout opponents of reform but played the game of the thorough-going reformers. To-day, strong Conservatives and fervid Churchmen cry "No surrender" when the question of Ireland's *State* Church is mooted, and declare that if the Irish Establishment falls, the English and Scotch Establishments must fall with it. Had they not better take warning from the past, lest in again opposing all change, and refusing every compromise, they find in the end that they have but been helping forward the cause of the ultra-opponents of all Church Establishments whatever? As regards the Church of England, her dangers come from within. Let her heal, if possible, her own unhappy divisions—above all, let her preserve an essentially Protestant character and teaching—for if she do not, she will assuredly lose her hold on the hearts and consciences of England's great, free, and Protestant people. That hold once lost, the fall of England's Church, as a national establishment, is certain.

THE UNITED STATES CONSTITUTION AND THE SECESSIONISTS.

Reprinted from the " Westminster Review" of 1st April 1866.

1. *The Life and Public Services of Abraham Lincoln, Sixteenth President of the United States.* By HENRY J. RAYMOND. New York: Derby and Miller.
2. *The Constitution of the United States of America.* By W. HICKLEY. Philadelphia, 1854.
3. *Bacon's Guide to American Politics.* London: Sampson Low, Son, & Co.
4. *The Presidential Message, Dec.* 3, 1865, *of Andrew Johnson, Seventeenth President of the United States.*

A TRAVELLER landing in America for the first time has much difficulty in forming a true idea of the political condition of the country. The first impression is that of so much confusion, of such a Babel of meetings, of speeches, of pamphlets, of papers, of such an endless variety of party names, often amusing and always puzzling, that it is no easy task to form a sound judgment upon public affairs. It is not only the diversity of opinions which embarrasses the stranger, but also the violence with which the Americans frequently put forward their political views. It is not merely the animosity of parties which strikes him, but equally the vehemence of the attacks often directed against the President and his Cabinet, against the highest authorities, civil and military.

Sometimes the elections, always warmly contested, appear as if they would end in a general overthrow; and be it borne in mind that they are of such constant occurrence as to seem both endless and perpetual.

Every man forms upon every subject his own judgment, to which he gives full and free utterance. In the railway may be seen the labourer or the artisan conning over his paper with evident relish. If spoken to, he will give his opinion upon political subjects without any hesitation. He will discuss freely the policy of the President, the last despatch of the Secretary of State, the proposition of one of the senators, the tactics of a general, or any other matter of public interest. He minces neither his praise nor his blame, as the case may be; for he considers himself as one of the sovereign people judging men of the people's choice. If a stranger from the Old World should hint that he would do better to attend more to his own work and less to politics, the American's wonder at such an idea would change quickly into something like pity for his foreign fellow-traveller, in whom he would see but a serf of feudal Europe, which he pictures to himself as in the last stage of decrepitude.

As to the contents of American papers, whose name is legion, the result of their perusal upon the newly-arrived stranger is that of confusion worse confounded. One journal paints the character and policy of the President and his Cabinet in colours so black that they might be supposed, without any great stretch of imagination, to be monsters of scarcely human origin sitting in the high places of Washington, itself little better than an earthly pandemonium. Another draws these same personages in characters of beatific perfection, worthy of angelic messengers directing a federal government in possession of a terrestrial paradise. Should the stranger reasonably conceive both of these pictures somewhat overdrawn, he will find numberless writers and speakers representing every shade of opinion which can possibly lie between these two extremes. He has only to choose; but there lies the difficulty.

Yet this very country, the surface of whose public life presents so much apparent confusion and disorder, has just traversed victoriously one of the most terrible crises to which a nation has ever been exposed. It has presented to the world the marvellous spectacle of its people going through the great political contest of a presidential election in the midst of a civil war which threatened the very existence of the State—a war which covered with vast armies an extent of territory the size of half Europe, which cost tens of thousands of lives and millions of money. The national laws and liberties have, notwithstanding, survived intact. Generals in all the prestige of victory, commanding numerous and disciplined armies, have respected the constitution and bowed to the authority of the civil power. During the war people continued to discuss public affairs. Elections, campaigns, expeditions, defeats, victories, followed in rapid and constant succession; but the final result was the complete victory of the United States government, crowned by a moderation of which history offers but few examples. What was the cause of this result, so little anticipated by the enemies of the American Republic? Whence sprang that deep devotion to the Federal Union which led the majority of the nation to lavish upon its government the means for crushing the violent attack upon its authority?

One of its chief sources is the love of his country's institutions which the American drinks in from his earliest childhood. That love is inculcated equally at home, at school, and at college. It plays a very important part in the educational system of the United States of America, constitutes in a great measure their strength, and produces results of vast importance to the country. In order thoroughly to appreciate the extent of its influence in the formation of the national character, it is necessary to touch upon the leading features of this system of public instruction. Spreading itself over the length and breadth of the land, it embraces all classes, from the richest to the poorest, throughout the whole of the Northern States. In the South it has not received the same full development, and has been far less generally encouraged. It is worthy of remark that the Federal Congress at Washington has absolutely nothing whatever to do with the system of education—a most singular and abnormal fact according to the ideas prevalent in European countries. It is, indeed, the exception when even the legislature of a particular State interferes in the matter of schools. In new States, however, where the population is still scanty, the legislature of the State sometimes aids by grants of land or money. To the township belongs the real management of its popular instruction. In each township a Committee of Education is elected by the inhabitants, which votes and levies the money destined to this object; to it belongs the regulation of all details, such as the erection and maintenance of the school-buildings, the appointment of masters and mistresses, their salaries, the selection of school-books, and the method of instruction to be followed. Another marked feature in the system is the absolute prohibition of all denominational religious teaching—that is, of all doctrinal or dogmatical instruction characteristic of any particular church. That general morality which is common to all religious denominations is alone permitted, but all dogmas are forbidden. In many, perhaps the majority of schools, the Lord's prayer or a psalm is read daily at the opening of the school, but it is not allowed to make this practice the occasion for giving religious instruction. The school committee of the township decide whether or not such a practice is to be followed in the schools under its authority. The object of this exclusion of all dogmatic teaching is, to avoid the innumerable difficulties arising from difference of religious views; the questions which spring from such difference creating almost insuperable obstacles to the establishment of a really effective system of national education. All such difficulties are thus got rid of. The religious instruction of the children is left exclusively to the parents and to the Sunday schools. These latter are completely in the hands of the various religious bodies, all of whom are wholly unconnected with the State, and entirely supported by the voluntary contributions of their respective members.

As to the quality of the instruction given under this system of public education, it may be said, without exaggeration, not to be surpassed in excellence by that of any country. The greatest attention is paid in the teaching of those elementary matters which lie at the foundation of all instruction, and which form by far the most difficult part of education; the tender age of the children, and the great simplicity of the primary notions to be taught them, requiring all the tact, gentleness, and patience of which the teacher is capable. Nor does the care thus taken at all fall off in the instruction given to the elder pupils. So deeply have the native-born Americans become convinced of the excellence of a sound education, (especially throughout the Northern and Western States, where such a feeling is universal, and where

THE CONSTITUTION AND THE SECESSIONISTS. 289

the school is ever one of the first buildings erected in a new township,) that the greatest punishment which can be inflicted is that of forbidding a child to attend school during a given time. The little culprit usually gets punished at home for having allowed matters to reach such a climax. Parents or friends will come to inquire whether the punishment was really merited, and beg to have so severe a sentence remitted, or at least mitigated.

One of the subjects to which especial interest is attached in the schools of the United States is the history of their own country. The principles upon which the government is founded, and their practical application, are carefully inculcated. Not only is this subject taught in all its details, but the effort is made to impress the pupil with the utmost love and admiration for the institutions of the Republic. The starting-point is naturally the story of American independence. First is stated the origin of the resistance of the colonies to the mother country. Then it is shown that this resistance was not a mere capricious act arising from no particular cause of complaint, but that it originated in a legitimate opposition to certain illegal proceedings of the home government, which exceeded its powers by taxing the colonists, although they were wholly unrepresented in the British parliament. Thus the English government violated the principle of that inseparable union between taxation and representation which forms the basis of all constitutional liberties; nor did numerous and repeated demonstrations of the most lawful char-

T

acter, such as public meetings, protests, and petitions, avail to turn the home government from its unconstitutional policy. It must not be forgotten that the Americans are supported by very high authorities in accusing the then English ministers of pursuing a course opposed to the principles of their own constitution; for in England's parliament three of the most eminent statesmen of the day—William Pitt, (Lord Chatham,) Edmund Burke, and Lord Rockingham—protested against the acts of the home government. Pitt and Burke pleaded the cause of the colonists in parliament with great eloquence and unanswerable arguments. These facts are carefully recalled by the Americans, who draw from them strong evidence in support of their cause. This point established, they make every effort to demonstrate the excellence of their own institutions. They dwell especially upon the wisdom, patriotism, and political knowledge displayed by the men who gave to America her actual constitution; placing ever foremost the honoured name of Washington.

Youth is generous: nothing is easier than to make it admire that which is constantly held up to it as great and noble. It is therefore easy to imagine how immense is the effect of the teaching just described. It is yet further increased as the youths of America grow up and realise the vast resources, the immense extent, and the ever-increasing wealth of their country. This system deposits and develops in the hearts of all classes an affection, bordering upon idolatry, for their native land; but such a result is not without its defects and drawbacks. From it arises an exaggerated pride of country, often displayed by the American when away from home. He is apt to boast unbecomingly of his own country, and to speak of other nations and governments as quite inferior to his own. If, on the contrary, the European travels in the States, this same feeling has a very different effect, and is not unfrequently the source of much kindness and hospitality. The American is delighted to be questioned as well as to question. He willingly explains everything, and points out whatever is most worthy of observation. He is the most indefatigable of cicerones and the kindest of hosts. The traveller gives him real pleasure by studying the institutions of the country, and has every opportunity afforded him of doing so thoroughly. Proud of his country's system, and deeply attached to it, the American delights to see others examine carefully that which he so fondly loves himself. Let it not, however, be supposed that this love of country, excellent as is that feeling, is the only source whence springs that friendly hospitality which is so freely offered to the stranger in all parts of the United States.

These feelings had grown with the nation's growth, and were handed down from father to son. They were especially strong throughout the Northern States, where the national educational system has received its full and perfect development. Thus it was that, up to the memorable year 1860, the Constitution had ever been regarded as the sacred ark, so to speak, of the Republic. To touch or change it, except by those legal means prescribed by the Constitution itself, was to commit a veritable sacrilege. It was worthy of notice how both individuals and parties sought, in their discussions, to prove that their opponents were outstepping the limits of the Constitution. Such a charge, if brought home, was annihilation to the argument of a political adversary. A cry of general indignation quickly arose against any who were even supposed to harbour ideas subversive of the institutions of the country. Did any Northerner chance to use an expression which might seem to have such a tendency, when attacking some piece of pro-slavery legislation, the South and its supporters were the first to cry out against him as being untrue to the constitutional principles of the State. This sentiment of deep-rooted love to the Union and the Federal Constitution was shown to be especially strong throughout the North, inasmuch as its people had ever been scrupulous observers of the law, who bowed at once to the electoral decisions. For many years the South had carried their own candidate in the Presidential elections, and commanded the majority in Congress: thus it shaped and directed the policy of the United States. Whenever that policy displeased the Northern statesmen, they only opposed it by the admitted constitutional means; those once exhausted, .the national will, as expressed by the majority, was acknowledged and submitted to by all. These considerations at once explain the indignation of the North at the illegal conduct of the South, which sought to break up the Union by force, and trampled down the Constitution, merely because a President was elected who was not of their political party. For not only had the new President and his Cabinet no intention of perpetrating any illegal act, but they had not had even the opportunity of so doing. What was the course pursued by the South? It endeavoured to effect by *violence* a complete transformation in the constitutional order of things established by common consent, although the Constitution itself furnished, by its fifth article, the legal means of proposing, under form of amendment, any fundamental change in the Federal Union which might be thought desirable. Such a mode of proceeding, at once lawful and rational, would have given the whole nation, sole legitimate judge in such matters, the opportunity of discussing the proposed change, and deciding whether or not it should be carried into effect, according to the provisions of the Constitution.

The fifth article runs thus:—

"The Congress, whenever two-thirds of both Houses shall deem it necessary, shall propose amendments to this Constitution; or, on the application of the Legislatures of two-thirds of the several States, shall call a Convention for proposing amendments, which, in either case, shall be valid to all intents and purposes as part of this Constitution, when ratified by the Legislatures of three-fourths of the several States, or by Conventions in three-fourths thereof, as the one or other mode of ratification may be proposed by Congress;" . . . . .

Nothing could be more illegal, then, than the course

actually pursued by the South, nothing more legitimate than the resistance of the Federal Government. The first shot fired upon Fort Sumter was an act of unwarrantable violence against the constituted authority of the United States Government, which had in no way overstepped the bounds of its authority, and to which every official in every State had promised allegiance. From that moment the President of the United States had but one duty to perform— that of defending and maintaining by arms the legitimate authority of the government of which he was the responsible chief. Those who contend that he should have consented to the secession, forget that he had no power whatever to give such consent. As Mr Seward, the Secretary of State, justly laid it down, no State or States could of their own act secede; they could only do so by the consent of the people of the United States, assembled in national convention, according to the provisions of the Constitution. The oath of the President bound him to maintain and defend the Federal Constitution by force of arms against all enemies, from within or from without. This duty was, under the circumstances, terrible indeed. Mr Lincoln did not fail in its performance; that is one of his chief titles to the gratitude of all who duly value the maintenance of those rights which belong to a free government. He was able to maintain them, because supported by the majority of the nation, whose love for its institutions was such that it recoiled from no sacrifice when once convinced that it was necessary to arm the President against the violators of that Federal Union and its laws, which had been bequeathed to the country by the founders of American independence.

But what, it will be asked, was the policy of Mr Lincoln which so displeased the South? It was the policy known as the *Free-Soil* policy. The party which upheld it had for some years past been gaining strength, and, in November 1860, finally triumphed by the election of its candidate, Mr Lincoln, to the Presidency. This *Free-Soil* policy made no attempt to interfere with slavery in those States where it already existed; but it sought to prohibit that institution from passing those limits, and spreading over the territories not yet formed into States, which are under the immediate and entire control of the Federal Government and Congress at Washington. This was a really anti-slavery, though not an abolitionist policy. Mr Lincoln spoke of it as follows in 1858, during the elections for the nomination of a senator to represent the State of Illinois in the Senate at Washington: "We insist on a policy that shall restrict slavery to its present limits." And again: "We deal with slavery as with any other wrong, in so far as we can prevent its growing larger, and so deal with it, that in the run of time there may be some promise of an end to it." In another speech he says that the *Republican* or *Free-Soil* party

"Look upon slavery as being a moral, social, and political wrong; and while they contemplate it as such, they nevertheless have a due regard for its actual existence among us, and the difficulties of getting rid of it in any satisfactory way, and to all the constitutional obligations thrown about it. Yet, having a due regard for these, they desire a policy in regard to it that looks to its not creating any more danger. They insist that it should, as far as may be, be treated as a wrong, and one of the methods of treating it as a wrong is to make provision that it shall grow no larger. They desire a policy that looks to a peaceful end of slavery at some time as being wrong."

Pages might be filled with quotations from Mr Lincoln's public speeches to the same effect. He and all his party were bent upon opposing, by every constitutional means in their power, the further extension of slavery. In a speech delivered at the Cooper Institute, New York, in February 1860, Mr Lincoln went into the whole question with great minuteness and ability; indeed throughout his whole life, as well as at the time of his presidential election, he was a staunch supporter of this wise and moderate *Free-Soil* policy. There was no other essential difference between his political views and those of his predecessors in the presidential chair as regarded home politics.

The South, on the contrary, openly avowed its determination to carry slavery far and wide, to maintain and extend it in every direction. To this end all its efforts had been for many years unceasingly directed. Hardly had the Southern Secessionist Government been formed, when its Vice-President, Mr A. H. Stephens, declared, in a memorable speech, delivered at Savannah, that *slavery* was the " cornerstone " of the new Confederation, that it was "the immediate cause of the late rupture and present revolution."

Mr Lincoln, when candidate for the Presidency, when elected in November 1860, and when inaugurated on 4th March 1861, reiterated again and again his firm resolve in no way to infringe the Constitution; nor did he or his government ever break either the letter or the spirit of that promise. Yet scarcely was the result of the presidential election known, when South Carolina and others of the Slave States declared that they seceded from the Union, and flung off their allegiance to the Federal Government. In the meanwhile, numbers of deputations from all parts of the country waited on Mr Lincoln, both before and after his inauguration as President. Their almost exclusive subject of discussion was the slavery question, in one form or another. Again and again Mr Lincoln assured them that he intended to maintain the Constitution, and to confine himself strictly within its limits. He declared that he had no intention of interfering with slavery in those States where it already existed; but nothing would induce him to give up his *free-soil* policy, which sought to prohibit expressly the extension of slavery into the territories of the Union. One deputation, of which an ex-governor of a Slave State, Mr Morehead, was member, did its utmost to induce Mr Lincoln to modify this part of his programme. But Mr Lincoln replied that not under any state of the case would he consent to the extension of slavery into the Territories, to which he had been opposed all his life.

In the manifesto issued by the *Republican* or *Free-Soil* party, which nominated him as its candidate for the Presidency, it is affirmed " that the normal condition of the Territories of the United States is that of freedom, and that there is no power which has the right to make slavery a vital institution in any territory of the United States."

In December 1861, the Federal Congress, in which for the first time the *Free-Soil* party had the majority, passed a law expressly prohibiting slavery from being introduced into the Territories. It was further abolished on the 18th March 1862, in the district of Columbia, in which Washington stands, and which is under the sole authority of the Federal Government.

These facts clearly demonstrate that slavery was the real question at issue, and that the *Free-Soil* party, whose chosen leader was Mr Lincoln, had always been thoroughly consistent and firm in the maintenance of its policy. They also show how wide was the difference between the principles of the Free-Soilers and those of the pro-slavery Secessionists. Indeed, nothing could be more moderate or more able than the policy of the *Free-Soil* statesmen. For without infringing upon the constitutional principles of the United States system, that policy would have stopped the spread of slavery, thus reducing it to a mere local institution. In this manner barriers would have been erected against its further extension, and so its power diminished. By a slow and gradual process its strength would have been undermined, and its vitality weakened. Thus, without necessitating political or social convulsions, slavery would have had to modify itself, to soften down its worst features, and so have taken by degrees a new and less repulsive form, more adapted to the altered circumstances of the case. From that point to its final, but not too hasty extinction, both in fact and in law, would have been a comparatively easy matter. Such a prudent course, spread over a number of years, would have left uninjured the planter interest, which could have adapted itself almost insensibly to the gradual change; it would also have afforded ample time to prepare the negro for freedom.

But the sad error of the Southerners in clinging to this evil institution and maintaining it at all costs; in appealing to force rather than allow it to be legally circumscribed; in turning their arms against that old Union which had accorded to them all those rights and liberties given so abundantly to the citizens of the United States, prevented the carrying out of the wise and moderate policy of the *Free-Soil* statesmen. Thus it was that the Secessionists brought fearful calamities on the entire country, and swift destruction upon that slave system to which, alas, the South clung with culpable and fatal obstinacy.

Such, then, was the distinctive policy of that party which elected Mr Lincoln as President. Not many days after his inauguration in March 1861, two Southern gentlemen asked to have an interview with Mr Seward in their capacity as Commissioners of the Secessionist States. He refused to receive them in their assumed official capacity, sending them this reply:—

"That it could not be admitted that the States referred to had, in law or fact, withdrawn from the Federal Union, or that they could do so in any other manner than with the consent and concert of the people of the United States, to be given through a national convention, to be assembled in conformity with the provisions of the constitution of the United States."

The Secessionists made this incident the occasion of precipitating an armed rupture, by summoning Fort Sumter to surrender. This fortress, situated in Charleston harbour, belonged exclusively and absolutely to the Federal Government, the troops of which alone formed its garrison. The State of South Carolina had no right to exercise any authority whatever in or over the fort, which was the property of the national Federal Government, and was placed under its sole authority. The commander of the fortress refused to surrender it to the Carolinian general. The Secessionists at once attacked it, and after a bombardment of thirty-three hours, it fell into their power on the 14th of April 1861. The national flag was hauled down, and that of South Carolina hoisted in its place. This act, and the agreement entered into by the seceding States, constituted a flagrant violation of the First Article of the Constitution, which forbids any State to enter into agreement with any other State, or to levy war. These violations of the law were perpetrated, be it remembered, without the Federal Government having done, or having the intention to do, any illegal act whatever.

Thus, simply because the separatist minority had been beaten in the presidential election, it took up arms against the National government, and sought to overthrow that constitution to which the governors, senators, congressmen, and officials of each State, (as well as all members of the Federal executive and legislature,) had sworn allegiance. To admit that a minority has a right to appeal to arms because its particular policy is not adopted, and *that* when its government has committed no illegal act, is to render every form of free government impossible, is to annihilate order and liberty alike. It is the destruction of law and the triumph of anarchy.

Yet stronger still must be the condemnation of such proceedings when placed in juxtaposition with those words, already quoted, of Mr Stephens, the vice-president of the Secessionist Government, that *slavery* was the "corner-stone" of the new Confederation, that it was "the immediate cause of the late rupture and present revolution." Well, then, might one of the greatest statesmen of the present century declare his sympathy for the Northern cause. Not that he was a republican; on the contrary, he was a great admirer of English constitutional liberties; they were his model in framing the new structure of his country's freedom. But he knew that law and order are no less necessary to a nation's welfare than independence and liberty. Therefore it was that Count Cavour wrote thus to the Italian minister at Washington on the 22d of May 1861 :—" This reserve," that of non-intervention, " M. le Chevalier, will not prevent us from manifesting our sympathies for the triumph of the Northern States; for their cause is not only the cause of constitutional liberty, but of all humanity."

A thrill of indignation ran through the whole North at the news of the insult offered to the national flag, and of the attack made upon the Federal authority. There could no longer be any doubt as to the danger which threatened the Union. Up to the attack on Fort Sumter in April 1861, and its seizure by the separatists, the greater part of the North hoped that all would end, after much wordy war, in a peaceful arrangement of the differences between the South and the Federal Government. But the sad truth became clearer every day, and so decided the citizens of the Northern States to take up arms in good earnest in answer to the call of the government.

The varying phases of this gigantic struggle, the immense sacrifices of men and money made by the North, its tenacity despite frequent disasters, its ever firm belief in ultimate success, prove how deep was the devotion of the Northern States to the institutions of their country, and how rooted was the conviction of their excellence and stability. At the very commencement of the war, in July 1861, the Congress of Washington passed a resolution setting forth the motives which led them to carry it on. The resolution concluded with these words :—

. . . . "That this war is not waged on their part in any spirit of oppression, or for any purpose of conquest or subjugation, or purpose of overthrowing or interfering with the rights or established institutions of these States, but to defend and maintain the supremacy of the constitution, and to preserve the Union, with all the dignity, equality, and rights of the several States unimpaired; and that as soon as these objects are accomplished the war ought to cease."

Two acts of President Lincoln during the course of this war excited especial discussion both in Europe and in America. The one was the suspension of the privilege of Habeas Corpus, and the other the Emancipation Proclamation of 1st January 1863. As regards the first, the Constitution had declared that "the privilege of the writ of Habeas Corpus shall not be suspended unless when in cases of rebellion or invasion the public safety may require it," but it did not determine who was to exercise the power of suspension. Mr Lincoln and his cabinet were of opinion that this power belonged to the President as chief of the executive, and accordingly he proceeded to exercise such power in given cases. This was done while Congress was not in session. When again assembled, that body sanctioned the action of the President, and passed a resolution to the effect "that during the present insurrection the President of the United States is authorised to suspend the Habeas Corpus when, in his judgment, the public security requires it." These proceedings caused the warmest discussion. The government and its supporters maintained the perfect legality of the President's conduct; the opposition affirmed the contrary. Each party appealed to the law, and did its utmost to show that its opponents were violating the constitution. This was the good old ground of political disputes; and it is ever, in all free countries, whatever be their form of freedom, the only lawful battle-field upon which the members of one party have a right to challenge those of the other to meet them, there to discuss the question at issue, and then decide it at the polling-booth. The way, then, in which the Northern States treated this matter was the right and constitutional way. It but affords another proof of that respect for legal and constitutional methods of determining political questions which is so marked a feature in their character—a feature which ought to win for them the sympathy of the whole English race, one of whose finest characteristics is, that it combines the greatest love of freedom with the greatest respect for law.

On the 1st January 1863, Mr Lincoln proclaimed the emancipation of all slaves in those States which were in arms against the United States Government. It must be borne in mind that this act was no part of Mr Lincoln's original programme. He adopted it as commander-in-chief of the United States forces in a time of insurrection against their authority as a means tending to suppress that insurrection. Never let it be forgotten that Mr Lincoln had ever been a Free-Soiler, not an abolitionist. The President's first duty, according to his oath, was to maintain and defend, by all means within his power, the constitution of the United States, and to enforce its due observance. Such duty was perfectly compatible with the Free-Soil policy of prohibiting, by legal enactment, slavery from extending into the Territories, but to abolish slavery by his own mere motion was beyond the President's power; he could only do so as a war measure, for the re-establishment of the Federal government's authority, as against a State or States in overt act of rebellion against that authority.

As to those Slave States which remained faithful to the Union, Mr Lincoln desired that the Federal government should aid them in the gradual abolition of slavery. To this end Congress had already adopted, on the 10th of March 1862, the resolution "That the United States ought to lend their co-operation to every State which shall abolish slavery, according to it an indemnity, which the State should use according to its own discretion, to compensate for the public and private inconveniences arising from such a change of system." During the summer of this year the Congress authorised the government to recognise officially the negro States of Hayti and Liberia. It likewise strengthened and improved the treaty with England for the suppression of the slave-trade. It also prohibited, by express enactment to that effect, slavery throughout the territories of the United States.

Thus the policy of Mr Lincoln, anti-slavery from the commencement of his life, by means of the Free-

Soil principle, and not by the adoption of immediate abolition, took more and more this latter direction according to the necessities of the day and the growth of public opinion in favour of such a course. The President, however, took the utmost care never to infringe the principles of the constitution.

It does not fall within the scope of the present article to deal with the military operations of the war. It may, however, be permitted to say a few words with respect to the generals who conducted it.

Assuredly it would be most unjust not to recognise the courage of the Southern soldiers and the skill of their leaders. The frequent repulses and defeats of the Federal armies, the able and prolonged defence of Richmond and Petersburg, the successful resistance offered by Charleston to formidable naval armaments, and many other similar deeds, prove the valour of the Southerners and the great capacity of their commanders. No one, either in Europe or America, can hesitate a moment to give them credit for the possession of military qualities of the highest order. So that if the Southerners are obliged to say to-day with the captive King of France, "*Tout est perdu,*" they have assuredly the right to add with him, "*fors l'honneur.*" Who would not receive with all respect gallant General Lee? Who does not willingly render homage to his great military talents? Nor let it be forgotten that he is by no means the only one of the Southern generals whose courage and ability have excited upon all hands real and deserved admiration.

THE CONSTITUTION AND THE SECESSIONISTS. 307

As to the Northern generals, such as Grant, Sherman, and Sheridan, it is sufficient praise, from the military point of view, to say that they succeeded in defeating such adversaries. But this is not their greatest merit. They possess another and yet more enduring title to their country's gratitude. For, when at the head of victorious armies, numbering no less than one million of soldiers, none of them sought to make such a command the stepping-stone to his own aggrandisement. No Northern general, flushed with victory and inflated with vanity, proclaimed himself alone capable of saving the republic, and then, under pretext of so doing, sacrificed alike the lives and the rights of his fellow-countrymen to his own exaltation. None followed the evil course of those who have raised to themselves a blood-stained throne upon the wreck and ruin of their country's laws and liberties. Far other was the example that they kept in view. Ever did they remember him who set the rights and freedom of his native land above all other considerations—him whom the entire nation has with one voice proclaimed "first in peace, first in war, first in the hearts of his countrymen"—him whose name is dear, not to America alone, but to the freemen of every land and of every clime—the loved and honoured name of Washington.

The like praise must be given to the statesmen of the Federal government, for they, too, displayed that elevated patriotism which sought but to perform the duties of a faithful minister, instead of aiming at a dictator's baneful rule.

Can all the leading politicians of the South, who, both before and during the presidential election of 1860, sat in the Senate and Congress of Washington, some of whom held prominent positions, and even cabinet offices, in the Federal government, say that they were equally faithful to their high trust ? Were there none amongst them who abetted the overthrow of that very Federal government and constitution which they had solemnly sworn to uphold and to defend, whose bread they were eating, and whose highest offices they filled ? Were there not members of the outgoing administration who emptied the Federal forts in the North of arms and ammunition in order to fill those in the South, that they might thus be within reach of a hostile hand ? Did they not disperse the few armed forces that the United States possessed in those days, in order that their successors might find themselves without the means of defending the authority of the United States government in case it were attacked ? And if this be so, what other word can fitly be applied to such conduct unless it be that of *treason ?*

The truth is, that the sentiment of legality and respect for the constitution had been decreasing in the South for some years previous to Mr Lincoln's election. The traveller in the Southern States met with men of position and influence who avowed that they were prepared to break up the Union by force should a Free-Soil President be elected, and *that* even though there were nothing unconstitutional in his election or his public conduct. Thus they preferred lawless violence to constitutional opposition.

Another and yet more deplorable fact was the ever-increasing attachment of the Southerners to slavery, their determination to maintain it at all costs, and to spread it everywhere. It was no longer in their eyes an evil to be tolerated, but the normal condition of the two races, a good thing in itself, despite certain drawbacks in practice. There were not wanting those who maintained it to be a divine institution, and pleaded not only for negro slavery, but for all kinds of slavery in principle, to be applied according to circumstances. Nor, if what is *called* the Bible argument be used, is there any stopping short of this hideous conclusion. Some amongst them—men, too, of ability and standing—boldly demanded the reopening of the African slave-trade, and declared themselves for free trade in slaves as well as in all other branches of commerce. Or, as Mr Yancey put it with great force and clearness, "The South demands as free a trade in negroes from Africa as the North in mules from Malta."

Sad indeed was it to hear such monstrous sentiments propounded and enforced by every argument which a misguided ingenuity could suggest. Sadder still to find them daily gaining strength in a community so many of whose members possessed noble and charming qualities. Who that has travelled in the South can ever forget the kindness and hospitality he there received? What Christmas gatherings could be fuller of everything that can render such scenes delightful, than those which were to be met with beneath the roof of the Southern planter? Such pleasant recollections, mingled with the sad tales of suffering and war, were only too well calculated to fill with heaviness the heart of any one who had experienced the warm welcome of Southern hospitality.

Yet not by mere feeling, however natural and right, can be decided so great a question as that which divided for a time the United States Federal government and the Southern Secessionists. A careful appreciation of facts, and a just application of the great principles of order and liberty, are the only right means of judging between the conflicting parties.

The more carefully the criterion of those principles is applied to the subject in question, the clearer does it become that Italy's illustrious statesman, whose words have been already quoted, was right when he condemned the slave-owners' secession movement, and declared the Northern cause to be that "not only of constitutional liberty, but of all humanity."

History does not record a more complete victory or a more crushing defeat than that which marked the termination of the late American war. At its close were to be seen, on the one hand, victorious armies numbering a million of soldiers, perfectly equipped, ready in case of need to undertake fresh campaigns, supported by a powerful nation possessing resources which seemed almost boundless; on the other side were the broken remnants of valiant but defeated troops, encumbering a country once flourishing but now desolated, many of whose rich inhabitants were reduced to poverty and its poorer classes to want. Hence it was, that immediately after the fall of Richmond and Petersburg, Southern generals and soldiers gave up the struggle and submitted to the Federal government. Thus abruptly finished this gigantic conflict, which but a short time before did not seem so near its close.

Scarcely had the verdict of the sword to which the Southerners had appealed been given against them, than the North gave instant proofs of a desire for peace and reconciliation. The citizens of the loyal States declared that the South should have back all its former rights, liberties, and privileges, slavery excepted, on the single condition of an honest return to the Union—that Union whose perfect reconstruction was the hearty desire of men who had ever felt for it a love and respect bordering upon idolatry.

No one longed for such a result more than the upright President of the United States, Abraham Lincoln. Already words of pardon and peace fell from his lips, already his heart thrilled with joy at the prospect of brotherly union once again restored to his native land. Bowed down through four long years beneath the double burden of his country's woes and the awful responsibilities of his own high office, the hope of happier days now dawned upon his sight, and gladdened his soul, weary and worn with watching through the fearful night of his country's agony and peril. To him who had presided over the nation's destinies while the hurricane of civil war swept across the land, seemed now to be given the hallowed task of healing the Republic's wounds, of reconciling her contending sons, of releasing her once for all from slavery's hideous chain. Thus would he re-establish the pillars of the State wholly and without reserve upon justice, liberty, and law, those only sure foundations of a nation's weal, righteous and eternal even as their eternal Author. But the ways of the Infinite Father are not our ways: He had decreed that the earthly course of this noblehearted man was run—that the good and faithful servant was now to enter into that rest which lies beyond the grave. The nation was to be yet further tried, was to pass through another crisis, but momentary indeed, yet full of deepest sorrow.

No words can depict the anguish and horror of the American people when they learned that their truehearted President had been murdered. If anything can have lessened their bitter grief, it was the reprobation of that foul crime by every civilised nation, and the heartfelt expression of sympathy offered by every friend of justice and humanity. In a moment the shout of victory was hushed throughout the land. Its busy millions ceased from their accustomed labours. For a time no sound was heard save the long deep wail of a nation's grief. Every heart was heavy, every home was desolate. Hundreds of thousands, without distinction of creed or party, class or colour, mingled in that funeral procession which stretched a thousand miles from Washington to Springfield,

Illinois, where repose the mortal remains of Abraham Lincoln. Others have possessed more brilliant genius, others have shown as unyielding tenacity; but none have ever united clearness of intellect and firmness of purpose to a gentler heart or a purer patriotism. Henceforth there are in America two spots sacred to every friend of constitutional law and to every lover of human freedom—Mount Vernon, where lies buried "the father of his country," and Oak Ridge Cemetery, where rests from his labours her Martyr-President.

There were those who, untaught by past blunders, did not hesitate to predict a revolution, or at least a lengthened period of confusion and disorder. Some seemed to fancy that Northern soldiers, if not armies, maddened with rage, would rush South and commence a general massacre. Others declared nothing could save the nation but one of the generals seizing at once the reigns of power.

The Americans thought of nothing and followed nothing but the constitution. According to its provisions, Mr Johnson, the Vice-President, took the prescribed oath a few hours after Mr Lincoln's death, and so became President. Mr Hunter, one of the under-secretaries of the State Department, filled *ad interim* Mr Seward's post, who had been nearly assassinated while lying ill in bed. Thus everything followed the regular legal course without a moment's interruption or danger. There was but given to the world another proof of that deep-seated love of law, which is so potent an element in the system of the United States and in the character of its people. This fact is still further brought out by two incidents which occurred about this time, and which are worthy of mention.

Very shortly before President Lincoln's death an armistice was agreed upon between General Sherman and one of the Southern generals; the President, however, set it aside, because in his judgment Sherman had overstepped his powers in certain particulars. The ready and entire submission with which the general bowed to the President's decision affords a noteworthy proof of the power which constituted authorities possess in the United States.

It appears that after Mr Lincoln's murder some foreign paper had alluded to or suggested the idea of General Grant's instantly putting himself at the head of the government. This was told to the general not very long after, upon which he said quietly, that such a thought had never crossed his brain, and even if it had, he could not have put it in execution; for there was not in his army a single soldier who would have abetted him in such an enterprise. Such words in the mouth of the conqueror of Richmond and Vicksburg show what was the character of the man himself and of his army.

Many and bitter were the attacks which had been made on Abraham Lincoln—the like were now directed against his successor. Neither his origin nor his character was spared; his future policy was denounced beforehand as cruel and sanguinary. Andrew Johnson has given to these predictions the most complete of all replies—he has lived them down. He is now known to the world as one of the able men of the day. Born of poor parents in North Carolina, he migrated while still a youth to Tennessee, where he worked as a journeyman tailor. His education had been much neglected, and it was only about the age of twenty that he learned to read and write, by the assistance of his wife. But from that day he set to work at his own instruction with such ardour and perseverance that he soon made up for lost time. He gained quickly the confidence of his fellow-citizens, and after occupying various less important posts, he was elected senator for the State of Tennessee. Favourable to slavery, he was consequently unfavourable to the Free-Soil policy of which Mr Lincoln was already a well-known supporter. But he opposed from the very commencement the secessionist movement. Alone amongst the Southern senators, he resisted it with the whole weight of his influence and eloquence. He denounced the course taken by the Secessionists, both in the Senate at Washington and elsewhere, as utterly illegal, and as a flagrant breach of the constitution. He predicted that it would bring fearful calamities upon the whole country, especially upon the South. He went down in person to his own State of Tennessee, and did his utmost to turn her from the evil path of secession. This courageous and patriotic conduct nearly cost him his life, thanks to the outrageous violence of his separatist opponents. He was obliged at last to fly from Tennessee, and returned to Washington, where he remained throughout the war. Devoted to the maintenance of the Union, Mr Senator

Johnson, as he then was, supported the Washington government in its determination to maintain with a strong hand the just authority and rights of the Federal government. His views of public policy assimilated themselves more and more, as time went on, to those of Mr President Lincoln, and finally came into agreement with them. When the latter was elected President a second time, Mr Johnson was elected with him as Vice-President. It was a wise choice, for he had shown a rare mixture of courage and ability. He had remained faithful to the Union, and being, as he was, a Southern senator, the Northerners by such a selection clearly showed that it was not against the South, *as such*, that they were fighting, but against the violators of the law and the constitution. Since his accession to the presidency he has discharged the duties of his high office and directed the policy of the country with a firmness, moderation, and tact, which prove him to be a man of no ordinary capacity.* The work which Mr Johnson and his government have had to do has been of

* The conduct of Mr Johnson, during the course of his long dispute with Congress on the subject of reconstruction, (begun and carried on since the above estimate of him was written in February 1866,) has clearly proved that that estimate was far too favourable. Still, those who simply denounce him as wholly unfit for his high office appear to the writer to judge the President over-harshly. The fact seems to be, that he is one of those men who are well fitted to meet such a terrible national crisis as that brought on by the armed and revolutionary attack made upon the Federal Union and government of the United States by Mr Jefferson Davis and his compeers. Nor can Mr Johnson's conduct during that crisis be too highly praised. Again, the course he pursued from April 1865, when he unexpectedly became President, until the meeting of Congress at the close of that year, seems the most difficult and delicate kind. Dangers of the most opposite character beset the object to which all their efforts have been directed—that of reconstructing the Union. If too great leniency were shown, there was danger of losing in point of fact one of the

commendable. His first message to Congress, in December 1865, was worthy of the head of a great and free people. But Mr Johnson showed himself wanting in almost all the qualities necessary to his exalted position when questions involving delicate and intricate constitutional problems arose, upon which the best, the ablest, and the most loyal men might well disagree. The qualities needed in a President, when dealing with so arduous and unprecedented a matter as reconstruction, were moderation, tact, a willingness to compromise, a readiness to meet the views of those who differed with him, a desire to bring all parties, himself included, to take a middle course. Instead of that, when Mr Johnson found the majority of Congress opposed to his views, he did little else than lay them down more peremptorily than ever, and insist upon their full and instant adoption. No doubt he thought his own plan of reconstruction the best and the most constitutional, but that was just the question at issue. What was wanted was great tact, judgment, and skill; what Mr Johnson chiefly displayed was an obstinate determination to carry out only his own views, united to great intemperance of language, as more especially displayed in his western tour in the autumn of 1866. It must, however, be admitted that more than one prominent man among his opponents was equally guilty of the same faults. When, however, the whole circumstances of the case are considered, the writer, although not endorsing all that the Senate and House of Congress have done, prefers their policy in this great and difficult question of reconstruction to that of Mr President Johnson. But whatever hesitation the writer may feel with regard to the best solution of so arduous a problem, he has none in expressing his desire that the complete restoration of the Union may be effected upon the broad principles of justice, liberty, and right. His undivided sympathies were with the people and government of the United States throughout the fearful struggle into which their country was plunged by the Southern Secessionists; he therefore naturally hails with delight the prospect of a completely reconstructed Union, resting upon the sure foundation of the rights and freedom of all, without distinction of class or colour.

May the American republic, in this its new and better phase, enjoy best fruits of the crisis through which the nation had passed; for to abolish slavery, and yet leave the future of the former slaves *entirely* in the hands of their old masters, would have been to abolish it only in name—guarantees were necessary that this should be a *bona fide* abolition, carried into practical effect. It was also just to ask of the South tangible proofs, in one form or another, of its sincerity and loyalty in returning to the Union. On the other hand, it was most desirable, both as a matter of policy and of principle, not to be too severe or even too exacting. Such a course would have been wrong, and would, besides, have hindered the work of reconstruction which the United States government and people earnestly wished to further; it would, moreover, have irritated the South, and indisposed it towards that party among its own citizens which desired to return to their old allegiance in all good faith. Nor let it be forgotten that such a party not only existed in the South, but was both numerous and influential. A few facts will show that the Washington government has, at least to a very great extent, avoided both these opposite dangers—that it has followed a course which, speaking generally, may be pronounced worthy of an enlightened and free government, presiding, in

increasing and permanent prosperity; may every section of its people unite in upholding the lawful authority of the Federal government, and the acknowledged rights of the several States; so shall be realised in the political life of the republic both the letter and the spirit of its national motto—" *E pluribus unum.*"

J. W. P.

June 1868.

times of no little difficulty, over the destinies of a great and a Christian people.

Andrew Johnson succeeded to the presidency on the 15th of April 1865, (the day of Mr Lincoln's death,) but the session of Congress did not begin until December. The President and his cabinet had therefore to direct, during the interval, the general policy and affairs of the country. The government, while closely keeping within the limits of the constitution, and carefully abstaining from all entrenchment upon the prerogatives or action of the Federal Congress, used every lawful means to further the work of reconstruction.

The President, among other measures, decreed a general amnesty, one of whose clauses seemed hard —that clause which excluded from the benefits of this measure all persons who possessed a capital amounting to 20,000 dollars or more. Its real object was to oblige all such persons to ask a special pardon, which was at once given on their promise of renewed allegiance to the Union, and adherence to the late President's proclamation for the abolition of slavery. The demands for these pardons were so numerous that it cost an immense amount of time and labour to furnish them to the multitude of applicants who sought them. This able stroke of policy thus succeeded admirably. It rehabilitated the Southerners of influence and position, whilst it obliged them personally to acknowledge the wrong they had done, and ask for pardon. It further obtained from them an additional guarantee against the return of slavery, whilst awaiting its complete abolition, by passing to that effect an amendment to the constitution, according to the provisions of the fifth article.

The government also established throughout the South a vast number of " Freedmen's Bureaux," under the direction of that good and brave man, General Howard, who, it has been said, won for himself during the war the title of the " Hedley Vicars of the Federal army." The mission of these bureaux is to afford aid, work, and protection to the recently enfranchised negroes. Throughout the North, private societies have been formed with the same object, only yet further extended to all in need of such assistance, without distinction of race.

The President hastened to name provisional governors in the States recently in revolt. Their duty was to reassure the inhabitants, and to restore the machinery of government. They called together State conventions, for the double purpose of annulling the Secession ordinances and sanctioning the abolition of slavery. These were the only two acts which were demanded as a *sine qua non* of their full re-admission into the Union, with all their former rights, privileges, and liberties. As to the suffrage, the President decided nothing—believing the matter to lie beyond his power. It was left, like that of the time and manner of the final re-admission of the Southern representatives into the Federal Congress, to be settled by the nation through the action of the Senate and House of Representatives of the United States. This clement policy of the Washington government in the hour of victory was further manifested by the fact that no life was forfeited, excepting that of those who were proved to be accomplices in Mr Lincoln's murder, and that of a certain Wirz, convicted of heinous cruelty towards Northern prisoners incarcerated at Andersonville. Such lenient conduct was but right, yet rarely, if ever, has it marked the close of those civil strifes which have desolated in turn every country of the Old World. The reception of a numerous and influential Southern deputation by Mr Johnson at the White House brought out in all their force these sentiments of mercy and reconciliation. The deputation waited on him to make known their views and hopes upon the vital question of reconstruction. Nothing could be more kindly, more dignified, or more truly Christian than the words and bearing of the President of the United States upon that occasion. In a speech couched in noble and appropriate language, he expressed the pleasure it gave him to hear the deputation acknowledge the errors of the past. He assured those present of his sincere desire to give back to the South all its rights. He would adhere strictly to the constitution, maintain it in all its integrity, and make it the means of restoring the Southern States to their former position. The generous feelings expressed by the President, his reiterated assurances of good-will, his treatment of the Southerners as brothers—as sons of a common country—who had erred indeed, but who were and ever had been brothers, touched all present, and produced a deep impression. More than once the chief magistrate was interrupted by the approbation and emotion of his audience. The members of the deputation expressed their firm resolve to do all in their power towards the reconstruction of the Union. At length they retired, full of hope and confidence, renewing again their promise to join heartily in the work of restoring harmony and peace throughout the length and breadth of their common country.

How great is the contrast offered by this brotherly reconciliation between the chief of a free nation and some of its sons for a time led astray, and those scenes of bloody repression which have marked the triumph of many an European despot over his own subjects, whom long years of oppression and misrule had goaded into rebellion!

The policy of Mr Johnson may be summed up in these words: "The constitution in all its integrity!" He had been faithful to it in the hour of danger; he made it the supreme rule of his conduct in the hour of victory. But he determined to apply it, even in the case of those who had taken up arms against it, with all the leniency consistent with its due maintenance. Such conduct was worthy of the constitutional chief of a free government, when dealing with those who had ever been considered as erring brothers, and who were now completely at its mercy.

The last* and highest expression of the President's policy is to be found in the message which he addressed to the United States Senate and House of Representatives on the 4th December 1865. After

* It was the last when this was written, viz., in February 1866.

thanking God, in the name of the people, for the preservation of the state, the message set forth the object of the Union, and what it really was in the intention of its authors: " The ·Union of the United States was intended by its authors to last as long as the States themselves shall last. *The Union shall be perpetual!* are the words of the Confederation. '*To form a more perfect Union*' by an ordinance of the United States, is the declared purpose of the constitution." The prolonged labours and the earnest discussions by which this great work was accomplished are recalled, as is also the fact that all opinions and all feelings were ultimately united in its support. It is shown that the constitution possesses two most important powers: that of maintaining its authority and that of reforming itself when such reform is deemed necessary. Upon these points the message says :—

"The constitution to which life was thus imparted contains within itself ample resources for its own preservation. It has power to enforce the laws, punish treason, and insure domestic tranquillity. In case of the usurpation of the government of a State by one man or an oligarchy, it becomes a duty of the United States to make good the guarantee to that State of a republican form of government, and so to maintain the homogeneousness of all. Does the lapse of time reveal defects? A simple mode of amendment is provided in the constitution itself, so that its conditions can always be made to conform to the requirements of advancing civilisation. No room is allowed even for the thought of a possibility of its coming to an end. And these powers of self-preservation have always been asserted in their complete integrity by every patriotic chief magistrate

—by Jefferson and Jackson, not less than by Washington and Madison. The parting advice of the father of his country, while yet President, to the people of the United States, was, that 'the free constitution, which was the work of their hands, might be sacredly maintained;' and the inaugural words of President Jefferson held up 'the preservation of the general government, in its constitutional vigour, as the sheet-anchor of our peace at home and safety abroad.' The constitution is the work of 'the people of the United States,' and it should be as indestructible as the people."

The message fully admits that the various State governments have their rights, as well as the Federal government, but declares that all questions at issue can only be settled lawfully by the employment of those means which the constitution affords, and never by force. "The absolute acquiescence in the decisions of the majority was," says the message, "at the beginning of the present century enforced by Jefferson as the vital principle of republics." Indeed, it must ever be, in one form or another, the vital principle of every species of free government, for without it there is no other settlement but that of brute force.

The supremacy of the constitution is emphatically set forth in these words, taken from the constitution itself:—

"The constitution and the laws of the United States which shall be made in pursuance thereof, and all treaties made, or which shall be made, under the authority of the United States, shall be the supreme law of the land; and the judges in every State shall be bound thereby, anything in the constitution or laws of any State to the contrary notwithstanding."

That part of the message which touches on the reorganisation of the Southern States shows the extreme care of the Washington government to avoid alike over-indulgence and undue rigour, as well as its constant adherence to the law and to the constitution as its supreme guide. The following considerations, worthy of remark, are made touching the question of secession, and the position in which those States were placed who took part in it—

"The true theory is, that all pretended acts of secession were, from the beginning, null and void. The States cannot commit treason, nor screen the individual citizens who may have committed treason, any more than they can make valid treaties or engage in lawful commerce with any foreign power. The States attempting to secede placed themselves in a condition where their vitality was impaired, but not extinguished—their functions suspended, but not destroyed.

"But if any State neglects or refuses to perform its offices, there is the more need that the general government should maintain all its authority, and, as soon as practicable, resume the exercise of all its functions. On this principle I have acted, and have gradually and quietly, and by almost imperceptible steps, sought to restore the rightful energy of the general government and of the States. To that end provisional governors have been appointed for the States, conventions called," &c.

The final accomplishment of the work of reconstruction, the time and mode of re-admitting the Southern representatives into the Federal Congress, and the delicate question of the suffrage, are left undecided by the President. He desires to accomplish them in accordance with the united action of Congress, and by its aid.

With regard to the freedmen, the following admirable language is held :—

"But while I have no doubt that now, after the close of the war, it is not competent for the general government to extend the elective franchise in the several States, it is equally clear that good faith requires the security of the freedmen in their liberty and their property, their right to labour, and their right to claim the just return of their labour. I cannot too strongly urge a dispassionate treatment of this subject, which should be carefully kept aloof from all party strife. We must equally avoid hasty assumptions of any natural impossibility for the two races to live side by side in a state of mutual benefit and good-will. The experiment involves us in no inconsistency; let us, then, go and make that experiment in good faith, and not be too easily disheartened. The country is in need of labour, and the freedmen are in need of employment, culture, and protection. While their right of voluntary migration and expatriation is not to be questioned, I would not advise their forced removal and colonisation. Let us rather encourage them to honourable and useful industry, where it may be beneficial to themselves and to the country; and instead of hasty anticipations of the certainty of failure, let there be nothing wanting to the fair trial of the experiment."

As to the constitutional amendment for the abolition of slavery, since carried and become law, according to the provisions of the 5th article, the President earnestly advises its adoption. It is interesting to observe how he speaks of slavery as "essentially a monopoly of labour," as "the element which has so long perplexed and divided the country," and adds, further, "that the adoption of the amendment re-unites us beyond all power of disruption." Thus he admits that slavery was the real cause of the rupture which had taken place, and which it was now the common desire of all to heal for ever.

Such views of President Johnson fully agree with those set forth by Mr A. H. Stephens of Georgia, the ex-Vice-President of the ex-separatist government, who, but a few weeks after its formation, said at a great meeting in Savannah:—

"The new constitution" of the Secessionist Confederation "has set at rest for ever all agitating questions relating to our peculiar institution—African slavery as it exists among us—the proper state of the negro in our form of civilisation. This was the immediate cause of the late rupture and present revolution. Jefferson in his forecast had anticipated this as the rock upon which the old Union would split. He was right."

If there are still any persons prepared to assert that slavery had little or nothing to do with the Secessionist movement and war, let them meditate upon this united testimony of President Johnson and Mr A. H. Stephens.

The message concludes by an eloquent panegyric of the United States and its institutions. It is worth reading for its own sake, although in some respects it may be considered too highly coloured; but it is especially desirable to do so in order to compare it with another panegyric on the same subject, uttered by a very different man, in very different circumstances. That of the President's message runs thus:—

"Here is the great land of free labour, where industry is blessed with unexampled rewards, and the bread of the working man is sweetened by the consciousness that the cause of the country 'is his own cause, his own safety, his own dignity.' Here every one enjoys the free use of his faculties and the choice of activity as a natural right. Here, under the combined influences of a fruitful soil, genial climes, and happy institutions, population has increased fifteen-fold within a century. Here, through the easy development of boundless resources, wealth has increased with twofold greater rapidity than numbers, so that we have become secure against the financial vicissitudes of other countries, and, alike in business and in opinion, are self-centred and truly independent. Here more and more care is given to provide education for every one born on our soil. Here religion, released from political connection with the civil government, refuses to subserve the craft of statesmen, and becomes, in its independence, the spiritual life of the people. Here toleration is extended to every opinion, in the quiet certainty that truth needs only a fair field to secure the victory. Here the human mind goes forth unshackled in the pursuit of science, to collect stores of knowledge, and acquire an ever-increasing mastery over the forces of nature. Here the national domain is offered and held in millions of separate freeholds, so that our fellow-citizens, beyond the occupants of any other part of the earth, constitute in reality a people. Here exists the democratic form of government; and that form of government, by the confession of European statesmen, 'gives a power of which no other form is capable, because it incorporates every man with the State, and arouses everything that belongs to the soul.'

"Where, in past history, does a parallel exist to the public happiness which is within the reach of the people of the United States? Where, in any part of the globe, can institutions be found so suited to their habits or so entitled to their love as their own free constitution? Every one of them, then, in whatever part of the land he has his home, must wish its perpetuity. Who of them will not now acknowledge, in the words of Washington, that 'every step by which the people of the United States have advanced to the character of an independent nation, seems to have been distinguished by some token of providential agency?' Who will not join with me in the prayer that the invisible hand that has led us through the clouds that gloomed around our path, will so guide us onward to a perfect restoration of fraternal affection, that we of this day may be able to transmit our great inheritance of state governments in all their rights, of the general government in its whole constitutional vigour, to our posterity, and they to theirs, through countless generations?

"ANDREW JOHNSON.
"WASHINGTON, *Dec.* 4, 1865."

Let it be remarked, in passing, that these last words prove that, far from wishing to diminish the rights of the governments of the various States on account of the late rebellion, or on account of the abuse of the doctrine of states rights, the President would fully maintain them, just as he would preserve in all their vigour the rights of the Federal government. Or, as he puts it in another place, "So long as the constitution of the United States endures, the States will endure; the destruction of the one is the destruction of the other; the preservation of the one is the preservation of the other."

The second panegyric which has been alluded to forms part of a speech delivered on the 14th November 1860, before the legislature of the State of Georgia, with a view to dissuade it from joining the Secession movement. The man who delivered it was no other than Mr A. H. Stephens, who, in November 1860, opposed secession, and then in the following February became Vice-President of the Secessionist Confederation. His words are well worth a careful perusal :—

"I look upon this country, with our institutions, as the Eden of the world—the paradise of the universe. It may be, that out of it we may become greater and more prosperous, but I am candid and sincere in telling you that I fear, if we rashly evince passion, and without sufficient cause shall take that step [of secession], that instead of becoming greater, or more ·peaceful, prosperous and happy—instead of becoming gods, we will become demons, and at no distant day commence cutting each others' throats.

"The first question that presents itself is, Shall the people of the South secede from the Union in consequence of the election of Mr Lincoln to the presidency of the United States ? My countrymen, I tell you candidly, frankly, and earnestly, that I do not think that they ought. In my judgment, the election of no man constitutionally chosen to that high office is sufficient cause for any State to separate from the Union. It ought to stand by, and still aid in maintaining the constitution of the country. To make a point of resistance to the government, to withdraw from it because a man has been constitutionally elected, puts us in the wrong. . . . We went into the election with this people. The result was different from what we wished ; but the election has been constitutionally held. Were we to make a point of resistance to the government, and go out of the Union on this account, the record would be made up hereafter against us."

In another place Mr Stephens says:—

"This step, once taken, could never be recalled; and all the baleful and withering consequences that must follow [as they would see] will rest on the Convention for all coming time. . . . What right has the North assailed? What interest of the South has been invaded? What justice has been denied? And what claim, founded in justice and right, has been withheld? Can either of you to-day name one governmental act of wrong, deliberately and purposely done, by the government of Washington, of which the South has a right to complain? I challenge the answer."

He then enters into many details to show that no wrong has been done, and that the South has had its full share, and even more, of all the honours, offices, rights, and liberties of their common country and government. After which he concludes by asking why this scission:—

"Is it for the overthrow of the American government, established by our common ancestry, cemented and built up by their sweat and blood, and founded on the broad principles of right, justice, and humanity? and, as such—I must declare here, as I have often done before, and which has been repeated by the greatest and wisest of statesmen and patriots, that it is the best and freest of governments— the most equal in its rights, the most just in its decisions, the most lenient in its measures, and the most inspiring in its principles to elevate the race of men, that the sun of heaven ever shone upon. Now, for you to attempt to overthrow such a government as this, under which we have lived for more than three-quarters of a century—in which we have gained our wealth, our standing as a nation, our domestic safety while the elements of peril are around us, with peace and tranquillity, accompanied by unbounded prosperity, and rights unassailed—is the height of madness, folly, and wickedness, to which I can neither lend my sanction nor my vote."

Such words in the mouth of such a man need no commentary.

Do not, then, both facts and arguments prove that love of law and devotion to the constitution are indelible features of the American character; and that for them the majority of the nation is prepared to make the very greatest sacrifices? Is it not to-day clear what were the real motives which roused the government and people of the United States to vindicate the outraged authority of the Federal rule, and maintain, at all costs, its supreme and lawful rights?

Can an impartial mind any longer deny that the Secessionists, on the contrary, trampled npon the constitution and the law, and appealed to that sword which decided against them, although the Federal government had not overstepped, even by a hair's-breadth, its constitutional limits? And yet the cause of such conduct was even worse than the conduct itself; for it arose from the opposition of the South to the wise and moderate policy of the Free-Soil statesmen who, in 1861, came into the legal possession of constitutional power. The Southerners, rather than allow that policy to be adopted, broke through the law, took up arms, plunged the country into civil war, and sought by such lawless means to found a new confederation, based, according to the statement of their own Vice-President, upon "the corner-stone of slavery."

The war once closed, constitutional means and principles have alone guided the Federal government in the delicate work of reconstruction. And even these have been applied with all the leniency compatible with the Federal Union's laws and just authority.

But there is another aspect of this great question that must not be passed over. It is a matter of the highest import that the great principles of law and order should have been thus vindicated by a people which delights to call itself the freest upon earth, and which is certainly amongst the freest. It has thus by deeds, not words alone, declared that freedom cannot exist without order, that respect for the law is absolutely necessary to the possession of liberty. It is a lesson that can never be forgot, a precedent to be referred to through all future ages. The ultimate result of this tremendous conflict proves also that a free government is perfectly compatible with a strong government; and that such a government can enforce its constitutional laws without sacrificing its liberties, even though it should deem it necessary to suspend some of them for a time in a moment of danger. It demonstrates admirably that order must not be sacrificed to liberty, nor liberty to order. The United States of America have thus set their seal to the all-important truth, that these two great principles are essentially necessary to each other, that both are of vital importance to the existence of a free and well-governed people.

Now, there were none who sympathised more

heartily with the Northern States and the Federal government throughout the late war than the working classes of England, especially the artisans of her great cities. To their lasting honour it must be said that they judged well and truly the American question; they ever supported staunchly and manfully that cause which no less an authority than the great Cavour had declared to be "not only that of constitutional liberty, but of all humanity."

Let them, then, never forget the great lesson which the free government and people of the United States have inculcated upon the world. Let them remember, that just as order without freedom is little else than tyranny, so freedom without order is little better than anarchy. Let them bear in mind that liberty and law must ever go hand-in-hand; that the co-operation of the two is absolutely needful to the life of a free people. Thus continuing to think and act, the operative classes will add daily to the proofs already existing, that to admit them in a just proportion to a direct participation in the choice of England's representatives, is but to widen and strengthen the basis upon which repose those ancient laws and liberties which we English love so proudly and so well.

But one word more. There are those who dread the growing power of the United States, and that chiefly on account of its republican form of government. Yet, while believing that, in the Old World at any rate, constitutional monarchy is the best form of freedom, it is only just to add that the republican is but another form of that same freedom, and not a hostile system. What, after all, lies at the basis of America's republican institutions, if not our own English laws and liberties? Whence comes the system of her jurisprudence—whence her juries? From whence do her legal authorities draw their precedents? Her free press, her public meetings, the two Houses which in her every State form the legislature, are they not outgrowths of England's system? The principle of self-government, and that local application of it in every portion of American soil, is it not of English origin?

Wherever America's dominion extends, it ever carries with it the germ of these rich blessings, spreads abroad England's faith and mother tongue, thus advancing her free and Christian civilisation.

Is it, indeed, so terrible a thing to see them spreading throughout the New World?

Is it worthy of English hearts and intellects to tremble at such a prospect?

Would they not do better to rejoice and take courage? Should they not rather bid God speed to the younger branch of our great English family?

Such, assuredly, is the feeling of England's toiling millions; and they are right. There is no good reason for a wretched display of petty jealousy between the mother country and her stalwart son. Their prosperity and friendship are mighty elements of the world's order, freedom, and progress. Therefore England's people do well to say to their kinsmen of America: May brotherly union, with all its attendant blessings, be completely restored throughout the length and breadth of your vast dominion. So may all your federated States rally anew around your star-decked flag, planted by the hand of immortal Washington, and saved by that of your loved patriot and martyr, Abraham Lincoln. So may each one of your citizens, whether his State lie on the Atlantic or the Pacific shore, whether watered by the Northern lakes or by the Southern gulf, repeat from his heart those noble words of Daniel Webster, "I know no North, I know no South; I know only my country." So may your future be yet greater and more prosperous than your past, and that, not by means of crafty policy, not by the brutal force of arms, nor yet because your material wealth increases, but because now your institutions rest, without reserve, upon the sure foundations of justice, liberty, and right—because now you recognise those sacred principles as the common heritage of all, without distinction of class, or creed, or colour—because now the fair page of your constitution is no longer soiled by the foul stain of Slavery!

THE END.

Printed by Ballantyne & Co., Edinburgh.

WORKS

PUBLISHED BY

TRÜBNER & COMPANY,

60 PATERNOSTER ROW, LONDON.

THE POSITIVE PHILOSOPHY OF AUGUSTE COMTE. Freely Translated and Condensed by HARRIET MARTINEAU. Two volumes large post 8vo, pp. xlii. and 1042, cloth, 16s.

"A work of profound science."—*Edinburgh Review.*

THE CATECHISM OF POSITIVE RELIGION. Translated from the French of AUGUSTE COMTE, by RICHARD CONGREVE. 12mo, pp. 434, cloth, 6s. 6d.

A GENERAL VIEW OF POSITIVISM. Translated from the French of AUGUSTE COMTE, by Dr J. H. BRIDGES. Crown 8vo, pp. xii. and 428, cloth, 8s. 6d.

AUGUSTE COMTE AND POSITIVISM. By JOHN STUART MILL. Reprinted from the *Westminster Review.* Second Edition. Revised. 8vo, pp. 200, cloth, 6s.

REVIEW OF THE WORK OF MR JOHN STUART MILL, entitled "Examination of Sir William Hamilton's Philosophy." By GEORGE GROTE, Author of the "History of Ancient Greece," &c. 12mo, pp. 112, cloth, 3s. 6d.

SPEECH OF JOHN STUART MILL, M.P., ON THE ADMISSION OF WOMEN TO THE ELECTORAL FRANCHISE. Spoken in the House of Commons, May 20th, 1867. 8vo, stitched, 6d.

ENFRANCHISEMENT OF WOMEN. By Mrs STUART MILL. Reprinted from the *Westminster Review* for July 1851. 8vo, sewed, 1d.

THE CLAIM OF ENGLISHWOMEN TO THE SUFFRAGE CONSTITUTIONALLY CONSIDERED. By HELEN TAYLOR. Reprinted from the *Westminster Review*. 8vo, sewed, 1d.

LECTURES ON POLITICAL ECONOMY. By FRANCIS W. NEWMAN. Crown 8vo, pp. 342, cloth, 5s.

DISCOURSES OF SOCIAL SCIENCE. By the late THEODORE PARKER. In one volume crown 8vo, pp. 296, cloth, 6s.

LESSONS FROM THE WORLD OF MATTER AND THE WORLD OF MAN. By THEODORE PARKER. Selected from Notes of his unpublished Sermons, by RUFUS LEIGHTON. Edited by FRANCES POWER COBBE. Crown 8vo, pp. xx. and 332, cloth, 7s. 6d.

"The richest collection of golden words and precious thoughts in the English tongue."—*The Truth Seeker*.

JEREMY BENTHAM'S THEORY OF LEGISLATION. From the French Version of ÉTIENNE DUMONT. By R. HILDRETH. In one volume 8vo, pp. xvi. and 472, cloth, 7s. 6d.

ESSAYS AND LECTURES ON INDIAN HISTORICAL SUBJECTS.—I. A Native State and its Rulers.—II. Lord Lake of Laswarrie.—III. Count Lally.—IV. Havelock.—V. Hyder Ali's Last War.—VI. Sir Hugh Rose. By Major G. B. MALLESON, Bengal Staff Corps. Crown 8vo, pp. 348, cloth, 6s.

THE DERVISHES; or, Oriental Spiritualism. By JOHN P. BROWN, Secretary and Dragoman of the Legation of the United States of America at Constantinople. In one volume, with twenty-four illustrations, crown 8vo, pp. viii. and 416, cloth, 14s.

ESSAYS, POLITICAL AND MISCELLANEOUS. By BERNARD CRACROFT, M.A., Trinity College, Cambridge. In two vols. crown 8vo, pp. 674, cloth, 21s.

CONTENTS OF VOL. I.—The Session of 1866—The State of Affairs in January 1867—Analysis of the House of Commons in 1867—The Session of 1867. Social Articles: Magnanimity, Work, Praise, Vanity—The Talent of Looking Like a Fool with Propriety—Jealousy—Hatred—Cruelty—Intellectual Playfulness—Englishmen's Arguments—Manners—Private Theatricals—County Balls—Landladies and Laundresses—Man and Bee. CONTENTS OF VOL. II.—The Jews of Western Europe—Arabian Nights—Greek Anthology—Ovid as a Satirist—Plautus—Translation at Cambridge—On a Translation of Tacitus—Professor Conington's Horace—Professor Conington's Æneid—Hiawatha Translated into Latin—Sir Kingston James' Tasso—M. Karcher's Rienzi—The Etching Club—Macaroneana, &c.

These Essays are reprinted from the *Saturday Review*, *Spectator*, and other Journals.

LITERARY AND SOCIAL JUDGMENTS. By WILLIAM RATHBONE GREG. In one vol. crown 8vo, cloth.
[Nearly ready.

CONSIDERATIONS ON THE CONDITION OF IRELAND, AND ITS FUTURE. By the late Count CAVOUR. Translated by W. B. HODGSON, LL.D.
[Will shortly be published.

REVUE ANALYTIQUE DES OUVRAGES ÉCRITS EN CENTONS, depuis les Temps Anciens jusqu'au XIXième Siècle. Par un BIBLIOPHILE BELGE. In one vol. small 4to, pp. 512, beautifully printed by Whittingham. 112 copies only. Price 30s.

THE FOUNDERS OF CHRISTIANITY; or, Discourses upon the Men and Circumstances that Originated the Christian Religion. By the Rev. JAMES CRANBROOK, Edinburgh. Fcap. 8vo, pp. 336, cloth, price 6s.

CONTENTS—Lect. 1 and 2. The Sources of Information.—3. The Supernatural—4. Jewish Phases of Religious Thought.—5. The Historical Christ.—6. Christian Mythology: its Origin and Development.—7. The Mythological Christ.—8. The Alexandrine School of Philosophy.—9. Paul the Apostle.—10. The Fourth Gospel.—11. Summary and Conclusion.

Published by Her Majesty's Gracious Permission.

The Eleventh Thousand of

MEDITATIONS ON DEATH AND ETERNITY. From the German by FREDERICA ROWAN. Library Edition, 8vo, cloth, 10s. 6d.; crown 8vo edition, printed on toned paper, pp. 360, cloth, 6s.

MEDITATIONS ON LIFE AND ITS RELIGIOUS DUTIES. Translated from the German by FREDERICA ROWAN, being a Companion to the above. Library Edition, 8vo, cloth, 10s. 6d.; crown 8vo edition, printed on toned paper, pp. 343, cloth, 6s.

BY MAJOR EVANS BELL.

RETROSPECTS AND PROSPECTS OF INDIAN POLICY. 8vo, pp. 352, cloth, 10s. 6d.

REMARKS ON THE MYSORE BLUE-BOOK. With a Few Words to Mr R. D. Mangles. 8vo, pp. 86, sewed, 2s.

THE MYSORE REVERSION "AN EXCEPTIONAL CASE." Second Edition, revised. 8vo, pp. 308, cloth, 7s. 6d.

THE EMPIRE IN INDIA. Letters from Madras and other Places. Post 8vo, pp. 420, cloth, 8s. 6d.

THE ENGLISH IN INDIA. Letters from Nagpore, written in 1857-8. Post 8vo, pp. 206, cloth, 5s.

BY MISS FRANCES POWER COBBE.

HOURS OF WORK AND PLAY. Crown 8vo, pp. 274, cloth, 6s.

STUDIES, New and Old, on Ethical and Social Subjects. Crown 8vo, pp. 446, cloth, 10s. 6d.

ITALICS: Brief Notes on Politics, People, and Places in Italy in 1864. 8vo, pp. 534, cloth, 12s. 6d.

RELIGIOUS DUTY. Post 8vo, pp. 340, cloth, 7s. 6d.

BROKEN LIGHTS: an Inquiry into the Present Condition and Future Prospects of Religious Faith. Second Edition, with a new Preface. Crown 8vo, pp. 204, cloth, 5s.

THANKSGIVING: a Chapter on Religious Duty. 18mo, pp. 42, cloth, sewed, 1s.

THE RELIGIOUS DEMANDS OF THE AGE. 8vo, pp. 36, sewed, 1s.

LONDON:
TRÜBNER & CO., 60 PATERNOSTER ROW.

A CATALOGUE OF IMPORTANT WORKS,

IN ALL DEPARTMENTS OF

LITERATURE AND SCIENCE,

PUBLISHED BY

TRÜBNER & CO.,

60, PATERNOSTER ROW, LONDON.

ADDRESS OF THE ASSEMBLED STATES OF SCHLESWIG TO HIS MAJESTY THE KING OF DENMARK. 8vo. pp. 32. 1861. 1s.

Adler.—THE SECOND DAYS OF THE FESTIVALS. A Sermon delivered at the New Synagogue, Great St. Helen's, on the second day of Passover, 5628, by the Rev. Dr. Adler, Chief Rabbi. Printed by request. 8vo., pp. 16, sewed. 1868. 6d.

ADMINISTRATION (THE) OF THE CONFEDERATE STATES. Correspondence between Hon. J. A. Campbell and Hon. W. H. Seward, all of which was laid before the Provisional Congress, on Saturday, by President Davis. 8vo. sewed, pp. 8. 1861. 1s.

Æsop.—THE FABLES OF ÆSOP. With a Life of the Author, Illustrated with 111 Engravings, from Original Designs by Herrick, handsomely printed on toned paper. 8vo. pp. xiii. and 311. 1865. Cloth, extra gilt edges. 10s. 6d.

Agassiz.—AN ESSAY ON CLASSIFICATION. By Louis Agassiz. 8vo. pp. viii. and 381. Cloth. 1859. 12s.

Agassiz.—METHODS OF STUDY IN NATURAL HISTORY. By L. Agassiz. 12mo. pp. 319. Cloth. 1864. 5s. 6d.

Agassiz.—GEOLOGICAL SKETCHES. By L. Agassiz. With portrait and numerous Illustrations. 1 Vol., crown 8vo. cloth, pp. iv. and 311. 1866. 10s. 6d.

Agassiz.—JOURNEY IN BRAZIL. By Professor and Mrs. Louis Agassiz. In 1 large 8vo. vol. with numerous Illustrations, 8vo. pp. xx. 540. 1868. 21s.

Agassiz.—SEA-SIDE STUDIES IN NATURAL HISTORY. By Elizabeth C. and Alexander Agassiz. With numerous Illustrations. 8vo. pp. vi. and 155. 1865. 12s.

Agüero.—BIOGRAFIAS DE CUBANOS DISTINGUIDOS. Por P. De Agüero. I. Don José Antonio Saco. En 8vo. mayor, 88 páginas, con retrato. 1860. 6s.

Agüero.—LA GUERRA DE ITALIA, y la Paz de Villafranca, con todos sus incidentes y sus complicaciones y consecuencias politicas hasta la nueva constitucion de la Peninsula. Coleccion de articulos publicados en varios Periódicos de Europa y América. Por P. de Agüero. Un tomo en 8vo. mayor, de 138 páginas. 1859. 12s.

Ahn.—Dr. F. Ahn's Practical Grammar of the German Language. A New Edition. By Dr. Dawson Turner, Head Master of Royal Institution School, Liverpool. Crown 8vo. pp. cxii. and 430. Cloth. 1866. 5s.

Ahn.—New, Practical, and Easy Method of Learning the German Language. By Dr. F. Ahn. First and Second Course. Bound in one vol. 12mo. cloth, pp. 86 and 120. 1866. 3s.

Ahn.—Key to Ditto. 12mo. sewed, pp. 40. 8d.

Ahn.—Manual of German and English Conversations, or Vade Mecum for English Travellers. 12mo. cloth, pp. 160. 1861. 2s. 6d.

Ahn.—German Commercial Letter Writer, with Explanatory Introductions in English, and an Index of Words in French and English. By Dr. F. Ahn. 12mo. cloth, pp. 248. 1861. 4s. 6d.

Ahn.—New, Practical, and Easy Method of Learning the French Language. By Dr. F. Ahn. First Course and Second Course, 12mo. cloth, each 1s. 6d. The Two Courses in one vol. 12mo. cloth, pp. 114 and 170. 1865. 3s.

Ahn.—New, Practical, and Easy Method of Learning the French Language. Third Course, containing a French Reader, with Notes and Vocabulary. By H. W. Ehrlich. 12mo. cloth, pp. viii. and 125. 1866. 1s. 6d.

Ahn.—Manual of French and English Conversations, for the use of Schools and Travellers. By Dr. F. Ahn. 12mo., pp. viii. and 200. Cloth. 1862. 2s. 6d.

Ahn.—French Commercial Letter Writer, on the same Plan. By Dr. F. Ahn. 12mo. cloth, pp. 228. 1866. 4s. 6d.

Ahn.—New, Practical, and Easy Method of Learning the Italian Language. By Dr. F. Ahn. First and Second Course. 12mo. pp. 198. 1863. 3s. 6d.

Ahn.—Key to Ditto. 12mo. sewed, pp. 22. 1865. 1s.

Ahn.—New, Practical, and Easy Method of Learning the Dutch Language, being a complete Grammar, with Selections. By Dr. F. Ahn. 12mo. cloth, pp. viii. and 166. 1862. 3s. 6d.

Ahn.—Ahn's Course. Latin Grammar for Beginners. By W. Ihne, Ph. D. 12mo. pp. vi. and 184, cloth. 1864. 3s.

Alcock.—A Practical Grammar of the Japanese Language. By Sir Rutherford Alcock, Resident British Minister at Jeddo. 4to. pp. 62, sewed, 18s.

Alcock.—Familiar Dialogues in Japanese, with English and French Translations, for the Use of Students. By Sir Rutherford Alcock. 8vo. pp. viii. and 40, sewed. 1863. 5s.

Alger.—A Critical History of the Doctrine of a Future Life. With a complete Bibliography of the Subject. By William Rounseville Alger. 4th Edition, thoroughly revised. 8vo. cloth, pp. x. and 914. 1866. 18s.

Alger.—The Friendships of Women. By William Rounseville Alger. 12mo. cloth, pp. xvi. and 416. 1867. 8s.

Alger.—THE GENIUS OF SOLITUDE. The Solitudes of Nature and of Man, or the Loneliness of Human Life. By Rev. W. R. Alger. 16mo. pp. 412, cloth. 1867. 9s.

Alger.—THE POETRY OF THE ORIENT. By William Rounseville Alger. 12mo., pp. xii. and 337, cloth. 1867. 9s.

Allibone.—A CRITICAL DICTIONARY OF ENGLISH LITERATURE, AND BRITISH AND AMERICAN AUTHORS, from the Earliest Accounts to the Middle of the Nineteenth Century. By S. Austin Allibone. Vol. I. royal 8vo. pp. 1,006, cloth. 1859. £1 4s. (Vol. II. nearly ready).

Althaus.—A TREATISE ON MEDICAL ELECTRICITY, THEORETICAL AND PRACTICAL. By Julius Althaus, M.D. 8vo. pp. viii. and 352. 1859. 7s. 6d.

Althaus.—THE SPAS OF EUROPE. By Julius Althaus, M.D. 8vo. cloth, pp. 516. 1862. 12s.

"This is decidedly the most elaborate and complete work on mineral waters which has hitherto appeared in the English language."—*British Medical Journal*.

"A book of research and authority, written by one who is evidently master of his subject, and which we can confidently recommend to the reader."—*Lancet*.

"The book is well timed and well done."—*Cornhill Mag.*

"We can recommend Dr. Althaus's work as by far the best that has been written in our language, with a medical object in view."—*Athenæum*.

Althaus.—ON THE VALUE OF GALVANISM IN THE TREATMENT OF PARALYSIS, NEURALGIA, LOSS OF VOICE, RHEUMATISM, AND OTHER DISEASES. By Julius Althaus, M.D. Fourth Edition. 12mo. cloth, pp. viii. and 236. 1866. 3s. 6d.

American Bible Union.—REVISED VERSION OF THE HOLY SCRIPTURES, viz.:—

BOOK OF JOB. The common English Version, the Hebrew Text, and the Revised Version. With an Introduction and Notes. By T. J. Conant. 4to. boards, pp. xxx. and 166. 1859. 7s. 6d.

GOSPEL BY MATTHEW. The Common English Version and the Received Greek Text; with a Revised Version, and Critical and Philological Notes. By T. J. Conant, D.D. Pp. xl. and 172. With an APPENDIX on the Meaning and Use of Baptizein. Pp. 106. 4to. boards. 8s.

GOSPEL ACCORDING TO MARK. Translated from the Greek, on the Basis of the Common English Version, with Notes. 4to. boards, pp. vi. and 134. 1858. 5s.

GOSPEL BY JOHN. Ditto. 4to. boards, pp. xv. and 172. 1859. 5s.

ACTS OF THE APOSTLES. Ditto. 4to. boards, pp. iv. and 224. 1858. 6s.

EPISTLE TO THE EPHESIANS. Ditto. 4to. boards, pp. vi. and 40. 1857. 3s. 6d.

EPISTLES OF PAUL TO THE THESSALONIANS. Ditto. 4to. boards, pp. viii. and 74. 1858. 4s. 6d.

EPISTLES OF PAUL TO TIMOTHY AND TITUS. Ditto. 4to. boards, pp. vi. and 78. 1860. 2s. 6d.

EPISTLE OF PAUL TO PHILEMON; Ditto. 4to. sewed, pp. 404. 1s. 6d. 12mo. cloth, 2s. 1860.

EPISTLE TO THE HEBREWS. 4to. boards, pp. iv. and 90. 1857. 4s.

SECOND EPISTLE OF PETER, EPISTLES OF JOHN AND JUDE, AND THE REVELATION. Ditto. 4to. pp. 254. 5s.

THE NEW TESTAMENT OF OUR LORD AND SAVIOUR, JESUS CHRIST. Forty-fifth Thousand. 32mo. cloth, pp. 488. 1866. 1s. 6d.

Ditto. Thirty-eighth Thousand. 12mo. cloth, pp. 488. 1866. 4s. 6d.

Ditto. Demy 8vo. cloth, pp. 488. 1866. 7s. 6d.

American Bible Union.—IL NUOVO TESTAMENTO. Traduizione dal Greco per Cura di G. Achilli. Post 8vo. roan, pp. 343. New York, 1854. 7s. 6d.

Americans (The) Defended. By an American. Being a Letter to one of his Countrymen in Europe, in answer to inquiries concerning the late imputations of dishonour upon the United States. 8vo. sewed, pp. 38. 1844. 1s.

Anderson.—PRACTICAL MERCANTILE CORRESPONDENCE. A collection of Modern Letters of Business, with Notes, Critical and Explanatory, and an Appendix, containing a Dictionary of Commercial Technicalities, pro forma Invoices, Account Sales, Bills of Lading, and Bills of Exchange; also an explanation of the German Chain Rule. 17th Edition, revised and enlarged. By William Anderson. 12mo. cloth, pp. 288. 1866. 5s.

Anderson and Tugman.—MERCANTILE CORRESPONDENCE, containing a collection of Commercial Letters, in Portuguese and English, with their translation on opposite pages, for the use of Business Men and of Students in either of the Languages, treating in modern style of the system of business in the principal Commercial Cities of the World. Accompanied by pro forma Accounts, Sales, Invoices, Bills of Lading, Drafts, etc. With an Introduction and copious Notes. By William Anderson and James E. Tugman. 12mo. cloth, pp. xi. and 193. 1867. 6s.

Andrews.—A DICTIONARY OF THE HAWAIIAN LANGUAGE, to which is appended an English-Hawaiian Vocabulary, and a Chronological Table of remarkable Events. By Lorrin Andrews. 8vo. cloth, pp. xvi. and 560. Honolulu, 1865. £1 11s. 6d.

Anglicus.—A VOICE FROM THE MOTHERLAND, answering Mrs. H. Beecher Stowe's Appeal. By Civis Anglicus. 8vo. sewed, pp. 46. 1863. 1s.

Anthropological Review, THE. Vol. I. 1863. 8vo. cloth, pp. xxxiv. and 499. 18s.
Ditto Ditto, Vol. II. 1864. 8vo. cloth, pp. 347 and ccxcii. 18s.
Ditto Ditto, „ III. 1865. Ditto pp. 378 and cccxviii. 18s.
Ditto Ditto, „ IV. 1866. Ditto pp. 408 and ccxiv. 18s.
Ditto Ditto, „ V. 1867. Ditto pp. 376 and cclxxii. 18s.

Anthropological Society.—INTRODUCTORY ADDRESS ON THE STUDY OF ANTHROPOLOGY, delivered before the Anthropological Society of London, on the 24th of February. By James Hunt, Ph. D., F.S.A., F.R.S.L., President. Post 8vo. sewed, pp. 20. 1863. 6d.

Anthropological Society.— MEMOIRS read before the Anthropological Society of London, 1863—1864. In one vol., 8vo. cloth, pp. 542. 21s.

CONTENTS.—I. On the Negro's Place in Nature. By James Hunt, Ph. D., F.S.A., F.R.S.L., F.A.S.L., President of the Anthropological Society of London.—II. On the Weight of the Brain in the Negro. By Thomas B. Peacock, M.D., F.R.C.P., F.A.S.L.—III. Observations on the Past and Present Populations of the New World. By W. Bollaert, Esq., F.A.S.L.—IV. On the Two Principal Forms of Ancient British and Gaulish Skulls. By J. Thurnam, Esq., M.D., F.A.S.L. With Lithographic Plates and Woodcuts.—V. Introduction to the Palæography of America; or, Observations on Ancient Picture and Figurative Writing in the New World; on the Fictitious Writing in North America; on the Quipu of the Peruvians, and Examination of Spurious Quipus. By William Bollaert, Esq., F.A.S.L.—VI.—Viti and its Inhabitants. By W. T. Pritchard, Esq., F.R.G.S., F.A.S.L.—VII. On the Astronomy of the Red Man of the New World. By W. Bollaert, Esq., F.A.S.L.—VIII. The Neanderthal Skull: its peculiar formation considered anatomically. By J. Barnard Davis, M.D., F.S.A., F.A.S.L.—IX. On the Discovery of large Kist-vaens on the "Muckle Heog," in the Island of Unst (Shetland), containing Urns of Chloritic Schist. By George E. Roberts, Esq., F.G.S., Hon. Sec. A.S.L. With Notes on the Human Remains. By C. Carter Blake, Esq., F.A.S.L., F.G.S.—X. Notes on some Facts connected with the Dahoman. By Capt. Richard F. Burton, V.P.A.S.L—XI. On certain Anthropological Matters connected with the South Sea Islanders (the Samoans). By W. T. Pritchard, Esq., F.R.G.S., F.A.S.L.—XII. On the Phallic Worship of India. By Edward Sellon.—XIII. The History of Anthropology. By T. Bendyshe, M.A., F.A.S.L., Vice-President A.S.L.—XIV. On the Two Principal Forms of Ancient British and Gaulish Skulls. Part II. with Appendix of Tables of Measurement. By John Thurnam, M.D., F.S.A., F.A.S.L.—APPENDIX. On the Weight of the Brain and Capacity of the Cranial Cavity of the Negro. By Thomas B. Peacock, M.D., F.R.C.P., F.A.S.L.

Anthropological Society.—MEMOIRS read before the Anthropological Society of London, 1865—1866. Vol. II. 8vo. cloth, pp. x. and 464. 1866. 21s.

CONTENTS.—I. The Difference between the Larynx of the White Man and Negro. By Dr. Gibb.—II. On the Dervishes of the East. By Arminius Vambéry.—III. Origin and Customs of the Gallinas of Sierra Leone. By J. Meyer Harris.—IV. On the Permanence of Anthropological Types. By Dr. Beddoe.—V. The Maya Alphabet. By Wm. Bollaert.—VI. The People of Spain. By H. J. C. Beavan.—VII. Genealogy and Anthropology. By G. M. Marshall.—VIII. Simious Skulls. By C. Carter Blake.—IX. A New Goniometer. By Dr Paul Broca.—X. Anthropology of the New World. By Wm. Bollaert.—XI. On the Psychical Characteristics of the English. By Luke Owen Pike.—XII. Iconography of the Skull. By W. H. Wesley.—XIII. Orthographic Projection of the Skull. By A. Higgins.—XIV. On Hindu Neology. By Major S. R. I. Owen.—XV. The Brochs of Orkney. By George Petrie.—XVI. Ancient Caithness Remains. By Jos. Anderson.—XVII. Description of Living Microcephalo. By Dr. Shortt.—XVIII. Notes on an Hermaphrodite. By Captain Burton.—XIX. On the Sactí Puja. By E. Sellon. XX. Resemblance of Inscriptions on British and American Rocks. By Dr. Seemann.—XXI. Sterility of the Union of White and Black Races. By R. B. N. Walker.—XXII. Analogous Forms of Flint Implements. By H. M. Westropp.—XXIII. Explorations in Unst, Brassay, and Zetland. By Dr. Hunt, President.—XXIV. Report of Expedition to Zetland. By Ralph Tate.—XXV. The Head-forms of the West of England. By Dr. Beddoe.—XXVI. Explorations in the Kirkhead Cave at Ulverstone. By J. P. Morris.—XXVII. On the Influence of Peat on the Human Body. By Dr. Hunt.—XXVIII. On Stone Inscriptions in the Island of Brassay. By Dr. Hunt.—XXIX. The History of Ancient Slavery. By Dr. John Bower.—XXX. Blood Relationship in Marriage. By Dr. Arthur Mitchell.

Anthropology.—ANTHROPOLOGY AND THE BRITISH ASSOCIATION. Reprinted from The Anthropological Review for October, 1865. Post 8vo. sewed, pp. 22. 1865. 6d.

Anthropological Society.—ANNIVERSARY ADDRESSES, 1863, 1864, and 1865. Each 1s.

Apel.—PROSE SPECIMENS FOR TRANSLATION INTO GERMAN, with copious Vocabularies and Explanations. By H. Apel. 12mo. cloth, pp. viii. and 246. London, 1862. 4s. 6d.

Arago.—LES ARISTOCRATIES. A Comedy in Verse. By Etienne Arago. Edited, with English Notes and Notice on Etienne Arago, by the Rev. P. H. Brette, B.D., Head Master of the French School, Christ's Hospital, Examiner in the University of London. Fcap. 8vo. pp. 244, cloth. 1868. 4s.

Asher.—ON THE STUDY OF MODERN LANGUAGES in general, and of the English Language in particular. An Essay. By David Asher, Ph. D. 12mo. cloth, pp. viii. and 80. 1859. 2s.

Asiatic Society.—JOURNAL OF THE ROYAL ASIATIC SOCIETY OF GREAT BRITAIN AND IRELAND, from the Commencement to 1863. First Series, complete in 20 Vols. 8vo., with many Plates. Price £10; or in single Numbers, as follows:—Nos. 1 to 14, 6s. each; No. 15, 2 Parts, 4s. each; No. 16, 2 Parts, 4s. each; No. 17, 2 Parts, 4s. each; No. 18, 6s. These 18 Numbers form Vols. I. to IX.—Vol. X., Part 1, op.; Part 2, 5s.; Part 3, 6s.—Vol. XI., Part 1, 6s.; Part 2 not published.—Vol. XII., 2 Parts, 6s. each.—Vol. XIII., 2 Parts, 6s. each.—Vol. XIV., Part 1, 5s.; Part 2 not published.—Vol. XV.., Part 1, 6s.; Part 2, with Maps, 10s.—Vol. XVI., 2 Parts, 6s. each.—Vol. XVII., 2 Parts, 6s. each.—Vol. XVIII., 2 Parts, 6s. each.—Vol. XIX., Parts 1 to 4, 16s.—Vol. XX., 3 Parts, 4s. each.

Asiatic Society.—JOURNAL OF THE ROYAL ASIATIC SOCIETY OF GREAT BRITAIN AND IRELAND. New Series. Vol. I. 8vo. sewed, pp. 32 and 490. 16s.

CONTENTS.—I. Vajra-chhediká, the "Kin Kong King," or Diamond Sútra. Translated from the Chinese by the Rev. S. Beal, Chaplain, R.N.—II. The Páramitá-hridaya Sútra, or, in Chinese, "Mo-ho-pô-ye-po-lo-mih-to-sin-king," i.e. "The Great Páramitá Heart Sútra." Translated from the Chinese by the Rev. S. Beal, Chaplain, R.N.—III. On the Preservation of National Literature in the East. By Colonel F. J. Goldsmid.—IV. On the Agricultural, Commercial, Financial, and Military Statistics of Ceylon. By E. R. Power, Esq.—V. Contributions to a

Knowledge of the Vedic Theogony and Mythology. By J. Muir, D.C.L., LL.D.—VI. A Tabular List of Original Works and Translations, published by the late Dutch Government of Ceylon at their Printing Press at Colombo. Compiled by Mr. Mat. P. J. Ondaatje, of Colombo.—VII. Assyrian and Hebrew Chronology compared, with a view of showing the extent to which the Hebrew Chronology of Usaher must be modified, in conformity with the Assyrian Canon. By J. W. Bosanquet, Esq.—VIII. On the existing Dictionaries of the Malay Language. By Dr. H. N. van der Tuuk.—IX Bilingual Readings: Cuneiform and Phœnician. Notes on some Tablets in the British Museum, containing Bilingual Legends (Assyrian and Phœnician). By Major-General Sir H. Rawlinson, K.C.B., Director R.A.S.—X. Translations of Three Copperplate Inscriptions of the Fourth Century A.D., and Notices of the Chálukya and Gurjjara Dynasties. By Professor J. Dowson, Staff College, Sandhurst.—XI. Yama and the Doctrine of a Future Life, according to the Rig-Yajur-, and Atharva-Vedas. By J. Muir, Esq., D.C.L., LL.D. —XII. On the Jyotisha Observation of the Place of the Colures, and the Date derivable from it. By William D. Whitney, Esq., Professor of Sanskrit in Yale College, New Haven, U.S.— Note on the preceding Article. By Sir Edward Colebrooke, Bart., M.P., President R.A.S.— XIII. Progress of the Vedic Religion towards Abstract Conceptions of the Deity. By J. Muir, Esq., D.C.L., LL.D.—XIV. Brief Notes on the Age and Authenticity of the Work of Aryabhata, Varáhamihira, Brahmagupta, Bhattotpala, and Bháskaráchárya. By Dr. Bháu Dájí, Honorary Member R.A.S.—XV. Outlines of a Grammar of the Malagasy Language. By H. N. Van der Tuuk.—XVI. On the Identity of Xandrames and Krananda. By Edward Thomas, Esq.

Vol. II. In Two Parts. pp. 522. Price 16s.

CONTENTS.—I. Contributions to a Knowledge of Vedic Theogony and Mythology. No. 2. By J. Muir, Esq.—II. Miscellaneous Hymns from the Rig-and Atharva-Vedas. By J. Muir, Esq. —III. Five Hundred questions on the Social Condition of the Natives of Bengal. By the Rev. J. Long.—IV. Short account of the Malay Manuscripts belonging to the Royal Asiatic Society. By Dr. H. N. Van der Tuuk.—V. Translation of the Amitábha Sûtra from the Chinese. By the Rev. S. Beal, Chaplain Royal Navy.—VI. The initial coinage of Bengal. By Edward Thomas, Esq.—VII. Specimens of an Assyrian Dictionary. By Edwin Norris, Esq.—VIII. On the Relations of the Priests to the other classes of Indian Society in the Vedic age. By J. Muir, Esq.—IX. On the Interpretation of the Veda. By the same. -X. An Attempt to Translate from the Chinese a work known as the Confessional Services of the great compassionate Kwan Yin, possessing 1,000 hands and 1,000 eyes. By the Rev. S. Beal, Chaplain Royal Navy. —XI. The Hymns of the Gaupâyanas and the Legend of King Asamâti. By Professor Max Müller, M.A., Honorary Member Royal Asiatic Society.—XII. Specimen Chapters of an Assyrian Grammar. By the Rev. E. Hincks, D.D., Honorary Member Royal Asiatic Society.

Asiatic Society.—TRANSACTIONS OF THE ROYAL ASIATIC SOCIETY OF GREAT BRITAIN AND IRELAND. Complete in 3 vols. 4to., 80 Plates of Facsimiles, etc., cloth. London, 1827 to 1835. Published at £9 5s.; reduced to £1 11s. 6d. The above contains contributions by Professor Wilson, G. C. Haughton, Davis, Morrison, Colebrooke, Humboldt, Dorn, Grotefend, and other eminent oriental scholars.

Atharva VEDA PRÂTIÇÂKHYA, THE, OR ÇAUNAKÎYÂ CATURÂDHYÂYIKÂ. Text, Translation and Notes. By William D. Whitney, Professor of Sanskrit in Yale College. 8vo., pp. 286. Boards. 1862. 12s.

Atkinson.—CHANGE OF AIR considered with regard to Atmospheric Pressure and its Electric and Magnetic Concomitants, in the Treatment of Consumption and Chronic Disease; with a General Commentary on the most Eligible Localities for Invalids. By J. C. Atkinson, M.D. Crown 8vo. cloth, pp. viii. and 142. 1867. 4s. 6d.

Atkinson and Martineau.—LETTERS ON THE LAWS OF MAN'S NATURE AND DEVELOPMENT. By Henry George Atkinson, F.G.S., and Harriet Martineau. Post 8vo. cloth, pp. xii. and 390. 1851. 5s.

Auctores Sanscriti. Edited for the Sanskrit Text Society, under the supervision of Theodor Goldstücker, Vol. I., containing the Jaiminîya-Nyâya-Mâlâ-Vistara. Parts I. to V., large 4to. sewed, pp. 400. 1865. 10s. each.

Augier.—DIANE. A Drama in Verse. By Émile Augier. Edited with English Notes and Notice on Augier. By Theodore Karcher, LL.B., of the Royal Military Academy and the University of London. 12mo. cloth, pp. xiii. and 146. 1867. 2s. 6d.

Austin.—A PRACTICAL TREATISE on the Preparation, Combination, and Application of Calcareous and Hydraulic Limes and Cements. To which is added many useful Recipes for various Scientific, Mercantile, and Domestic Purposes. By James G. Austin, Architect. 12mo. cloth, pp. 192. 1862. 5s.

Awas I Hind; or, A VOICE FROM THE GANGES. Being a Solution of the true Source of Christianity. By an Indian Officer. Post 8vo. cloth, pp. xix. and 222. 1861. 5s.

Baconi, Francisci, VERULAMIENSIS SERMONES FIDELES, sive interiora rerum, ad Latinam orationem emendatiorem revocavit philologus Latinus. 12mo. cloth, pp. xxvi. and 272. 1861. 3s.

Bader.—THE NATURAL AND MORBID CHANGES OF THE HUMAN EYE, and their Treatment. By C. Bader, Ophthalmic Assistant-Surgeon to Guy's Hospital. Medium 8vo. cloth, pp. viii. and 506. 1868. 16s.

Bader.—PLATES ILLUSTRATING THE NATURAL AND MORBID CHANGES OF THE HUMAN EYE. By C. Bader, Ophthalmic Assistant-Surgeon to Guy's Hospital. Six Chromo-Lithographic Plates, each containing the figures of six Eyes, and four Lithographed Plates with figures of Instruments. With an explanatory text of 32 pages. Medium 8vo. in a Portfolio. 21s.
Price for Text and Atlas taken together, 32s.

Baital Pachisi (The); OR TWENTY-FIVE TALES OF A DEMON. A New Edition of the Hindí text, with each word expressed in the Hindústání character immediately under the corresponding word in the Nágarí; and with a perfectly literal English interlinear translation, accompanied by a free translation in English at the foot of each page, and explanatory notes. By W. Burckhardt Barker, M.R.A.S., Oriental Interpreter and Professor of the Arabic, Turkish, Persian, and Hindústání languages at Eton. Edited by E. B. Eastwick, F.R.S., Professor of Oriental languages, and Librarian in the East India College. 8vo., pp. viii. and 370. Cloth. 1855. 12s.

Baker.—LIPIDHÁRÁ. A Murathi Primer, compiled expressly for the use of accepted candidates for the Bombay Civil Service, by F. P. Baker formerly Superintendent of Government Murathi and Canarese Schools in the Bombay Presidency, and lithographed under his supervision. 8vo., pp. 60, sewed. 1868. 5s.

Ballantyne.—ELEMENTS OF HINDI AND BRAJ BHAKHA GRAMMAR, Compiled for the use of the East India College at Haileybury. By James R. Ballantyne. Second Edition. Crown 8vo., pp. 38. Cloth. 1868. 5s.

Barlow.—FRANCESCA DA RIMINI, HER LAMENT AND VINDICATION; with a brief notice of the Malatesti, e'l Mastin Vecchio, e'l nuovo da Verrucchio. By Henry Clark Barlow, M.D., Academico Correspondente de Quiritti di Roma etc., etc. 8vo. sewed, pp. 52. 1859. 1s. 6d.

Barlow.—IL GRAN RIFIUTO, WHAT IT WAS, WHO MADE IT, AND HOW FATAL TO DANTE ALLIGHIERI. A dissertation on Verses 58 to 65 of the Third Canto of the Inferno. By H. C. Barlow, M.D., Author of "Francisca da Rimini, her Lament and Vindication"; "Letteratura Dantesca," etc., etc., etc. 8vo. sewed, pp. 22. 1862. 1s.

Barlow.—IL CONTE UGOLINO E L'ARCIVESCOVO RUGGIERI, a Sketch from the Pisan Chronicles. By H. C. Barlow, M.D. 8vo. sewed, pp. 24. 1862. 1s.

Barlow.—THE YOUNG KING AND BERTRAND DE BORN. By H. C. Barlow, M.D. 8vo. sewed, pp. 35. 1862. 1s.

Barnstorff.—A KEY TO SHAKSPEARE'S SONNETS. By D. Barnstorff. Translated from the German by T. J. Graham. 8vo. cloth, pp. 216. 1862. 6s.

Bartlett.—DICTIONARY OF AMERICANISMS. A Glossary of Words and Phrases colloquially used in the United States. By John Russell Bartlett. Second Edition, considerably enlarged and improved. 1 vol. 8vo. cloth, pp. xxxii. and 524. 1860. 16s.

Barton.—THE REALITY, BUT NOT THE DURATION OF FUTURE PUNISHMENT, IS REVEALED. An Appeal to Scripture. By John Barton, M.A. 8vo. sewed, pp. 40. 1866. 1s. 6d.

Beal.—THE TRAVELS OF THE BUDDHIST PILGRIM FAH HIAN, translated from the Chinese, with Notes and Prolegomena. By S. Beal, a Chaplain in H. M.'s Fleet, a member of the Royal Asiatic Society, and formerly of Trinity College, Cambridge. Crown 8vo.

Beeston.—THE TEMPORALITIES OF THE ESTABLISHED CHURCH as they are and as they might be; collected from authentic Public Records. By William Beeston. 8vo. sewed, pp. 36. 1850. 1s.

Beigel.—THE EXAMINATION AND CONFESSION OF CERTAIN WITCHES AT CHELMSFORD, IN THE COUNTY OF ESSEX, ON THE 26TH DAY OF JULY, 1556. Communicated and Prefaced by Hermann Beigel, M.D. Small 4to., pp. 49. 1864. 10s. 6d.

Bell.—VISIBLE SPEECH. The Science of Universal Alphabetics; or, Self-Interpreting Physiological Letters, for the Writing of all Languages in One Alphabet. Illustrated by Tables, Diagrams, and Examples. By Alexander Melville Bell, F.E.I.S., F.R.S.S.A., Professor of Vocal Physiology, Lecturer on Elocution in University College, London; Author of "Principles of Speech and Cure of Stammering," "Elocutionary Manual," "Standard Elocutionist," "Emphasized Liturgy," "Reporter's Manual," etc., etc. Inaugural Edition. 4to. cloth, pp. 126. 1867. 15s.

Bell.—ENGLISH VISIBLE SPEECH FOR THE MILLION, for communicating the Exact Pronunciation of the Language to Native or Foreign Learners, and for Teaching Children and illiterate Adults to Read in a few Days. By Alexander Melville Bell, F.E.I.S., F.R.S.S.A., Lecturer on Elocution in University College, London. 4to. sewed, pp. 16. 1867. 1s.

Bell.—THE ENGLISH IN INDIA. Letters from Nagpore. Written in 1857-8. By Captain Evans Bell. Post 8vo. cloth, pp. 202. 1859. 5s.

Bell.—THE EMPIRE IN INDIA; Letters from Madras and other Places. By Major Evans Bell. Crown 8vo. cloth, pp. vi. and 412. 1864. 8s. 6d.

"We commend the letters of Major Bell to every friend of India. He is not only an ardent lover of justice in the abstract, but he has gone deeply into the questions which he discusses and reasons on them with a force of argument quite irresistible."—*Athenæum.*

Bell.—REMARKS ON THE MYSORE BLUE BOOK, with a Few Words to Mr. R. D. Mangles. By Major Evans Bell. 8vo. sowed, pp. xi. and 74. 1866. 2s.

Bell.—THE MYSORE REVERSION. By Major Evans Bell. Second Edition. With Remarks on the Parliamentary Papers, and a few Words to Mr. R. D. Mangles. 8vo. cloth, pp. xvi. and 292. London, 1866. 7s. 6d.

Bell.—RETROSPECTS AND PROSPECTS OF INDIAN POLICY. By Major Evans Bell, late of the Madras Staff Corps, author of "The Empire in India," "The Mysore Reversion," etc. 8vo. pp. vi. and 344, cloth, 1868. 10s. 6d.

Bellew.—A Dictionary of the Pukkhto or Puksiito Language, in which the Words are traced to their Sources in the Indian and Persian Languages. With a Reversed Part, or English and Pukkhto. By Henry Walter Bellew, Assistant Surgeon, Bengal Army. Small 4to., pp. 356. 1867. 42s.

Bellew.—A Grammar of the Pukkhto or Puksiito Language, on a New and Improved System, combining Brevity with practical Utility, and including Exercises and Dialogues, intended to facilitate the Acquisition of the Colloquial. By Henry Walter Bellew, Assistant Surgeon, Bengal Army. Small 4to., pp. 155. London, 1867. 1l. 1s.

Bellows.—English Outline Vocabulary for the use of Students of the Chinese, Japanese, and other Languages. Arranged by John Bellows. With Notes on the Writing of Chinese with Roman Letters. By Professor Summers, King's College, London. 1 vol. crown 8vo., pp. vi. and 368, cloth. 1867. 6s.

Bellows.—Outline Dictionary for the use of Missionaries, Explorers, and Students of Language. By Max Müller, M.A., Taylorian Professor in the University of Oxford. With an Introduction on the proper use of the ordinary English Alphabet in transcribing Foreign Languages. The Vocabulary compiled by John Bellows. Crown 8vo. limp morocco, pp. xxxi. and 368. 1867. 7s. 6d.

Bellows.—Tous les Verbes. Conjugations of all the Verbs in the French and English Languages. By John Bellows. Revised by Professor Beljame, B.A., LL.B. of the University of Paris, and Official Interpreter to the Imperial Court, and George B. Strickland, late Assistant French Master, Royal Naval School, London. Also a New Table of Equivalent Values of French and English Money, Weights, and Measures. 32mo. sewed, 76 Tables. 1867. 1s.

Bellows.—The New Dictionary of the French and English Languages, showing both divisions on the same page, distinguishing the genders at sight by different types, and giving Conjugations of all the Irregular Verbs in French, each Irregular Preterite and Past Participle, and the accent of every word in English, the respective Prepositions to be used, etc. By John Bellows, Gloucester. Revised and corrected by Professor Beljame, B.A. and LL.B. of the University, Official Interpreter to the Imperial Court, Paris; G. Beauchamp Strickland, late French Preceptor at the Royal Naval School, London. Dedicated by special permission to Prince Louis Lucien Bonaparte. [In the Press.

Bellows.—Two Days' Excursion from Gloucester to Llanthony Abbey and the Black Mountains. By John Bellows. Fcap. 8vo. pp. 32 sewed, Illustrated. 1868. 6d.

Benedix.—Der Vetter. Comedy in Three Acts. By Roderich Benedix. With Grammatical and Explanatory Notes by F. Weinmann, German Master at the Royal Institution School, Liverpool, and G. Zimmermann, Teacher of Modern Languages. Post 8vo., pp. 128, cloth. 1863. 2s. 6d.

Benfey.—A Practical Grammar of the Sanskrit Language, for the use of Early Students. By Theodor Benfey, Professor of Sanskrit in the University of Göttingen. Second, revised and enlarged, edition. Royal 8vo., pp. viii. and 296, cloth. 1868. 10s. 6d.

Benisch.—Travels of Rabbi Petachia of Ratisbon: who, in the latter end of the twelfth century, visited Poland, Russia, Little Tartary, the Crimea, Armenia, Assyria, Syria, the Holy Land, and Greece. Translated from Hebrew, and published together with the original on opposite pages. By Dr. A. Benisch; with Explanatory Notes, by the Translator and William F. Ainsworth, Esq., F.S.A., F.G.S., F.R.G.S. 12mo. cloth, pp. vii. and 106. 1856. 5s.

Benjamin.—SPEECH OF HON. J. P. BENJAMIN, of Louisiana, on the Right of Secession, delivered in the Senate of the United States, Dec. 31st, 1860. Royal 8vo. sewed, pp. 16. 1860. 1s.

Benjumea.—GIBRALTAR TO SPAIN; or, the Important Question of the Cession of that Fortress by England, as recently brought before the Spanish Public. Being an Accurate Translation of a Pamphlet just published at Madrid, and written by Nicolas Diaz Benjumea, Esq. 8vo. sewed, pp. 92. 1863. 1s. 6d.

Bentham.—THEORY OF LEGISLATION. By Jeremy Bentham. Translated from the French of Etienne Dumont by R. Hildreth. Post 8vo., pp. xv. and 472. Cloth. 1864. 7s. 6d.

Bentham.—ANALYSIS OF JEREMY BENTHAM'S THEORY OF LEGISLATION. By G. W. H. Fletcher, LL.B. 12mo. cloth, pp. ix. and 86. 1864. 2s. 6d.

Bethune.—EARLY LOST, EARLY SAVED; or, Consolation for Bereaved Parents. By the Rev. George W. Bethune, D.D., LL.D., of New York, Author of "Lectures on the Heidelberg Catechism," etc. Edited by the Rev. A. Pope, late of Leamington. In 1 vol. Crown 8vo. cloth, pp. xii. and 173. 1866. 3s.

Beurmann.—VOCABULARY OF THE TIGRÉ LANGUAGE. Written down by Moritz von Beurmann. Published with a Grammatical Sketch. By Dr. A. Merx, of the University of Jena. pp. viii. and 78, cloth. 1868. 3s. 6d.

Bible.—THE HOLY BIBLE. First division, the Pentateuch, or Five Books of Moses, according to the authorised version, with Notes, Critical, Practical, and Devotional. Edited by the Rev. Thomas Wilson, M.A., of Corpus Christi College, Cambridge. 4to. Part I. pp. vi. and 84; part II. pp. 85 to 176; part III. pp. 177 to 275, sewed. 1863—4. Each pt. 5s., the work complete 20s.

Biblia Hebraica Secundum Editiones J. Athiæ, Joannis Leusdeni, J. Simonis, aliorumque. Imprimis E. Van der Hooght, recensuit Augustus Hahn. 8vo. bound, pp. 1396. 1868. 6s.

Bibliomane, Le.—REVUE DE LA BIBLIOGRAPHIE ANTIQUAIRE. Texte et gravures par J. Ph. Berjeau. Nos. 1 and 2. 8vo. pp. 20 and 42, sewed. 1861. 1s. each part.

Bibliophile, Le.—REVUE DE LA BIBLIOGRAPHIE ANTIQUAIRE, Texte et gravures par J. Ph. Berjeau. Nos. 1, 2, 3. 8vo. pp. 16, 32, and 48, sewed. 1861. 1s. each part.

Bicknell.—IN THE TRACK OF THE GARIBALDIANS THROUGH ITALY AND SICILY. By Algernon Sidney Bicknell. Cr. 8vo. cloth, pp. xx. and 344. 1861. 10s. 6d.

Bigandet.—THE LIFE OR LEGEND OF GAUDAMA, the Budha of the Burmese, with Annotations. The ways to Neibban, and Notice on the Phongyies, or Burmese Monks. By the Right Reverend P. Bigandet, Bishop of Ramatha, Vicar Apostolic of Ava and Pegu. 8vo. sewed, pp. xi., 538, and v. 1866. 18s.

Bigelow.—AUTOBIOGRAPHY OF BENJAMIN FRANKLIN. Edited from his manuscript, with Notes and an Introduction. By John Bigelow. With a portrait of Benjamin Franklin. Post 8vo., pp. 410. Cloth. 1868. 10s.

Biglow Papers (The).—By James Russell Lowell. Newly Edited, with a Preface, by the Author of "Tom Brown's School Days." In 1 vol. crown 8vo. cloth, pp. lxviii. and 140. 1861. 2s. 6d.

Ditto. People's Edition. 12mo. sewed, fancy cover. 1865. 1s.

Biglow Papers (The).—MELIBÆUS-HIPPONAX. The Biglow Papers, Second Series. With a Portrait of the Author. Post 8vo. cloth, pp. lxiii. and 190. 1867. 3s. 6d.

"Masterpieces of satirical humour, they are entitled, as such, to a permanent place in American, which is English Literature."—*Daily News.*

"No one who ever read the *Biglow Papers* can doubt that true humour of a very high order is within the range of American gift."—*Guardian.*

"The book undoubtedly owed its first vogue to party feeling; but it is impossible to ascribe to that cause only, so wide and enduring a popularity as it has now."—*Spectator.*

Blasius.—A List of the Birds of Europe. By Professor I. H. Blasius. Reprinted, from the German, with the Author's Corrections. 8vo. sewed, pp. 24. 1862. 1s.

Bleek.—A Comparative Grammar of South African Languages. By Dr. W. H. I. Bleek. Will be completed in Four parts. Part I., sewed, pp. 104. 1862. 5s.

Bleek.—Formenlehre der lateinischen Sprache zum ersten Unterricht, Von W. H. I. Bleek. 8vo. pp. 68, sewed. 1863. 1s.

Bleek.—Reynard the Fox in South Africa; or, Hottentot Fables and Tales, chiefly Translated from Original Manuscripts in the Library of His Excellency Sir George Grey, K.C.B. By W. H. I. Bleek, Ph.D. Post 8vo. cloth, pp. xxvi. and 94. 1864. 3s. 6d.

Blyth and Speke.—Report on a Zoological Collection from the Somali Country. By Edward Blyth, Curator of the Royal Asiatic Society's Museum, Calcutta. Reprinted from the Twenty-fourth volume of the Journal of the Royal Asiatic Society of Bengal; with Additions and Corrections by the Collector, Capt. J. H. Speke, F.R.G.S., etc. 8vo. pp. 16. One Coloured Plate. 1860. 2s. 6d.

Bohlen, Von.—Historical and Critical Illustrations of the First Part of Genesis, from the German of Professor Von Bohlen. Edited by James Heywood, M.A., F.R.S. Revised. 2 vols. 8vo., pp. xxxii. and 336, iv. and 298. Cloth. 1868. 6s.

Bojesen.—A Guide to the Danish Language. Designed for English Students. By Mrs. Maria Bojesen. 12mo, cloth, pp. 250. 1863. 5s.

Boke of Nurture (The); or, Schoole of Good Maners, for Men-Servants, and Children, with stans puer ad mensam. Newly corrected, very necessary for all youth and children. Compyled by Hugh Rhodes of the Kinges Chappell, born and bred in Deuonshyre, p. 13 and ii. Imprinted at London in Fleetestreete, beneath the Conduite, at the sign of S. John Euaungelist. By H. Jackson, 1577. 4to., pp. xxx. and 56. Cloth. London, 1868. 10s. 6d.

Bollaert.—Antiquarian, Ethnological, and other Researches, in New Granada, Equador, Peru, and Chili; with Observations on the Pre-Incarial, Incarial, and other Monuments of Peruvian Nations. With numerous Plates. By William Bollaert. 8vo. cloth, pp. 279. 1860. 15s.

Bollaert.—The Expedition of Pedro de Ursua and Lope de Aguirre in Search of Eldorado and Amagua in 1560-1. Translated from Fray Pedro Simon's "Sixth Historical Notice of the Conquest of Tierra Firme." By William Bollaert, Esq., F.R.G.S. With an Introduction by Clements R. Markham, Esq. 8vo. cloth, pp. 237. 1861. 10s. 6d.

Boltz.—A NEW COURSE OF THE ENGLISH LANGUAGE, after a New Practical and Theoretical Method, by T. Robertson. For the use of schools and for private tuition, with numerous analogies of English words, with the corresponding French or German expressions. Translated from his fourth German edition into Russian by Dr. August Boltz, Professor of the Russian, the English, the Spanish, etc., Languages at the Royal Military Academy and the Royal Navy Institution at Berlin. 2 vols. Post 8vo., pp. 166 and 160, cloth. 1865. 7s.

BOOK OF GOD. THE APOCALYPSE OF ADAM OANNES. Post 8vo. cloth, pp. 648. 1867. 12s. 6d.

BOOK OF GOD. An Introduction to the Apocalypse. In 1 vol. crown 8vo. pp. iv and 752, cloth. 14s.

Bowditch.—SUFFOLK SURNAMES. By N. L. Bowditch. Third Edition. 8vo. cloth. pp. xxvi. and 758. 1861. 7s. 6d.

Bowles.—LIFE'S DISSOLVING VIEWS. By G. C. Bowles. 12mo., pp. 108. 1865. 3s.

Bowring.—ON RELIGIOUS PROGRESS BEYOND THE CHRISTIAN PALE. An Address delivered at St. Martin's Hall, London, by Sir John Bowring, LL.D., F.R.S., etc., on Sunday, 14th January, 1866. Post 8vo. sewed, pp. 16. 1866. 3d.

Bowring.—SIAM AND THE SIAMESE. A Discourse delivered by Sir John Bowring at St. Martin's Hall, on February 17th, 1867. Also the Introductory Address of J. Baxter Langley, Esq., M.R.C.S., F.L.S. 8vo. sewed, pp. 12. 1867. 2d.

Boyce.—A GRAMMAR OF THE KAFFIR LANGUAGE. By William B. Boyce, Wesleyan Missionary. Third Edition, augmented and improved, with Exercises, by William J. Davis, Wesleyan Missionary. 12mo., pp. xii. and 164, cloth, 8s.

Bracton AND HIS RELATION TO THE ROMAN LAW. A Contribution to the History of the Roman Law in the Middle Ages. By Carl Güterbock, Professor of Law in the University of Koenigsberg. Translated by Brinton Coxe. 8vo., pp. 182, cloth. 1866. 9s.

Brazil, THE EMPIRE OF, at the Paris International Exhibition of 1867. Post 8vo., sewed, pp. 139. Rio de Janeiro. 1867. 2s. 6d.
Ditto, Ditto, with Maps and Catalogue of the Articles sent to the Universal Exhibition at Paris, in 1867. Post 8vo. sewed, pp. 139, iii. and 197. Rio de Janeiro. 1867. 7s. 6d.

Brentano.—HONOUR: OR, THE STORY OF THE BRAVE CASPAR AND THE FAIR ANNERL. By Clemens Brentano. With an Introduction, and a Biographical Notice of the Author. By T. W. Appell. Translated from the German. 12mo. cloth, pp. 74. 1847. 2s. 6d.

Bretschneider.—A MANUAL OF RELIGION AND OF THE HISTORY OF THE Christian Church, for the use of upper classes in public schools in Germany, and for all educated men in general. By Karl Gottlieb Bretschneider. Translated from the German. 12mo. cloth, pp. 296. 1857. 2s. 6d.

Brice.—A ROMANIZED HINDUSTANI AND ENGLISH DICTIONARY, designed for the Use of Schools and for Vernacular Students of the Language. Composed by Nathaniel Brice. New Edition, revised and enlarged. Post 8vo., cloth, pp. 366, 1864. 8s.

Bridges.—THE UNITY OF COMTE'S LIFE AND DOCTRINE: A Reply to Strictures on Comte's Later Writings, addressed to J. S. Mill, Esq., M.P. By Dr. J. H. Bridges, Translator of Comte's General View of Positivism. 8vo., sewed, pp. 70. 1866. 2s

Brinton.—THE MYTHS OF THE NEW WORLD. A Treatise on the Symbolism and Mythology of the Red Race of America. By Daniel G. Brinton, A.M., M.D. Crown 8vo., pp. viii. and 308. Cloth. 1868. 10s. 6d.

Brown.—THE DERVISHES; OR, ORIENTAL SPIRITUALISM. By John P. Brown, Secretary and Dragoman of the Legation of the United States of America at Constantinople. Crown 8vo., cloth, pp. viii. and 416, with 24 Illustrations. 1868. 14s.

Buchner.—FORCE AND MATTER. By Dr. Louis Buchner. Edited from the Eighth Edition of "Kraft and Stoff," by J. Frederick Collingwood, F.R.S.L., F.G.S. Post 8vo. cloth, pp. 320. 1865. 7s. 6d.
"The work is valuable on account of its close and logical reasoning, and the profound and in many cases striking views taken of the subjects discussed."—*Observer*.

Buckle.—HISTORIA DE LA CIVILIZACION EN ESPAÑA POR ENRIQUE TOMAS BUCKLE. Capitulo Iº del segundo tomo de la historia de la civilizacion en Inglaterra. Traducido de la primera edicion Inglesa por F. G. y T. Post 8vo., cloth, pp. xvi. and 188. 1861. 2s. 6d.

Bumstead.—THE PATHOLOGY AND TREATMENT OF VENEREAL DISEASES. By F. J. Bumstead, M.D. 8vo. cloth, pp. xvi. and 640. 1866. 21s.

Bunsen.—MEMOIR ON THE CONSTITUTIONAL RIGHTS OF THE DUCHIES OF SCHLESWIG AND HOLSTEIN, presented to Viscount Palmerston, by Chevalier Bunsen, on the 8th of April, 1848. With a Postscript of the 15th of April. Published with M. de Gruner's Essay, on the Danish Question, and all the official Documents, by Otto Von Wenkstern. Illustrated by a Map of the Two Duchies. 8vo., sewed, pp. 160. 1848. 2s. 6d.

Burgess.—THE PHOTOGRAPHIC MANUAL. A Practical Treatise containing the cartes-de-visite process, and the method of taking stereoscopic pictures, including the Albumen process, the dry Collodion process, the Tanning process, the various Alkaline Toning baths, etc., etc., etc. To which is added an Appendix containing all the recent improvements in the art. By N. G. Burgess. 12mo. cloth, pp. 283. 1865. 6s.

Burgh.—THE MANUFACTURE OF SUGAR AND THE MACHINERY EMPLOYED FOR COLONIAL AND HOME PURPOSES. Read before the Society of Arts, Adelphi, London, April 4th, 1866. By N. P. Burgh, Engineer. 8vo. sewed, pp. 31. 1866. 1s.

Burgh.—THE PRINCIPLES THAT GOVERN THE FUTURE DEVELOPMENT OF THE MARINE BOILER, ENGINE, AND SCREW PROPELLER. Read before the Society of Arts, Adelphi, London, December 18th, 1867. By N. P. Burgh, Engineer. 8vo., sewed, pp. 30. 1868. 2s.

Burton.—CAPTAIN RICHARD F. BURTON'S HANDBOOK FOR OVERLAND EXPEDITIONS: being an English Edition of the "Prairie Traveller," a Handbook for Overland Expeditions; with Illustrations and Itineraries of the Principal Routes between the Mississippi and the Pacific, and a Map. By Captain Randolph B. Marcy (now General and Chief of the Staff, Army of the Potomac). Edited (with Notes) by Captain Richard F. Burton. Crown 8vo., cloth, pp. 270. Numerous Woodcuts, Itineraries, and Map. 1863. 6s. 6d.

Busch.—GUIDE FOR TRAVELLERS IN EGYPT AND ADJACENT COUNTRIES SUBJECT TO THE PASHA. Translated from the German of Dr. Moritz Busch. By W. C. Wrankmore. Square 12mo., cloth, pp. xxxviii. and 182, with 14 Illustrations, a Travelling Map, and Plan of Cairo. 1858. 7s. 6d.

Busch.—MANUAL OF GERMAN CONVERSATION: A choice and comprehensive collection of sentences on the ordinary subjects of every-day life, with a copious Vocabulary on an entirely new and simple plan. By Dr. Oscar Busch, Teacher of Ancient and Modern Languages at the establishment of Dr. Krause at Dresden. 12mo., cloth, pp. x. and 340. 1861. 4s.

Butchers.—A WAIF ON THE STREAM. By S. M. Butchers. 12mo. cloth, pp. viii. and 200. London, 1866. 3s. 6d.

Calvert.—LECTURES ON COAL-TAR COLOURS AND ON RECENT IMPROVEMENTS AND PROGRESS IN DYEING AND CALICO PRINTING. Embodying Copious Notes taken at the International Exhibition of 1862, and Illustrated with numerous specimens of Aniline and other colours. By Dr. F. Crace Calvert, F.R.S. 8vo. sewed, pp. 64. 2s.

Callaway.—IZINGANEDWANE, NENSUMANSUMANE, NEZINDABA ZABANTU (Nursery Tales, Traditions, and Histories of the Zulus. In their own words.) With a Translation into English and Notes. By the Rev. Canon Callaway, M.D. Volume I. 8vo. pp. vii. and 390. cloth. Springvale (Natal), Pietermaritzburg (Natal) and London. 1868. 16s.

Camerini.—L'ECO ITALIANO; A PRACTICAL GUIDE TO ITALIAN CONVERSATION. By E. Camerini. With a Vocabulary. 12mo. cloth, pp. 98. 1860. 4s. 6d.

Campbell.—NEW RELIGIOUS THOUGHTS. By Douglas Campbell. Post 8vo. cloth, pp. xii. and 425. 1860. 6s. 6d.

Canones LEXICOGRAPHICI: or Rules to be observed in editing the New English Dictionary of the Philological Society, prepared by a Committee of the Society. 8vo. sewed, pp. 12. 1860. 6d.

Canticum Canticorum, reproduced in facsimile, from the Scriverius copy in the British Museum. With an Historical and Bibliographical Introduction by I. Ph. Berjeau. Folio, pp. 36, with Sixteen Tables of Illustrations. Vellum. 1860. £2 2s.

Carey.—THE SLAVE TRADE, DOMESTIC AND FOREIGN, WHY IT EXISTS AND HOW IT MAY BE EXTINGUISHED. By H. C. Carey, Author of "Principles of Political Economy," "The Past, the Present, and the Future," etc., etc. 8vo. cloth, pp. 426. 1853. 6s.

Carey.—THE PAST, THE PRESENT, AND THE FUTURE. By H. C. Carey. Second Edition. 8vo. cloth, pp. 474. 1856. 10s. 6d.

Carey.—PRINCIPLES OF SOCIAL SCIENCE. By H. C. Carey. In Three Volumes. 8vo. cloth, pp. 474, 480, and 511. 1858—1867. 42s.

Cape Town.—PICTORIAL ALBUM OF CAPE TOWN, with Views of Simon's Town, Port Elizabeth, and Graham's Town, from original Drawings by T. W. Bowler. With Historical and Descriptive Sketches by W. R. Thomson. Oblong 4to. With Twelve Plates, pp. 44. 1866. 25s.

Carpenter.—THE LAST DAYS IN ENGLAND OF THE RAJAH RAMMOHUN ROY. Edited by Mary Carpenter, of Bristol. With Illustrations. 8vo. cloth, pp. v. and 255. 1866. 7s. 6d.

Catherine II., MEMOIRS OF THE EMPRESS. Written by herself. With a Preface by A. Herzen. Translated from the French. 12mo., boards, pp. xvi. and 352. 1859. 7s. 6d.

Catherine II., Mémoires de l'Impératrice. Ecrits par elle-même et précédés d'une préface par A. Herzen. Seconde édition. Revue et augmentée, de huit lettres de Pierre III., et d'une lettre de Catherine II. au Comte Poniatowsky. 8vo., pp. xvi. and 370. 1859. 10s. 6d.

Catholic, The New Church. Second Edition. 8vo., sewed, pp. 15. 1867. 6d.

Catlin.—The Breath of Life. By G. Catlin. 8vo., with Illustrations. Pp. 76. 1864. 2s. 6d.

Catlin.—O-Kee-Pa. A Religious Ceremony; and other Customs of the Mandans. By George Catlin. With Thirteen coloured Illustrations. Small 4to. cloth, pp. vi. and 52. 1867. 14s.

Cavour.—Considerations on the Condition of Ireland, and its Future. By the late Count Cavour. Translated by W. B. Hodgson, LL.D.

Caxton.—The Game of Chess. A reproduction of William Caxton's Game of Chess, the first work printed in England. 4to. 1862. In cloth, £1 1s. Ditto, full morocco antique, £2 2s.

Frequently as we read of the works of Caxton, and the early English Printers, and of their black letter books, very few persons have ever had the opportunity of seeing any of these productions, and forming a proper estimate of the ingenuity and skill of those who first practised the "Noble Art of Printing."
This reproduction of the first work printed by Caxton at Westminster, containing 23 woodcuts, is intended, in some measure, to supply this deficiency, and bring the present age into somewhat greater intimacy with *the Father of English Printers.*
The type has been carefully imitated, and the cuts traced from the copy in the British Museum. The paper has also been made expressly, as near as possible like the original.

Cazeaux.—A Theoretical and Practical Treatise on Midwifery. By J. Cazeaux. Translated by W. R. Bullock. 4th edition, royal 8vo. Pp. 988. 1866. Cloth. 24s.

Centoniana.—Revue Analytique des Ouvrages écrits en Centons, depuis les temps anciens, jusqu'au XIXieme Siecle. Par un Bibliophile Belge. Small 4to., pp. 508. 1868. 30s.

Chalmers.—The Origin of the Chinese. An Attempt to trace the connection of the Chinese with Western Nations in their Religion, Superstitions, Arts, Language, and Traditions. By John Chalmers, A.M. Fcap. 8vo., pp. 80, cloth. 1868. 2s. 6d.

Chalmers.—The Speculations on Metaphysics, Polity, and Morality of "The Old Philosopher" Lau-tsze. Translated from the Chinese, with an Introduction by John Chalmers, M.A. Fcp. 8vo. cloth, pp. xx. and 62. 1868. 4s. 6d.

Channing.—Self-Culture. By William E. Channing. Post 8vo. Cloth. Pp. 56. 1844. 1s.

Chapman.—George Chapman's Tragedy of Alphonsus, Emperor of Germany. Edited with an Introduction and Notes, by Karl Elze, Ph. D., Hon. M.R.S.L. 12mo. sewed, p. 152. 1867. 3s. 6d.

Chapman.—The Cotton and Commerce of India, considered in relation to the Interests of Great Britain: with Remarks on Railway Communication in Bombay Presidency. By John Chapman, Founder of the Great India Peninsula Railway Company. 8vo. cloth, pp. xvii. and 412. 1851. 6s.

Chapman.—BARODA AND BOMBAY; their Political Morality. A Narrative drawn from the Papers laid before Parliament in relation to the Removal of Lieut.-Col. Outram, C.B., from the Office of Resident at the Court of the Gaekwar. With Explanatory Notes, and Remarks on the Letter of L. R. Reid, Esq., to the Editor of the *Daily News.* By J. Chapman. 8vo. sewed, pp. iv. and 174. 1853. 3s.

Chapman.—INDIAN POLITICAL REFORM. Being Brief Hints, together with a Plan for the Improvement of the Constituency of the East India Company, and the Promotion of Public Works. By John Chapman. 8vo. sewed pp. 36. 1853. 1s.

Chapman.—REMARKS ON THE LEGAL BASIS REQUIRED BY IRRIGATION IN INDIA. By John Chapman. 8vo. sewed, pp. 20. 1854. 1s.

Chapman.—CHLOROFORM AND OTHER ANÆSTHETICS; their History and Use during Childbed. By John Chapman, M.D. 8vo. sewed, p. 52. 1859. 1s.

Chapman.—CHRISTIAN REVIVALS; THEIR HISTORY AND NATURAL HISTORY. By John Chapman, M.D. 8vo. sewed, pp. 53. 1860. 1s.

Chapman.—FUNCTIONAL DISEASES OF WOMEN. Cases illustrative of a New Method of Treating them through the Agency of the Nervous System, by means of Cold and Heat. With Appendix, containing Cases illustrating a New Method of Treating Epilepsy, Infantile Convulsions, Paralysis, and Diabetes. By John Chapman, M.D. 8vo. sewed, pp. xviii. and 74. 1863. 2s. 6d.

Chapman.—SEA-SICKNESS: ITS NATURE AND TREATMENT. By John Chapman, M.D. 8vo. sewed, pp. 72. 1864. 2s. 6d.

Chapman.—DIARRHŒA AND CHOLERA; their NATURE, ORIGIN, AND TREATMENT THROUGH THE AGENCY OF THE NERVOUS SYSTEM. By John Chapman, M.D., M.R.C.P., M.R.C.S. 2nd edition. Enlarged. 8vo. cloth, pp. xix. and 248. 1866. 7s. 6d.

Charnock.—VERBA NOMINALIA: or Words derived from Proper Names. By Richard Stephen Charnock, Ph.D., F.S.A., F.R.G.S., etc. 8vo. cloth, pp. iv. and 357. London. 1866. 14s.

Charnock.—LUDUS PATRONYMICUS; or, The Etymology of Curious Surnames. By Richard Stephen Charnock, Ph.D., F.S.A., F.R.G.S. Crown 8vo. cloth, pp. 182. 1868. 7s. 6d.

Chauvenet.—A MANUAL OF SPHERICAL AND PRACTICAL ASTRONOMY, embracing the general problems of Spherical Astronomy, the special applications to Nautical Astronomy, and the theory and use of fixed and portable Astronomical Instruments. With an Appendix on the method of least squares. By William Chauvenet, Professor of Mathematics and Astronomy. Library edition, revised and corrected. 2 vols. 8vo., pp. 708 and 632. With fourteen plates. Cloth. 1864. £2 16s. 0d.

Chess.—ONE HUNDRED CHESS GAMES, played between Mr. J. F. Emmett and Mr. Vivian Fenton, during the Winter of 1864. Small 4to. sewed, pp. 60. Boulogne and London. 1865. 2s.

Chess-Strategy.—A Collection of the Most Beautiful Chess Problems, composed by "J. B., of Bridport," and contributed by him to the chief Chess Periodicals during the last fifteen years. Illustrated by Diagrams, and accompanied by Solutions. Post 8vo. cloth, pp. 118. 1865. 5s.

Chess World (The).—Volumes 1, 2, and 3, each 12s. 1865, 1866, 1867. Continued in monthly numbers at 1s. each.

Childe.—Investigations in the Theory of Reflected Ray-Surfaces, and their Relation to Plane Reflected Caustics. Also, in the Appendix, A Theory of Plane Caustic Curves, Identified with the Evolute of the Auxiliary Curve of Equiangular Intersection. By Rev. G. F. Childe, M.A., Mathematical Professor in the South African College, Cape of Good Hope. 8vo. Boards. Pp. 140. 1857. 7s.

Chronique de Abou-Djafar-Mohammed Ben-Djarir Ben-Yezid Tabari. Traduite par Monsieur Hermann Zotenberg. Volume I., 8vo., pp. 608, sewed. 7s. 6d. 1867. (To be completed in four volumes).

Claim (The) of Englishwomen to the Suffrage Constitutionally Considered. Reprinted by permission from the *Westminster Review*, for January, 1867. Post 8vo. sewed, pp. 19. London. 1867. 6d.

Clayton and Bulwer Convention, of the 19th April, 1850, between the British and American Governments, concerning Central America. 8vo. Pp. 64, sewed. 1856. 1s.

Clegg.—A Practical Treatise on the Manufacture and Distribution of Coal Gas, its Introduction and Progressive Improvement. Illustrated by Engravings from Working Drawings, with General Estimates. By Samuel Clegg, Jun., M. Inst. C.E., F.G.S. Fifth Edition. Greatly enlarged, and with numerous Additional Engravings. 4to. Pp. xii. and 412, cloth. 1868. 21s.

Cobbe.—Female Education, and How it would be Affected by University Examinations. A Paper read at the Social Science Congress, London, 1862. By Frances Power Cobbe. Third Edition. 18mo. sewed, pp. 20. 1862. 2d.

Cobbe.—Friendless Girls and How to Help Them. Being an Account of the Preventive Mission at Bristol. From a Paper read at the Social Science Congress in Dublin, 1861. By Frances Power Cobbe. Fourth Thousand. 18mo. sewed, pp. 14. 1862. 2d.

Cobbe.—The Workhouse as an Hospital. By Frances Power Cobbe. 18mo. sewed, pp. 16. 1862. 2d.

Cobbe.—The Religious Demands of the Age. A Reprint of the Preface to the Collected Works of Theodore Parker. By Frances Power Cobbe. 8vo. sewed, pp. 36. 1863. 1s.

Cobbe.—Thanksgiving. A Chapter of Religious Duty. By Frances Power Cobbe. 18mo. pp. 40, cloth. 1863. 6s.

Cobbe.—The Cities of the Past. By Frances Power Cobbe. 12mo. cloth, pp. 216. 1864. 3s. 6d.

Cobbe.—An Essay on Intuitive Morals. Being an attempt to popularise Ethical Science. By Frances Power Cobbe. Part I. Theory of Morals. New Edition. Crown 8vo. cloth, pp. xv. and 289. 1864. 5s.

Cobbe.—Italics: Brief Notes on Politics, People, and Places in Italy, in 1864. By Frances Power Cobbe. 8vo. cloth, pp. 534. 1864. 12s. 6d.

Cobbe.—Religious Duty. Second Edition. Crown 8vo., cloth, pp. vi. and 332. 1864. 7s. 6d.

Cobbe.—BROKEN LIGHTS. A Survey of the Religious Controversies of our Times. By Frances Power Cobbe. Second Edition. Crown 8vo., cloth, pp. ix. and 192. 1865. 6s.

Cobbe.—STUDIES, NEW AND OLD, ON ETHICAL AND SOCIAL SUBJECTS. By Frances Power Cobbe. Post 8vo. cloth, pp. 446. 1865. 10s. 6d.

CONTENTS.—I. Christian Ethics and the Ethics of Christ.—II. Self-Abnegation and Self-Development.—III. The Sacred Books of the Zoroastrians.—IV. Hades.—V. The Philosophy of the Poor Laws—VI. The Rights of Man and the Claims of Brutes.—VII. The Morals of Literature—VIII. The Hierarchy of Art.

Cobbe.—HOURS OF WORK AND PLAY. By Frances Power Cobbe. Post 8vo., cloth, pp. 374. 1867. 6s.

Cobden.—RICHARD COBDEN, ROI DES BELGES; par un ex-Colonel de la Garde Civique. Dédié aux blessés de Septembre. Deuxième Edition. 12mo. sewed, pp. 62. 1863. 2s. 6d.

Colecção DE VOCABULOS E FRASES usados na Provincia de S. Pedro de Rio Grande do Sul no Brazil. 16mo., pp. 32, sewed, 2s. 6d.

Ditto ditto, large paper, small 4to. 1856. 5s.

Coleccion DE DOCUMENTOS ineditos relativos al Descubrimiento y á la Historia de las Floridas. Los ha dado á luz el Señor Don Buckingham Smith, segun los manuscritos de Madrid y Sevilla. Tomo primero, folio, pp. 216, con retrato del Rey D. Fernando V. 1851. 28s.

Colenso.—FIRST STEPS IN ZULU-KAFIR: An Abridgement of the Elementary Grammar of the Zulu-Kafir Language. By the Right Rev. John W. Colenso, Bishop of Natal. 8vo., pp. 86, cloth. Ekukanyeni, 1859. 4s. 6d.

Colenso.—ZULU-ENGLISH DICTIONARY. By the Right Rev. John W. Colenso, Bishop of Natal. 8vo., pp. viii. and 552, sewed. Pietermaritzburg, 1861. 15s.

Colenso.—FIRST ZULU-KAFIR READING BOOK, two parts in one. By the Right Rev. John W. Colenso, Bishop of Natal. 16mo., pp. 44, sewed. Natal. 1s.

Colenso.—SECOND ZULU-KAFIR READING BOOK. By the same. 16mo. pp. 108, sewed. Natal. 3s.

Colenso.—FOURTH ZULU-KAFIR READING BOOK. By the same. 8vo. pp. 160, cloth. Natal, 1859. 7s.

Colenso.—THREE NATIVE ACCOUNTS OF THE VISITS OF THE BISHOP OF NATAL, IN SEPTEMBER AND OCTOBER, 1859, TO UPMANDE, KING OF THE ZULUS. With Explanatory Notes and a Literal Translation, and a Glossary of all the Zulu words employed in the same. Designed for the use of Students of the Zulu Language. By the Right Rev. John W. Colenso, Bishop of Natal. 16mo., pp. 160. Stiff cover. Maritzburg, Natal. 1860. 4s. 6d.

Colenso.—TWO SERMONS Preached by the Lord Bishop of Natal, in St. Paul's, D'Urban, on Sunday, November 12, 1865; and in the Cathedral Church of St. Peter's, Maritzburg, on Sunday, November 19, and Sunday, November 26, 1865. 8vo., sewed, pp. 12. 1866. 6d.

Colenso.—THE PREFACE AND CONCLUDING REMARKS OF PART V. OF THE PENTATEUCH AND BOOK OF JOSHUA CRITICALLY EXAMINED. By the Right Rev. John William Colenso, D.D., Bishop of Natal. Printed separately by request. 8vo., sewed, pp. xlvi. and pp. 305 to 320. 1865. 1s.

Colenso.—ON MISSIONS TO THE ZULUS IN NATAL AND ZULULAND. A Lecture by the Right Rev. J. W. Colenso, D.D., Bishop of Natal. 8vo. sewed, pp. 24. 1866. 6d.

Colenso.—NATAL SERMONS. A Series of Discourses Preached in the Cathedral Church of St. Peter's, Maritzburg. By the Right Rev. John William Colenso, D.D., Bishop of Natal. 8vo., cloth, pp. viii. and 373. 1866. 7s. 6d.

Colenso.—NATAL SERMONS. The Second Series. Preached in the Cathedral Church of St. Peter's, Maritzburg. By the Right Reverend John William Colenso, D.D., Bishop of Natal. Crown 8vo. 1868. 5s.

Coleridge.— A GLOSSARIAL INDEX to the Printed English Literature of the Thirteenth Century. By Herbert Coleridge. 8vo. cloth. Pp. 104. 1859. 2s. 6d.

Collet.—GEORGE JACOB HOLYOAKE AND MODERN ATHEISM. A Biographical and Critical Essay. By Sophia Dobson Collet. 12mo., pp. 54, sewed. 1855. 1s.

Comte.—THE POSITIVE PHILOSOPHY OF AUGUSTE COMTE. Translated and Condensed. By Harriet Martineau. 2 Vols. Large post 8vo. Cloth. Vol. 1, pp. xxxvi. and 480. Vol. 2, pp. xvi. and 561. 1853. 16s.

Comte.—THE CATECHISM OF POSITIVE RELIGION. Translated from the French of Auguste Comte. By Richard Congreve. 12mo. cloth. Pp. vi. and 428. 1858. 6s. 6d.

Comte.—A GENERAL VIEW OF POSITIVISM. By Auguste Comte. Translated by Dr. J. H. Bridges. Crown 8vo. cloth. Pp. xi. and 426. 1865. 8s. 6d.

Conant.—THE MEANING AND USE OF BAPTIZEIN PHILOLOGICALLY AND HISTORICALLY INVESTIGATED. By T. J. Conant, D.D. 8vo. cloth. Pp. 164. 1861. 2s. 6d.

Confessions (The) of a Catholic Priest. Post 8vo. cloth. Pp. v. and 320. 1858. 7s. 6d.

Congreve.—THE ROMAN EMPIRE OF THE WEST. Four Lectures delivered at the Philosophical Institution, Edinburgh, February, 1855, by Richard Congreve, M.A. 8vo. pp. 176, cloth. 1855. 4s.

Congreve.—INDIA. By Richard Congreve. 8vo. sewed. Pp. iv. and 35. 1857. 1s.

Congreve.—THE CATECHISM OF POSITIVE RELIGION. Translated from the French of Auguste Comte. By Richard Congreve, M.A. 12mo. cloth, pp. 428. 1858. 6s. 6d.

Congreve.—THE NEW RELIGION IN ITS ATTITUDE TOWARDS THE OLD. A Sermon. By Richard Congreve. 12mo. sewed, pp. 34. 1859. 3d.

Congreve.— ITALY AND THE WESTERN POWERS. By Richard Congreve. 8vo. sewed, pp. 18. 1860. 6d.

Congreve.—THE PROPAGATION OF THE RELIGION OF HUMANITY. A Sermon preached at South Fields, Wandsworth, 10th January, 1860, on the Anniversary of the Birth of Auguste Comte, 19th January, 1798. By Richard Congreve. 8vo. sewed, pp. 22. 1860. 1s.

Congreve.—THE LABOUR QUESTION. By Richard Congreve. Post 8vo. sewed, pp. 24. 1861. 4d.

Congreve.—ELIZABETH OF ENGLAND. Two Lectures delivered at the Philosophical Institution, Edinburgh, January, 1862. By Richard Congreve. 18mo. sewed. Pp. 114. 1862. 2s. 6d.

Congreve.—GIBRALTAR; OR, THE FOREIGN POLICY OF ENGLAND. By Richard Congreve, M.A. Second Edition. 8vo., pp. 70, sewed. 1864. 1s. 6d.

Congreve.—IRELAND. By Richard Congreve, M.A., M.R.C.P.L. 8vo. pp. 40, sewed. 1868. 1s.

Contopoulos.—A LEXICON OF MODERN GREEK-ENGLISH AND ENGLISH MODERN GREEK. By N. Contopoulos. First Part, Modern Greek-English, 8vo., pp. 460, cloth. 1868. 12s.

Constitution of the United States, with an Index to each Article and Section. By a Citizen of Washington. 8vo. Pp. 64, sewed. 1860. 2s.

Cornelia.—A NOVEL. Post 8vo., pp. 250. Boards. 1863. 1s. 6d.

Cornet.—A MANUAL OF RUSSIAN AND ENGLISH CONVERSATION. By Julius Cornet. 12mo. Boards. Pp. 424. 1858. 3s. 6d.

Cornwallis.—SELECTIONS FROM THE LETTERS OF CAROLINE FRANCES CORNWALLIS, Author of "Pericles," "Small Books on Great Subjects," etc. Also some Unpublished Poems, Original and Translated. 1 Vol. 8vo. cloth, pp. xv. and 482. 1864. 12s.

Cotta, Von.—GEOLOGY AND HISTORY. A popular Exposition of all that is known of the Earth and its inhabitants in pre-historic times. By Bernhard Von Cotta, Professor of Geology at the Academy of Mining, Freiberg, in Saxony. 12mo., pp. iv. and 84, cloth. 1865. 2s.

Cotton.—THE FAMINE IN INDIA. Lecture by Major-General Sir Arthur Cotton, R.E., K.C.S.I. (late Chief Engineer, Madras). Read at the Social Science Congress, at Manchester, October 12, 1866, and printed at the request of a Special Committee by the Cotton Supply Association. 8vo. sewed. Pp. 46. 1866. 1s.

Coupland.—SHALL WE NOT GO FORWARD? A Discourse delivered in the Unitarian Chapel, Bridgewater. By William Chatterton Coupland, B.A., B.Sc. 8vo. sewed, pp. 20. 1865. 1s.

Coupland.—INCENTIVES TO A HIGHER LIFE. Discourses by William Chatterton Coupland, B.A., B.Sc. Fcap, 8vo. cloth. Pp. xi. and 148. 1866. 2s. 6d.

Courtenay.—RELIGIOUS PERSECUTION. Report of the Prosecution at Bow Street. The Queen versus Dumergue. From the shorthand Notes of John Kelley Courtenay. 8vo. sewed, pp. 12. 1867. 2d.

Cousin.—ELEMENTS OF PSYCHOLOGY: included in a Critical Examination of Locke's Essay on the Human Understanding, and in additional pieces. Translated from the French of Victor Cousin, with an Introduction and Notes. By Caleb S. Henry, D.D. Fourth improved Edition, revised according to the Author's last corrections. Crown 8vo., cloth, pp. 568. 1864. 7s.

Cousin.—THE PHILOSOPHY OF KANT. Lectures by Victor Cousin. Translated from the French. To which is added a Biographical and Critical Sketch of Kant's Life and Writings. By A. G. Henderson. Large post 8vo., cloth, pp. xciv. and 194. 1864. 9s.

Cowan.—Curious Facts in the History of Insects. By Frank Cowan. Crown 8vo., pp. 396. Cloth. 1865. 7s. 6d.

Cowell.—Prakrita-Prakasa; or, the Prakrit Grammar of Vararuchi, with the Commentary (Manorama) of Bhamaha; the first complete Edition of the Original Text, with various Readings from a collection of Six MSS. in the Bodleian Library at Oxford, and the Libraries of the Royal Asiatic Society and the East India House; with Copious Notes, an English Translation, and Index of Prakrit Words, to which is prefixed an Easy Introduction to Prakrit Grammar. By Edward Byles Cowell, of Magdalen Hall, Oxford. Professor of Sanskrit at Cambridge. Cloth. New Edition, with New Preface, Additions, and Corrections. Second Issue. 8vo., pp. xxxi. and 204. Cloth. 1868. 14s.

Cowper.—Popery and Common Sense. A Poem. By William Cowper. Post 8vo., sewed, pp. 8. 1866. 6d.

Cox.—A Monograph of Australian Land Shells. By James C. Cox, M.D. Univ. Edin., F.R.C.S. Edin., Corresponding Member of the Zoological Society of London, Correspondent of the Academy of Natural Sciences of Philadelphia, Member of Royal Medical Society of Edinburgh, Royal and Entomological Societies of New South Wales. 8vo. pp. v. and 112. Illustrated by 18 plates, sewed. 1868. £2 2s.

Cracroft.—Essays, Political and Miscellaneous. By Barnard Cracroft, M.A., Trinity College, Cambridge. Reprinted from various sources. Two Volumes. Crown 8vo., pp. xvi. and 322, pp. xvi. and 320, cloth. 21s.

CONTENTS OF VOL. I.

The Session of 1866.
The State of Affairs in January, 1867.
Analysis of the House of Commons in 1867.
The Session of 1867.

SOCIAL ARTICLES:—
Magnanimity.
Work.
Praise.
Vanity.
The Talent of looking like a Fool with propriety.
Jealousy.
Hatred.
Cruelty.
Intellectual Playfulness.
Englishmen's Arguments.
Manners.
Private Theatricals.
County Balls.
Landladies and Laundresses.
Man and Bee.

CONTENTS OF VOL. II.

The Jews of Western Europe.
Arabian Nights.
Greek Anthology.
Ovid as a Satirist.
Plautus.
Translation at Cambridge.
On a Translation of Tacitus.
Professor Conington's Horace.
Professor Conington's Æneid.
Hiawatha translated into Latin.
Sir Kingston James' Tasso.
M. Karcher's Rienzi.
The Etching Club.
Macaroneans.
Professor Tyndall on Heat.
Professor Tyndall on Sound.
Burton's Anatomy of Melancholy.
Dreamthorp.
Mr. Forsyth's Life of Cicero.
The worldly Wisdom of Bacon.
Life and Times of Sir Joshua Reynolds.
Mr. Robert Leslie Ellis.
Madame de Tracy.
Madame de Sevigné.

Cranbrook.—Credibilia; or, Discourses on Questions of Christian Faith. By the Rev. James Cranbrook, Edinburgh. Reissue. Post 8vo., pp. iv. and 190, cloth. 1868. 3s. 6d.

Cranbrook.—The Founders of Christianity; or, Discourses upon the Origin of the Christian Religion. By the Rev. James Cranbrook, Edinburgh. Post 8vo., pp. xii. and 324. 1868. 6s.

Crawfurd.—The Plurality of the Races of Man. A Discourse delivered by John Crawfurd, Esq., F.R.S., President of the Ethnological Society at Martin's Hall, January 13th, 1867, with Explanatory Notes. Also the Inaugural Address of J. Baxter Langley, Esq., M.R.C.S., F.L.S. 8vo., sewed, pp. 12. 1867. 2d.

Crosskey.—A Defence of Religion. By Henry W. Crosskey. Pp. 48. 12mo. sewed. 1854. 1s.

Current (The) Gold and Silver Coins of all Countries, their Weight and Fineness, and their Intrinsic Value in English Money, with Facsimiles of the Coins. By Leopold C. Martin, of Her Majesty's Stationery Office, and Charles Trübner. In one volume, medium 8vo., 141 Plates, printed in Gold and Silver, and representing about 1,000 Coins, with 160 pages of Text, handsomely bound in embossed cloth, richly gilt, with Emblematical Designs on the Cover, and gilt edges. 1863. £2 2s.

This work, which the Publishers have much pleasure in offering to the Public, contains a series of the Gold and Silver Coins of the whole world, current during the present century. The collection amounts, numerically, to nearly a thousand specimens, comprising, with their reverses, twice that number; and the Publishers feel confident that it is as nearly complete as it was possible to make it.

It seems almost superfluous to allude to the utility of the work. It is evident that it must become a highly valuable Handbook to the Bullion-dealer and the Money-changer; and to the Merchant and Banker it will prove a sure and safe work of reference, from the extreme accuracy of its details and computations.

The elegance and splendour of the work admirably adapt it as a choice and instructive ornament to the drawing room table; the amusement to be found in the comparison of the taste of different countries as exemplified in their Coins, may chase away many a half-hour's ennui.

In the valuation of the substantial Coins, and the notation of their relative worth in English money, the minutest accuracy has been observed, as also in the statements of their relative purity, which are given according to the legal Mint regulations of each country. In exceptional cases only, where official information was not to be obtained of the weight and fineness of the Coins, assays as found at different places, are reported.

The exact weight of the Coins is expressed both in English troy grains and in French grammes, and the fineness by the English technical terms, as well as in French milliémes; the general tendency of our time towards the decimal metrical system making such a notation almost indispensable. For easier reference, tables of British reports for milliémes of gold and silver have been affixed.

Da Costa.—Medical Diagnosis: with Special References to Practical Medicine. By J. M. Da Costa, M.D. 2nd edition revised. 8vo. cloth. pp. 784. 1866. 24s.

Dadabhai.—The European and Asiatic Races. Observations on Mr. Crawfurd's Paper read before the Ethnological Society. By Dadabhai Navroji. 8vo. sewed, pp. 32. 1866. 1s.

Dalton.—A Treatise on Human Physiology. For the Use of Students and Practitioners of Medicine. By John C. Dalton, Jun., M.D. Third Edition, revised and enlarged. 8vo. cloth, pp. 706. 1866. 21s.

Dana.—A Text-Book of Geology, designed for Schools and Academies. By J. D. Dana, LL.D. Illustrated by 375 Woodcuts. Crown 8vo., cloth, pp. vi. and 354. 1864. 7s. 6d.

Dana.—Manual of Geology; treating of the Principles of the Science, with Special Reference to American Geological History. For the Use of Colleges, Academies, and Schools of Science. By James D. Dana, M.A., LL.D. Illustrated by a Chart of the World, and over One Thousand Figures, mostly from American Sources. 8vo. cloth, pp. 798. 1866. 21s.

Dana.—Manual of Mineralogy; including Observations on Mines, Rocks, Reduction of Ores, and the Applications of the Science to the Arts; designed for the Use of Schools and Colleges. By James D. Dana. New edition, revised and enlarged. With 260 Illustrations. 12mo., pp. xii. and 456. 1867. 7s. 6d.

Dana.—A SYSTEM OF MINERALOGY, DESCRIPTIVE MINERALOGY, comprising the most recent Discoveries. By James Dwight Dana and George Jarvis Brush. Fifth edition. 1 vol. 8vo., pp 874. 1868. £1 16s.

Darby.—RUGGIERO VIVALDI and other Lays of Italy. By Eleanor Darby. 8vo. cloth. pp. viii. and 208. 1865. 5s.

Day.—THE LAND OF THE PERMAULS, or Cochin, its Past and its Present. By Francis Day, Esq., F.L.S. 8vo. cloth, pp. 577. 1863. 25s.

Deichmann.—NEW TABLES to facilitate the Practice of Great Circle Sailing, together with an Application of the Theory of the great Circle on the Globe to the sailing, and an Appendix, containing some mathematical demonstrations. Accompanied by a scale of great circles on a blank chart, to determine without calculation the great circle which passes through two given places, and to show the places at which the spherical courses expressed in fourths of the point, take place on the great circle's arc between the two given places. By A. H. Deichmann. 8vo. boards. pp. viii. and 88. 1857. 5s.

Delepierre.—HISTOIRE LITTERAIRE DES FOUS. Par Octave Delepierre. 184. 1860. 5s.

Delepierre.—ANALYSE DES TRAVAUX DE LA SOCIETE DES PHILOBIBLON DE LONDRES. Par Octave Delepierre. Small 4to., pp. viii. and 134, bound in the Roxburghe style. 1862. 10s. 6d.

"It is probably not generally known, that among the numerous learned associations of the British metropolis there exists one called the Philobiblon Society. This somewhat exclusive union of bibliographic philosophers was established in 1853, under the auspices of the late Prince Consort, and after its model of the French Academy—it being one of the fundamental rules of the Society never to depass in number the immortal Forty. . . . The statutes of the Philobiblon provided for the annual issue of a volume of historical, biographical, critical, and other essays, contributed by any of the forty members, and printed in a very limited edition —not a single book to be disposed of for money. To enhance the value of the works thus published, it was arranged that every member should receive only two copies of each volume, to be signed by the president and secretary of the society, and with the name of the possessor on the title-page. . . . The contents of this half-a dozen semi-mysterious and rare works have just been revealed in a curious little book published by Messrs. Trübner and Co., and got up in exact imitation of the products of Caxton's press. The work is dedicated by M. Octave Delepierre, the author, to the Duke D'Aumale, the patron of the Philobiblon since the decease of Prince Albert, and one of the leading members from the beginning."—*Spectator.*

"Two unpretending but very useful books have been lately compiled by M. Delepierre and Mr. Nichols. The former, whose 'History of Flemish Literature' has already been noticed in these columns, has printed an abstract of the multifarious works issued by the Philobiblon Society of London, of which, by the way, he is the honorary secretary. . . . How great a boon such catalogues as these are to historical and literary enquirers can only be estimated by those who have experienced the want of them. . . The gentlemen whose works we have named at the head of this paper, have done, in their way and degree, a service to literature which may be compared with those rendered by the compilers of the Calendars of the State Papers."—*Saturday Review.*

"M. Delepierre, the secretary, is also a very important contributor. By way of tantalizing the public he issues this 'Analyse,' which is a descriptive catalogue of the precious rarities collected by the society."—*Literary Budget.*

"The account which M. Delepierre gives of these volumes makes us regret that their contents have remained, as he tells us, almost unknown to the public, since many of the contributions appear to be of much interest."—*Parthenon.*

Delepierre.—MACARONEANA ANDRA; overum Nouveaux Mélanges de Litterature Macaronique. Par Octave Delepierre. Small 4to., pp. 180, printed by Whittingham, and handsomely bound in the Roxburghe style. 1862. 10s. 6d.

This Volume, together with the one published by the Author in 1852, form the completest collection of that peculiar form of poetry in existence.

Deliberation or Decision? being a Translation from the Danish, of the Reply given by Herr Raasløff to the accusations preferred against him on the part of the Danish Cabinet; together with an Introductory Article from the Copenhagen "Dagbladet," and Explanatory Notes. 8vo., pp. 40, sewed. 1861. 1s.

Delpech.—THE BEGINNER'S COMPREHENSIVE FRENCH BOOK. By J. Delpech, French Master at Christ's Hospital. Crown 8vo. cloth, pp. viii. and 326. 1866. 4s. 0d.

Demarteau.—GALVANIZED IRON, AND ITS APPLICATION: A Treatise by A. Demarteau on J. and G. Winniwarter's Galvanizing and Lead Works at Gumpoldskirchen. Oblong royal 8vo., pp. viii. 42. 1862. 2s. 6d.

Dennys.—THE TREATY PORTS OF CHINA AND JAPAN. A complete Guide to the open Ports of those Countries, together with Peking, Yedo, Hong-Kong, and Macao. Forming a Guide Book and Vade Mecum for Travellers, Merchants, and Residents in general. With 29 Maps and Plans. With Index to Hong Kong, Canton, Macao, Swatow, Amoy, Foochow, Formosa (General), Takao, Taiwanfoo, Tamsui, Kelung, Ningpo, Shanghai, Yangtz River, Chinkiang, Nanking, Kinkiang, Hankow, Chefoo, Taku, Tientsing, Peking, Newchang, Japan (General), Nagasaki, Yokohama, Yedo, Hakodadi and Hiogo. Appendices, viz., Means of Transport between England, France, and America, and China and Japan. French Mail Steam Ships, Compagnie des Services Maritimes des Messageries Impériales. Extract from Handbook of Information. Overland Route to India, China, and Japan. The Pacific Mail Steamship Company. Alfred Holt's Line of Steamers from Liverpool to China, via the Cape of Good Hope. Distances in Nautical Miles from Shanghae to Towns on the Yang-tse-Kiang, and Catalogue of Books, etc., in China and Japan. By William Frederick Mayers, F.R.G.S., Her Majesty's Consular Service, N. B. Dennys, late Her Majesty's Consular Service, and Charles King, Lieutenant Royal Marine Artillery. Compiled and Edited by N. B. Dennys. 8vo. Half bound. pp. 668, xlviii. and 26. 1867. 42s.

De Tracy.—ESSAIS DIVERS, LETTRES ET PENSÉES de Madame de Tracy. 3 volumes. 12mo., paper covers, pp. iv. 404, 360, and 388. 1852, 1854, and 1855. 1l. 1s.

De Veitelle.—MERCANTILE DICTIONARY; a Complete Vocabulary of the Technicalities of Commercial Correspondence, Names of Articles of Trade, and Marine Terms in English, Spanish, and French. With Geographical Names, Business Letters, and Tables of the Abbreviations in Common Use in the three Languages. By J. De Veitelle. Crown 8vo. cloth, pp. 302. 1864. 7s.

De Vere.—STUDIES IN ENGLISH; or, Glimpses of the Inner Life of our Language. By M. Schele de Vere, LL.D., Professor of Modern Languages in the University of Virginia. 8vo. cloth, pp. vi. and 365. 1867. 10s. 6d.

Dewey.—AMERICAN MORALS AND MANNERS. By Orville Dewey, D.D. 8vo., pp. 32, sewed. 1844. 1s.

Diary of a Poor Young Gentlewoman. Translated from the German, by M. Anna Childs. Crown 8vo. cloth, pp. 224. 1860. 3s. 6d.

Dickinson's, (John), Pamphlets relating to Indian Affairs.

    THE FAMINE IN THE NORTH-WEST PROVINCES OF INDIA: How we might have prevented it, and may prevent another. 8vo. pp. 36, sewed. 1861. 1s.

    OBSTRUCTIONS TO TRADE IN INDIA. A Letter to P. C. Brown, Esq., of Tellicherry. With his Reply. Edited by John Dickinson. 8vo. pp. 15, sewed. 1861. 6d.

DICKINSON'S (JOHN), Pamphlets relating to Indian Affairs—(*continued*).

ADDRESS TO THE MEMBERS OF THE HOUSE OF COMMONS on the Relation between the Cotton Crisis and Public Works in India. 8vo. pp. 39, sewed. 1862. 6*d*.

OBSTRUCTIONS TO TRADE IN INDIA. A Letter. By F. C. Brown, Esq., of Tellicherry. Edited by John Dickinson. 8vo. pp. 20, sewed. 1862. 6*d*.

REMARKS ON THE INDIAN RAILWAY REPORTS PUBLISHED BY THE GOVERNMENT, and Reasons for a Change of Policy in India. 8vo. pp. 32, sewed. 1862. 6*d*.

A LETTER TO LORD STANLEY, M.P., etc., etc., on the Policy of the Secretary of State for India. By John Dickinson. 8vo. pp. 40, sewed. 1863. 6*d*.

DHAR NOT RESTORED, in Spite of the House of Commons and of Public Opinion. By John Dickinson. 8vo. pp. 110, cloth. 1864. 1*s*.

SEQUEL TO "DHAR NOT RESTORED," and a Proposal to Extend the Principle of Restoration. By John Dickinson. 8vo. sewed, pp. 35. 1865. 1*s*.

LETTERS TO MALCOLM MOSS, ESQ., President of the Manchester Chamber of Commerce. By John Dickinson, F.R.A.S, etc., etc., and John Malcolm Ludlow, Barrister at Law, author of "British India, its Races and its History," "The War in Oude," etc., etc. 8vo. pp. 16, sewed. 1866. 6*d*.

RESULTS OF IRRIGATION WORKS IN GODAVERY DISTRICT, and Reflections upon them. By Major-General Sir Arthur Cotton, R.E. Part I. 8vo. pp. 15, and Appendix, sewed. 1866. 6*d*. Part II. 8vo. pp. 11, sewed. 1866. 6*d*.

Dictionary AND COMMERCIAL PHRASEOLOGY in the German, Dutch, English, French, Italian, and Spanish Languages, including a complete Catalogue of Goods, and Five Tables of References in the above Languages. Compiled by Prof. Dr. Brutzer, Prof. Dr. Binder, Messrs. J. Bos Iz, M. W. Brasch and others. 8vo. pp. 544, cloth. 1868. 10*s*.

Dircknick-Holmfeld.—ATTIC TRACTS ON DANISH AND GERMAN MATTERS. By Baron C. Dirckinck-Holmfeld. 8vo. sewed, pp. 116. 1861. 1*s*.

Dircks.—THE CENTURY OF INVENTIONS, written in 1655; by Edward Somerset, Marquis of Worcester. Now first translated into French from the first edition, London, 1663. Edited by Henry Dircks, C.E., LL.D., F.R.S.E., M.R.S.L., etc., Author of "The Life of the Marquis of Worcester," "Worcesteriana," etc., etc. Crown 8vo. sewed, pp. 62. 1868. 1*s*.

Discussion (A) AMONG UPWARDS OF 250 THEOLOGICAL INQUIRERS ON THE UNITY, DUALITY, AND TRINITY OF THE GODHEAD. With Discussions on the Creation, Fall, Incarnation, Atonement, Resurrection, Infallibility of Scripture, Inspiration, Miracles, Future Punishment, Revision of the Bible, etc. 8vo. cloth, pp. 206. 1864. 6*s*.

Doherty.—ORGANIC PHILOSOPHY; or, Man's True Place in Nature. Vol. I. Epicosmology. By Hugh Doherty, M.D. 8vo. cloth, pp. 408. 1864. 10*s*.

Doherty.—ORGANIC PHILOSOPHY. Volume II. Outlines of Ontology, Eternal Forces, Laws, and Principles. By Hugh Doherty, M.D. 8vo. pp. vi. and 462. 1867. 12*s*.

Doherty.—PHILOSOPHY OF RELIGION. By Hugh Doherty, M.D. 8vo. sewed, pp. 48. 1865. 1*s*.

Dohne.—THE FOUR GOSPELS IN ZULU. By the Rev. J. L. Dohne, Missionary to the American Board C. F. M. 8vo. pp. 208, cloth. Pietermaritzburg, 1866. 5*s*.

Dohne.—A ZULU-KAFIR DICTIONARY, etymologically explained, with copious illustrations and examples, preceded by an introduction on the Zulu-Kafir Language. By the Rev. J. L. Dohne. Royal 8vo. pp. xlii. 418, sewed. Cape Town, 1867. 21s.

Dolgoroukow.—LA VÉRITÉ SUR LE PROCÈS du Prince Pierre Dolgoroukow, par un Russe. 32mo. sewed. pp. 144. 1862. 8s.

Dolgoroukow.—LA FRANCE SOUS LE RÉGIME BONAPARTISTE, par le Prince Pierre Dolgoroukow. 2 volumes. 12mo. paper, pp. 478. 1864. 10s.

D. O. M.—THE TRIUNE; or, the New Religion. By Scrutator. 8vo. cloth, pp. ii. and 50. 1867. 2s.

Dominguey's HISTORY OF THE ARGENTINE REPUBLIC. Volume I. (1492 to 1807), Translated from the Spanish. By J. W. Williams. Royal 8vo. sewed, pp. vii. and 149. Buenos Ayres. 1865. 9s.

D'Orsey.—COLLOQUIAL PORTUGUESE; or, Words and Phrases of Every-day Life. Compiled from Dictation and Conversation. For the Use of English Tourists in Portugal, Brazil, Madeira, etc. By A. J. D. D'Orsey. Third Edition, enlarged. 12mo. cloth, pp. viii. and 126. 1868. 3s. 6d.

D'Orsey.—A PRACTICAL GRAMMAR OF PORTUGUESE AND ENGLISH, exhibiting in a Series of Exercises, in Double Translation, the Idiomatic Structure of both Languages, as now written and spoken. Adapted to Ollendorff's System by the Rev. Alexander J. D. D'Orsey, of Corpus Christi College, Cambridge, and Professor of the English Language in that University. Third edition. In one vol. 12mo. cloth, pp. viii. and 298. 1868. 7s. 6d.

D'Orsey.—A PORTUGUESE-ENGLISH AND ENGLISH-PORTUGUESE DICTIONARY. By Rev. Alex. J. D. D'Orsey. [*In preparation.*

Dour and Bertha. A Tale. 18mo. pp. vi. and 72, sewed. 1848. 1s.

Drummond.—PRESIDENT LINCOLN AND THE AMERICAN WAR. A Funeral Address, delivered on Sunday, April 30th, 1865. By Robert Blackley Drummond, B.A. 8vo. sewed, pp. 12. 1865. 3d.

Duncanson.—THE PROVIDENCE OF GOD MANIFESTED IN NATURAL LAW. By John Duncanson, M.D. Post 8vo. cloth, pp. v. and 354. 1861. 7s.

Dunglison.—MEDICAL LEXICON. A Dictionary of Medical Science, containing a concise explanation of the various subjects and terms of Anatomy, Physiology, Pathology, Hygiene, Therapeutics, Pharmacology, Pharmacy, Surgery, Obstetrics, Medical Jurisprudence, and Dentistry. Notices of Climate and of Mineral Waters. Formulæ for Official, Empirical, and Dietetic Preparations, with the accentuation and etymology of the terms, and the French and other Synonymes, so as to constitute a French as well as English Medical Lexicon. By Robley Dunglison, M.D., LL.D., Professor of the Institute of Medicine, etc., in the Jefferson Medical College of Philadelphia. New edition, thoroughly revised, and very greatly modified and augmented. Roy. 8vo. cloth, pp. 1048. 1866. 24s.

Dunlop.—BRAZIL AS A FIELD FOR EMIGRATION. Its Geography, Climate, Agricultural Capabilities, and the Facilities afforded for Permanent Settlement. By Charles Dunlop. Post 8vo. sewed, pp. 32. 1866. 6d.

Dwight.—MODERN PHILOLOGY; its Discoveries, History and Influence. With Maps, Tabular Views, and an Index. By Benjamin W. Dwight. First Series. Third edition, revised and corrected. 8vo. cloth, pp. xviii. and 360. 1864.

Second Series. 8vo. cloth, pp. 504. 1864. 2 vols. 8vo. 24s.

Early English Meals and Manners. — John Russell's Boke of Nurture, Wynkyn de Worde's Boke of Kervynge, the Boke of Curtasye, R. Weste's Booke of Demeanor, Seager's Schoole of Vertue, the Babee's Book, Aristotle's A B C, Urbanitatis, Stans Puer ad Mensam, the Lytylle Childrenes Lytil Boke, for to serve a Lord, Old Symon, the Birched School-Boy, etc., etc. With some Forewords on Education in Early England. Edited by Frederick J. Furnivall, M.A., Trinity Hall, Cambridge. 4to., pp. c. and 388. With 16 tables of Illustrations. Cloth. 1868. 42s.

Early English Text Society's Publications.

1864.

1. EARLY ENGLISH ALLITERATIVE POEMS. In the West-Midland Dialect of the Fourteenth Century. Edited by R. Morris, Esq., from an unique Cottonian MS. 16s.
2. ARTHUR (about 1440 A.D.). Edited by F. J. Furnivall, Esq., from the Marquis of Bath's unique M.S. 4s.
3. ANE COMPENDIOUS AND BREUE TRACTATE CONCERNYNG YE OFFICE AND DEWTIE OF KYNGIS, etc. By William Lauder. (1556 A.D.) Edited by F. Hall, Esq., D.C.L. 4s.
4. SIR GAWAYNE AND THE GREEN KNIGHT (about 1320-30 A.D.). Edited by R. Morris, Esq., from an unique Cottonian M.S. 10s.

1865.

5. OF THE ORTHOGRAPHIE AND CONGRUITIE OF THE BRITAN TONGUE; a treates, noe shorter than necessarie, for the Schooles, be Alexander Hume. Edited for the first time from the unique MS. in the British Museum (about 1617 A.D.), by Henry B. Wheatley, Esq. 4s.
6. LANCELOT OF THE LAIK. Edited from the unique M.S. in the Cambridge University Library (about 1500), by the Rev. Walter W. Skeat, M.A. 8s.
7. THE STORY OF GENESIS AND EXODUS, an Early English Song, of about 1250 A.D. Edited for the first time from the unique MS. in the Library of Corpus Christi College, Cambridge, by R. Morris, Esq. 8s.
8. MORTE ARTHURE; the Alliterative Version. Edited from Robert Thornton's unique MS. (about 1440 A.D.) at Lincoln. By the Rev. George Perry, M.A., Prebendary of Lincoln. 7s.
9. ANIMADVERSIONS UPPON THE ANNOTACIONS AND CORRECTIONS OF SOME IMPERFECTIONS OF IMPRESSIONES OF CHAUER'S WORKES, reprinted in 1598; by Francis Thynne. Edited from the unique MS. in the Bridgewater Library. By G. H. Kingsley, Esq., M.D. 4s.
10. MERLIN, OR THE EARLY HISTORY OF KING ARTHUR. Edited for the first time from the unique MS. of the Cambridge University Library (about 1450 A.D.). By Henry B. Wheatley, Esq. Part I. 2s. 6d.
11. THE MONARCHE, and other Poems of Sir David Lyndesay. Edited from the first edition by Johne Skott, in 1552. By Fitzedward Hall, Esq., D.C.L. Part I. 3s.
12. THE WRIGHT'S CHASTE WIFE, a Merry Tale, by Adam of Cobsam (about 1642 A.D.), from the unique Lambeth MS. 306. Edited for the first time by F. J. Furnivall, Esq., M.A. 1s.

1866.

13. SEINTE MARHERETE, YE MEIDEN ANT MARTYR. Three Texts of about 1200, 1310, 1330 A.D. First edited in 1862. By the Rev. Oswald Cockayne, M.A., and now re-issued. 2s.
14. KYNG HORN, with fragments of Floriz and Blanucheflur, and the Assumption of the Blessed Virgin. Edited from the MS. in the Library of the University of Cambridge and the British Museum. By the Rev. J. Rawson

Early English Text Society's Publications—*(continued).*

Latyn, þ Hermys þ prophete and king of Egipt after þ flood of Noe, fader of Philosophris, hadde by reuelacioun of an aungil of God to him sente. Edited from the Sloane MS. 73. By F. J. Furnivall, Esq., M.A. 1s.

17. PARALLEL EXTRACTS from 29 Manuscripts of PIERS PLOWMAN, with Comments, and a Proposal for the Society's Three-text edition of this Poem. By the Rev. W. Skeat, M.A. 1s.
18. HALI MEIDENHEAD, about 1200 A.D. Edited for the first time from the MS. (with a translation) by the Rev. Oswald Cockayne, M.A. 1s.
19. THE MONARCHE, and other Poems of Sir David Lyndesay. Part II., the Complaynt of the King's Papingo, and other minor Poems. Edited from the first edition by F. Hall, Esq., D.C.L. 3s. 6d.
20. SOME TREATISES BY RICHARD ROLLE DE HAMPOLE. Edited from Robert of Thorntone's MS. about 1440 A.D. By the Rev. George G. Perry, M.A. 1s.
21. MERLIN, OR THE EARLY HISTORY OF KING ARTHUR. Part II. Edited by Henry B. Wheatley, Esq. 4s.
22. THE ROMANS OF PARTENAY, OR LUSIGNEN. Edited for the first time from the unique MS. in the Library of Trinity College, Cambridge, by the Rev. W. W. Skeat, M.A. 6s.
23. DAN MICHEL'S AYENBITE OF INWYT, or Remorse of Conscience, in the Kentish dialect, 1340 A.D. Edited from the unique MS. in the British Museum, by Richard Morris, Esq. 10s. 6d.

1867.

24. HYMNS OF THE VIRGIN AND CHRIST; THE PARLIAMENT OF DEVILS, and Other Religious Poems. Edited from the Lambeth MS. 853, by F. J. Furnivall, M.A. 3s.
25. THE STACIONS OF ROME, and the Pilgrim's Sea-Voyage and Sea-Sickness, with Clene Maydenhod. Edited from the Vernon and Porkington MSS., etc. By F. J. Furnivall, Esq., M.A. 1s.
26. RELIGIOUS PIECES IN PROSE AND VERSE. Containing Dan Jon Gaytrigg's Sermon; The Abbaye of S. Spirit; Sayne Jon, and other pieces in the Northern Dialect. Edited from Robert of Thorntone's MS. (about 1460 A.D.) by the Rev. George G. Perry, M.A. 2s.
27. MANIPULUS VOCABULORUM: a Rhyming Dictionary of the English Language, by Peter Levens (1570). Edited, with an Alphabetical Index, by Henry B. Wheatley. 12s.
28. THE VISION OF WILLIAM CONCERNING PIERS PLOWMAN, together with Vita de Dowel, Dobet et Dobest. 1362 A.D. By William Langland. The earliest or Vernon Text; Text A. Edited from the Vernon MS., with full Collations. By Rev. W. W. Skeat, M.A. 7s.
29. ENGLISH GILDS, their Statutes and Customs, with an Introduction and an Appendix of translated Statutes. Edited from the MSS. 1389 A.D. By Toulmin Smith, Esq. [*In the press.*
30. PIERCE THE PLOUGHMAN'S CREDE (about 1394). Edited from the MSS. by the Rev. W. W. Skeat, M.A. 2s.

1868.

31. INSTRUCTIONS FOR PARISH PRIESTS. By John Myrc. Edited from Cotton MS. Claudius A. II. By Edward Peacock, Esq., F.S.A., etc., etc. 4s.
32. THE BABEES BOOK, Aristotle's A B C, Urbanitatis, Stans Puer ad Mensam, The Lytille Childrenes Lytil Boke. The Bokes of Nurture of Hugh Rodes and John Russell, Wynnyn de Worde's Boke of Kervynge, the Booke of Demeanor, the Boke of Curtasye, Seager's Schoole of Vertue, etc., etc. With some French and Latin Poems on like subjects, and some Forewords on Education in Early England. Edited by F. J. Furnivall, M.A., Trinity Hall, Cambridge. 15s.
33. THE BOOK OF THE KNIGHT DE LA TOUR LANDRY, 1372. A Father's Book for his Daughters. Edited from the Harleian MS. 1764. By Thomas Wright, Esq., M.A., and Mr. William Rossiter. 8s.

Eastwick.—KHIRAD AFROZ (the Illuminator of the Understanding). By Maulaví Hafízu'd-dín. A New Edition of the Hindústaní Text, carefully revised, with Notes, Critical and Explanatory. By Edward B. Eastwick, F.R.S., F.S.A., M.R.A.S., Professor of Hindústaní at Haileybury College. Imperial 8vo. cloth, pp. xiv. and 319. Re-issue, 1867. 18s.

Echo (Deutsches).—THE GERMAN ECHO. A Faithful Mirror of German Conversation. By Ludwig Wolfram. With a Vocabulary. By Henry P. Skelton. Post 8vo., pp. 130 and 70. Cloth. 1863. 3s.

Echo Français.—A PRACTICAL GUIDE TO CONVERSATION. By Fr. de la Fruston. With a complete Vocabulary. By ;Anthony Maw Border. Post 8vo., pp. 120 and 72. Cloth. 1860. 3s.

Eco Italiano (L').—A PRACTICAL GUIDE TO ITALIAN CONVERSATION. By Eugene Camerini. With a complete Vocabulary. By Henry P. Skelton. Post 8vo., pp. vi., 128 and 98. Cloth. 1860. 4s. 6d.

Eco de Madrid.—THE ECHO OF MADRID. A Practical Guide to Spanish Conversation. By J. E. Hartzenbusch, and Henry Lemming. With a complete Vocabulary, containing Copious Explanatory Remarks. By Henry Lemming. Post 8vo., pp. xii., 144 and 83. Cloth. 1860. 5s.

Edalji.—A DICTIONARY, GUJARÁTÍ AND ENGLISH. By Shápurjí Edalji. Second edition. 8vo. pp. xxiv. 874, cloth. 1868. £1 1s.

Edalji.—A GRAMMAR OF THE GUJARÁTÍ LANGUAGE. By Shapurji Edalji. Crown 8vo. cloth, pp. 127. 1867. 10s. 6d.

Edda SÆMUNDAR HINNS FRODA. The Edda of Sœmund the Wise. Translated from the Old Norse, with a Mythological Index. Part First. Mythological. 12mo. cloth, pp. viii. and 152. 1866. 3s. 6d.

Edda SÆMUNDAR HINNS FRODA. The Edda of Sœmund the Learned. From the Old Norse or Icelandic. Part II., Historical. 12mo. cloth, pp. viii. and 170. London, 1866. 4s.

Edda SÆMUNDAR HINNS FRODA. The Edda of Sœmund the Learned. Translated from the Old Norse, by Benjamin Thorpe. Complete in 1 vol. fcap. 8vo. cloth, pp. viii. 152, and pp. viii. 170. 1866. 7s. 6d.

Edgar.—MODERN TIMES, THE LABOUR QUESTION, AND THE FAMILY. A Brief Statement of Facts and Principles. By Henry Edgar. 12mo. sowed, pp. 24. 3d.

Edgar.—THE POSITIVIST'S CALENDAR; or, Transitional System of Public Commemoration, instituted by Auguste Comte, Founder of the Positive. Religion of Humanity. With a Brief Exposition of Religious Positivism. By Henry Edgar. 12mo. sewed, pp. 103. 1856. 2s. 6d.

Edge.—MAJOR-GENERAL MCCLELLAN AND THE CAMPAIGN ON THE YORKTOWN PENINSULA. By Frederick Milnes Edge. With a map of the Peninsula, drawn expressly for this work, by James Wyld, Geographer to the Queen. 12mo. pp. iv. and 204. 1865. 4s.

Edwards.—MEMOIRS OF LIBRARIES, together with a Practical Handbook of Library Economy. By Edward Edwards. 2 vols. roy. 8vo. Numerous illustrations. Cloth. Vol. 1, pp. xxviii. and 841. Vol. 2. pp. xxxvi. and 1104. 1859. £2 8s.

Ditto, large paper, imperial 8vo. cloth. £4 4s.

Edwards.—CHAPTERS OF THE BIOGRAPHICAL HISTORY OF THE FRENCH ACADEMY. 1629—1863. With an Appendix relating to the Unpublished Chronicle "Liber de Hyda." By Edward Edwards, Esq. 1 vol. 8vo., pp. 180. cloth. 1864. 6*s*.
Ditto, large paper. Roy. 8vo. 10*s*. 6*d*.

Edwards.—LIBRARIES AND FOUNDERS OF LIBRARIES. By Edward Edwards. 8vo. cloth, pp. xix. and 506. 1865. 18*s*.
Ditto, large paper, imperial 8vo. cloth. £1 10*s*.

Edkins.—A GRAMMAR OF THE CHINESE COLLOQUIAL LANGUAGE, COMMONLY CALLED THE MANDARIN DIALECT. By Joseph Edkins. 8vo., pp. viii. and 266, sewed. 1857. 20*s*.

Edkins.—PROGRESSIVE LESSONS IN THE CHINESE SPOKEN LANGUAGE, with Lists of Common Words and Phrases, and an Appendix, containing the laws of tones in the Peking dialect. 8vo., pp. vi. and 104, sewed. 1862. 12*s*.

Eger and Grime.—AN EARLY ENGLISH ROMANCE. Edited from Bishop Percy's Folio Manuscripts, about 1650 A.D. By John W. Hales, M.A., Fellow and late Assistant Tutor of Christ's College, Cambridge, and Frederick J. Furnivall, M.A., of Trinity Hall, Cambridge. 4to. large paper. Half bound, Roxburgh style, pp. 64. 1867. 10*s*. 6*d*.

Elder.—BIOGRAPHY OF ELISHA KENT KANE. By William Elder. 8vo. pp. 416. Cloth. 1858. 12*s*.

Ellet.—THE MISSISSIPPI AND OHIO RIVERS: containing Plans for the Protection of the Delta from inundation, and Investigations of the Practicability and Cost of Improving the Navigation of the Ohio, and other Rivers, by means of Reservoirs. With an Appendix on the Bars at the Mouths of the Mississippi. By Charles Ellet, Junior, Civil Engineer. 8vo. pp. 368. Cloth. 1853. 16*s*.

Elliott.—THE HISTORY OF INDIA AS TOLD BY ITS OWN HISTORIANS. The Muhammadan Period. Edited from the Posthumous Papers of the late Sir H. M. Elliott, K.C.B., East India Company's Bengal Civil Service. By Professor John Dowson, M.R.A.S., Staff College, Sandhurst. Vol. I. 8vo. cloth, pp. xxxii. and 541. 1867. 18*s*. To be completed in three volumes.

Elliott.—MEMOIRS ON THE HISTORY, PHILOLOGY, AND ETHNIC DISTRIBUTION OF THE RACES OF THE NORTH-WEST PROVINCES OF INDIA: being an amplified Edition of the Glossary of Indian Terms. By the late Sir H. M. Elliott, K.C.B. Arranged from M.S. materials collected by him, and Edited by Reinhold Rost, Ph. D., Secretary to the Royal Asiatic Society. 2 vols. 8vo. In the press.

Emerson.—THE YOUNG AMERICAN. A Lecture. By Ralph Waldo Emerson. 8vo., pp. 24. 1844. 1*s*.

Emerson.—REPRESENTATIVE MEN. Seven Lectures. By R. W. Emerson. Post 8vo., pp. 215, cloth. 1850. 6*s*.

Emerson.—ESSAYS. By Ralph Waldo Emerson. First Series, embodying the Corrections and Editions of the last American edition; with an Introductory Preface, by Thomas Carlyle, reprinted by permission, from the first English Edition. Post 8vo. pp. viii. and 192, sewed. 1853. 2*s*.

Emerson.—ESSAYS. By Ralph Waldo Emerson. Second Series, with Preface by Thomas Carlyle. Post 8vo. cloth, pp. vi. and 190, 1858. 3*s*. 6*d*.

Emerson.—POEMS. By Ralph Waldo Emerson. 16mo. cloth. Blue and Gold Series, pp. 254. With portrait. 1865. 5s.

Emerson.—ESSAYS. By Ralph Waldo Emerson. First and Second Series. Blue and Gold Edition. 16mo. cloth, gilt edges, pp. iv. and 515. 5s.

Emperor OF AUSTRIA VERSUS LOUIS KOSSUTH. A few words of Common Sense. By an Hungarian. 8vo. pp. 28. 1861. 1s.

Epistle, AN. In Familiar Verse. To a Young Statesman. By a Loyal Subject. Post 8vo. sewed, pp. 11. 1867. 6d.

Ethnological Journal.—A Monthly Record of Ethnological Research and Criticism. Edited by Luke Burke. July, 1865, to March, 1866. Nos. 1 to 7, 1s, each; 8 and 9, 4d. each.

Ethnological Journal.—A MAGAZINE OF ETHNOGRAPHICAL AND ANTIQUARIAN SCIENCE. Edited by Luke Burke. New Series. No. 1. January, 1854. 8vo. pp. 90, sewed. 3s. 6d. (No more published.)

Everett.—SELF GOVERNMENT IN THE UNITED STATES. By the Hon. Edward Everett. 8vo., pp. 44, sewed. 1860. 1s.

Everett.—THE QUESTIONS OF THE DAY. An Address. By Edward Everett. Royal 8vo. sewed, pp. 46. 1861. 1s. 6d.

Ewbank.—A DESCRIPTIVE AND HISTORICAL ACCOUNT OF HYDRAULIC AND OTHER MACHINES FOR RAISING WATER, Ancient and Modern, with Observations on various Subjects connected with the Mechanic Arts: including the progressive Development of the Steam Engine; Descriptions of every variety of Bellows, Piston, and Rotary Pumps; Fire Engines, Water Rams, Pressure Engines, Air Machines, Eolipiles, etc.; Remarks on Ancient Wells, Air Beds, Cog Wheels, Blow Pipes, Bellows of various People, Magic Goblets, Steam Idols, and other Machinery of Ancient Temples. To which are added, Experiments of Blowing and Spouting Tubes, and other original Devices, Natures, Modes, and Machinery for raising Water; Historical Notices respecting Siphons, Fountains, Water Organs, Clepsydræ, Pipes, Valves, Cocks, etc. In Five Books, illustrated by nearly 300 Engravings. 15th edition, with additional matter. By Thomas Ewbank. 8vo. cloth, pp. 624. 1864. 21s.

Exposition (AN), OF SPIRITUALISM; comprising Two Series of Letters, and a review of the *Spiritual Magazine*, No. 20. As published in the *Star and Dial*. With Introduction, Notes, and Appendix. By Sceptic. Crown 8vo. sewed, pp. xiv. and 314. Cloth. 1862. 6s.

Falkener.—A DESCRIPTION OF SOME IMPORTANT THEATRES AND OTHER REMAINS IN CRETE. From a MS. History of Candia, by Onorio Belli, in 1586. Being a Supplement to the "Museum of Classical Antiquities." Illustrations and nine Plates. By Edward Falkener. Pp. 32, royal 8vo. cloth. 1854. 5s. 6d.

Farm (HOW TO GET A) AND WHERE TO FIND ONE. Showing that Homesteads may be had by those desirous of securing them, with the Public Law on the subject of Free Homes, and suggestions from Practical Farmers, together with numerous successful experiences of others, who, though beginning with little or nothing, have become the owners of ample farms. By the Author of "Ten Acres Enough." Second edition, pt. 8vo. pp. 345. Cloth. 6s.

Faulkner.—A Dictionary of Commercial Terms, with their Synonyms in various Languages. By Alexander Faulkner, Assistant Commissioner of Customs, Salt and Opium. Author of the "Orientalist's Grammatical Vade-Mecum," etc. 12mo., pp. iii. and 158, and vii. Half-bound. 1866. 4s.

Fay.—Great Outline of Geography for High Schools and Families. By Theodore S. Fay. With an Atlas of 8 plates in folio. 12mo., pp. viii. and 238. Boards. 1867. 16s.

Felton.—Selections from Modern Greek Writers, in Prose and Poetry. With Notes. By Dr. C. C. Felton. 8vo. cloth, pp. xv. and 216. 1857. 6s.

Felton.—Greece, Ancient and Modern. Lectures delivered before the Lowell Institute. By C. C. Felton, LL.D., late President of Harvard University. Two vols., 8vo. cloth, pp. vi. 511, and iv. 549. 1867. 28s.

Feuerbach.—The Essence of Christianity. By Ludwig Feuerbach. Translated from the Second German Edition, by Marian Evans, translator of Strauss's "Life of Jesus." Large post 8vo. cloth, pp. xx. and 340. 1864. 10s. 6d.

Fichte.—The Characteristics of the Present Age. By Johann Gottlieb Fichte. Translated from the German by William Smith. Post 8vo. cloth, pp. xi. and 271. 1847. 6s.

"We accept these lectures as a true and most admirable delineation of the present age; and on this ground alone we should bestow on them our heartiest recommendation; but it is because they teach us how we may rise above the age, that we bestow on them our most emphatic praise.

"He makes us think, and perhaps more sublimely than we have ever formerly thought, but it is only in order that we may the more nobly act.

"As a majestic and most stirring utterance from the lips of the greatest German prophet, we trust that the book will find a response in many an English soul, and potently help to regenerate English society."—*The Critic.*

Fichte.—The Vocation of a Scholar. By Johann Gottlieb Fichte. Translated from the German by William Smith. Post 8vo. cloth. Pp. 78, sewed, 1847. 2s.

"'The Vocation of a Scholar .... is distinguished by the same high moral tone, and manly, vigorous expression' which characterise all Fichte's works in the German, and is nothing lost in Mr. Smith's clear, unembarrassed, and thoroughly English translation."—*Douglas Jerrold's Newspaper.*

"We are glad to see this excellent translation of one of the best of Fichte's works presented to the public in a very neat form .... No class needs and earnest and sincere spirit more than the literary class; and therefore the 'Vocation of the Scholar,' the 'Guide of the Human Race,' written in Fichte's most earnest, most commanding temper, will be welcomed in its English dress by public writers, and be beneficial to the cause of truth."—*Economist.*

Fichte.—The Vocation of Man. By Johann Gottlieb Fichte. Translated from the German by William Smith. Post 8vo. cloth, pp. xii. and 198. 1848. 4s.

"In the progress of my present work, I have taken a deeper glance into religion than ever I did before. In me the emotions of the heart proceed only from perfect intellectual clearness; it cannot be but the clearness I have now attained on this subject shall also take possession of my heart."—*Fichte's Correspondence.*

"'The Vocation of Man' is, as Fichte truly says, intelligible to all readers who are really able to understand a book at all; and as the history of the mind in its various phases of doubt, knowledge, and faith, it is of interest to all. A book of this stamp is sure to teach you much because it excites thought. If it rouses you to combat his conclusions, it has done a good work; for in that very effort you are stirred to a consideration of points which have hitherto escaped your indolent acquiescence.—*Foreign Quarterly.*

"This is Fichte's most popular work, and is every way remarkable."—*Atlas.*

"It appears to us the boldest and most emphatic attempt that has yet been made to explain to man his restless and unconquerable desire to win the True and the Eternal."—*Sentinel.*

Fichte.—ON THE NATURE OF THE SCHOLAR, AND ITS MANIFESTATIONS. By Johann Gottlieb Fichte. Translated from the German by William Smith. Second Edition. Cloth. Post 8vo. Pp. vii. and 131. 1848. 3s.

"With great satisfaction we welcome this first English translation of an author who occupies the most exalted position as a profound and original thinker; as an irresistible orator in the cause of what he believed to be the truth; as a thoroughly honest and heroic man.... The appearance of any of his works in our language is, we believe, a perfect novelty.... These orations are admirably fitted for their purpose; so grand is the position taken by the lecturer, and so irresistible their eloquence."—*Examiner*.

"This work must inevitably arrest the attention of the scientific physician, by the grand spirituality of its doctrines, and the pure morality it teaches ... Shall we be presumptuous if we recommend these views to our professional brethren? or if we say to the enlightened, the thoughtful, the serious. This—if you be true scholars—is *your* Vocation? We know not a higher morality than this, or more noble principles than these: they are full of truth."—*British and Foreign Medico-Chirurgical Review*.

Fichte.—MEMOIR OF JOHANN GOTTLIEB FICHTE. By William Smith. Second Edition. Post 8vo. Cloth. Pp. 168. 1848. 4s.

"..... A Life of Fichte, full of nobleness and instruction, of grand purpose, tender feeling, and brave effort ! ... the compilation of which is executed with great judgment and fidelity."—*Prospective Review*.

"We state Fichte's character as it is known and admitted by men of all parties among the Germans, when we say that so robust an intellect, a soul so calm, so lofty, so massive, and immoveable, has not mingled in philosophical discussion since the time of Luther .... Fichte's opinions may be true or false; but his character can be slightly valued only by such as know it ill; and as a man, approved by action and suffering, in his life and in his death, he ranks with a class of men who were common only in better ages than ours."—*State of German Literature, by Thomas Carlyle.*

Fichte.—THE WAY TOWARDS A BLESSED LIFE; OR, THE DOCTRINE OF RELIGION. By Johann Gottlieb Fichte. Translated by William Smith. Post 8vo. Cloth. Pp. viii. and 221. 1849. 5s.

Fichte.—THE POPULAR WORKS OF JOHANN GOTTLIEB FICHTE. Translated from the German, with a Memoir of the Author, by William Smith. 2 vols. Post 8vo. Cloth. Pp. 554, and pp. viii. and 529. 1859. 20s.

Fichte.—THE SCIENCE OF KNOWLEDGE. By J. G. Fichte. Translated from the German by A. E. Kroeger. Crown 8vo., pp. 378. Cloth. 1868. 8s.

Filippo Malincontri; OR, STUDENT LIFE IN VENETIA. An Autobiography. Edited by Girolamo Volpe. Translated from the unpublished Italian MS. by C. B. Cayley, B.A. Two vols., post 8vo. Pp. xx. and 646. 1861. 18s.

Fitzgerald.—THE BOSTON MACHINIST. Being a Complete School for the Apprentice as well as the Advanced Machinist, showing how to make and use every tool in every branch of the business, with a Treatise on Screw and Gear Cutting. By Walter Fitzgerald, Inventor and Mechanical Engineer. 12mo. cloth, pp. 80. 1866. 2s. 6d.

Fletcher.—ANALYSIS OF BENTHAM'S THEORY OF LEGISLATION. By G. W. H. Fletcher, LL.B., of the Civil Service Commission. 12mo. cloth, pp. ix. and 86. 1864. 2s. 6d.

Fox.—THE SERVICE IN COMMEMORATION OF WILLIAM JOHNSON FOX, late M.P. for Oldham, and Minister at South Place, Finsbury. At Finsbury Chapel, on Sunday Morning, June 12, 1864. By M. D. Conway. Post 8vo., sewed, pp. 23. 1864. 6d.

Fox.—Memorial Edition of Collected Works, by W. J. Fox :—
Vol. 1. Lectures, Lessons, etc., prior to 1824. 8vo. cloth, pp. 390. 1865. 5s.
Vol. 2. Christ and Christianity. 8vo. cloth, pp. 355. 1865. 5s.
Vol. 3. Miscellaneous Lectures and Sermons, and Twenty Sermons on Principles of Morality Inculcated in Holy Scripture. 8vo. cloth, pp. 350. 1865. 5s.
Vol. 4. Anti-Corn Law Speeches and occasional Speeches. 8vo. cloth, pp. 378. 1866. 5s.
Vol. 5. Letters on the Corn Laws. By a Norwich Weaver Boy, and Extracts from Letters by Publicola. 8vo. cloth, pp. 325. 1866. 5s.
Vol. 6. Miscellaneous Essays, Political, Literary, Critical, and Biographical. From the *Retrospective Review, Westminster Review, Monthly Repository, Morning Chronicle*, etc. 8vo. cloth, pp. 424. 1867. 5s.
Vol. 7. Reports of Lectures at South Place Chapel, Finsbury. 8vo. cloth, pp. 312. 1865. 5s.
Vol. 8. Reports of Lectures at South Place Chapel, Finsbury. 8vo. cloth, pp. 321. 1865. 5s.
Vol. 9. Reports of Lectures at South Place Chapel, Finsbury, supplementary to the Course on the Religious Ideas. 8vo. cloth, pp. 323. 1867. 5s.
Vol. 10. Reports of Lectures at South Place Chapel, Finsbury, supplementary to the Course on the Religious Ideas, and Miscellaneous Lectures. 8vo. cloth, pp. 314. 1867. 5s.
Vol. 11. Reports of Miscellaneous Lectures at South Place Chapel, Finsbury. 8vo. cloth, pp. vi. and 322. 1868. 5s.
Vol. 12. Reports of Miscellaneous Lectures at South Place Chapel, Finsbury. 8vo. cloth, pp. viii. and 358. 1868. 5s.

Foxton.—The Priesthood and the People. By Frederick J. Foxton, A.B., Author of "Popular Christianity," etc. 8vo., pp. 58, sewed. 1862. 1s. 6d.

Foxton.—Popular Christianity; its Transition State, and Probable Development. By Frederick J. Foxton, A.B., formerly of Pembroke College, Oxford, and Perpetual Curate of Stoke Prior and Docklow, Herefordshire. Post 8vo. cloth, pp. ix. and 226. 1849. 5s.

Francis.—Lowell Hydraulic Experiments. Being a selection from experiments on Hydraulic Motors, on the Flow of Water over Weirs, in Open Canals of Uniform Rectangular Section and through Submerged Orifices and Diverging Tubes, made at Lowell, Massachusetts. By James B. Francis, Civil Engineer, Member of the American Society of Civil Engineers and Architects, Fellow of the American Academy of Arts and Sciences, Member of the American Philosophical Society, etc. Second Edition. Revised and enlarged. With many new experiments and additional illustrations. 4to., pp. 250, 23 plates. Cloth. 1868. £3 3s.

Franklin.—Life and Times of Benjamin Franklin. By James Parton. With Steel Portraits. Two vols. 8vo., pp. 1,336. 1864. 21s.

Free Press (Publications of the):
Reasons for demanding Investigations into the Charges against Lord Palmerston. 8vo., pp. 19. 1840. 1s.
The Crisis—France in Face of the Four Powers. With Supplement, by David Urquhart. 8vo., pp. 58. 1840. 1s.
The Sulphur Monopoly. By David Urquhart. 8vo., pp. 8. 1840. 3d.
The Edinburgh Review and the Affghan War. By David Urquhart. 8vo., pp. 61. 1843. 6d.
A Fragment of the History of Servia, 1843. By David Urquhart. 8vo., pp. 96. 6d.
An Appeal against Faction. By David Urquhart. 8vo., pp. 56. 1843. 1s.

FREE PRESS (Publications of the)—*continued*.
- CANADA UNDER SUCCESSIVE ADMINISTRATIONS. By David Urquhart. 8vo., pp. 100. 1844. 1s.
- THE CHANNEL ISLANDS—NORMAN LAWS AND MODERN PRACTICE. 8vo., pp. 32. 1844. 6d.
- PUBLIC OPINION AND ITS ORGANS. By David Urquhart. 8vo., pp. 94. 1855. 6d.
- THE SERF AND THE COSSACK. By Francis Marx. 8vo., pp. 60. 1855. 6d.
- TUCKER'S POLITICAL FLY SHEETS. 8vo. 1855. 3s. Containing:—Palmerston and Poland; Palmerston, what has he done? England's Part in Turkey's Fall; War *for* Russia—not against Russia; Louis Napoléon, Russia, Circassia; the Invasion of the Crimea; the Words of Palmerston; the Spider and the Fly; the Home Face of the Four Points.
- THE FREE PRESS SERIALS. 8vo. 1855-56. Containing:—The Nation Cheated out of its Food; Visit of David Urquhart to the Hungarian Exiles at Kutayah; Contradictions of Lord Clarendon in reference to Corn; The Story of the Life of Lord Palmerston; the Affghan War; the Will of Peter the Great.
- PARLIAMENTARY USURPATIONS in reference to Money Cognizance and Suppression of Treason by leading Statesmen and Diplomatists; Betrayal of Denmark to Russia; the Chartist Correspondence; Selections from the Blue Books as Materials for Study, by Gustavus; the Danger of the Political Balance of Europe; Crimes of Louis Philip; Report of the Newcastle Committee on the Union of the Principalities.
- REPORTS OF COMMITTEES OF THE BIRMINGHAM CONFERENCE, ON THE RIGHT OF SEARCH AND NEWSPAPER FOLIO. 6d.
- THE PROPOSED BASIS OF PACIFICATION KNOWN AS THE FOUR POINTS. 1855. 1s.
- NEWCASTLE COMMITTEE REPORTS, ON THE LIMITATION OF THE SUPPLY OF GRAIN, AND CONSTITUTIONAL REMARKS. 8vo., pp. 48. 1855. 6d.
- FAMILIAR WORDS AS AFFECTING ENGLAND AND THE ENGLISH. 8vo., pp. 350. 1856. 2s.
- THE TURKISH BATH, WITH A VIEW TO ITS INTRODUCTION INTO THE BRITISH DOMINIONS. 8vo., pp. 68. 1856. 1s.
- THE QUEEN AND THE PREMIER. 8vo., pp. 32. 1857. 6d.
- THE REBELLION OF INDIA. By David Urquhart. 8vo., pp. 46. 1s.
- THE HOSTILITIES AT CANTON. By Augustus G. Stapleton. 8vo., pp. 16. 1857. 6d.
- THE IMMEDIATE CAUSE OF THE INDIAN MUTINY. By G. Crawshay. 8vo., pp. 28. 1857. 6d.
- THE REPORT OF THE EAST INDIAN COMMITTEE OF THE COLONIAL SOCIETY ON THE MILITARY OPERATIONS IN CHINA. 8vo., pp. 67. 1857. 6d.
- THE REPORT OF THE BRADFORD COMMITTEE WHAT CONSTITUTES LAWFUL WAR. 8vo., pp. 24. 1857.
- THE SRADDHA, THE KEYSTONE OF THE BRAHMINICAL, BUDDHISTIC, AND ARIAN RELIGIONS. By David Urquhart. 8vo., pp. 43. 1858. 1s.
- THE GROWTH OF RUSSIAN POWER, CONTINGENT ON THE DECAY OF THE BRITISH CONSTITUTION. 8vo., pp. 18. 1858. 6d.
- PROSELYTISM DESTRUCTIVE OF CHRISTIANITY, 8vo., pp. 44. By G. Crawshay. 1858. 1s.
- CATASTROPHE OF THE EAST INDIA COMPANY. By G. Crawshay. 8vo., pp. 21. 1858. 6d.
- KOSSUTH AND URQUHART. Estrath di una Corrispondenza. 8vo., pp. 40. 1859. 1s.
- HOW RUSSIA TRIES TO GET INTO HER HANDS THE SUPPLY OF CORN OF THE WHOLE OF EUROPE. 8vo., pp. 24. 1859. 6d.
- THE EUROPEAN COMPLICATION EXPLAINED. By G. Crawshay. 8vo., pp. 10 1859. 6d.

FREE PRESS (Publications of the)—*continued*.

DAVID URQUHART ON THE ITALIAN WAR. To which is added a Memoir of Europe, drawn up for the Instruction of the present Emperor of Russia. 8vo., pp. 40. 1859. 1s.

THE RUSSO-DUTCH QUESTION. Obligations of England to Russia contracted to ensure the maintenance of the Kingdom of Poland, and paid for its Suppression. 4to., pp. 15. 6d.

A LETTER ON THE DANGER TO ENGLAND OF AUSTRIA'S SUBJUGATION. 8vo., pp. 8. 1859. 6d.

THE AFFGHAN PAPERS. Report and Petition of the Newcastle Foreign Affairs Association. 8vo., pp. 32. 1860. 6d.

THE INVASION OF ENGLAND. By David Urquhart. 8vo., pp. 18. 3d.

THE DUKE OF COBURG'S PAMPHLET. THE DESPOTS AS REVOLUTIONISTS. 8vo., pp. 31. 1s.

PALMERSTON UNMASKED. Answer to Ismail's Reply to the Duke of Coburg's Pamphlet. By Edward Fischel. 8vo., pp. 51. 1s.

SUCCESSION TO THE CROWN OF DENMARK. Speech of Lord R. Montague. 8vo., pp. 24. 1861. 1s.

THE PACIFIC AND THE AMAAR. By Francis Mark. 8vo., pp. 28. 1s.

THE DEFENCE OF ENGLAND. Nine Letters by a Journeyman Shoemaker. 8vo., pp. 34. 1862. 6d.

CIRCASSIA. Speech of S. E. Rolland at Preston. 8vo., dp. 34. 1862. 1s.

THE RIGHT OF SEARCH. Two Speeches, by David Urquhart. January 20 and 27. 8vo., pp. 103. 1862. 1s.

THE CIRCASSIAN WAR AND POLISH INSURRECTION. SECRET OF RUSSIA IN THE CASPIANA EUXINE. 8vo., pp. 102. 1863. 1s.

THE EXPEDITION OF THE CHESEPEAKE TO CIRCASSIA. 8vo., pp. 18 1864. 6d.

THE NEW HERESY—PROSELYTISM SUBSTITUTED FOR RIGHTEOUSNESS. By David Urquhart. 4to., pp. 19. 1862. 6d.

THE REASON FOR ABROGATING THE TREATY OF LONDON OF MAY 8TH, 1852. Presented by a Deputation from the Lancashire Foreign Affairs Committee. 4to., pp. 15. 6d.

THE STORY OF THE CRIMEAN WAR. From the *Times* and *Herald* Correspondents, and the evidence before the Sebastopol Committee. 4to., pp. 24. 3d.

DEBATES ON THE MOTION FOR PAPERS, WITH A VIEW TO THE IMPEACHMENT OF VISCOUNT PALMERSTON. 4to., pp. 59. 1s. 6d.

Friedrich.—PROGRESSIVE GERMAN READER, with Copious Notes to the First Part. By P. Friedrich. Crown 8vo., pp. 166. Cloth. 1868. 4s. 6d.

Froembling.—GRADUATED GERMAN READER, consisting of a selection from the most popular writers, arranged progressively; with a complete Vocabulary for the first part. By Friedrich Otto Froembling. 12mo., pp. viii. and 256. Cloth. 1867. 3s. 6d.

Frœmbling.—GRADUATED EXERCISES FOR TRANSLATION INTO GERMAN. Consisting of Extracts from the best English Authors, arranged progressively; with an Appendix, containing Idiomatic Notes. By Friedrich Otto Frœmbling, Ph.D., Principal German Master at the City of London School. Crown 8vo., cloth, pp xiv. and 322. With Notes, pp. 66. 1867. 4s. 6d. Without Exercises, 4s.

Froude.—THE BOOK OF JOB. By J. A. Froude, M.A., late Fellow of Exeter College, Oxford. Reprinted from the *Westminster Review*. New Series, No. 7. 8vo., sewed, pp. 38. 1853. 8*d*.

Fruston.—ECHO FRANÇAIS. A Practical Guide to French Conversation. By F. de la Fruston. With a Vocabulary. 12mo., pp. vi. and 192. Cloth. 3*s*.

Fulton.—THE FACTS AND FALLACIES OF THE SABBATH QUESTION CONSIDERED SCRIPTURALLY. By Henry Fulton. 12mo., limp cloth, pp. 108. 1858. 1*s*. 6*d*.

Furnivall.—EDUCATION IN EARLY ENGLAND. Some Notes used as forewords to a Collection of Treatises on "Manners and Meals in Olden Times," for the Early English Text Society. By Frederick J. Furnivall, M.A. 8vo., sewed, pp. 4 and lxxiv. 1867. 1*s*.

Furnivall.—A CONCISE MIDDLE-ENGLISH DICTIONARY FOR THE PERIOD, 1250—1526, THE BEGINNING OF EARLY ENGLISH TO THE DATE OF THE FIRST ENGLISH NEW TESTAMENT. Edited by F. J. Furnivall, Esq., M.A. 8vo.

Galitzin.—EMANCIPATION-FANTASIA. Dedicated to the Russian people. By Prince George Galitzin. Partition to Orchestra and Piano Duet. Fol. pp. 38, sewed. 1861. 5*s*.

Galitzin.—THE HERZEN VALSE, for two performers on the pianoforte. Composed by Prince George Galitzin. Folio, pp. 20, sewed. 5*s*.

Gavazzi.—LECTURE. By Signor Gavazzi, on "Garibaldi," delivered at the Liverpool Institute, October 3rd, 1864. 12mo., sewed, pp. 20. 1864. 2*d*.

Geiger.—JUDAISM AND ITS HISTORY. By Dr. Abraham Geiger, Rabbi of the Israelitish Congregation at Frankfort. Translated by M. Mayer. Vol. I. Closing with the Destruction of the Second Temple. To which is added an Appendix. "Strauss and Rénan." 8vo., half-bound, pp. x. and 344. 1866. 10*s*. 6*d*.

Geological Magazine (The) ; OR MONTHLY JOURNAL OF GEOLOGY, with which is incorporated "The Geologist." Edited by Henry Woodward, F.G.S., F.Z.S., Honorary Member of the Geological Societies of Glasgow and Norwich; Corresponding Member of the Natural History Society of Montreal. Assisted by Professor John Morris, F.G.S., etc., etc., and Robert Etheridge, F.R.S.E., F.G.S. Volume III. 8vo. pp. 592, cloth. January to December, 1866. 20*s*. Volume IV. 8vo. pp. iv. and 584, cloth. January to December, 1867. 20*s*. Continued monthly.

Germany and Italy.—ANSWER TO MAZZINI'S "ITALY AND GERMANY." By Rodbertus, De Berg, and L. Bucher. 8vo., pp. 20, sewed. 1861. 1*s*.

Gervinus.—THE MISSION OF THE GERMAN CATHOLICS. By G. G. Gervinus, Professor of History in the University of Heidelberg. Translated from the German. Post 8vo., sewed, pp. iv. and 66. 1846. 1*s*.

Gesenius.—HEBREW GRAMMAR. Translated from the 17th edition by Dr. T. J. Conant, including the corrections and additions of Dr. E. Rödiger, with Grammatical Exercises and Chrestomathy, by the Translator. 8vo. cloth. pp. xv. and 297. Exercises, pp. 20. Chrestomathy, pp. 64. 1864. 10s. 6d.

Gesenius.—HEBREW AND ENGLISH LEXICON OF THE OLD TESTAMENT, including the Biblical Chaldee. Translated by Edward Robinson, with corrections and additions by the Author. 14th Edition. Royal 8vo. cloth, pp. ix. and 1160. 1855. 25s.

Gessner.—LE DROIT DES NEUTRES SUR MER. Par L. Gessner. 8vo. Paper covers, pp. 437. 1865. 7s.

Ghose.—THE OPEN COMPETITION FOR THE CIVIL SERVICE OF INDIA. By Manomohan Ghose, of the Calcutta University and Lincolns' Inn. 8vo., sewed, pp. 68. 1866. 1s. 6d.

Giles.—HEBREW RECORDS. An Historical Enquiry concerning the Age, Authorship, and Authenticity of the Old Testament. By Rev. Dr. Giles, late Fellow of Corpus Christi College, Oxford. Second Edition. 8vo. pp. 356, cloth. 1853. 10s. 6d.

Gillespie.—A TREATISE ON LAND-SURVEYING; comprising the Theory developed from Five Elementary Principles; and the Practice with the Chain alone, the Compass, the Transit, the Theodolite, the Plain Table, etc. Illustrated by 400 Engravings and a Magnetic Chart. By W. M. GILLESPIE, LL.D., C.E. 8vo., cloth, pp. 424 and 84. 8th Edition. 1867. 16s.

Gillespie.—A MANUAL OF THE PRINCIPLES AND PRACTICE OF ROAD MAKING; comprising the Location, Construction, and Improvement of Roads (common, Macadam, paved, planked, etc.) and Railroads. By W. M. Gillespie, LL.D., C.E. Ninth Edition, with Additions. Post 8vo., cloth, pp. 372. 1867. 9s.

Gillmore.—ENGINEER AND ARTILLERY OPERATIONS against the Defences of Charleston Harbour in 1863, comprising the Descent upon Morris Island, the Demolition of Fort Sumter, the Reduction of Forts Wagner and Gregg, with Observations on Heavy Ordnance, Fortifications, etc. By G. A. Gillmore. Illustrated by 76 Plates and Engraved Views. 8vo. cloth, pp. vi. and 354. 1865. 45s.

Glennie.—KING ARTHUR; or, the Drama of the Revolution. By John S. Stuart Glennie, M.A., F.S.A., F.R.A.S., etc. Volume I., Prologue and Overture. 12mo. cloth, pp. vi. and 279. 1867. 7s. 6d.

Gliddon.—ANCIENT EGYPT. Her monuments, hieroglyphics, history, and archæology, and other subjects connected with hieroglyphical literature. By George R. Gliddon, late United States Consul at Cairo. Fifteenth edition. Revised and corrected, with an Appendix. 4to. pp. 68, sewed. 2s. 6d.

God's COMMANDMENTS, according to Moses, according to Christ, and according to our present knowledge. A Sketch suggestive of a New Westminster Confession of Faith. For the Laity of the 19th Century. Addressed to all who deem it their highest duty, as well as right, to think for themselves. 8vo., sewed, pp. 24. 1867. 6d.

Goethe.—FEMALE CHARACTERS OF GOETHE. From the original Drawings of William Kaulbach. With explanatory text, by George Henry Lewes. Folio, 21 full page steel engravings. Cloth, gilt. 1868. £7 7s.

Goethe's CORRESPONDENCE WITH A CHILD. 8vo., pp. viii. and 498. 1860. 7s. 6d.

Golden A. B. C.—Designed by Gustav König. Engraved by Julius Thater. Oblong, cloth. 6s.

Goldstücker.—A COMPENDIOUS SANSKRIT-ENGLISH DICTIONARY, for the Use of those who intend to read the Easier Works of Classical Sanskrit Literature. By Theodore Goldstücker. Small 4to., pp. 900, cloth. [In preparation.

Goldstücker.—A COMPENDIOUS GRAMMAR OF THE SANSKRIT LANGUAGE FOR BEGINNERS. By Theodore Goldstücker. 8vo. [In preparation.

Goldstücker.—A DICTIONARY, SANSKRIT AND ENGLISH, extended and improved from the second edition of the Dictionary of Professor H. H. Wilson, with his sanction and concurrence; together with a Supplement, Grammatical Appendices, and an Index, serving as a Sanskrit-English Vocabulary. By Theodore Goldstücker. Parts I. to VI. pp. 480. 1854-1864. Each 6s.

Goldstücker.—PANINI: His Place in Sanskrit Literature. An Investigation of some Literary and Chronological Questions which may be settled by a study of his Work. By Theodore Goldstücker. A separate impression of the Preface to the Facsimile of M.S. No. 17 in the Library of Her Majesty's Home Government for India, which contains a portion of the Manava-Kalpa-Sutra, with the Commentary of Kumarila-Swamin. Imperial 8vo., pp. 268, cloth. 1861. 12s.

Goldstücker. — MANAVA-KALPA-SUTRA; being a portion of this ancient work on Vaidik Rites, together with the Commentary of Kumarila-Swamin. A Facsimile of the MS. No. 17 in the Library of Her Majesty's Home Government for India. With a Preface by Theodore Goldstücker. Oblong folio, pp. 268, of letter press, and 121 leaves of facsimiles. Cloth. 1861. £4. 4s.

Goldstücker.—AUCTORES SANSCRITI. Edited for the Sanskrit Text Society, under the supervision of Theodore Goldstücker. Vol. I., containing the Jaiminiya-Nyâya-Mâlâ-Vistara. Parts I. to V. pp. 400, large 4to., sewed. 1865-7. 10s. each.

Golovin.—THE NATIONS OF RUSSIA AND TURKEY, AND THEIR Destiny. By Ivan Golovin, author of "The Caucasus." 2 vols. crown 8vo. pp. xvi. and 172; xvi. and 170. Cloth. 1854. 10s.

Gooroo Simple.—Strange Surprising Adventures of the Venerable G. S. and his Five Disciples, Noodle, Doodle, Wiseacre, Zany, and Foozle; adorned with Fifty Illustrations, drawn on wood, by Alfred Crowquill. A companion Volume to "Münchhausen" and "Owlglass," based upon the famous Tamul tale of the Gooroo Paramartan, and exhibiting, in the form of a skilfully-constructed consecutive narrative, some of the finest specimens of Eastern wit and humour. Elegantly printed on tinted paper, in crown 8vo., richly gilt ornamental cover, gilt edges, pp. 223. 1861. Price 10s. 6d.

Gould.—GOOD ENGLISH, OR POPULAR ERRORS IN LANGUAGE. By Edward S. Gould, author of "Abridgment of Alison's Europe. Crown 8vo. cloth, pp. v. and 228. 1867. 6s.

Grammatography.—A MANUAL OF REFERENCE to the Alphabets of Ancient and Modern Languages. Based on the German Compilation of F. Ballhorn. In one vol. royal 8vo. cloth. pp. 80. 1861. 7s. 6d.

The "Grammatography" is offered to the public as a compendious introduction to the reading of the most important Ancient and Modern Languages. Simple in its design, it will be consulted with advantage by the Philological Student, the Amateur Linguist, the Bookseller, the Corrector of the Press, and the diligent Compositor.

ALPHABETICAL INDEX.

Afghan (or Pushto).	German.	Numidian.
Amharic.	Glagolitic.	Old Slavonic (or Cyrillic).
Anglo-Saxon.	Gothic.	Palmyrenian.
Arabic.	Greek.	Persian.
Arabic Ligatures.	Greek Ligatures.	Persian Cuneiform.
Aramaic.	Greek (Archaic).	Phœnician.
Archaic Characters.	Gujerati (or Guzerattee)	Polish.
Armenian.	Hieratic.	Pushto (or Afghan).
Assyrian Cuneiform.	Hieroglyphics.	Romaic (or Modern Greek).
Bengali.	Hebrew.	Russian.
Bohemian (Czechian).	Hebrew (Archaic).	Runes.
Bugis.	Hebrew (Rabbinical).	Samaritan.
Burmese.	Hebrew (Judæo-German).	Sanscrit.
Canarese (or Carnâtaca).	Hebrew (current hand).	Servian.
Chinese.	Hungarian.	Slavonic (Old).
Coptic.	Illyrian.	Sorbian (or Wendish).
Croato-Glagolitic.	Irish.	Swedish.
Cufic.	Italian (Old).	Syriac.
Cyrillic (or Old Slavonic).	Japanese.	Tamil.
Czechian (or Bohemian).	Javanese.	Telugu.
Danish.	Lettish.	Tibetan.
Demotic.	Mantshu.	Turkish.
Estrangelo.	Median Cuneiform.	Wallachian.
Ethiopic.	Modern Greek (or Romaic).	Wendish (or Sorbian).
Etruscan.	Mongolian.	Zend.
Georgian.		

Grattan.—CONSIDERATIONS ON THE HUMAN MIND, its Present State and Future Destination. By Richard Grattan, Esq., M.D., ex M.P. 8vo. cloth, pp. 336. 1861. 8s.

Grattan.—THE RIGHT TO THINK. An Address to the Young Men of Great Britain and Ireland. By Richard Grattan, M.D. Crown 8vo. stiff covers, pp. 134. 1865. 2s. 6d.

Gray.—MANUAL OF THE BOTANY OF THE NORTHERN UNITED STATES, including Virginia, Kentucky, and all east of the Mississippi; arranged according to the Natural System. Third Revised Edition, with Garden Botany, etc. By Asa Gray. With six plates, illustrating the Genera of Ferns, etc. 8vo. half-bound. pp. xcviii. and 606. 1862. 10s. 6d.

Gray.—FIRST LESSONS IN BOTANY AND VEGETABLE PHYSIOLOGY. Illustrated by 360 wood engravings, with copious Dictionary of Botanical Terms. By Dr. Asa Gray. 8vo. half-bound, pp. xii. and 236. 1866. 6s.

Gray.—INTRODUCTION TO STRUCTURAL AND SYSTEMATIC BOTANY, AND VEGETABLE PHYSIOLOGY. By Dr. Asa Gray. With 1300 woodcuts. 8vo. cloth, pp. 1866. 10s. 6d.

Gray.—NATURAL SELECTION NOT INCONSISTENT WITH NATURAL THEOLOGY. A free examination of Darwin's treatise on the Origin of Species, and of its American reviewers. By Asa Gray, M.D., Fisher Professor of Natural Philosophy in Harvard University. 8vo. pp. 56, sewed. 1861. 1s. 6d.

Gray.—HOW PLANTS GROW: A Simple Introduction to Structural Botany. By Asa Gray, M.D. Square 8vo., boards. New edition. pp. 233. 1866. 6s.

Green.—SHAKESPEARE AND THE EMBLEM WRITERS OF HIS AGE; with Illustrations from the original Woodcuts and Engravings. By Henry Green, M.A. In one volume, demy 8vo., of about 400 pages, and upwards of 100 Illustrative Woodcuts or Engravings. [In the press.

Greg.—THE CREED OF CHRISTENDOM: its Foundation and Superstructure. By William Rathbone Greg. Second Edition. Crown 8vo. pp. xx. and 280. 1863. 6s.

Greg.—LITERARY AND SOCIAL JUDGMENTS. By William Rathbone Greg. In One Volume, cr. 8vo.

Grey.—HANDBOOK OF AFRICAN, AUSTRALIAN, AND POLYNESIAN PHILOLOGY, etc., as represented in the Library of His Excellency Sir George Grey, K.C.B., Her Majesty's High Commissioner of the Cape Colony. Classed, Annotated, and Edited by Sir George Grey and Dr. H. I. Bleek.

- Vol. I. Part 1.—South Africa.' 8vo. pp. 186, sewed. 1858. 7s. 6d.
- Vol. I. Part 2.—Africa (North of the Tropic of Capricorn). 8vo. pp. 70, sewed. 1858. 2s.
- Vol. I. Part 3.—Madagascar. 8vo. pp. 24, sewed. 1859. 1s.
- Vol. II. Part 1.—Australia. 8vo. pp. iv. and 44, sewed. 1858. 1s. 6d.
- Vol. II. Part 2.—Papuan Languages of the Loyalty Islands and New Hebrides, comprising those of the Islands of Nengone, Lifu, Aneitum, Tana, and others. 8vo. pp. 12, sewed, 1858. 6d.
- Vol. II. Part 3.—Fiji Islands and Rotuma (with Supplement to Part II., Papuan Languages, and Part I., Australia). 8vo. pp. 34, sewed. 1859. 1s.
- Vol. II. Part 4.—New Zealand, the Chatham Islands, and Auckland Islands. 8vo. pp. 76, sewed. 1858. 3s. 6d.
- Vol. II. Part 4.—(Continuation).—Polynesia and Borneo, 8vo. pp. 77–154, sewed. 1859 3s. 6d.
- Vol. III. Part 1.—Manuscripts and Incunables. 8vo. pp. viii. and 24. 1862. 2s.
- Vol. IV. Part 1.—England. Early Printed Books. 8vo. pp. 264, sewed. 1867. 12s.

Grey.—MAORI MEMENTOS: being a Series of Addresses, presented by the Native People to His Excellency Sir George Grey, K.C.B., F.R.S. With Introduction, Remarks, and Explanatory Notes. To which is added a small Collection of Laments, etc. By Charles Oliver B. Davis. 8vo. Pp. 227. Aukland, 1855. 12s.

Gross.—A SYSTEM OF SURGERY, PATHOLOGICAL, DIAGNOSTIC, THERAPEUTIC, AND OPERATIVE. By Samuel D. Gross, M.D. Illustrated by more than 1,300 engravings. Fourth Edition, much enlarged, and carefully revised. 2 vols. 8vo. sheep, pp. xxxi. 1049, and xxviii. 1087. 1866. £3 3s.

Grote.—REVIEW of the Work of Mr. John Stuart Mill, entitled "Examination of Sir William Hamilton's Philosophy." By George Grote, author of "The History of Ancient Greece," "Plato, and the other Companions of Socrates," etc. 12mo. pp. 112, cloth. 1868. 3s. 6d.

Grout.—THE ISIZULU. A Grammar of the Zulu Language; accompanied with a Historical Introduction, also with an Appendix. By Rev. Lewis Grout. 8vo. cloth, pp. liii. and 432. 1859. 21s.

Grout.—ZULU-LAND; or, Life among the Zulu-Kafirs of Natal and Zulu-Land, South Africa. With Map and Illustrations, largely from Original Photographs. By the Rev. Lewis Grout. Crown 8vo. cloth, pp. 352. 7s. 6d.

Groves.—JOHN GROVES. A Tale of the War. By S. E. De M——. 12mo. Pp. 16, sewed. London, 1846. 2d.

Guizot.—MÉDITATIONS SUR L'ESSENCE DE LA RELIGION CHRETIENNE. Par M. Guizot. 12mo. paper. Pp. 384. 1864. 4s. 6d.

Gunderode.—CORRESPONDENCE OF FRÄULEIN GUNDERODE and BETTINA VON ARNIM. Cr. 8vo. cloth, pp. 356. 1861. 6s.

Gutenberg, John, First Master Printer, his Acts, and most remarkable Discourses, and his Death. From the German. By C. W. 8vo. cloth, pp. 141. 1860. 10s. 6d.

Hagen.—Norica; or, Tales from the Olden Time. Translated from the German of August Hagen. Fcap. 8vo., ornamental binding, suitable for presentation. Pp. xiv. and 374. 1850. 5s.

"This pleasant volume is got up in that style of imitation of the books a century ago, which has of late become so much the vogue. The typographical and mechanical departments of the volume speak loudly for the taste and enterprise bestowed upon it. Simple in its style, pithy, reasonably pungent—the book smacks strongly of the picturesque old days of which it treats. A long study of the art-antiquities of Nürnburg, and a profound acquaintance with the records, letters, and memoirs, still preserved, of the times of Albert Durer and his great brother artists, have enabled the author to lay before us a forcibly-drawn and highly-finished picture of art and household life in that wonderfully art-practising and art-reverencing old city of Germany."—*Atlas*.

"A delicious little book. It is full of a quaint garrulity, and characterised by an earnest simplicity of thought and diction, which admirably conveys to the reader the household and artistic German life of the times of Maximilian, Albert Durer, and Hans Sachs, the celebrated cobbler and 'master singer,' as well as most of the artist celebrities of Nürnberg in the 16th century. Art is the chief end and aim of this little history. It is lauded and praised with a sort of unostentatious devotion, which explains the religious passion of the early moulders of the Ideal and the beautiful; and, perhaps, through a consequent deeper concentration of thought, the secret of their success."—*Weekly Dispatch*.

"A volume full of interest for the lover of old times; while the form in which it is presented to us may incite many to think of art and look into its many wondrous influences with a curious earnestness unknown to them before. It points a moral also, in the knowledge that a people may be brought to take interest in what is chaste and beautiful as in what is coarse and degrading."—*Manchester Examiner*.

Hall.—The Law of Impersonation as applied to Abstract Ideas and Religious Dogmas. By S. W. Hall. Third edition, with an Appendix on the Dual Constitution of First Causation. 12mo. cloth, pp. xxiv. and 135. 1863. 4s. 6d.

Hall.—A Contribution towards an Index to the Bibliography of the Indian Philosophical Systems. By Fitzedward Hall, M.A., Inspector of Public Instruction, Saugor and Nerbudda Territories, Published by order of the Government of the North Western Provinces. 8vo. sewed, pp. iv. and 236. 1859. 7s. 6d.

Hambleton.—The Song of Songs; the Voice of the Bridegroom and the Voice of the Bride; divided into Acts and Scenes, with the Dialogues apportioned to the different Interlocutors, chiefly as directed by M. the Professor Ernest Renan, Membre de l'Institut. Rendered into Verse, from the received English Translation and other Versions. By Joseph Hambleton. Post 8vo., sewed, pp. 70. 1864. 2s. 6d.

Hamilton.—A Practical Treatise on Fractures and Dislocations. By Frank H. Hamilton, M.D. 3rd edition, revised, 8vo. cloth, pp. 777. 1866. 25s.

Hammond.—Military Medical and Surgical Essays. Prepared for the United States Sanitary Commission. Edited by W. A. Hammond, M.D., Surgeon-General. 8vo. cloth, pp. 552. 1864. 15s.

Harkness.—Latin Ollendorff. Being a Progressive Exhibition of the Principles of the Latin Grammar. By Albert Harkness, Ph. D. 12mo. cloth, pp. xii. and 355. 1858. 6s.

Harris.—A Dictionary of Medical Terminology, Dental Surgery, and the Collateral Sciences. By Chapin A. Harris, M.D., D.D.S., Professor of the Principles of Dental Surgery in the Baltimore College. Third edition, carefully revised and enlarged, by Ferdinand J. S. Gorgas, M.D., D.D.S., Professor of Dental Surgery in the Baltimore College. 8vo. cloth,

Harrison.—The Meaning of History; Two Lectures delivered by Frederic Harrison, M.A. 8vo., pp. 80, sewed. 1862. 1s.

Harrison.—Sundays and Festivals. A Lecture delivered by Frederic Harrison, Esq., M.A., at St. Martin's Hall, on Sunday evening, March 10th, 1867. 8vo. sewed, pp. 15. 1867. 2d.

Hartzenbusch, J. E., and H. Lemming.—Eco de Madrid: A Practical Guide to Spanish Conversation. Post 8vo. cloth, pp. 240. 1860. 5s.

Haslett.—The Mechanics', Machinists', and Engineers' Practical Book of Reference, containing Tables and Formulæ for use in superficial and solid Mensuration; Strength and Weight of Materials; Mechanics, Machinery, Hydraulics, Hydrodynamics, Marine Engines, Chemistry, and miscellaneous Recipes. Adapted to and for the use of all Practical Mechanics. Together with the Engineer's Field Book; containing Formulæ for the various Methods of running and changing Lines, locating Side-tracks and Switches, etc., etc.; Tables of Radii and their Logarithms, natural and logarithmic versed Sines and external Secants, natural Sines and Tangents to every Degree and Minute of the Quadrant, and Logarithms of natural Numbers from 1 to 10,000. By Charles Haslett, Civil Engineer. Edited by Charles W. Hackley, Professor of Mathematics. Fcap. 8vo. tuck, pp. 533. 1866. 12s.

Hasty Conclusions; or, the Sayings that went Abroad. 16mo. sewed, pp. 20. 1866. 1s.

Haug.—Essays on the Sacred Language, Writings, and Religion of the Parsees. By Martin Haug, Dr. Phil. Superintendent of Sanskrit Studies in the Poona College. 8vo. cloth, pp. 278. 1862. 31s. 6d.

Haug.—Outline of a Grammar of the Zend Language. By Martin Haug, Ph. D. 8vo., sewed, pp. 82. 1862. 18s.

Haug.—The Aitareya Brahmanam of the Rig Veda: containing the Earliest Speculations of the Brahmans on the meaning of the Sacrificial Prayers, and on the Origin, Performance, and Sense of the Rites of the Vedic Religion. Edited, Translated, and Explained by Martin Haug, Ph. D., Superintendent of Sanskrit Studies in the Poona College, etc., etc. In 2 Vols. Crown 8vo. Vol. I. Contents, Sanskrit Text, with Preface, Introductory Essay, and a Map of the Sacrificial Compound at the Soma Sacrifice, pp. 312. Vol. II. Translation with Notes, pp. 544. 1863. £2 2s.

Haug.—A Lecture on an Original Speech of Zoroaster (Yasna 45), with remarks on his age. By Martin Haug, Ph. D. 8vo. pp. 28, sewed. 1865. 2s.

Haug.—An Old Zand-Pahlavi Glossary. Edited in the Original Characters, with a Transliteration in Roman Letters, an English Translation, and an Alphabetical Index. By Destur Hoshengji Jamaspji, High-priest of the Parsis in Malwa, India. Revised with Notes and Introduction by Martin Haug, Ph. D., late Superintendent of Sanscrit Studies in the Poona College, Foreign Member of the Royal Bavarian Academy. Published by order of the Government of Bombay. 8vo. sewed, pp. lvi. and 132. 1867. 15s.

Haug.—The Religion of the Zoroastrians, as contained in their Sacred Writings. With a History of the Zend and Pehlevi Literature, and a Grammar of the Zend and Pehlevi Languages. By Martin Haug, Ph. D., late Superintendent of Sanscrit Studies in the Poona College. 2 vols. 8vo. [In preparation.]

Haupt.—MILITARY BRIDGES: with Suggestions of New Expedients and Constructions for Crossing Streams and Chasms. Including also Designs for Trestle and Truss Bridges for Military Railroads. Adapted especially to the wants of the Service in the United States. By Hermann Haupt, A.M., Civil Engineer. Illustrated by 69 Lithographic engravings. 8vo. cloth, pp. xix. and 310. 1864. 25s.

Haupt.—GENERAL THEORY OF BRIDGE CONSTRUCTION: containing Demonstrations of the Principles of the Art and their Application to Practice; furnishing the means of calculating the Strains upon the Chords, Ties, Braces, Counter-braces, and other parts of a Bridge or Frame of any description. With practical Illustrations. By Herman Haupt, A.M., Civil Engineer. New Edition. Royal 8vo. cloth, pp. 268. Plates. 1867. 16s.

Hazard.—ESSAY ON LANGUAGE AND OTHER PAPERS. By Rowland G. Hazard. Edited by E. P. Peabody. 8vo. cloth, pp. 348. 1857. 7s. 6d.

Hazard.—FREEDOM OF MIND IN WILLING; OR, EVERY-BEING THAT WILLS A CREATIVE FIRST CAUSE. By Rowland G. Hazard. 8vo. cloth, pp. xviii. and 456. 1865. 7s. 6d.

Hazard.—OUR RESOURCES. A Series of Articles on the Financial and Political Condition of the United States. By Rowland G. Hazard. 8vo. sewed, pp. 32. 1864. 1s.

Hearts IN MORTMAIN, and CORNELIA. Two Novels. Post 8vo. Fancy boards. Pp. 206 and 252. 1863. Each 1s. 6d.

Heatherington.—A PRACTICAL GUIDE FOR TOURISTS, MINERS, AND INVESTORS, and all Persons interested in the Development of the Gold Fields of Nova Scotia. By A. Heatherington, Author of Cosmopolite's Statistical Chart and Petraglot Reviews, adopted by the Department of Mines, and the Paris Exhibition Committee, etc., etc. 12mo. cloth, pp. 180. 1868. 2s.

Heaviside.—AMERICAN ANTIQUITIES; or, the New World the Old, and the Old World the New. By John T. C. Heaviside. 8vo. sewed, pp. 46. 1s. 6d.

Hecker.—THE EPIDEMICS OF THE MIDDLE AGES. Translated by G. B. Babington, M.D., F.R.S. Third Edition, completed by the Author's Treatise on Child-Pilgrimages. By J. F. C. Hecker. 8vo. cloth, pp. 384. 1859. 9s. 6d.
Contents:—The Black Death—The Dancing Mania—The Sweating Sickness—Child Pilgrimages.

Heine.—SELECTIONS FROM THE POETRY OF HENRICH HEINE. Translated by John Ackerlos. 12mo. pp. viii. and 66, stiff cover. 1854. 1s.

Heine.—PICTURES OF TRAVEL. Translated from the German of Henry Heine. By Charles G. Leland. Fifth revised edition. Crown 8vo. cloth, pp. 472. 1866. 10s. 6d.

Heine.—HEINE'S BOOK OF SONGS. By Heinrich Heine. Translated by Charles G. Leland, author of " Meister Karl's Sketch-book, and Sunshine in Thought." Cloth, fcap. 8vo. pp. xiv. and 240. 1868. 7s.

Hennell.—AN ESSAY ON THE SCEPTICAL TENDENCY OF BUTLER'S "Analogy." By Sara S. Hennell. 12mo. sewed, pp. 66. 1859. 1s.

Hennell.—THOUGHTS IN AID OF FAITH. Gathered chiefly from recent works in Theology and Philosophy. By Sara S. Hennell. Post 8vo. cloth, pp. 428. 1860. 10s. 6d.

Hennell.—PRIZE ESSAY. Christianity and Infidelity, an Exposition of Arguments on both sides. By Sara S. Hennell. 8vo. cloth, pp. 173. 1857. 3s. 6d.

Hennell.—THE EARLY CHRISTIAN ANTICIPATION OF AN APPROACHING END OF THE WORLD, and its bearing upon the Character of Christianity as a Divine Revelation. Including an investigation into the primitive meaning of the Antichrist and Man of Sin; and an examination of the argument of the Fifteenth Chapter of Gibbon. By Sara S. Hennell. 12mo. cloth, pp. 136. 1860. 2s. 6d.

Hennell.—PRESENT RELIGION, as a Faith owning Followship with Thought. Part I. By Sara S. Hennell, Author of "Thoughts in Aid of Faith." Crown 8vo. cloth, pp. 570. 1865. 7s. 6d.

Hepburn.—A JAPANESE AND ENGLISH DICTIONARY. With an English and Japanese Index. By J. C. Hepburn, A.M., M.D. Imperial 8vo. cloth, pp. xii., 560 and 132. 1867. £5 5s.

Herbert.—THE SANITARY CONDITION OF THE ARMY. By the Right Honourable Sidney Herbert, M.P. 8vo. sewed, pp. 48. 1859. 1s. 6d.

Hernisz.—A GUIDE TO CONVERSATION in the English and Chinese Languages, for the Use of Americans and Chinese, in California and elsewhere. By Stanislas Hernisz. Square 8vo. sewed, pp. 274. 1855. 10s. 6d.

_{The Chinese characters contained in this work are from the collections of Chinese groups, engraved on steel, and cast into moveable types, by Mr. Marcellin Legrand, Engraver of the Imperial Printing Office at Paris; they are used by most of the Missions to China.}

Hervey.—THE POEMS OF THOMAS KIBBLE HERVEY. Edited by Mrs. Hervey. With a Memoir. 16mo. cloth, pp. viii. and 437. 1866. 6s.

Herzen.—DU DEVELOPPEMENT DES IDÉES REVOLUTIONNAIRES EN RUSSIE. Par Alexander Herzen. 12mo. sewed, pp. xxiii. and 144. 1853. 2s. 6d.

Herzen.—LA FRANCE OU L'ANGLETERRE? Variations Russes sur le thême de l'attentat du 14 Janvier 1858. Par Iscander. 1858. 1s.

Herzen.—FRANCE OR ENGLAND? 8vo. 1858. 6d.

Herzen.—NOUVELLE PHASE DE LA LITTÉRATURE RUSSE. Par A. Herzen. 8vo. sewed, pp. 81. 1864. 2s. 6d.

Hester and Elinor; OR, THE DISCIPLINE OF SUFFERING.—A Tale. Crown 8vo., fancy boards, pp. 473. 1863. 2s.

Hickok.—A SYSTEM OF MORAL SCIENCE. By Lawrens P. Hickok, D.D., Author of "Rational Psychology." Royal 8vo. cloth, pp. viii. and 432. 1853. 12s.

Higginson.—WOMAN AND HER WISHES. An Essay. By Thomas Wentworth Higginson. Post 8vo. sewed, pp. 23. 1854. 1s.

Hincks.—SPECIMEN CHAPTERS OF AN ASSYRIAN GRAMMAR. By the Rev. E. Hincks, D.D., Honorary Member Royal Asiatic Society of Great Britain and Ireland. 8vo. sewed, pp. 40. 1866. 1s.

Histoire DU GRAND ORIENT DE FRANCE. 8vo sewed, pp. 528.

Historical SKETCHES OF THE OLD PAINTERS. By the Author of
"Three Experiments of Living," etc. Crown 8vo. sewed, pp. 181. 1858. 2s.

Hitchcock.—RELIGIOUS LECTURES ON PECULIAR PHENOMENA OF THE
FOUR SEASONS. Delivered to the Students in Amhurst College, in 1845-47-48-49. By Edward Hitchcock. 12mo. sewed, pp. 72. 1852. 1s.

Hittell.—THE RESOURCES OF CALIFORNIA. Third edition, by John
S. Hittell. Cloth, pp. xvi. and 461. 10s.

Hoffmann.—SHOPPING DIALOGUES in Japanese, Dutch, and English.
By J. Hoffmann. Oblong 8vo., sewed, pp. xiii. and 44. 1861. 3s.

Hole.—LECTURES ON SOCIAL SCIENCE AND THE ORGANIZATION OF
LABOUR. By James Hole. 8vo. sewed, pp. xi. and 182. 1851. 2s. 6d.

Holley.—ORDNANCE AND ARMOUR: embracing a Description of
Standard European and American Ordnance, Rifling, and Projectiles, and their Materials, Fabrications, and Test, and the Results of Practice; also a Detailed Account of Experiments against Armour. By Alex. L. Holley, B.P. With 480 Engravings and 150 Tables of Results. One vol. 8vo., pp. 950. Half morocco. 1865. £2 5s.

Hollister.—THE MINES OF THE COLORADO. By Ovando J. Hollister.
With map, pp. vii. and 450. 1867. 10s.

Holly.—THE CARPENTER'S AND JOINER'S HAND-BOOK, containing a
Complete Treatise on Framing Hip and Valley Roofs. Together with much valuable instruction for all Mechanics and Amateurs, useful rules, tables, etc., never before published. By H. W. Holly, Practical Architect and Builder. Illustrated by 37 Engravings. 12mo. cloth, pp. 50. 1868. 2s. 6d.

Holly.—THE ART OF SAW-FILING, SCIENTIFICALLY TREATED AND
EXPLAINED ON PHILOSOPHICAL PRINCIPLES. With full and explicit Directions for putting in Order all kinds of Saws, from a Jeweller's Saw to a Steam Sawmill. Illustrated by forty-four engravings. By H. W. Holly, Author of "The Carpenter's and Joiner's Hand-book." 12mo. cloth, pp. 56. 1864. 2s. 6d.

Holmes.—THE POEMS OF OLIVER WENDELL HOLMES. Blue and
Gold Series. 12mo. cloth, pp. xi. and 410. 1866. 6s.

Home.—PLAIN THOUHTS, by a Plain Man, on the State of the
Church of England. By Jeremiah Home, Esq. 8vo. sewed, pp. 8. 1868. 2d.

Horrocks.—ZENO. A Tale of the Italian War, and other Poems.
To which are added Translations from Modern German Poetry. By James D. Horrocks. 12mo., pp. vii. and 286, cloth. 1854. 5s.

Houghton.—AN ESSAY ON THE CANTICLES, OR THE SONG OF SONGS.
With a Translation of the Poem and short Explanatory Notes. By the Rev. W. Houghton, M.A., F.L.S., Rector of Preston on the Wild Moors, Shropshire. 8vo. cloth, pp. 67. 1865. 2s. 6d.

Howells.—VENETIAN LIFE. By William D. Howells, formerly
United States Consul at Venice. Crown 8vo. cloth. Second Edition. Pp. 401. 1867. 7s. 6d.

Howitt.—THE DÜSSELDORF ARTISTS' ALBUM. Twenty-seven superb
Litho-tint Illustrations, from Drawings by Achenbach, Hubner, Jordan, Lessing, Leutze, Schadow, Tidemand, etc. With Contributions, original and translated, by Mary Howitt, Anne Mary Howitt, Francis Bennoch, etc. Edited by Mary Howitt. 4to, elegantly bound in cloth, 18s.; or, in fancy leather binding, £1 1s. 1862.

Howse.—A GRAMMAR OF THE CREE LANGUAGE. With which is combined an analysis of the Chippeway Dialect. By Joseph Howse, Esq., F.R.G.S. 8vo. cloth, pp. xx. and 324. 1865. 7s. 6d.

Hugh Bryan: THE AUTOBIOGRAPHY OF AN IRISH REBEL. 8vo. cloth, pp. 478. 1866. 10s. 6d.

Humboldt.—LETTERS OF WILLIAM VON HUMBOLDT TO A FEMALE FRIEND. A complete Edition. Translated from the Second German Edition by Catherine M. A. Couper, with a Biographical Notice of the Writer. Two vols. Crown 8vo. cloth, pp. xxviii. and 592. 1867. 10s.

Humboldt.—THE SPHERE AND DUTIES OF GOVERNMENT. Translated from the German of Baron Wilhelm Von Humboldt, by Joseph Coulthard, Jun. Post 8vo. cloth, pp. xv. and 203. 1854. 5s.

Humboldt (ALEX. VON).—LETTERS TO VARNHAGEN VON ENSE. Authorised English Translation, with Explanatory Notes, and a full Index of Names. 8vo. cloth, pp. xxvi. and 334. 1860. 12s.

Hunt.—ON THE CHEMISTRY OF THE GLOBE. A Manual of Chemical Geology. By Dr. T. Sterry Hunt, F.R.S. 2 vols. 8vo. [*In preparation.*]

Hunt.—POPULAR LECTURES ON CHEMICAL AND PHYSICAL GEOLOGY. Delivered before the Lowell Institute, by Dr. T. Sterry Hunt, F.R.S. 1 vol. 8vo. [*In preparation.*]

Hunt.—THE RELIGION OF THE HEART. A Manual of Faith and Duty. By Leigh Hunt. Fcap. 8vo. cloth, pp. xxiv. and 259. 1853. 6s.

Hunt.—INTRODUCTORY ADDRESS ON THE STUDY OF ANTHROPOLOGY, delivered before the Anthropological Society of London, February 24th, 1863. By James Hunt, Ph. D., F.S.A., F.R.S.L., President. 8vo. sewed, pp. 20. 1863. 6d.

Hunt.—ANNIVERSARY ADDRESS delivered before the Anthropological Society of London, January 5th, 1864. By James Hunt, Ph. D., F.S.A., F.R.S.L., F.A.S.L., etc., etc. 8vo. sewed, pp. 32. 1864. 6d.

Hunt.—ANNIVERSARY ADDRESS delivered before the Anthropological Society of London, January 3rd, 1865. Dedicated to the British Association for the Advancement of Science. By James Hunt, Ph. D., F.S.A., F.R.S.L., F.A.S.L., etc., etc. 8vo. sewed, pp. viii. and 32. 1865. 6d.

Hunt.—A LETTER addressed to the Members of the British Association for the Advancement of Science, on the desirability of appointing a Special Section for Anthropology. By James Hunt, Ph. D., F.S.A., F.R.S.L., F.A.S.L. Post 8vo., sewed, pp. 8. Printed for Private Circulation. 6d.

Hunt.—ON THE NEGRO'S PLACE IN NATURE. By James Hunt, Esq., Ph. D., F.S.A., F.R.S.L., President of the Anthropological Society of London. 8vo., sewed, pp. 60. 1863. 1s.

Hurst.—HISTORY OF RATIONALISM: embracing a Survey of the Present State of Protestant Theology. By the Rev. John F. Hurst, A.M. With Appendix of Literature. Revised and enlarged from the Third American Edition. Small 8vo., cloth, pp. xvii. and 525. 1867. 10s. 6d.

Hutton.—MODERN WARFARE; its Positive Theory and True Policy. With an application to the Russian War, and an Answer to the Question "What shall we do?" By Henry Dix Hutton, Barrister. 8vo. sewed, pp. 74. 1855. 1s.

Ibis (The).—A MAGAZINE OF GENERAL ORNITHOLOGY. Edited by Philip Lutley Sclater, M.A. Vol. i. 1859. 8vo. cloth. Coloured Plates.
  Vol. ii., 1860.
  Vol. iii., 1861. £1 6s.
  Vol. iv., 1862. £1 6s.
  Vol. v., 1863. £1 6s.
  Vol. vi., 1864. £1 6s.

Ihne.—A LATIN GRAMMAR FOR BEGINNERS. By W. H. Ihne, late Principal of Carlton Terrace School, Liverpool. Crown 8vo. cloth, pp. vi. and 184. 1864. 3s.

India.—BREACH OF FAITH IN; or, Sir John Lawrence's Policy in Oudh. 8vo. sewed, pp. 40. 1s. 6d.

Indian Annexations.—BRITISH TREATMENT OF NATIVE PRINCES. Reprinted from the *Westminster Review*. New Series, No. xlv. January, 1863. Revised and corrected. 8vo. sewed, pp. 48. 1863. 1s.

Indian INVESTMENTS, A GUIDE TO, interesting to Shareholders or or intending Shareholders in the following Joint Stock Companies:—East Indian Railway, Great Indian Peninsular Railway, Madras Railway, Scinde Railway, Indus Flotilla, Punjaub Railway, Bombay and Baroda Railway, Eastern of Bengal Railway, Calcutta and South Eastern Railway, Madras Irrigation Company, Oriental Inland Steam Company, Peninsular and Oriental Steam Company. By a Manchester Man. Second edition. With an introduction exposing the hollowness of Indian guarantees. 8vo. sewed, pp. viii. and 40. 1861. 1s.

Inman.—ANCIENT FAITHS EMBODIED IN ANCIENT NAMES. By Thomas Inman, M.D. Vol. 1, 8vo., containing pp. viii. and 790, and illustrated with 5 Plates and numerous Woodcuts. 30s.

Inspiration.—By J. B. 24mo. sewed, pp. 51. 1865. 1s.

Inspiration; HOW IS IT RELATED TO REVELATION AND THE REASON? With a few remarks suggested by recent criticisms on Mansel's Bampton Lectures. 8vo. limp cloth, pp. 64. 1859. 2s.

International Exhibition of 1862.—OFFICIAL CATALOGUE OF THE MINING AND METALLURGICAL PRODUCTS; Class 1, in the Zollverein Department of the International Exhibition, 1862. Compiled under the immediate direction of Mr. Von Dcohen. By Dr. Hermann Wedding. Royal 8vo. sewed, pp. 106. 1862. 1s.

International Exhibition of 1862.—AUSTRIA AT THE INTERNATIONAL EXHIBITION OF 1862. Upon Orders from the J. R. Ministry for Commerce and National Economy. By Professor Dr. Jos. Arenstein, Vienna, 1862. Royal 8vo., paper covers, pp. 125. 1862. 1s.

International Exhibition of 1862.—SPECIAL CATALOGUE OF THE ZOLLVEREIN DEPARTMENT. Edited by authority of the Commissioners of the Zollverein-Governments, together with Advertisements, Recommendations, and Illustrations. Royal 8vo., sewed, pp. 180 and lxxix. 1862. 1s.
  Ditto ditto, in German, pp. 196 and cxv. 1s.

Jackson's GYMNASTIC EXERCISES FOR THE FINGERS AND WRIST. With numerous Illustrations. Post 8vo., cloth, pp. x. and 90. 1865. 3s. 6d.

Jackson.—ECHOES FROM MY YOUTH, AND OTHER POEMS. By J. W. Jackson. 12mo., cloth, pp. 126. 1864. 2s. 6d.

Jackson.—ETHNOLOGY AND PHRENOLOGY AS AN AID TO THE HISTORIAN. By J. W. Jackson. Crown 8vo., cloth, pp. 324. 1863. 4s.

Jacobus.—REFLECTIONS ON THE PSALMS OF DAVID AS INSPIRED COMPOSITIONS; and as indicating "the Philosophy of Jewish Faith." By Jacobus. 8vo. sewed, pp. iv. and 32. 1863. 1s.

Jaeschke.—A SHORT PRACTICAL GRAMMAR OF THE TIBETAN LANGUAGE, with Special Reference to the Spoken Dialects. By H. A. Jaeschke, Moravian Missionary. 8vo., pp. 60. 1865. 2s. 6d.

Jamison.—THE LIFE AND TIMES OF BERTRAND DU GUESCLIN. A History of the Fourteenth Century. By D. F. Jamison, of South Carolina. Portrait. Two vols. 8vo., elegantly printed, extra cloth, pp. xvi. 287, and viii. 314. 1864. £1 1s.

Jay.—THE AMERICAN REBELLION; its History, its Aims, and the Reasons why it must be Suppressed. An Address. By John Jay. Post 8vo. sewed, pp. 50. 1861. 1s.

Jay.—THE GREAT CONSPIRACY. An Address. By John Jay. 8vo. sewed, pp. 50. 1861. 1s.

Jenkins's VEST-POCKET LEXICON. A Dictionary of all except the common Words which everybody knows. By omitting these it contains the less familiar Words, and the principal Scientific and Technical Terms, Foreign Moneys, Weights and Measures; also the common Latin and French Phrases of two and three Words, Law Terms, etc.

"A little book, entitled, 'Jenkins's Vest-pocket Lexicon,' has just been published by Messrs. Trübner and Co., of Paternoster-row, which has a somewhat novel but very useful design. The object of the work is to compress within the smallest practicable compass a full lexicon of all the words used in writing or speaking English, except—and in the exception lies the essence of the undertaking—those which may fairly be considered familiar to every one. Thus every word which any reader but the most ignorant, and any reader but the most amazingly learned, could need to look for in a dictionary, is to be found in the columns of this little book. We have put it to several tests, by looking out for peculiar scientific words, terms used in art, legal phrases, names of foreign coins, titles of foreign officials, etc., and, so far as our examination went, have not found it to fail in any instance. We can, therefore, cordially recommend it to writers as well as to readers. It really does fit in the waistcoat pocket, and may literally be made a constant companion.—*Morning Star, July 17.*
64mo. limp morocco, pp. 560. 1861. 2s. 6d.

Jewish (A) REPLY TO DR. COLENSO'S CRITICISM ON THE PENTATEUCH. Issued by the Jewish Association for the Diffusion of Religious Knowledge. 8vo. cloth, pp. ix. and 147. 1865. 3s.

'Ιοαννες.—Φιλολογικὰ παρέργα ὑπὸ Φιλίππου Ἰωάννου Καθηγητοῦ τῆς φιλοσοφίας παρὰ τῷ πανεπιστημίῳ Ἀθηνῶν. (Literary Miscellanies. By Philippe Joannes, Professor of Philosophy at the University of Athens). 8vo. cloth, pp. 488. 10s. 6d.

John Groves.—A TALE OF THE WAR. By S. E. de M—. 12mo. sewed, pp. 16. 1856. 2d.

Jolowicz.—THE FIRST EPISTLE OF BARUCH. Translated from the Syriac, with an Introduction. By the Rev. Dr. H. Jolowicz, ordinary Member of the German Oriental Society. Read at the meeting of the Syro-Egyptian Society, December 12, 1854. John Lee, Esq., LL.D., F.R.S., in the Chair. 8vo. sewed, pp. 12. 1855. 1s.

Jomini.—THE ART OF WAR. By Baron de Jomini, General and Aide-de-Camp to the Emperor of Russia. A New Edition, with Appendices and Maps. Translated from the French. By Capt. G. H. Mendell, and Capt. W. O. Craighill. Crown 8vo. cloth, pp. 410. 1864. 9s.

Jomini.—TREATISE ON GRAND MILITARY OPERATIONS, or a Critical and Military History of the Wars of Frederick the Great, as contrasted with the modern system. Together with a few of the most important principles of the Art of War. By Baron Jomini, Commander-in-Chief, and Aide-de-Camp to the Emperor of Russia. Translated from the French by Col. S. B. Holabird, U.S.A. Illustrated with Maps and Plans. 2 vols. 8vo. cloth, pp. 448, 496; and an Atlas, containing 39 maps and plans of battles, 1741-1762. 1865. £3.

Jomini.—THE MILITARY AND POLITICAL LIFE OF THE EMPEROR NAPOLEON. By Baron Jomini, General-in-Chief, and Aide-de-Camp to the Emperor of Russia. Translated from the French, with Notes, by H. W. Halleck, LL.D., Major-General U.S. Army. 4 vols., royal 8vo. cloth, pp. 395, 451, 414, 453, with an Atlas of 60 Maps and Plans. 1864. £4 4s.

Jomini.—THE POLITICAL AND MILITARY HISTORY OF THE CAMPAIGN OF WATERLOO. Translated from the French of General Baron de Jomini, by Captain S. V. Benét, United States Ordnance. Third Edition. 12mo. cloth, pp. . 6s.
This is a separate reprint of the twenty-second chapter of "Jomini's Life of Napoleon," and forms a capital summary of the campaign.

Jones.—WARNING; OR, THE BEGINNING OF THE END. An Address to the Jews. By C. Jones. 8vo. sewed, pp. 58. 1866. 2s.

Justi.—HANDBUCH DER ZENDSPRACHE, VON FERDINAND JUSTI. Altbactrisches Woerterbuch. Grammatik Chrestomathie. Four parts, 4to. sewed, pp. xxii. and 424. Leipzig, 1864. 24s.

Kafir Essays, AND OTHER PIECES; with an English Translation. Edited by the Right Rev. the Bishop of Grahamstown. 32mo. sewed, pp. 84. 1861. 2s. 6d.

Karcher.—LES ECRIVAINS MILITAIRES DE LA FRANCE. Par Theodore Karcher, Professeur à l'Académie Royale Militaire de Woolwich, etc. 8vo. cloth, with numerous Illustrations. Pp. viii. and 348. 1866. 7s. 6d.

Karcher. — QUESTIONNAIRE FRANÇAIS. Questions on French Grammar, Idiomatic Difficulties, and Military Expressions. By Theodore Karcher, LL.B. 12mo. cloth, pp. 111. 1865. 2s. 6d.
Interleaved with writing paper. 3s.

Kaulbach.—ALBUM-THIERFABELN, GESCHICHTEN UND MÄRCHEN IN BILDERN. Nach Original-Federzeichnungen von Wilhelm von Kaulbach, In Holz-schitten von J. G. Flegel. Text von Dr. Julius Grosse. 12 plates. oblong folio. 10s. 6d.

Kendrick.—GREEK OLLENDORFF. A Progressive Exhibition of the Principles of the Greek Grammar. By Asahel C. Kenrick. 8vo. cloth, pp. 371. 1857. 6s.

Keyne.—SPELLS AND VOICES. By Ada Keyne. 12mo. cloth, pp. 124. 1865. 2s. 6d.

Khirad-Afroz (The Illuminator of the Understanding). By Maulavi Hafisu'd-din. A New Edition of the Hindústáni Text, carefully Revised, with Notes, Critical and Explanatory. By Edward B. Eastwick, F.R.S., F.S.A., M.R.A.S., Professor of Hindústáni at the late East India Company's College at Haileybury. 8vo. cloth, pp. xiv. and 321. 1868. 18s.

Kidd.—Catalogue of the Chinese Library of the Royal Asiatic Society. By the Rev. S. Kidd. 8vo. sewed, pp. 58. 1s.

Kidder.—A Treatise on Homiletics; designed to Illustrate the True Theory and Practice of Preaching the Gospel. By Daniel P. Kidder, D.D., Professor in the Garratt Biblical Institute. Crown 8vo. cloth, pp. 495. 1864-5. 6s.

King.—The Patriot. A Poem. By J. W. King. 12mo. sewed, pp. 56. 1853. 1s.

King.—Lessons and Practical Notes on Steam, the Steam Engine, Propellers, etc., etc., for young Engineers, Students, and others. By the late W. H. King, U.S.N. Revised by Chief-Engineer J. W. King, U.S.N. Ninth Edition. Enlarged. 8vo. cloth, pp. 229. 1865. 9s.

Kingsford.—An Essay on the Admission of Women to the Parliamentary Franchise. By Ninon Kingsford. 8vo. sewed, pp. 40. 1868. 1s.

Knight.—The Indian Empire and our Financial Relations Therewith. A Paper read before the London Indian Society, May 25, 1866. By Robert Knight ("Times of India"). 8vo. sewed, pp. 42. 1866. 1s.

Knight.—Letter to the Right Hon. Sir Stafford Northcote, Baronet, Her Majesty's Secretary of State for India, upon the present condition of Bombay, with suggestions for its relief. By Robert Knight, "Times of India." 8vo. sewed, pp. 24. 1867. 1s.

Kohl.—Travels in Canada and through the States of New York and Pennsylvania. By I. J. Kohl. Translated by Mrs. Percy Sinnett. Revised by the Author. Two vols., post 8vo. cloth, pp. xiv. and 794. 1861. 21s.

Kortum.—The Jobsiad; a grotesco-comico-heroic Poem. From the German of Dr. Carl Arnold Kortum. By Charles T. Brooks, Translator of "Faust," "Titan," etc., etc. Crown 8vo. cloth, pp. xviii. and 182. 1863. 5s.

Kossuth.—Speeches of Louis Kossuth in America. Edited, with his sanction, by F. W. Newman. Post 8vo. cloth. pp. 388. 1853. 5s.

Kossuth.—Sheffield and Nottingham Evening Speeches. Edited by himself. 1854. 2d.

Kossuth.—Glasgow Speeches. Edited by himself. 2d.

Krapf.—Travels, Researches, and Missionary Labours, during an Eighteen Years' Residence on the Eastern Coast of Africa. By the Rev. Dr. J. Lewis Krapf, late Missionary in the service of the Church Missionary Society in Eastern and Equatorial Africa; to which is prefixed a concise Account of Geographical Discovery in Eastern Africa, up to the present time, by J. E. Ravenstein, F.R.G.S. In demy 8vo., with a Portrait, two Maps, and twelve Plates. Cloth, pp. li. and 566. 1866. £1 1s.

Kühner.—An Elementary Grammar of the Greek Language. By Raphael Kühner. Translated by Samuel H. Taylor. One vol. Twentieth Edition. 8vo. half-bound, pp. xii. and 355. 1865. 6s.

Kühner.—Grammar of the Greek Language for the use of High Schools and Colleges. Translated from the German by B. B. Edwards and S. H. Taylor. By Raphael Kühner. Fourth Edition. 8vo. cloth, pp. xvi. and 620. 1862. 10s. 6d.

Küstel.—NEVADA AND CALIFORNIA PROCESSES OF SILVER AND GOLD EXTRACTION FOR GENERAL USE, and especially for the Mining Public of California and Nevada, with full explanations and directions for all Metallurgical Operations connected with Silver and Gold, from a preliminary examination of the ore to the final casting of the ingot. Also a description of the General Metallurgy of Silver Ores. By Guido Küstel, Mining Engineer and Metallurgist. Illustrated by accurate engravings. 8vo. cloth, pp. 328. 1868. 14s.

Lady Nurses FOR THE SICK POOR IN OUR LONDON WORKHOUSES. Report of Proceedings at the Strand Union Board of Guardians, September 4, 1866. From the Short Hand Notes of Mr. John White. With an Appendix. 8vo. sewed, pp. 15. 1866. 6d.

Laghu Kaumudí.—A SANSKRIT GRAMMAR. By Varadarája. With an English Version, Commentary and References. By James R. Ballantyne, LL.D., Principal of the Sanskrit College, Benares. 8vo. cloth, pp. xxxvi. and 424. 1867. £1 11s. 6d.

Lange.—THE UPPER RHINE. Illustrating its finest Cities, Castles, Ruins, and Landscapes. From Drawings by Messrs. Rohbock, Louis and Julius Lange. Engraved by the most distinguished Artists. With a History and Topographical Text. Edited by Dr. Gaspey. 8vo., pp. 494. 134 Plates. 1859. £2 2s.

Langford.—ENGLISH DEMOCRACY; its History and Principles. By John Alfred Langford. Fcap. 8vo., stiff cover. Pp. 88. 1855. 1s. 6d.

Langford.—RELIGION AND EDUCATION IN RELATION TO THE PEOPLE. By John Alfred Langford. 12mo. cloth, pp. iv. and 133. 1852. 2s.

Langford.—RELIGIOUS SCEPTICISM AND INFIDELITY; their History, Cause, Cure, and Mission. By John Alfred Langford. Post 8vo. cloth, pp. iv. and 246. 1850. 2s. 6d.

Lathe (THE) AND ITS USES; or, Instruction in the Art of Turning Wood and Metal. Including a description of the most modern appliances for the ornamentation of plane and curved surfaces. With an Appendix, in which is described an entirely novel form of lathe for eccentric and rose engine turning; a lathe and planing machine combined; and other valuable matter relating to the art. Copiously illustrated. 8vo. cloth, pp. 290. 1868. 15s.

Lawrence, SIR JOHN, G.C.B., AND THE TALOOQDARS OF OUDH. A series of articles contributed to "The Press," showing how the Viceroy of India proposes to undermine and destroy the proprietary rights of the landowners of that province. 8vo. sewed, pp. 46. 1865. 6d.

Layman's Faith (A).—DOCTRINES AND LITURGY. By a Layman. 12mo. cloth, pp. viii. and 150. 1866. 2s. 6d.

Lea.—AN HISTORICAL SKETCH OF SACERDOTAL CELIBACY IN THE CHRISTIAN CHURCH. By Henry Carey Lea. 8vo. cloth, pp. 601. 1867. 15s.

Lea.—SUPERSTITION AND FORCE. Essays on the Wager of Law— the Wager of Battle—the Ordeal—Torture. By Henry C. Lea. 8vo. cloth. pp. 408. 1866. 10s. 6d.

Lees. AN INQUIRY INTO THE REASONS AND RESULTS OF THE PRESCRIPTION OF INTOXICATING LIQUORS IN THE PRACTICE OF MEDICINE.— By Dr. F. R. Lees, F.S.A. 12mo. cloth, pp. iv. and 144. 1866. 1s. 4d.

Leeser.—THE TWENTY-FOUR BOOKS OF THE HOLY SCRIPTURES: carefully Translated according to the Massoretic Text, after the best Jewish Authorities. By Isaac Leeser. 18mo. bound, pp. xii. and 1243. 1865. 7s. 6d.

Legge.—THE LIFE AND TEACHINGS OF CONFUCIUS. With explanatory Notes. By James Legge, D.D. Reproduced for General Readers from the Author's work, containing the Original Text. Post 8vo. cloth, pp. vi. and 338. 1867. 10s. 6d.

Legge.—THE CHINESE CLASSICS. With a Translation, Critical and Exegetical, Notes, Prolegomena, and copious Indexes. By James Legge, D.D., of the London Missionary Society. In seven Vols.

Vol. 1, containing Confucian analects, the great learning, and the doctrine of the mean. 8vo. cloth, pp. 526. 1861. 42s.

Vol. 2, containing the works of Mencius. 8vo. cloth, pp. 634. 1861. 42s.

Vol. 3, part 1, containing the first parts of the Shoo-King, or the Books of T'ang, the Books of Yu; the Books of Hea; the Books of Shang, and the Prolegomena. 8vo. cloth, pp. 291. 1865. 42s.

Vol. 3, part 2, containing the fifth part of the Shoo-King, or the Books of Chow, and the indexes. 8vo. cloth, pp. 453. 1865. 42s.

Legge.—THE CHINESE CLASSICS: translated into English. With Preliminary Essays and Explanatory Notes. Popular Edition. Reproduced for General Readers from the Author's work, containing the Original Text. By James Legge, D.D. Vol. 1—The Life and Teachings of Confucius. 8vo. cloth, pp. vi. and 338. 1867. 10s. 6d.

Leitner.—THE RACES AND LANGUAGES OF DARDISTAN. By G. W. Leitner, M.A., Ph. D., Honorary Fellow of King's College, London, etc. late on Special Duty in Kashmir. 4 vols. 4to. 1868. [*In the press.*

Lesley.—MAN'S ORIGIN AND DESTINY, Sketched from the Platform of the Sciences, in a Course of Lectures delivered before the Lowell Institute, in Boston, in the Winter of 1865-6. By J. P. Lesley, Member of the National Academy of the United States, Secretary of the American Philosophical Society. Numerous Woodcuts. Crown 8vo. cloth, pp. 392. 1868. 10s. 6d.

CONTENTS.—Lecture 1. On the Classification of the Sciences; 2. On the Genius of the Physical Sciences, Ancient and Modern; 3. The Geological Antiquity of Man; 4. On the Dignity of Mankind; 5. On the Unity of Mankind; 6. On the Early Social Life of Man; 7. On Language as a Test of Race; 8. The Origin of Architecture; 9. The Growth of the Alphabet; 10. The Four Types of Religious Worship; 11. On Arkite Symbolism. Appendix.

Lessing.—NATHAN THE WISE. A Dramatic Poem. By Gotthold Ephraim Lessing. Translated from the German. With an introduction on Lessing and the "Nathan;" its antecedents, character, and influence. Crown 8vo. cloth, pp. xxviii. and 214. 1868. 6s.

Lessing.—LETTERS ON BIBLIOLATRY. By Gotthold Ephraim Lessing. Translated from the German by the late H. H. Bernard, Ph. Dr. 8vo. cloth, pp. 184. 1862. 5s.

Three Generations of British Reviewers on LESSING.

"The work before us is as genuine sour-krout as ever perfumed a feast in Westphalia."—*Edinburgh Review, April,* 1806.

"As a poet, as a critic, a philosopher, or controversialist, his style will be found precisely such as we of England are accustomed to admire most. Brief, nervous, vivid; yet quiet, without glitter or antithesis; idiomatic, pure without purism; transparent, yet full of character and reflex hues of meaning."—*Edinburgh Review, October,* 1827.

"The first foreigner who had the glory of proclaiming Shakespeare to be the greatest dramatist the world had ever seen, was Gotthold Ephraim Lessing."—*Edinburgh Review.*

Lessing.—THE LIFE AND WORKS OF G. E. LESSING. From the German of Adolph Stahr. By E. P. Evans, Ph. D. 2 vols., crown 8vo. cloth, pp. xvi. and 383, iv. and 442. 1867. 25*s*.

Letter TO LORD PALMERSTON, CONCERNING THE QUESTION OF SCHLESWIG-HOLSTEIN. 8vo. sewed, pp. 32. 1850. 1*s*.

Letters FROM THE ARCHBISHOP OF CANTERBURY, THE BISHOP OF CAPETOWN, AND THE BISHOP OF NATAL. With some Observations on the Archbishop of Canterbury's reply to the Bishop of Natal. 8vo. pp. 30. 1866. 1*s*.

Letter TO THE RIGHT HONORABLE THE EARL OF DERBY ON POLITICAL REFORM. By one of the People. 8vo. sewed, pp. 46. 1867. 1*s*.

Leverson.—THE REFORMER'S REFORM BILL. Being a Proposed New and complete Code of Electoral Law for the United Kingdom. By Montague R. Leverson. Post 8vo. sewed, pp. 36. 1866. 1*s*.

Levy (M.).—THE HISTORY OF SHORTHAND WRITING. By Matthias Levy. To which is appended the System used by the Author. Crown 8vo. cloth, pp. viii. and 194. 1862. 5*s*.

Lima.—SKETCHES OF THE CAPITAL OF PERU, HISTORICAL, STATISTICAL, ADMINISTRATIVE, COMMERCIAL, AND MORAL. By Manuel A. Fuentes, Advocate. With numerous Illustrations. 8vo. half bound, pp. ix. and 224. 1867. 21*s*.

Little French Reader (THE).—Extracted from "The Modern French Reader." Crown 8vo. cloth. 1868. 2*s*. (See p. 63.)

Liturgy.—Ἡ θεία λειτουργία τοῦ ἐν ἁγίοις πατρὸς ἡμῶν Ἰωάννου τοῦ Χρυσοστόμου. Παραφρασθεῖσα κατὰ τὸ κείμενον τὸ ἐκδοθὲν ἐγκρίσει τῆς ἱερᾶς Συνόδου τοῦ βασιλείου τῆς Ἑλλάδος. (The divine Liturgy of our holy father St. Chrysostome, paraphrased according to the text published with the sanction of the Holy Synod of the kingdom of Greece.) 12mo. cloth, gilt edges, pp. 76. 2*s*. 6*d*.

Lobscheid.—ENGLISH AND CHINESE DICTIONARY, with the Punti and Mandarin Pronunciation. By the Rev. W. Lobscheid, Knight of Francis Joseph, C.M.I.R.G.S.A., N.Z.B.S.V., etc. Parts I. and II., folio, pp. iv. and 1 to 980. (Will be completed in Four Parts). 1867. Price, each part, £1 16*s*.

Log Cabin (THE); OR, THE WORLD BEFORE YOU. Post 8vo. cloth, pp. iv. and 120. 1844. 2*s*. 6*d*.

Longfellow.—FLOWER DE LUCE. By Henry Wadsworth Longfellow. With Illustrations. Small 4to., extra cloth, gilt edges, pp. 72. 1867. 10*d*. 6*d*.

Longfellow.—EVANGELINE. A Tale of Acadie. By Henry W. Longfellow. With Illustrations by F. O. C. Darley. Small 4to. extra cloth, gilt edges, pp. 157. 1867. 12*s*.

Longfellow.—THE POETICAL WORKS OF HENRY WADSWORTH LONGFELLOW. Revised Edition. 4 vols., crown 8vo. cloth, gilt top, pp. 318, v. 283, v. 351, 372. 1866. 40*s*.

Longfellow.—THE PROSE WORKS OF HENRY WADSWORTH LONGFELLOW. Revised Edition. 3 vols. crown 8vo., gilt top, pp. 364, 391, 365. 1866. 30*s*.

Loomis.—AN INTRODUCTION TO PRACTICAL ASTRONOMY, with a Collection of Astronomical Tables. By Elias Loomis, LL.D. Seventh Edition. 8vo. sheep, pp. xi. and 499. 1866. 10s. 6d.

Loomis.—A TREATISE ON ASTRONOMY. By Elias Loomis, Professor of Natural Philosophy and Astronomy in Yale College, Author of "An Introduction to Practical Astronomy," and of a series of Mathematics for Schools and Colleges. 8vo. sheep, pp. 338. With eight Plates. 1868. 10s. 6d.

Lorgion.—THE PASTOR OF VLIETHUIZEN, or Conversations about the Groningen School, the Doctrine of the Church, the Science of Theology, and the Bible. By E. J. Diest Lorgion, D.D. Translated from the Dutch. Post 4to., pp. iv. and 128. 1861. 7s. 6d.

Lowe.—SPEECH OF THE RIGHT HON. ROBERT LOWE, M.P., on the Irish Tenant Right Bill, and a Letter of Lord Oranmore's to the *Times*. 8vo. sewed, pp. 22. 1866. 6d.

Lowell.—THE VISION OF SIR LAUNFAL. By James Russell Lowell. With Illustrations by S. Eytinge, jun. Small 4to. 28 leaves, printed on one side only. 1867. 10s. 6d.

Lowell.—THE POETICAL WORKS OF JAMES R. LOWELL. Complete in two volumes. Blue and Gold Series. 24mo. cloth, pp. ix. 315, 322. With Portrait. 1863. 10s.

Ludewig.—THE LITERATURE OF AMERICAN ABORIGINAL LANGUAGES, with Additions and Corrections by Professor Wm. W. Turner. Edited by Nicolas Trübner. 8vo. fly and general Title, 2 leaves; Dr. Ludewig's Preface, pp. v.—viii.; Editor's Preface, pp. ix.—xii.; Biographical Memoir of Dr. Ludewig, pp. xiii., xiv.; and Introductory Bibliographical Notices, pp. xv.—xxiv., followed by List of Contents. Then follow Dr. Ludewig's Bibliotheca Glottica, alphabetically arranged, with Additions by the Editor, pp. 1—209; Professor Turner's Additions, with those of the Editor to the same, also alphabetically arranged, pp. 210—246; Index, pp. 247—256; and list of Errata, pp. 257, 258. By Hermann E. Ludewig. 8vo. cloth. London. 1858. 10s. 6d.

This work is intended to supply a great want, now that the study of Ethnology has proved that exotic languages are not mere curiosities, but essential and interesting parts of the natural history of man, forming one of the most curious links in the great chain of national affinities, defining as they do the reciprocity existing between man and the soil he lives upon. No one can venture to write the history of America without a knowledge of her aboriginal languages; and unimportant as such researches may seem to men engaged in the mere bustling occupations of life, they will at least acknowledge that those records of the past, like the stern-lights of a departing ship, are the last glimmers of savage life, as it becomes absorbed or recedes before the tide of civilization. Dr. Ludewig and Prof. Taylor have been most diligent in the use of the public and private collections in America, access to all of which was most liberally granted to them. This has placed at their disposal the labours of the American Missionaries, so little known on this side of the Atlantic that they may be looked upon almost in the light of untrodden ground. But English and Continental libraries have also been ransacked; and Dr. Ludewig kept up a constant and active correspondence with scholars of "the Fatherland," as well as with men of similar tastes and pursuits in France, Spain, and Holland, determined to leave no stone unturned to render his labours as complete as possible. The volume, perfect in itself, is the first of an enlarged edition of Vater's "*Linguarum totius orbis Index.*" The work has been noticed by the press of both Continents, and we may be permitted to refer particularly to the following.

OPINIONS OF THE PRESS.

"This work, mainly the production of the late Herr Ludewig, a German, naturalized in America, is devoted to an account of the literature of the aboriginal languages of that country. It gives an alphabetical list of the various tribes of whose languages any record remains, and refers to the works, papers, or manuscripts, in which such information may be found. The work has evidently been a labour of love; and as no pains seem to have been spared by the editors, Prof. Turner and Mr. Trübner, in rendering the work as accurate and complete as possible, those who are most interested in its contents will be best able to judge of the labours and assiduity bestowed upon it by author, editors, and publisher."—*Athenæum*, 5th April, 1858.

"This is the first instalment of a work which will be of the greatest value to philologists; and is a compendium of the aboriginal languages of the American continents, and a digest of all the known literature bearing upon those languages. Mr. Trübner's hand has been engaged *passim*, and in his preface he lays claim to about one-sixth of the whole; and we have no doubt that the encouragement with which this portion of the work will be received by scholars, will be such as to inspire Mr. Trübner with sufficient confidence to persevere in his arduous and most honourable task."—*The Critic*, 15th Dec., 1857.

"Few would believe that a good octavo volume would be necessary to exhaust the subject; yet so it is, and this handsome, useful, and curious volume, carefully compiled by Mr. Ludewig, assisted by Prof. Turner, and edited by the careful hand of Mr. Trübner, the well-known publisher, will be sure to find a place in many libraries."—*Bent's Advertiser*, 6th Nov., 1857.

"The lovers of American linguistics will find in the work of Mr. Trübner scarcely any point omitted calculated to aid the comparative philologer in tracing the various languages of the great Western Continent."—*Galway Mercury*, 30th Jan., 1858.

"Only those deeply versed in philological studies can appreciate this book at its full value. It shows that there are upwards of seven hundred and fifty aboriginal American languages,"—*Gentleman's Magazine*, Feb., 1858.

"The work contains an account of no fewer than seven hundred different aboriginal dialects of America, with an introductory chapter of bibliographical information; and under each dialect is an account of any grammars or other works illustrative of it."—*The Bookseller*, Jan., 1858.

"We have here the list of monuments still existing, of an almost innumerable series of languages and dialects of the American Continent. The greater part of Indian grammars and vocabularies exist only in MS., and were compiled chiefly by Missionaries of the Christian Church; and to Dr. Ludawig and Mr. Trübner, we are, therefore, the more indebted for the great care with which they have pointed out where such are to be found, as well as for enumerating those which have been printed, either in a separate shape, in collections, or in voyages and travels, and elsewhere."—*Leader*, 11th Sept., 1858.

"I have not time, nor is it my purpose, to go into a review of this admirable work, or to attempt to indicate the extent and value of its contents. It is, perhaps, enough to say, that apart from a concise but clear summeration and notice of the various general philological works which treat with greater or less fulness of American languages, or which incidentally touch upon their bibliography, it contains not less than 256 closely-printed octavo pages of bibliographical notices of grammars, vocabularies, etc., of the aboriginal languages of America. It is a peculiar and valuable feature of the work that not only the titles of printed or published grammars or vocabularies are given, but also that unpublished or MS. works of those kinds are noticed, in all cases where they are known to exist, but which have disappeared among the *debris* of the suppressed convents and religious establishments of Spanish America."—E. G. Squier, in a paper read before the American Ethnological Society, 12th Jan., 1858.

"In consequence of the death of the author before he had finished the revisal of the work it has been carefully examined by competent scholars, who have also made many valuable additions."—*American Publishers' Circular*, 30th Jan., 1858.

"It contains 256 closely-printed pages of titles, or printed books and manuscripts, and notices of American aboriginal languages, and embraces references to nearly all that has been written or published respecting them, whether in special works or incidentally in books of travel, periodicals, or proceedings of learned societies."—*New York Herald*, 26th Jan., 1858.

"The manner in which this contribution to the bibliography of American languages has been executed, both by the author, Mr. Ludewig, and the able writers who have edited the work since his death, is spoken of in the highest terms by gentlemen most conversant with the subject."—*American Historical Magazine*, Vol. II., No. 5, May, 1858.

"Je terminerai en annonçant le premier volume d'une publication appelée à rendre de grands services à la philologie comparée et à la linguistique générale. Je veux parler de la Bibliotheca Glottica, ouvrage devant renfermer la liste de tous les dictionnaires et de toutes les grammaires des langues connues, tant imprimés que manuscrits. L'éditeur de cette précieuse bibliographie est M. Nicolas Trübner, dont le nom est honorablement connu dans le monde oriental. Le premier volume est consacré aux idiomes Américains; le second doit traiter des langues de l'Inde. Le travail est fait avec le soin le plus consciencieux, et fera honneur à M. Nicolas Trübner, surtout s'il poursuit son œuvre avec la même ardeur qu'il a mise à la commencer."—L. Léon de Rosny. *Revue de l'Orient*, Février, 1858.

"Mr. Trübner's most important work on the bibliography of the aboriginal languages of America is deserving of all praise, so eminently useful to those who study that branch of literature. The value, too, of the book, and of the pains which its compilation must have cost, will not be lessened by the consideration that it is first in this field of linguistic literature."—*Petermann's Geographische Mittheilungen*, p. 79, Feb., 1858.

"Undoubtedly this volume of Trübner's Bibliotheca Glottica ranks amongst the most valuable additions which of late years have enriched our bibliographical literature. To us Germans it is most gratifying, that the initiative has been taken by a German bookseller, himself one of the most intelligent and active of our countrymen abroad, to produce a work which has higher aims than mere pecuniary profit, and that he, too, has laboured at its production with his own hands; because daily it is becoming a circumstance of rarer occurrence that, as in this case, it is a bookseller's primary object to serve the cause of literature rather than to enrich himself."—P. Tromel, *Börsenblatt*, 4th Jan., 1858.

"In the compilation of the work the editors have availed themselves not only of the labours of Vater, Barton, Duponceau, Gallatin, De Souza, and others, but also of the MS. sources left by the missionaries, and of many books of which even the library of the British Museum is deficient, and furnish the fullest account of the literature of no less than 525 languages. The value of the work, so necessary to the study of ethnology, is greatly enhanced by the addition of a good Index."—*Berliner National-Zeitung*, 22nd Nov., 1857.

"The name of the author, to all those who are acquainted with his former works, and who know the thoroughness and profound character of his investigations, is a sufficient guarantee that this work will be one of standard authority, and one that will fully answer the demands of the present time."—*Petzholdt's Anzeiger*, Jan., 1858.

"The chief merit of the editor and publisher is to have terminated the work carefully and lucidly in contents and form, and thus to have established a new and largely augmented edition of '*Vater's Linguarum totius orbis Index*,' after Professor Jülg's revision of 1847. In order to continue and complete this work the editor requires the assistance of all those who are acquainted with this new branch of science, and we sincerely hope it may be accorded to him."—*Magazin für die Literatur des Auslandes*, No. 38, 1858.

"As the general title of the book indicates, it will be extended to the languages of the other continents, in case it meets with a favourable reception, which we most cordially wish it."—*A. F. Pott, Preussische Jahrücher*, Vol. II., part 1.

"Cette compilation savante est, sans contredit, le travail bibliographique le plus important que notre époque ait vu surgir sur les nations indigènes de l'Amérique."—*Nouvelles Annales des Voyages*, Avril, 1859.

"La Bibliotheca Glottica, dont M. Nicolas Trübner a commencé la publication, est un des livres les plus utiles qui aient jamais été rédigés pour faciliter l'étude de la philologie comparée. Le premier tome de cette grande bibliographie linguistique comprend la liste textuelle de toutes les grammaires, de tous les dictionnaires et des vocabulaires même les moins étendus qui ont été imprimés dans les différents dialectes des deux Amériques; en outre, il fait connaître les ouvrages manuscrits de la même nature renfermés dans les principales bibliothèques publiques et particulières. Ce travail a dû nécessiter de longues et patientes recherches; aussi mérite-t-il d'attirer tout particulièrement l'attention des philologues. Puissent les autres volumes de cette bibliothèque être rédigés avec le même soin et se trouver bientôt entre les mains de tous les savants auxquels ils peuvent rendre des services inappréciables."—*Revue Americaine et Orientale*, No. 1, Oct., 1858.

"To every fresh addition to the bibliography of language, of which we have a most admirable specimen in this work, the thoughtful linguist will ever, as the great problem of the unity of human speech approaches towards its full solution, turn with increasing satisfaction and hope.

"But Mr. Nicolas Trübner, however, has, perhaps, on the whole, done the highest service of all to the philologer, by the publication of "The Literature of American Aboriginal Languages." He has, with the aid of Professor Turner, greatly enlarged, and at the same time most skilfully edited, the valuable materials acquired by his deceased friend, M. Ludewig. We do not, indeed, at this moment, know any similar work deserving of full comparison with it. In its ample enumeration of important works of reference, and careful record of the most recent facts in the literature of its subject, it, as might have been expected, greatly surpasses Jülg's 'Vater,' valuable and trustworthy though that learned German's work undoubtedly is."—*North British Review*, No. 59, Feb., 1859.

The Editor has also received most kind and encouraging letters respecting the work from Sir George Grey, the Chevalier Bunsen, Dr. Th. Goldstücker, Mr. Watts (of the Museum), Professor A. Fr. Pott (of Halle), Dr. Julius Petzholt (of Dresden), Hofrath Dr. Grasse (of Dresden), M. F. F. de la Figanière (of Lisbon), E. Edwards (of Manchester), Dr. Max Müller (of Oxford), Dr. Buschmann (of Berlin), Dr. Jülg (of Cracow), and other linguistic scholars.

Luvini.—Tables of Logarithms with Seven Places of Decimals. By John Luvini. Crown 8vo, cloth, pp. viii. and 368. 1866. 5s.

Lyman.—Cotton Culture. By Joseph B. Lyman, late of Louisiana. With an additional chapter on Cotton Seed, and its Uses. By J. R. Sypher. Cloth, pp. VII. and 190. 6s.

Lysons.—Our Vulgar Tongue. A Lecture on Language in general, with a few words on Gloucestershire in particular. Delivered before the Literary and Scientific Association at Gloucester, January 17th, 1868, with Appendix containing tables of the world-wide affinity of Languages. By the Rev. Samuel Lysons, M.A., F.S.A., Hon. Canon of Gloucester Cathedral, and Rector of Rodmarton, Author of "Our British Ancestors," "The Model Merchant of the Middle Ages," etc., etc. 8vo. stiff cover, pp. 51 and 62. 1868. 2s. 6d.

Maccall, W.—NATIONAL MISSIONS. A Series of Lectures. 8vo. pp. viii. and 382. 1855. 10s. 6d.

Maccall.—SACRAMENTAL SERVICES. 12mo. sewed, pp. 20. 1847. 6d.

Maccall.—THE AGENTS OF CIVILIZATION. A Series of Lectures. 12mo. cloth, pp. 126. 1843. 1s. 6d.

Maccall.—THE DOCTRINE OF INDIVIDUALITY. A Discourse delivered at Crediton, on the 28th of May, 1843. 12mo. sewed, pp. 22. 1843. 6d.

Maccall.—THE EDUCATION OF TASTE. A Series of Lectures. 12mo. sewed, pp. 104. 1846. 1s.

Maccall.—THE ELEMENTS OF INDIVIDUALISM. A Series of Lectures. 8vo. cloth, pp. 358. 1847. 7s. 6d.

Maccall.—THE INDIVIDUALITY OF THE INDIVIDUAL. A Lecture delivered at Exeter on the 29th March, 1844, before the Literary Society. 12mo. sewed, pp. 40. 1844. 6d.

Maccall.—THE LESSONS OF THE PESTILENCE. A Discourse delivered at Royston, on the 23rd September, 1849. 12mo. sewed, pp. 22. 1849. 6d.

Maccall.—THE UNCHRISTIAN NATURE OF COMMERCIAL RESTRICTIONS. A Discourse delivered at Bolton, on Sunday, the 27th September, 1840. 12mo. sewed, pp. 14. 1840. 3d.

Macfarlane.—A LETTER TO OUR GRANDCHILDREN. By William Macfarlane, Esq., Brighton, Author of "A Letter to the Bishop of Natal." 8vo. sewed, pp. 15. 1862. 2d.

Macfarlane.—A LETTER TO THE RIGHT REVEREND DR. COLENSO, Bishop of Natal, remonstrating against his leaving the Church of England. By William Macfarlane, Esq., Brighton. 8vo. sewed, pp. 8. 1862. 1d.

Macfarlane.—A PRACTICAL LETTER to the Citizens of the World on the Civil Wars among the Bishops and Clergy. By William Macfarlane, Esq., Brighton, Author of "A Letter to our Grandchildren," and "A Letter to the Bishop of Natal." 8vo. sewed, pp. 18. 1863. 3d.

Mackellar.—THE AMERICAN PRINTER. A Manual of Typography, containing complete instructions for beginners, as well as practical directions for managing all departments of a Printing Office. With several useful tables, schemes for imposing forms in every variety, hints to Authors and Publishers, etc., etc. By Thomas Mackellar. Crown 8vo. cloth, pp. 336. 1867. 9s.

Mackenzie.—CONDENSED TEMPERANCE FACTS FOR CHRISTIANS. With remarks on ancient and modern wines and malt liquors. By J. Mackenzie, M.D., Justice of the Peace, Provost of Inverness. 12mo. sewed, pp. 40. 1868. 3d.

Madeira.—A BRIEF LETTER OF ADVICE TO AN INVALID, in reply to a request for information about Madeira as a winter residence. By an ex-invalid. 8vo. sewed, pp. 8. 1859. 6d.

M'Caul.—JERUSALEM: its Bishop, its Missionaries, and its Converts; being a Series of Letters addressed to the Editor of the "Daily News" in the Year 1858, by the late Rev. Alexander M'Caul, D.D., with other Letters, etc., illustrative thereof. Collected and Edited by his Son, Samuel M'Caul, B.C.L., of St. John's College, Oxford, etc. 8vo. sewed, pp. 80. 1866. 1s. 6d.

McCulloch.—A TREATISE on the Circumstances which determine the Rate of Wages and the Condition of the Labouring Classes. By J. R. McCulloch, Esq. 12mo. cloth, pp. x. and 114. 1868. 1s.

McPherson.—THE POLITICAL HISTORY OF THE UNITED STATES OF AMERICA during the Great Rebellion, from November 6, 1860, to July 4, 1864; with Summary of the Legislation thereon, and the Executive, Judicial, and Politico-Military Facts; together with an Account of the Rebel Administration. By Edward McPherson, of Gettysburg, Pennsylvania, Clerk of the House of Representatives. Royal 8vo., bound. 1864. 18s.

Mahan.—AN ELEMENTARY COURSE OF MILITARY ENGINEERING. Part I. Comprising Field Fortifications, Military Mining and Siege Operations. By D. H. Mahan, LL.D., Professor of Military and Civil Engineering in the U. S. Military Academy. 8vo. cloth, pp. xxx. and 284. 1865. 16s.

"The best treatise on its subject we know—lucid, accurate, full, and yet concise..it is the book by which most can be learned about the art of war."—*United States Service Magazine.*

Mahan.—AN ELEMENTARY TREATISE ON MILITARY ENGINEERING Part II. Permanent Fortifications. By D. H. Mahan, LL.D. With Plates. 8vo. cloth, pp. 176. 25s.

Mahan.—SUMMARY OF THE COURSE OF PERMANENT FORTIFICATIONS, and of the Attack and Defence of Permanent Works. For the Use of the Cadets of the United States Military Academy. By D. H. Mahan, Professor of Military Engineering, at the United States Military Academy. 2 vols. 4to. with folio Plates. Lithographed at the United States Military Academy Press. 25s.

Mahan.—AN ELEMENTARY COURSE OF CIVIL ENGINEERING for the use of Cadets of the United States Military Academy. By D. H. Mahan, M.A. New Edition, with large Addenda, and many new Cuts. 8vo. cloth, pp. 410. 18s.

Maharajahs.—HISTORY OF THE SECT OF MAHARAJAHS; or, Vallabhacharyas in Western India. With a Steel Plate. 1 vol. 8vo. cloth, pp. xv. and 183. 1865. 12s.

Malleson.—ESSAYS AND LECTURES ON INDIAN HISTORICAL SUBJECTS. I. A Native State and its Rulers.—II. Lord Lake of Laswarrie.—III. Count Lallay.—IV. Havelock.—V. Hyder Ali's Last War.—VI. Sir Hugh Rose. By Major G. B. Malleson, Bengal Staff Corps. Crown 8vo. cloth, pp. 360. 1868. 6s.

Manava-Kalpa-Sutra.—Being a portion of this ancient Work on Vaidik Rites, together with the Commentary of Kumarila-Swamin. A Facsimile of the MS. No. 17, in the Library of Her Majesty's Home Government for India. With a Preface by Theodor Goldstücker. Oblong folio, pp. 268 of letter-press, and 121 leaves of facsimiles. Cloth. 1863. £4 4s.

Manipulus Vocabulorum.—A RHYMING DICTIONARY OF THE ENGLISH Language. By Peter Levins (1570). Edited, with an Alphabetical Index, by Henry B. Wheatley. 8vo. cloth, pp. xvi. and 370. 1867. 14s.

Mann.—A FEW THOUGHTS FOR A YOUNG MAN. A Lecture delivered before the Boston Mercantile Library Association, on its 29th anniversary. By Horace Mann. Second Edition. 12mo. sewed., 56 pp. 1854. 6d.

Mannheimer.—THE STUDY OF GERMAN SIMPLIFIED in a New Systematic and Practical Grammar, according to the Systems of Ollendorff and Dr. Ahn. By H. Mannheimer. Third Edition, carefully revised, greatly enlarged, and improved. Post 8vo., stiff covers, pp. 270. 1864. 4s. 6d.
Ditto. Ditto. Key to. 1s.

Manning.—INQUIRY INTO THE CHARACTER AND ORIGIN OF THE POSSESSIVE, AUGMENT, IN ENGLISH AND COGNATE DIALECTS. By James Manning, Q.A.S., Recorder of Oxford. Reprinted from the "Transactions of the Philological Society," with an Appendix and Index. 1 vol. crown 8vo., sewed, Pp. ii. and 90. 1864. 2s.

Manning.—THOUGHTS UPON SUBJECTS CONNECTED WITH PARLIAMENTARY REFORM. By James Manning, Her Majesty's Ancient Serjeant-at-Law. 8vo., sewed. Pp. 20. 1866. 1s.

Manual OF PUNCTUATION (A), for Self-teaching and for Schools. By a Practical Printer. 12mo. pp. 40, limp cloth. 1859. 1s.

Maritime CAPTURE.—Shall England uphold the Capture of Private Property at Sea? By a Lawyer. Post 8vo. sewed. Pp. 40. 1866. 1s.

Markham.—QUICHUA GRAMMAR AND DICTIONARY. Contributions towards a Grammar and Dictionary of Quichua, the Language of the Yncas of Peru; collected by Clements R. Markham, F.S.A., Corr. Mem. of the University of Chili, Author of "Cuzco and Lima," and "Travels in Peru and India." In one vol., crown 8vo., pp. 150, cloth. 1864. 10s. 6d.

Marmontel.—BÉLISAIRE. Par Marmontel. Nouvelle édition, revue et corrigée par Ernest Brette, Chas. Cassal, Theod Karker. 12mo. cloth, pp. xii. 123. 1867. 2s. 6d.

Martin.—THE AGE OF LOUIS XIV. By Henri Martin. Translated from the Fourth Paris Edition, with the author's sanction and co-operation. By Mary L. Booth. 2 vols. 8vo. cloth, pp. xxii. and 563; viii. and 543. 1865. £1 16s.

Martineau.—LETTERS FROM IRELAND. By Harriet Martineau. Reprinted from the "Daily News." Post 8vo. cloth, pp. viii. and 220. 1852. 6s. 6d.

Martineau.—A HISTORY OF THE AMERICAN COMPROMISES. Reprinted (with additions) from the "Daily News." By Harriet Martineau. 8vo. pp. 35. 1856. 1s.

Martineau.—ESSAYS, PHILOSOPHICAL AND THEOLOGICAL. By James Martineau. Crown 8vo. cloth, pp. iv. and 424. 1866. 10s. 6d.

Marx.—THE SERF AND THE COSSACK. A Sketch of the Condition of the Russian People. By Francis Marx. Second Edition, enlarged. 12mo. sewed, pp. 60. 1865. 1s.

Mason.—BURMAH: ITS PEOPLE AND NATURAL PRODUCTIONS; or, Notes on the Nations, Fauna, Flora, and Minerals of Tenasserim, Pegu, and Burmah; with systematic Catalogues of the known Mammals, Birds, Fish, Reptiles, Insects, Molluscs, Crustaceans, Annelids, Radiates, Plants, and Minerals, with Vernacular Names. By Rev. F. Mason, D.D., M.R.A.S., Corresponding Member of the American Oriental Society, etc., etc. Second Edition, 8vo. cloth, pp.xvii. and 913. 1860. 30s.

Massey, Gerald.—HAVELOCK'S MARCH; and other Poems. 12mo. cloth, pp. vii. and 269. 1861. 5s.

Mathura.—A TRILINGUAL DICTIONARY, being a comprehensive Lexicon in English, Urdú, and Hindí, exhibiting the Syllabication, Pronunciation, and Etymology of English Words, with their Explanation in English, and in Urdú and Hindí in the Roman Character. By Mathurá Prasáda Misra, Second Master, Queen's College, Benares. 8vo. cloth, pp. xiv. and 1330. 1865. £2 2s.

Matthay.—DEUTSCHE LITERATUR UND LESE-BUCH. German Literature and Reader. By T. Matthay, M.R.C.P., Professor to the Wimbledon College, Clapham Grammar School, and other Military and Ladies' Colleges, etc. Post 8vo., cloth, pp. viii. and 575. 1866. 7s. 6d.

Matthew.—SCHLESWIG-HOLSTEIN. By Patrick Matthew. 8vo. sewed, pp. 62. 1864. 1s.

Mayer PAPYRI, and the Palimpsest Manuscripts of Uranius belonging to M. Simonides, Report of the Council of the Royal Society of Literature, with letters from Messrs. Pertz, Ehrenberg, and Dindorf. 8vo. sewed, pp. 30. 1863. 1s.

Mayne.—THE LOST FRIEND. A Crimean Memory. And other Poems. By Colbourn Mayne, Esq. 12mo., cloth, pp. viii. and 134. 1857. 3s. 6d.

Mazzini.—AN ADDRESS TO POPE PIUS IX., on his Encyclical Letter. By Joseph Mazzini. 8vo., sewed, pp. 24. 4th Edition. 1865. 6d.

Medhurst.—CHINESE DIALOGUES, QUESTIONS, AND FAMILIAR SENTENCES, literally rendered into English, with a view to promote commercial intercourse, and assist beginners in the Language. By the late W. H. Medhurst, D.D. A new and enlarged edition. 8vo. sewed, pp. 225. 1863. 18s.

Meditations ON LIFE AND ITS RELIGIOUS DUTIES. Translated from the German by Frederica Rowan. Dedicated to H.R.H. Princess Louis of Hesse. Published by Her Majesty's gracious permission. Being the Companion Volume to "Meditations on Death and Eternity." 8vo. cloth, pp. 1863. 10s. 6d.

Ditto. Smaller Edition, crown 8vo., printed on toned paper, pp. 338. 1863. 6s.

Meditations ON DEATH AND ETERNITY. Translated from the German by Frederica Rowan. Published by Her Majesty's gracious permission. 8vo. cloth, pp. 386. 1862. 10s. 6d.

Ditto. Smaller Edition, crown 8vo. cloth, printed on toned paper, pp. 352. 1863. 6s.

Mellet.—SUNDAY AND THE SABBATH. Translated from the French of Louis Victor Mellet, Pastor of Yvorne. 12mo., sewed, pp. viii. 106. 1856. 1s.

Menke, Dr. T.—ORBIS ANTIQUI DESCRIPTIO: an Atlas illustrating Ancient History and Geography, for the Use of Schools; containing 18 Maps engraved on Steel and Coloured, with Descriptive Letter-press. 4th edition. Folio, half-bound morocco. 1866. 5s.

Mercer.—MOUNT CARMEL: A Poem. By Edward Smith Mercer. 12mo. sewed, pp. 80. 1867. 1s.

Mérimée.—COLOMBA. Par Prosper Mériméo, de l'Académie Francaise. 12mo. cloth, pp. viii. and 210. 1867. 3s. 6d.

Mertens.—Huit Jours à Londres, Guide du touriste et du voyageur. Par Constant Mertens. Small 4to. sewed, pp. 82. 1867. 3s.

Michael.—The Social Gospel. By R. J. Michael. First English Edition. To be continued by "The Social Code." Crown 8vo. sewed, pp. 294. 1867. 2s. 6d.

Michælis.—A New System of Stenography or Short-hand, on the Principles of W. Stolze. By Dr. Gustav Michælis. With 32 lithographic plates. 12mo. stiff covers, pp. viii. and 135. 1864. 3s.

Michælis.—The Little Tiro.—A Practical Compendium of English Shorthand. By Gustav Michælis. With Sixteen Lithographic Plates. 12mo. stiff covers, pp. 28. 1864. 1s.

Michel.—Les Écossais en France, Les Français en Écosse. Par Francisque Michel, Correspondant de l'Institut de France, etc. Handsomely bound in two Volumes, 8vo., in rich blue cloth, with emblematical designs. Pp. vii. 547 and 551, with upwards of 100 Coats of Arms, and other Illustrations. Price £1 12s.—Also a Large Paper Edition (limited to 100 Copies), printed on Thick Paper. Two Volumes, 4to., half morocco, with three additional Steel Engravings. 1862. £3 3s.

Michelena y Rójas.—Exploracion Oficial por la primera vez desde el Norte de la América del Sur siempre por Rios, entrando por las Bocas del Orinóco, de los Valles de este mismo y del meta, casiquiare, Rio-Negro ó Guaynia y Amazónas, hasta nauta en el alto Marañon ó Amazónas, arriba de las Bocas del Ucayali bajada del Amazónas Hasta el Atlántico. Comprendiendo en ese inmenso espacio los Estados de Venezuela, Guayana Inglesa, Nueva-Granada, Brásil, Ecuador, Péru y Bolivia. Viaje a Rio de Janeiro desde belen en el Gran Pará, por el Atlántico, tocando en las Capitales de las principales provincias del Imperio en los años, de 1855 hasta 1859. Por F. Michelena y Rójas, Viajero al Rededor del Mundo, Miembro de la Real Sociedad Economica Matritense y de la Real Academia de Arqueologia y de Geografia de la Misma. Publicado bajo los Auspicios del Gobierno de los Estados Unidosdo Venezuela. Royal 8vo. With Map. Sewed, pp. 684. 1867. 18s.

Miles.—The Social, Political and Commercial Advantages of Direct Steam Communication and Rapid Postal Intercourse between Europe and America, viâ Galway, Ireland. By Pliny Miles. Illustrated by a Map. 8vo. sewed, pp. 122. 1859. 1s.

Mill.—The Enfranchisement of Women. By Mrs. Stuart Mill. (Reprinted from the "Westminster Review.") 8vo. sewed, pp. 16. 1868. 1d.

Mill.—Auguste Comte and Positivism. By John Stuart Mill, Esq., M.P. 8vo. cloth, pp. 200. 1866. 6s.

Mill.—Speech of John Stuart Mill, Esq., M.P., on the Admission of Women to the Electoral Franchise, spoken in the House of Commons, May 20th, 1867. 8vo. sewed, pp. 18. 1867. 6d.

Millhouse.—New English and Italian Pronouncing and Explanatory Dictionary. By John Millhouse. Vol. I. English-Italian. Vol. II. Italian-English. Two vols. square 8vo. cloth. 3rd edition, with Numerous Additions and Improvements. Pp. 608 and 740. 1867. 12s.

Millhouse, John.—Manual of Italian Conversation. For the Use of Schools. 18mo. cloth, pp. 126. 1866. 2s.

Miscegenation: THE THEORY OF THE BLENDING OF THE RACES, applied to the American White Man and Negro. 12mo. cloth, pp. 92. 1864. 2s. 6d.

Modern FRENCH READER (The). Edited by the Rev. P. H. Ernest Brette, B.D., of Christ's Hospital, London; Professor Ch. Cassal, LL.D., of University College, London, and Theodor Karcher, LL.B., of the Royal Military Academy, Woolwich, former and present Examiner in the University of London, and for the Civil Service of India. Crown 8vo. cloth. 1868. 2s. 6d.

Moffat.—THE "STANDARD-ALPHABET" PROBLEM; or, the Preliminary Subject of a General Phonic System considered, on the basis of some important Facts in the Sechwana Language of South Africa, and in Reference to the Views of Professors Lepsius, Max Müller, and others. A Contribution to Phonetic Philology, by Robert Moffat, jun., Fellow of the Royal Geographical Society. 8vo. cloth, pp. xxviii. and 174. 1864. 7s. 6d.

Molesworth.—A DICTIONARY, MÁRATHI AND ENGLISH. Compiled by J. T. Molesworth, assisted by George and Thomas Candy. Second Edition, revised and enlarged, by J. T. Molesworth. Royal 4to. pp. xxx. and 922, boards. 1857. £3 3s.

Moor.—THE HINDU PANTHEON. By Edward Moor, F.R.S. A New Edition, with additional Plates, Condensed and Annotated, by the Rev. W. O. Simpson. 8vo. cloth, pp. xvi. and 402. With a Frontispiece and 59 Plates. 1864. £2 8s.

Morell.—RUSSIA AND ENGLAND; their Strength and their Weakness. By John Reynell Morell, Author of "Russia as it is," etc. 12mo. sewed, pp. 104. 1854. 1s.

Morgan.—A DICTIONARY OF TERMS USED IN PRINTING. By H. Morgan, Government Printing Establishment. 8vo. cloth, pp. 136. 1863. 7s. 6d.

Morgan.—THE DUKE'S DAUGHTER. A Classic Tragedy, Acting Edition. Pp. 78, roan. 5s.

Morley.—A DESCRIPTIVE CATALOGUE of the Historical Manuscripts in the Arabic and Persian Languages preserved in the Library of the Royal Asiatic Society of Great Britain and Ireland. By William H. Morley, M.R.A.S. 8vo., pp. viii. and 160, sewed. 1854. 2s. 6d.

Morley.—SUNRISE IN ITALY, etc. Reveries. By Henry Morley. 4to. cloth, pp. 164. 1848. 7s. 6d.

Morrison.—A DICTIONARY OF THE CHINESE LANGUAGE. By the Rev. R. Morrison, D.D. New Edition. 2 vols. small 4to. cloth. Vol. 1, pp. ix. and 762. Vol. 2. pp. 827. 1865. £4 4s.

Motley.—CAUSES OF THE CIVIL WAR IN AMERICA. By John Lothrop Motley, LL.D. Reprinted from the "Times." 8vo. sewed, pp. 30. 1861. 1s.

Muhammed.—THE LIFE OF MUHAMMED. Based on Muhammed Ibn Ishak. By Abd El Malik Ibn Hisham. Edited by Dr. Ferdinand Wüstenfeld. One volume containing the Arabic Text. 8vo. sewed, pp. 1026. 21s. Another Volume, containing Introduction, Notes, and Index in German. 8vo. sewed, pp. lxxii. and 266. 7s. 6d. Each part sold separately.

The text based on the Manuscripts of the Berlin, Leipsic, Gotha, and Leyden Libraries, has been carefully revised by the learned editor, and printed with the utmost exactness.

Muir.—ORIGINAL SANSKRIT TEXTS, on the Origin and History of the People of India, their Religion and Institutions. Collected, Translated, and Illustrated by J. Muir, Esq., D.C.L., LL.D. Volume First: Mythical and Legendary Accounts of the Origin of Caste, with an inquiry into its existence in the Vedic age. Second Edition. Re-written and greatly enlarged. 8vo. pp. xx. and 532, cloth. 1868. 21s.

Muir.—ORIGINAL SANSKRIT TEXTS, on the Origin and History of the People of India, their Religion and Institutions. Collected, Translated, and Illustrated by J. Muir, Esq., D.C.L., LLD. Volume Third. The Vedas: Opinions of their Authors, and of later Indian Writers, on their Origin, Inspiration, and Authority. Second Edition, Enlarged. [In the press.]

Muir.—ORIGINAL SANSKRIT TEXTS, on the Origin and History of the People of India, their Religion and Institutions. Collected, Translated into English, and Illustrated by Remarks, by J. Muir, D.C.L., LL.D. Vol. Fourth. Comparison of the Vedic with the later representation of the principal Indian Deities. 8vo. cloth, pp. xii. and 440. 1863. 15s.

Mulhall.—COTTON FIELDS OF PARAGUAY AND CORRIENTES; being an Account of a Tour through these Countries, preceded by Annals of Cotton Planting in the River Plate Territories, from 1862 to 1864. By Michael G. Mulhall. Square 8vo. sewed, pp. 120. 1866. 5s.

Müller.—PARALLÈLE ENTRE JULES CÉSAR, par Shakspeare, et La Mort de César, par Monsieur de Voltaire. Faite par Robert Müller, Philos. Doctor. 12mo. sewed, pp. 20. 1864. 1s.

Müller.—THE SACRED HYMNS OF THE BRAHMINS, as Preserved to us in the Oldest Collections of Religious Poetry, "The Rig Veda-Sanhita." Translated and Explained. By Max Müller, M.A., Taylorian Professor of Modern European Languages in the University of Oxford, Fellow of All Souls College. In 8 vols. [Vol. I. in the press.]

Müller.—OUTLINE DICTIONARY for the Use of Missionaries, Explorers and Students of Language. With an Introduction on the proper Use of the Ordinary English Alphabet in transcribing Foreign Languages. By Max Müller, M.A., Taylorian Professor in the University of Oxford. The Vocabulary compiled by John Bellows. 12mo. morocco, pp. 368. 1867. 7s. 6d.

Munch.—WILLIAM AND RACHAEL RUSSELL; A Tragedy, in Five Acts. By Andreas Munch. Translated from the Norwegian, and Published under the Special Sanction of the Poet. By John Heyliger Burt. 12mo. pp 126. 1862. 3s. 6d.

Münchausen, Baron.—THE TRAVELS AND SURPRISING ADVENTURES OF. With Thirty original Illustrations (Ten full-page coloured plates and twenty woodcuts), by Alfred Crowquill. Crown 8vo. ornamental cover, richly gilt front and back, pp. xii. and 194. 1859. 7s. 6d.

Munroe.—THE PHYSIOLOGICAL ACTION OF ALCOHOL. A Lecture delivered at the Royal Institution, Hull. By Henry Munroe, M.D., F.L.S. 8vo. sewed, pp. 35. 1865. 6d.

Nahl.—INSTRUCTIONS IN GYMNASTICS. By Arthur and Charles Nahl. Illustrated with 53 plates. Containing several hundred figures, Designed and Engraved by the Authors, representing the various exercises on the ground, the Vaulting Horse, Parallel Bars, Horizontal Bars, Rings, etc., including construction of Pyramids. Plan of Apparatus, etc. 4to. cloth, pp. 67. 1865. £1 1s.

Nayler.—An Appeal from the Prejudices to the Judgments of the Thinking Inhabitants of Pembrokeshire on the Sabbath Question. By B. S. Nayler. Small 4to. sewed, pp. 64. 1859. 1s.

Neale.—My Comrade and my Colours; or, Men who know not when they are Beaten. By Rev. E. Neale. 12mo. sewed, pp. 135. 1854. 1s.

Neutrals and Belligerents.—The Rights of Neutrals and Belligerents, from a Modern Point of View. By a Civilian. 8vo. sewed, pp. 41. 1862. 1s.

New Universal Dictionary of the English, French, Italian, and German Languages, arranged after a new system. Small 8vo. cloth, pp. 1200. 1865. 7s. 6d.

Newman—The Difficulties of Elementary Geometry, especially those which concern the straight line, the plane, and the theory of parallels. By Francis William Newman, formerly Fellow of Balliol College, Oxford. 8vo. boards, pp. viii. and 144. 1841. 5s.

Newman.—On the Relations of Free Knowledge to Moral Sentiment. A Lecture delivered in University College, London, on the 13th of October, 1847, as introductory to the Session of 1847-1848. By Francis W. Newman, Professor of Latin, and formerly Fellow of Balliol College, Oxford. 8vo. sewed, pp. 24. 1847. 1s.

Newman.—Lectures on Political Economy. By Francis William Newman. Post 8vo. cloth, pp. vi. and 342. 1851. 5s.

"The most able and instructive book, which exhibits, we think, no less moral than economical wisdom."—*Prospective Review.*

Newman.—A Reply to the Eclipse of Faith; being Chapter IX. of the Second Edition of the Phases of Faith. By F. W. Newman. Post 8vo. sewed, pp. 28. 1853. 6d.

Newman.—The Odes of Horace. Translated into Unrhymed Metres, with Introduction and Notes. By F. W. Newman, Professor of Latin, University College, London. Post 8vo. cloth, pp. xxi. and 247. 1853. 5s.

Newman.—The Crimes of the House of Hapsburg against its own Liege Subjects. By F. W. Newman. 8vo. sewed, pp. 60. 1853. 1s.

Newman.—The Iliad of Homer, faithfully translated into Unrhymed Metre. By F. W. Newman, Professor of Latin in University College, London. Crown 8vo. cloth, pp. xxii. and 436. 1856. 6s. 6d.

Newman.—Theism, Doctrinal and Practical; or, Didactic Religious Utterances. By Francis W. Newman. 4to. cloth, pp. 184. 1858. 8s. 6d.

Newman.—The Relations of Professional to Liberal Knowledge. A Lecture delivered in University College, London, October 12, 1859. Introductory to the Session of the Faculty of Arts and Laws, 1859-1860. By Francis W. Newman, Professor of Latin, and formerly Fellow of Balliol College, Oxford. 8vo. sewed, pp. 30. 1859. 1s.

Newman.—Homeric Translation in Theory and Practice. A Reply to Matthew Arnold, Esq., Professor of Poetry, Oxford. By Francis W. Newman, a Translator of the Iliad. Crown 8vo. stiff covers, pp. 104. 1861. 2s. 6d.

Newman.—HIAWATHA: Rendered into Latin. With Abridgment. By Francis William Newman, Professor of Latin in University College, London. 12mo. sewed, pp. vii. and 110. 1862. 2s. 6d.

Newman.—THE SOUL: Her Sorrows and her Aspirations. An Essay towards the Natural History of the Soul, as the Basis of Theology. By Francis William Newman, formerly Fellow of Balliol College, Oxford. New ed., post 8vo. cloth, pp. xi. and 162. 1868. 3s. 6d.

Newman.—A DISCOURSE AGAINST HERO-MAKING IN RELIGION, delivered in South Place, Finsbury. By Francis W. Newman. Printed by request, with enlargements. 8vo. sewed, pp. 30. 1864. 1s.

Newman.—CATHOLIC UNION: Essays towards a Church of the future, as the organization of Philanthropy. By F. W. Newman. Post 8vo. cloth, pp. 113. 1864. 3s. 6d.

Newman.—A HISTORY OF THE HEBREW MONARCHY from the Administration of Samuel to the Babylonish Captivity. By Francis William Newman, formerly Fellow of Balliol College, Oxford, and Author of "The Soul; its Sorrows and Aspirations," etc. Third edition, crown 8vo. cloth, pp. x. and 354. 1865. 8s. 6d.

Newman.—PHASES OF FAITH; or, Passages from the History of my Creed. New Edition; with Reply to Professor Henry Rogers, Author of the "Eclipse of Faith." Crown 8vo. cloth, pp. 212. 1865. 3s. 6d.

Newman.—ENGLISH INSTITUTIONS AND THEIR MOST NECESSARY REFORMS. A Contribution of Thought. By Francis W. Newman. 8vo. pp. 32. 1865. 6d.

Newman.—THE PERMISSIVE BILL MORE URGENT THAN ANY EXTENSION OF THE FRANCHISE. An Address at Ramsgate, February 17th, 1865. By F. W. Newman. 8vo. sewed, pp. 12. 1865. 1d.

Newman.—A HANDBOOK OF MODERN ARABIC: consisting of a Practical Grammar, with numerous examples, etc. By F. W. Newman. Crown 8vo. cloth, pp. xxx. and 190. 1866. 6s.

Newman.—ON THE PHILOSOPHICAL CLASSIFICATION OF NATIONAL INSTITUTIONS. A Lecture delivered at the Bristol Institution for the Advancement of Science, Literature, and the Arts, March 4th, 1867. By F. W. Newman. Published by Request. 8vo. sewed, pp. 24. 1867. 6d.

Newman.—THE TEXT OF THE IGUVINE INSCRIPTIONS. With Interlinear Latin Translation and Notes. By Francis W. Newman. 8vo. sewed, pp. 56. 1868. 2s.

Newman.—TRANSLATIONS OF ENGLISH POETRY INTO LATIN VERSE. Designed as Part of a New Method of Instructing in Latin. By Francis W. Newman, Emeritus Professor of University College, London, formerly Fellow of Balliol College, Oxford. In 1 crown 8vo. vol. cloth, pp. xiv. and 202. 1868. 6s.

Newton.—THE OPERATION OF THE PATENT LAWS, with Suggestions for their better Administration. By A. V. Newton. 8vo. sewed, pp. 31. 1864. 6d.

Nicholson.—E PUR SI MUOVE. By N. A. Nicholson, M.A., Trinity College, Oxford. 8vo. cloth, pp. 115. 1866. 2s. 6d.

Nicholson.—ONE RESERVE OR MANY? Thoughts Suggested by the Crisis of 1866. By N. A. Nicholson, M.A., Trinity College, Oxford. Post 8vo. sewed, pp. 21. 1867. 1s.

Nicholson.—THE CONTROVERSY ON FREE BANKING, being a few observations on an Article in "Fraser's Magazine," January, 1868. By N. A. Nicholson, M.A., Trinity College, Oxford. 8vo. sewed, pp. 32. 1868. 1s.

Nicholson.—OBSERVATIONS ON COINAGE, SEIGNORAGE, etc., etc. By N. A. Nicholson, M.A., Trinity College, Oxford. 8vo. sewed, pp. 22. 1868. 1s.

Norton.—A TREATISE ON ASTRONOMY, SPHERICAL AND PHYSICAL; with Astronomical Problems, and Solar, Lunar, and other Astronomical Tables, for the use of Colleges, and Scientific Schools. By William A. Norton, M.A., Professor of Civil Engineering in Yale College. Fourth Edition. Revised, remodelled, and enlarged. 8vo. cloth, pp. 574. With numerous plates. 1867. 15s.

Notes and Queries ON CHINA AND JAPAN. Edited by N. B. Dennys. Vol. I. January to December, 1867. Royal 8vo., double columns, pp. 186, sewed. £1 1s.

Nott.—LECTURES ON BIBLICAL TEMPERANCE. By Eliphalet Nott, D.D. With an Introduction. By Taylor Lewis, LL.D. Post 8vo. cloth, pp. 268. 1863. 6s.

Ditto. Ditto. sewed. 1863. 1s.

Nott and Gliddon.—TYPES OF MANKIND; or, Ethnological Researches based upon the Ancient Monuments, Paintings, Sculptures, and Crania of Races, and upon their Natural, Geographical, Philological, and Biblical History. By J. C. Nott, M.D., Mobile, Alabama; and Geo. R. Gliddon, formerly U.S. Consul at Cairo. Plates. Royal 8vo. cloth, pp. 738. 1854. £1 5s.

Nott and Gliddon.—THE SAME, in 4to. £1 16s.

Nott and Gliddon.—INDIGENOUS RACES OF THE EARTH: or, New Chapters of Ethnological Inquiry: including Monographs on Special Departments of Philology, Iconography, Cranioscopy, Palæontology, Pathology, Archæology, Comparative Geography, and Natural History, contributed by Alfred Maury, Francis Pulszky, and J. Aitken Meigs, M.D.; presenting Fresh Investigations, Documents, and Materials, by J. C. Nott, M.D., and Geo. R. Gliddon. Plates and Maps. 4to. pp. 656, sewed. 1857. £1 16s.

Nott and Gliddon.—THE SAME, royal 8vo. £1 5s.

Nouvelles PLAISANTES RECHERCHES d'un Homme Grave sur quelques Farceurs. 8vo. pp. 53. 1863. 10s. 6d.

Novalis.—CHRISTIANITY OF EUROPE. By Novalis (Frederick Von Hardenberg). Translated from the German by the Rev. John Dalton. Post 8vo. cloth, pp. 34. 1844. 1s.

Nugent's IMPROVED FRENCH AND ENGLISH AND ENGLISH AND FRENCH POCKET DICTIONARY. Par Smith. 24mo. cloth, pp. 489 and 320. 1867. 3s.

Nyström.—POCKET BOOK OF MECHANICS AND ENGINEERING, containing a Memorandum of Facts and Connection of Practice and Theory. By John W. Nyström, C.E. 10th Edition, pp. 326. Revised with additional matter, 12mo. roan with tuck. 1867. 7s. 6d.

Oehlschlager's GERMAN-ENGLISH AND ENGLISH-GERMAN Pocket Pronouncing Dictionary. New edition, 24mo. strongly bound in cloth. 4s.

Ogareff.—ESSAI SUR LA SITUATION RUSSE. Lettres à un Anglais. Par N. Ogareff. 12mo. sewed, pp. 150. 1862. 3s.

Oliver.—A TRANSLATION OF THE SYRIAC PESHITO VERSION OF THE PSALMS OF DAVID, with notes, critical and explanatory. By the Rev. Andrew Oliver, M.A. Crown 8vo. cloth, pp. xiv. and 332. 1861. 7s. 6d.

Ollendorff.—MÉTODO PARA APRENDU A LEER, escribir y hablar el Inglés segun el sistema de Ollendorff. Por Ramon Palenzuela y Juan de la Carreño. 8vo. cloth, pp. xlvi. and 460. 1867. 7s. 6d.
Key to ditto. 12mo. cloth, pp. 111. 1863. 5s.

Omnibus, The.—A SATIRE. Crown 8vo. limp cloth, pp. 44. 1865. 2s. 6d.

O'Neill.—THE FINE ARTS AND CIVILIZATION OF ANCIENT IRELAND, illustrated with chromo and other lithographs, and several woodcuts. By Henry O'Neill, author of the work on "The most interesting of the Sculptured Crosses of Ancient Ireland." 4to. pp. vi. and 118, cloth. 1863. 15s.

Oriental Text Society Publications.

1. THEOPHANIA, or Divine Manifestations of our Lord and Saviour. By Eusebius, Bishop of Caesarea, Syriac. Edited by Professor S. Lee. 8vo. 1842. 15s.
2. ATHANASIUS' FESTAL LETTERS, discovered in an ancient Syriac version. Edited by the Rev. W. Cureton. 8vo. 1848. 15s.
3. SHAHRASTANI: Book of Religious and Philosophical Sects, in Arabic. Two parts. 8vo. 1842. 30s.
4. UMDAT AKIDAT ahl al Sunnat wa al Tamaat; Pillar of the Creed of the Sunnites. Edited in Arabic by the Rev. W. Cureton. 8vo. 1843. 5s.
5. HISTORY OF THE ALMOHADES. Edited in Arabic by Dr. R. P. A. Dozy. 8vo. 1847. 10s. 6d.
6. SAMA VEDA. Edited in Sanskrit by the Rev. G. Stevenson. 8vo. 1843. 12s.
7. DASA KUMARA CHARITA. Edited in Sanskrit by Professor H. H. Wilson. 8vo. 1846. 15s.
8. MAHA VIRA CHARITA, or a History of Rama. A Sanskrit Play. Edited by F. H. Trithen. 8vo. 1848. 15s.
9. MAKHZAN UL ASRAR; the Treasury of Secrets. By Nizami. Edited in Persian by N. Bland. 4to. 1844. 10s. 6d.
10. SALAMAN-U-URSAL; a Romance of Jami (Dahami). Edited in Persian by F. Falconer. 4to. 1843. 10s.
11. MIRKHOND'S HISTORY OF THE ATABEKS. Edited in Persian by W. H. Morley. 8vo. 1850. 12s.
12. TUHFAT-UL-AHRAR; the Gift of the Noble. A Poem by Jami (Dshami). Edited in Persian by F. Falconer. 4to. 1843. 10s.

Oswald.—AUSTRIA IN 1868. By Eugene Oswald. Reprinted from the "English Leader." 8vo. sewed, pp. 40. 1868. 1s.

Orthodox Catholic Review (THE). Edited by Professor J. J. Overbeck. Vol. 1. 8vo. cloth, pp. iv. and 290. 1868. 7s. 6d.

Osburn.—THE MONUMENTAL HISTORY OF EGYPT, as recorded on the Ruins of her Temples, Palaces, and Tombs. By William Osburn, F.S.L. Illustrated with Maps, Plates, etc. 2 vols. 8vo. cloth, pp. xii. and 461; vii. and 643. 1854. £2 2s.
  Vol. I. From the Colonization of the Valley to the Visit of the Patriarch Abram.
  Vol. II. From the Visit of Abram to the Exodus.

Ott.—THE ART OF MANUFACTURING SOAP AND CANDLES, including the most recent discoveries, embracing all kinds of ordinary Hard, Soft, and Toilet Soaps, especially those made by the Cold Process, the modes of detecting frauds, and the making of Tallow and Composite Candles. By Adolph Ott, Ph. D., Practical and Analytical Chemist. 8vo. cloth, pp. xxi. and 193. 1867. 10s. 6d.

Our North-West Frontier. With Map. 8vo. sewed, pp. 20. 1856. 1s.

Our Resources. A Series of Articles on the Financial and Political Condition of the United States. 8vo. sewed, pp. 32. 1864. 1s.

Overbeck.—CATHOLIC ORTHODOXY AND ANGLO-CATHOLICISM. A Word about the Intercommunion between the English and Orthodox Churches. By J. J. Overbeck, D.D. 8vo. cloth, pp. viii. and 209. 1866. 5s.

Overman.—MECHANICS FOR THE MILLWRIGHT, MACHINIST, ENGINEER, CIVIL ENGINEER, ARCHITECT, AND STUDENT; containing a clear elementary exposition of the Principles and Practice of Building Machines. By Frederick Overman, Author of "The Manufacture of Iron," and other scientific treatises. Illustrated by 154 fine Wood Engravings by William Gihon. Post 8vo. cloth, pp. 420. 1864. 7s.

Overman.—PRACTICAL MINERALOGY, ASSAYING AND MINING, with a Description of the useful Minerals, and instructions for Essaying and Mining according to the simplest methods. By Frederick Overman, mining engineer, Author of "Manufacture of Iron," and other works of applied sciences. Fifth Edition. Post 8vo. cloth, pp. 230. 1862. 4s. 6d.

Overman.—THE MANUFACTURE OF STEEL; containing the Practice and Principles of working and making Steel. A hand-book for blacksmiths and workers in steel and iron, wagon-makers, die-sinkers, cutlers, and manufacturers of files and hardware, of steel and iron, and for men of science and art. By Frederick Overman, Mining Engineer; Author of the "Manufacture of Iron," etc. Post 8vo. cloth, pp. 226. 1860. 4s. 6d.

Overman.—THE MOULDER'S AND FOUNDER'S POCKET GUIDE. A Treatise on moulding and founding in green-sand, dry-sand, loam, and cement; the moulding of machine frames, mill-gear, hollow ware, ornaments, trinkets, bells, and statues; description of moulds for iron, bronze, brass, and other metals; plaster of Paris, sulphur, wax, and other articles commonly used in casting; the construction of melting furnaces, the melting and foundering of metals; the composition of alloys and their nature. With an Appendix, containing receipts for alloys, bronze, varnishes and colours for castings, also tables on the strength and other qualities of cast metals. By Frederick Overman, Mining Engineer; Author of "The Manufacture of Iron," "a Treatise on Steel," etc., etc. With 42 Wood Engravings. Post 8vo. cloth, pp. 252. 1866. 4s. 6d.

Owen.—FOOTFALLS ON THE BOUNDARY OF ANOTHER WORLD. An enlarged English Copyright Edition. Ten editions of this work have been sold within a very short time in America. In the present edition, the author has introduced a considerable quantity of new matter. Post 8vo. cloth, pp. xx. and

Owlglass (MASTER TYLL).—THE MARVELLOUS ADVENTURES AND RARE CONCEITS OF. Edited, with an Introduction, and a Critical and Bibliographical Appendix. By Kenneth R. H. Mackenzie, F.S.A., with six coloured full-page Illustrations, and twenty-six Woodcuts, from original designs by Alfred Crowquill. Cloth gilt, pp. xix. and 255. 1860. 10s. 6d.

Oyster (THE): WHERE, HOW, AND WHEN TO FIND, BREED, COOK, AND EAT IT. Second Edition, with a new chapter, 'The Oyster-Seeker in London.' 12mo. boards, pp. viii. and 106. 1863. 1s.

Page.—LA PLATA, THE ARGENTINE CONFEDERATION AND PARAGUAY. Being a Narrative of the Exploration of the Tributaries of the River La Plata and adjacent countries during the years 1853, 1854, 1855, and 1856, under the orders of the United States Government. By Thomas J. Page, U. S. N. Commander of the Expedition. With Map and numerous Engravings. New Edition. 8vo. cloth, pp. 632. £1 1s.

Palmer.—EGYPTIAN CHRONICLES, with a Harmony of Sacred and Egyptian Chronology, and an Appendix on Babylonian and Assyrian Antiquities. By William Palmer, M.A., and late Fellow of Magdalen College, Oxford. 2 vols. 8vo. cloth, pp. lxxiv. 428, viii. and 636. 1861. 12s.

Palmerston.—LORD PALMERSTON. By R. H. Reprinted from the *Westminster Review* for January, 1866. 8vo. sewed, pp. 36. 1866. 1s.

Pandit (THE).—A MONTHLY JOURNAL OF BENARES COLLEGE, devoted to Sanskrit Literature. Vol. 1. Nos. 1 to 24, November, 1866, to May, 1868. Folio sewed, pp. 184. £2 8s.

The object of the *Pandit* is to publish rare Sanskrit works which appear worthy of careful editing hereafter; to offer a field for the discussion of controverted points in Old Indian Philosophy, Philology, History, and Literature; to communicate ideas between the Aryan scholars of the East and of the West; between the Pandits of Benares and Calcutta and the Sanskritists of the Universities of Europe.

The Journal, which will be enlarged as soon as the subscriptions cover the actual expenses of publication, will contain also Original Articles in Sanskrit and English, Critical Notices of new Sanskrit Books, and Translations from and into Sanskrit.

Annual subscription, 24s. Intending subscribers are requested to address the European Publishers.

Papers ON PICTURE FLAYING AT THE NATIONAL GALLERY. Reprinted from the *Weekly Despatch*. By an Artist. Post 8vo. sewed, pp. 44. 1867. 1s.

Parker.—THE PUBLIC FUNCTION OF WOMAN. A Sermon preached at the Music Hall, March 27, 1853. By Theodore Parker. Post 8vo. sewed. 1855. 1s.

Parker.—THE COLLECTED WORKS OF THEODORE PARKER, Minister of the Twenty-Eighth Congregational Society at Boston, U.S. Containing his Theological, Polemical, and Critical Writings; Sermons, Speeches, and Addresses; and Literary Miscellanies. Edited by Frances Power Cobbe. In 12 vols. 8vo., 1863 to 1865.

    Vol. I. Containing Discourses on Matters pertaining to Religion; with Preface by the Editor, and a Portrait of Parker, from a medallion by Saulini. Cloht, pp. 380. 6s.
    Vol. II. Containing Ten Sermons and Prayers. Cloth, pp. 360. 6s.
    Vol. III. Containing Discourses of Religion. Cloth, pp. 318. 6s.
    Vol. IV. Containing Discourses on Politics. Cloth, pp. 312. 6s.
    Vol. V. Containing Discourses of Slavery, Vol. I. Cloth, pp. 336. 6s.
    Vol. VI. Containing Discourses of Slavery, Vol. II. Cloth, pp. 323. 6s.
    Vol. VII. Containing Discourses of Social Science. Cloth, pp. 296. 6s.
    Vol. VIII. Contains Miscellaneous Discourses. Cloth, pp. 230. 6s.
    Vol. IX. Containing Critical Writings, Vol. I. Cloth, pp. 292. 6s.
    Vol. X. Containing Critical Writings, Vol. II. Cloth, pp. 308. 6s.
    Vol. XI. Containing Sermons of Theism, Atheism, and Popular Theology. Cloth, pp. 257. 6s.
    Vol. XII. Autobiographical and Miscellaneous pieces. Cloth, pp. 356. 6s.

Parker.—LESSONS FROM THE WORLD OF MATTER AND THE WORLD OF MAN; being Selections from the unpublished Sermons of Theodore Parker. By Rufus Leighton, and Edited by Frances Power Cobbe. Post 8vo. cloth, pp. xix. and 332. 1865. 7s. 6d.

Parker.—THE CRITICAL WRITINGS OF THEODORE PARKER. Edited by Frances Power Cobbe. 2 vols. 8vo., cloth, pp. 600. 1864-5. 12s.

Parrish.—A TREATISE ON PHARMACY; designed as a Text Book for the Student, and as a Guide to the Physician and Pharmaceutist. Containing the official and many unofficial formulas, and many examples of extemporaneous prescriptions. By Edward Parrish, Professor of Materia Medica in the Philadelphia College of Pharmacy. Third Edition, revised with important additions. 238 Illustrations. 8vo. cloth, pp. 850. £1 4s.

Partnership, WITH LIMITED LIABILITY. Reprinted, with additions, from the *Westminster Review*. New Series, No. 8, October, 1853. Post 8vo., sewed, pp. 63. 1854. 1s.

Partridge.—THE MAKING OF THE AMERICAN NATION; or, the Rise and Decline of Oligarchy in the West. Showing how the American Nation and Democracy have been made, and what they are, with considerations on their tendency and destiny. 8vo. cloth, pp. xxxvii. and 523. 1866. 16s.

Partridge.—ON DEMOCRACY. By J. Arthur Partridge. 8vo. cloth, pp. 418. 1866. 10s.

Parvula; OR A FEW LITTLE RHYMES ABOUT A FEW LITTLE FLOWERS, A FEW LITTLE BIRDS, AND A FEW LITTLE GIRLS; to which are added a Few Little Songs, and a Few other Little Things, by Minimus. 18mo. cloth, pp. 192. 1864. 5s.

Patell.—COWASJEE PATELL'S CHRONOLOGY, containing corresponding dates of the different eras used by Christians, Jews, Greeks, Hindus, Mohamedans, Parsees, Chinese, Japanese, etc. By Cowasjee Sorabjee Patell, 4to. cloth, pp. viii. and 183. 1866. £2 10s.

Paterson.—TREATISE ON MILITARY DRAWING. With a Course of 25 Progressive Plates. By Captain W. Paterson, Professor of Military Drawing at the Royal Military College, Sandhurst. Oblong 4to. cloth, pp. xii. and 31. 1862. £1 1s.

Paton.—RESEARCHES ON THE DANUBE AND THE ADRIATIC; or, Contributions to the Modern History of Hungary and Transylvania, Dalmatia, and Croatia, Servia and Bulgaria. By A. A. Paton, F.R.G.S. In 2 vols. 12mo., cloth, pp. 830. 1861. 12s.

Paton.—A HISTORY OF THE EGYPTIAN REVOLUTION, from the Period of the Mamelukes to the Death of Mohammed Ali; from Arab and European Memoirs, Oral Tradition, and Local Research. By A. A. Paton, F.R.G.S., Author of "Researches on the Danube and the Adriatic." 2 vols. 8vo. cloth, pp. xii., 395, and viii. 352. 1863. £1 4s.

Paton.—SKETCHES OF THE UGLY SIDE OF HUMAN NATURE. By A. A. Paton. Crown 8vo. cloth, pp. 302. 1868. 7s. 6d.

Percy.—Bishop Percy's Folio Manuscript—Ballads and Romances. Edited by John W. Hales, M.A., Fellow and late Assistant Tutor of Christ's College, Cambridge; and Frederick J. Furnivall, M.A., of Trinity Hall, Cambridge; assisted by Professor Child, of Harvard University, U.S.A., W. Chappell, Esq., etc. In 3 vols. Vol. 1, pp. 610. Vol. 2, pp. 681. Vol. 3, pp. 640. Demy 8vo., half-bound, £2 2s. Extra demy 8vo., half-bound, on Whatman's ribbed paper, £3 15s. Extra royal 8vo., paper covers, on Whatman's best ribbed paper, £5 5s. Large 4to., paper covers, on Whatman's best ribbed paper, £10 10s.

Perrin.—An English-Zulu Dictionary. By J. Perrin. New Edition, revised by J. A. Brickhiel, Interpreter to the Supreme Court of Natal. 16mo. cloth, pp. 226. Pietermaritzburg. 1865. 5s.

Petöfi.—Poems, Selected from the Works of the Great Hungarian Bard, Alexander Petöfi. Translated from the Magyar, with a Biographical and Critical Introduction by Sir John Bowring, K.C.B., LL.D., etc., etc. Fcap. 8vo. cloth, pp. viii. and 239. 1866. 5s.

Petruccelli.—Preliminaires de la Question Romaine de M. Ed. About. Par F. Petruccelli de la Gattina. 8vo. cloth, pp. xv. and 364. 1860. 7s. 6d.

Petzholdt.—Bibliotheca Bibliographica. Kritisches Verzeichniss der das Gesammtgebiet der Bibliographie betreffenden Litteratur des In-und Auslandes. In Systematischer Ordnung bearbeitet von Dr. Julius Petzholdt. Mit Alphabetischem Namen-und Sachregister. Royal 8vo., paper covers, pp. 939. 1866. 12s.

Philological Society.—Proposals for the Publication of a New English Dictionary. 8vo. sewed, pp. 32. 1859. 6d.

Pick.—A New Method of Studying Foreign Languages. By Dr. Edward Pick. The French Language, Part 1, the Genders and Irregular Verbs. Part 2, New Method of Studying the Language. 12mo. cloth, pp. viii. and 212. 1863. 3s. 6d.

Pick.—On Memory and the Rational Means of Improving It. By Dr. Edward Pick. Fourth Edition, with new Applications to the Study of the French and German Languages. Royal 18mo. cloth, pp. vi. and 20. 1866. 3s. 6d.

Pick.—On Memory. By Dr. Edward Pick. A Condensed Edition. Royal 18mo. limp, pp. 140. 1866. 1s. 6d.

Pickering.—The Geographical Distribution of Animals and Plants. By Charles Pickering, M.D. 4to. cloth, pp. 214. 1864. 15s.

Picture Flaying (Papers on) at the National Gallery. Reprinted from the *Weekly Dispatch*. By an Artist. 8vo. sewed, pp. 44. 1867. 1s.

Piggot.—Chemistry and Metallurgy, as applied to the study and practice of Dental Surgery. By A. Snowden Piggot, M.D., late Professor of Anatomy and Physiology in the Washington University of Baltimore. With numerous Illustrations. 8vo. cloth, pp. 516. 1854. 18s.

Piggot.—The Chemistry and Metallurgy of Copper, including a description of the principal Copper Mines of the United States and other countries, the art of mining and preparing ores for market, and the various processes of Copper Smelting, etc. By A. Snowden Piggot, M.D., Analytical and Consulting Chemist. With Illustrations. Post 8vo. cloth, pp. 388. 1858. 7s. 6d.

Pilgrims of Fashion.—A Novel. By R. C. 8vo. pp. xvi. and 338. Cloth. 1862. 16s.

Pim.—The Negro and Jamaica. By Commander Bedford Pim, R.N. Read before the Anthropological Society of London, February 1st, 1866, at St. James's Hall. Post 8vo. sewed, pp. vii. and 32. 1866. 1s.

Pirazzi.—L'Angleterre et l'Allemagne à propos du Schleswig-Holstein. Par Emile Pirazzi. Mémoire envoyé à plusieurs membres du parlement Anglais et suivi d'un article à l'adresse du *Times*. 8vo. sewed, pp. 180. 1865. 2s. 6d.

Plain Papers.—By Pikestaff. Vol. I. 12mo. cloth, pp. vii. and 144. 1866. 1s.

Plumb-Line (The); or the True System of the Interpretation of Scripture. Also Queries on the Foregoing Subjects. 8vo. sewed, pp. iv. and 63. 1861. 1s.

Poe.—The Works of Edgar Allan Poe. In 4 vols., crown 8vo. cloth. Vol. 1, pp. lv. and 483. Vol. 2, pp. xxvi. and 495. Vol. 3, pp. 607. Vol. 4, pp. 447. 1866. £1 12s.

Policy of the Danish Government and the "Misunderstandings." A Key to the Budget Dispute. 8vo. sewed, pp. 74. 1861. 1s.

Political (The).—Problem of the Day. Mr. Gladstone the Man to Solve It. 8vo. sewed, pp. 21. 1865. 1s.

Ponsard.—Charlotte Corday. A Tragedy. By F. Ponsard. Edited with English Notes and Notice on Ponsard, by Professor C. Cassal, LL.D., of University College, London. 12mo. cloth, pp. xi. and 133. 1867. 2s. 6d.

Popes' Rights and Wrongs. An Historical Sketch. 12mo. cloth, pp. xiv. and 97. 1860. 2s 6d.

Popes (The).—Their Temporal Dominion and Infallibility. An Argument between a Lady and an Italian. 12mo. sewed, pp. 8. 2d.

Porcari.—The Senate of Rome and the Pope. S. P. Q. R. By Stephano Porcari. 8vo. sewed, pp. 30. 1867.

Powell.—A Working Man's View of Tennyson's "Enoch Arden." By J. H. Powell. 12mo. sewed, pp. 29. 1866. 6d.

Powell.—Life Incidents and Poetic Pictures. By J. H. Powell. Post 8vo. cloth, pp. iv. and 264. 1865. 5s.

Preaching Suited to the Times. A Charge from Utopia. 16mo. sewed, pp. 39. 1865. 1s.

Preciosa; A Tale. Fcap. 8vo. cloth, pp. 326. 1852. 7s. 6d.

Prescott.—Life of William Hickling Prescott. By George Ticknor. 4to., pp. x. and 492. Printed on Toned Paper. With Portrait and Illustrations. Ornamental Binding, uncut. Gilt top. 1864. £1 16s.

Prescott.—Sir Rohan's Ghost. A Romance. By Miss Prescott. Crown 8vo. cloth, pp. x. and 352. 1860. 5s.

Prescott.—History, Theory, and Practice of the Electric Telegraph. By George B. Prescott, Superintendent of Electric Telegraph

Priaulx.—QUESTIONES MOSAICÆ, or the First Part of the Book of Genesis, compared with the Remains of Ancient Religions. By Osmond de Beauvoir Priaulx. Second Edition, corrected and enlarged. 8vo. cloth, pp. vii. and 548. 1854. 12s.

Pritchard.—ADMIRALTY DIGEST. A Digest of the Law and Practice of the High Court of Admiralty of England, with Notes from Text Writers, and the Scotch, Irish, and American Reports. By William Tarn Pritchard, Proctor in Doctors Commons. Second edition, omitting Prize and Slave Cases. By Robert A. Pritchard, D.C.L., of the Inner Temple, Barrister-at-Law, and William Tarn Pritchard. With Notes of Cases from French Maritime Law. By Algernon Jones, Avocat à la Cour Impériale de Paris, in 2 vols. roy. 8vo. 1865. £3.

Probyn.—ESSAYS ON ITALY, IRELAND, AND THE UNITED STATES OF AMERICA. By John W. Probyn, Esq. 1 vol., crown 8vo. [*In the press.*

Pulszky.—THREE CHRISTMAS PLAYS FOR CHILDREN. The Sleeper awakened. The Wonderful Bird. Crinolina. By Theresa Pulszky. With Music by Professor L. Jansa, and Illustrations by Charles Armytage. Square 12mo. pp. 130, cloth. 1859. 3s. 6d.

Quentin.—AN ACCOUNT OF PARAGUAY. Its History, its People, and its Government. From the French of M. Ch. Quentin. 8vo. sewed, pp. 90. 1865. 1s.

Quinet.—ULTRAMONTISM; or, The Roman Church and Modern Society. By E. Quinet, of the College of France. Translated from the French (Third edition), with the Author's approbation. By C. Cocks, B.L. Post 8vo. pp. ix. and 184, cloth. 1845. 5s.

Raja-Niti.—A COLLECTION OF HINDU APOLOGUES, IN THE BRAJ BHA'SHA' LANGUAGE. Revised Edition. With a Preface, Notes, and supplementary glossary. By Fitzedward Hall, Esq. 8vo. cloth, pp. 204. 1854. £1 1s.

Ram Raz.—ESSAY ON THE ARCHITECTURE OF THE HINDUS. By Ram Raz, Native Judge and Magistrate of Bangalore, Corresponding Member of the R.A.S. of Great Britain and Ireland. With 48 Plates. 4to., pp. xiv. and 64, sewed. 1834. Original selling price, £1 11s. 6d., reduced (for a short time only) to 12s.

Randall.—FINE WOOL SHEEP HUSBANDRY. By Henry S. Randall, LL.D. Read before the New York State Agricultural Society, February 12, 1862. With an Appendix, containing valuable statistics in reference to wool culture, imports, prices of fine wool from 1840 to August 1, 1863, etc. Small 8vo. cloth, pp. 190. 5s.

Randall.—THE PRACTICAL SHEPHERD. A Complete Treatise on the Breeding, Management, and Diseases of Sheep. By Henry S. Randall, LL.D. With Illustrations. 8vo. cloth, pp. ix. and 454. 1864. 10s. 6d.

Rask.—GRAMMAR OF THE ANGLO-SAXON TONGUE, from the Danish of Erasmus Rask. By Benjamin Thorpe. Second edition, corrected and improved, with Plate. Post 8vo. cloth, pp. vi. and 191. 1865. 5s. 6d.

Rask.—A SHORT TRACTATE on the Longevity ascribed to the Patriarchs in the Book of Genesis, and its relation to the Hebrew Chronology; the Flood, the Exodus of the Israelites, the Site of Eden, etc. From the Danish of the late Professor Rask; with his manuscript corrections, and large additions from his autograph, now for the first time printed. With a Map of Paradise and the circumjacent Lands. Crown 8vo. cloth, pp. 134. 1863. 2s. 6d.

Ravenstein.—The Russians on the Amur; its Discovery, Conquest, and Colonization, with a Description of the Country, its Inhabitants, Productions, and Commercial Capabilities, and Personal Accounts of Russian Travellers. By E. G. Ravenstein, F.R.G.S., Correspondent F.G.S. Frankfurt, with an Appendix on the Navigation of the Gulf of the Amur. By Captain Prutz. In one volume, 8vo., 500 pp. of Letter Press, 4 tinted Lithographs, and 3 Maps, cloth. 1861. 15s.

Ravenstein and Hulley.—The Gymnasium and its Fittings. By E. G. Ravenstein and John Hulley. With 14 Plates of Illustrations. 8vo. sewed, pp. 32. 1867. 2s. 6d.

Ravenstein and Hulley.— A Hand-book of Gymnastics and Athletics. By E. G. Ravenstein, F.R.G.S., etc., President of the German Gymnastic Society, London, and John Hulley, Gymnasiarch of Liverpool. With numerous Woodcut Illustrations from original designs. 8vo. cloth, pp. viii. and 408. 1867. 8s. 6d.

Rawlinson.—A Commentary on the Cuneiform Inscriptions of Babylonia and Assyria, including Readings of the Inscription on the Nimrud Obelisk, and a brief Notice of the ancient Kings of Nineveh and Babylon. Read before the Royal Asiatic Society, by Major H. C. Rawlinson. 8vo. pp. 84, sewed. London, 1850. 2s. 6d.

Rawlinson.—Outlines of Assyrian History, from the Inscriptions of Nineveh. By Lieut.-Colonel Rawlinson, C.B., followed by some Remarks, by A. H. Layard, Esq., D.C.L. 8vo. pp. xliv., sewed. 1852. 1s.

Read.—Poems. By Thomas Buchanan Read. Illustrated by Kenny Meadows. 12mo. cloth, pp. vii. and 275. 1852. 6s.

Reade—White Lies; a Story. By Charles Reade. In 3 volumes, 8vo., Vol. I., pp. 300; Vol. II., pp. 238; Vol. III., pp. 232. 1857. £1 1s.

Reade.—Cream. Contains "Jack of all Trades;" "A Matter-of-Fact Romance," and "The Autobiography of a Thief." By Charles Reade. 8vo. pp. 270. 1858. 10s. 6d.

Reade.—Love me Little, Love me Long. By Charles Reade. In 2 vols. post 8vo. Vol. I. pp. 390; Vol. II., pp. 35. 8vo. cloth. 1859. 21s.

Reade.—The Eighth Commandment. By Charles Reade. 8vo., pp. 380. 1860. 14s.

Reade.—The Cloister and the Hearth; a Tale of the Middle Ages. By Charles Reade. In four volumes. Third edition. Vol. I., pp. 360; Vol. II., pp. 376; Vol. III., pp. 328; Vol. IV., pp. 435. 1861. £1 11s. 6d.

The Same. Fourth edition. In 3 vols. Crown 8vo. cloth, pp. 328, 391, 338. 1862. 15s.

Reform.—Letter to the Right Honourable the Earl of Derby, on Political Reform. By One of the People. Post 8vo. sewed, pp. 46. 1867. 1s.

Reiff.—ENGLISH-RUSSIAN GRAMMAR; or, Principles of the Russian Language for the Use of the English. With Synoptical Tables for the Declensions and Conjugations, Graduated Themes or Exercises for the Application of the Grammatical Rules, the Correct Construction of these Exercises, and the Accentuation of all the Russian Words. By Charles Philip Reiff. Third edition, carefully revised. 8vo. sewed, pp. viii. and 191. 1862. 6s.

Reiff.—LITTLE MANUAL OF THE RUSSIAN LANGUAGE. By Ch. Ph. Reiff. 12mo. sewed, pp. 80. 1863. 2s. 6d.

Renan.—AN ESSAY on the Age and Antiquity of the Book of Nabathæan Agriculture. To which is added, an Inaugural Lecture on the Position of the Shemitic Nations in the History of Civilization. By M. Ernest Renan, Membre de l'Institut. In 1 Vol., crown 8vo. cloth, pp. xvi. and 148. 1862. 3s. 6d.

Renan.—THE LIFE OF JESUS. By Ernest Renan. Authorised English Translation. 8vo. cloth, pp. xii. and 311. 1864. 10s. 6d.
Ditto. Crown 8vo. cloth, pp. xii. and 311. 1865. 2s. 6d.
Ditto. Crown 8vo. paper, pp. xii. and 311. New edition. 1867. 1s. 6d.

Report OF THE COMMITTEE APPOINTED BY THE CONFERENCE OF MEMBERS OF THE REFORM LEAGUE AND OTHERS, on Mr. Hare's Scheme of Representation, held at their Rooms, on 28th February, and 7th and 21st March, 1868. 8vo. 1s.

Report OF THE SUB-COMMITTEE of the Newcastle-on-Tyne Association for watching the war limitation of the supply of grain by the past action of British Diplomacy. 8vo. sewed, pp. 24. 1855. 1s.

Revised ARMY REGULATIONS.—Vol. I. Royal Warrant for the Pay and Promotion, Non-Effective, Pay and Allowances of Majesty's British Forces serving elsewhere than in India. To which are added Instructions to Commanding and Financial Officers. Part I. Pay dated February 3rd, 1866. 8vo. sewed, pp. 182. 1866. 1s.

Revolt (THE) OF REASON AGAINST THE REVEALED. In One Volume, 8vo. (Shortly).

Reynard THE FOX; after the German Version of Göthe. By Thomas J. Arnold, Esq.

"Fair jester's humour and ready wit
Never offend, though smartly they hit."

With Seventy Illustrations, after the designs of Wilhelm Von Kaulbach. Royal 8vo. pp. vi. 226. Printed by Clay, on toned paper, and elegantly bound in embossed cloth, with appropriate design after Kaulbach; richly tooled front and back. Price 16s. Best full morocco, same pattern. Price 24s.; or, neatly half-bound morocco, gilt top, uncut edges, Roxburgh style. 1860. Price 18s.

Richard Cobden, ROI DES BELGES. Par un Ex-Colonel de la Garde Civique. Dédié aux blessés de Septembre. Deuxième édition. Crown 8vo. sewed, pp. 64. 1863. 2s. 6d.

Richter.—TITAN; A Romance. From the German of Jean Paul Friedrich Richter. Translated by Charles T. Brooks. 2 vols. 12mo. cloth

Richter.—FLOWER, FRUIT, AND THORN PIECES; or, the Married Life, Death, and Wedding of the Advocate of the Poor, Firmian Stanislaus Siebenkäs. By Jean Paul Friedrich Richter. Translated from the German, by Edward Henry Noel. With a Memoir of the Author. By Thomas Carlyle. In two volumes. 12mo. cloth, pp. viii. 361, and v. 345. 1863. 21s.

Richter.—LEVANA; or, the Doctrine of Education. Translated from the German of Jean Paul Friedrich Richter. 12mo. cloth, pp. xvii and 400. 1864. 10s.

Richter.—LIFE OF JEAN PAUL FRIEDRICH RICHTER, compiled from various sources. Preceded by his Autobiography. By Eliza Buckminster Lee. 12mo. cloth, pp. xvi. and 539. 1864. 7s. 6d.

Richter.—HESPERUS; or, Forty-Five Dog-Post Days. A Biography, from the German of Jean Paul Friedrich Richter. Translated by Charles T. Brooks. 2 vols. 12mo. cloth, pp. xxviii. 498, and v. 478. 1865. 21s.

Riddell.—THE CARPENTER AND JOINER, AND ELEMENTS OF HAND-RAILING. By Robert Riddell. With 32 Plates. Folio cloth, pp. 26. 1868. £1 1s.

Rights (THE) OF NEUTRALS AND BELLIGERENTS. From a modern point of view. By a Civilian. 8vo. sewed, pp. 42. 1862. 1s.

Rig-Veda-Sanhita (THE). THE SACRED HYMNS OF THE BRAHMINS, as preserved to us in the oldest collection of Religious Poetry. The Rig-Veda-Sanhita, translated and explained. By Max Müller, M.A., Taylorian Professor of Modern European Languages in the University of Oxford, Fellow of All Soul's College. In 8 vols., 8vo. [*Vol. I. in the press.*

Rig-Veda Sanhita.—A COLLECTION OF ANCIENT HINDÚ HYMNS, constituting the first Ashtáka, or Book, of the Rig-Veda, the oldest authority for the religious and social institutions of the Hindús. Translated from the original Sanskrit. By the late H. H. Wilson, M.A., F.R.S., etc., late Boden Professor of Sanskrit in the University of Oxford. With a postscript, by Dr. Fitzedward Hall. Vol. I., 8vo. cloth, pp. lii. and 348. 1866. £1 1s.

Rig-Veda Sanhita.—A COLLECTION OF ANCIENT HINDÚ HYMNS, constituting the second Ashtáka, or Book, of the Rig-Veda; the oldest authority for the religious and social institutions of the Hindús. Translated from the original Sanskrit. By the late H. H. Wilson, M.A., F.R.S., late Boden Professor of Sanskrit in the University of Oxford. Vol. II. 8vo. cloth, pp. xxx. and 346. 1854. 21s.

Rig-Veda Sanhita.—A COLLECTION OF ANCIENT HINDÚ HYMNS, constituting the third and fourth Ashtákas, or Books, of the Rig-Veda; the oldest authority for the religious and social institutions of the Hindús. Translated from the original Sanskrit. By the late H. H. Wilson, M.A., F.R.S., late Boden Professor of Sanskrit in the University of Oxford. Vol. III. 8vo. cloth, pp. xxiv. and 525. 1857. 21s.

Rig-Veda Sanhita.—A COLLECTION OF ANCIENT HINDÚ HYMNS, constituting the first Ashtaka, or Book, of the Rig-Veda; the oldest authority for the religious and social institutions of the Hindus. Translated from the original Sanskrit by the late H. H. Wilson, M.A., F.R.S., etc., late Boden Professor of Sanskrit in the University of Oxford. Edited by E. B. Cowell, M.A., late Principal of the Sanskrit College, Calcutta, and now Professor of Sanskrit in the University of Cambridge. Vol. IV. 8vo. cloth, pp. viii. and 314. 1866. 14s.

Riley.—MEDIÆVAL CHRONICLES OF THE CITY OF LONDON.—Chronicles of the Mayors and Sheriffs of London, and the Events which happened in their Days, from the Year A.D. 1188 to A.D. 1274. Translated from the original Latin of the "Liber de Antiquis Legibus" (published by the Camden Society), in the possession of the Corporation of the City of London; attributed to Arnold Fitz-Thedmar, Alderman of London in the Reign of Henry III.— Chronicles of London, and of the Marvels therein, between the Years 44 Henry III., A.D. 1260, and 17 Edward III., A.D. 1343. Translated from the original Anglo-Norman of the "Croniques de London," preserved in the Cottonian Collection (Cleopatra A. iv.) in the British Museum. Translated, with copious Notes and Appendices, by Henry Thomas Riley, M.A., Clare Hall, Cambridge; of the Inner Temple, Barrister-at-Law. The Two Parts bound in one handsome Volume. 4to. cloth, pp. xii. and 319. 1863. 12s.

Ditto. Morocco, gilt edges, pp. xii. and 319. 1863. £1 1s.

Ditto. Vellum, red edges, pp. xii. and 319. 1863. £1 1s.

Ripley.—SACRED RHETORIC; or, Composition and Delivery of Sermons. By Henry I. Ripley, Professor of Sacred Rhetoric and Pastoral Duties in Newton Theological Institute. To which are added, Hints on Extemporaneous Preaching. By Henry Ware, Jun., D.D. 12mo. cloth, pp. 234. 1858. 2s. 6d.

River Plate (THE). (South America), as a Field for Emigration; its Geography, Climate, Agricultural Capabilities, and the Facilities afforded for permanent Settlement. With Maps, Third edition. Revised by the Legation of the Argentine Republic. 8vo. pp. 60, sewed. 1867. 1s.

Robertson.—PRIESTCRAFT. By F. Robertson, F.R., Astron. Soc., late of Royal Engineers. Part I. 8vo. cloth. Second edition, pp. 181. 1867. 4s.

Robertson.—AN EXPOSITION OF THE BOOK OF GENESIS. By F. Robertson, F.R.A.S., late Royal Engineers, author of "Priestcraft," etc. 8vo. boards, pp. viii. and 262. 1868. 5s.

Robinet.—NOTICE sur les Travaux et la Vie D'Auguste Comte. Par le Dr. Robinet. 8s.

Roche.—HISTOIRE DE FRANCE; Depuis les Temps les Plus Reculés. par Antonin Roche. Troisième edition. Two volumes, 12mo. sewed, pp. vii. 504 and 519. 1867. 7s.

Roche.—ENGLISH PROSE AND POETRY. Materials for Translation from English into French. By Antonin Roche. 12mo. cloth, pp. xi. 368. 1867. 4s. 6d.

Roche.—ABRÉGÉ DE LA GRAMMAIRE FRANÇAISE. Par Antonin Roche, ouvrage dont l'introduction dans les Ecoles publiques a été autorisée par arrêté du Ministre de l'Instruction publique. 12mo., pp. vi. and 132. 1861. 1s.

Roche.—CORRIGÉ DE LA SYNTAXE DES EXERCISES SUR LA GRAMMAIRE FRANÇAISE. Par Antonin Roche, Directeur de l'Educational Institute de Londres, Chevalier de la Légion d'honneur. 3rd éd. 12mo., pp. 140. 1s.

Roche.—EXERCICES SUR L'ABRÉGÉ DE LA GRAMMAIRE FRANÇAISE. Par Antonin Roche, Chevalier de la Légion d'honneur. 2nd éd. 12mo., pp. vi. and 140. 1s.

Roche.—EXERCICES SUR LA GRAMMAIRE FRANÇAISE. Par Antonin Roche. 12mo., pp. iv. and 244. 1s. 6d.

Roche.—GRAMMAIRE FRANÇAISE, Ouvrage adopté pour les Ecoles publiques par arrêté du Ministre de l'Instruction publique en date du 22 Août, 1859. Par Antonin Roche, Directeur de l'Educational Institute de Londres, Chevalier de la Légion d'honneur. 5th éd. 12mo., pp. 208. 1s 6d.

Roche.—HISTOIRE DES PRINCIPAUX ECRIVAINS FRANÇAIS, depuis l'origine de la Littérature jusqu'à nos jours, par Antonin Roche, Directeur de l'Educational Institute de Londres. 2 vols. 12mo. pp. 700. 1863. 6s.

Roche.—LES POËTES FRANÇAIS, Recueil de morceaux, choisis dans les meilleurs poëtes depuis l'origine de la littérature française jusqu'à nos jours, avec une notice biographique sur chaque auteur, par Antonin Roche, Directeur de l'Educational Institute de Londres, Chevalier de la Légion d'honneur 7th éd. augmentée. 12mo. pp. 532. 3s. 6d.

Roche.—LES PROSATEURS FRANÇAIS, Recueil de morceaux choisis dans les meilleurs prosateurs depuis l'origine de la littérature française jusqu'à nos jours avec une notice biographique sur chaque auteur par Antonin Roche. Directeur de l'Educational Institute de Londres, Chevalier de la Légion d'honneur. 8th éd. augmentée. 12mo. pp. 544. 1867. 4s.

Ronge.—THE AUTOBIOGRAPHY AND JUSTIFICATION OF JOHANNES RONGE (the German reformer), translated from the fifth German edition, by John Lord, A.M. 12mo. sewed, pp. x. and 84. 1856. 1s. 6d.

Rowley.—A PAPER upon the Egg of Æpyornis Maximus, the Colossal Bird of Madagascar. By George Dawson Rowley, M.A. 8vo. sewed, pp. 16. 1864. 1s.

Rowley.—THE REMAINS of Man and Extinct Mammalian Fauna, found in Eynesbury, near St. Neots, Huntingdonshire. By George Dawson Rowley, M.A., F.Z.S. 8vo. sewed, pp. 15. 1866. 1s.

Russia, CENTRAL ASIA, AND BRITISH INDIA. By a British Subject. Post 8vo. sewed, pp. 48. 1865. 1s.

Saint Petersburg, Sights of, Book First; Fact, Feeling, and Fun. Wahrheit und Dichtung. 8vo. pp. 76, sewed. 1860. 2s. 6d.

Samson.—ELEMENTS OF ART CRITICISM, comprising a Treatise on the Principles of Man's Nature as addressed by Art; together with a Historic Survey of the Methods of Art-Execution in the departments of Drawing, Sculpture, Architecture, Painting, Landscape Gardening, and the Decorative Arts. Designed as a Text-book for Schools and Colleges, and as a Handbook for Amateurs and Artists. By G. W. Samson, D.D., President of Columbia College, Washington D.C. 8vo. cloth, pp. 840. 1867. 16s.

Sand.—MOLIÈRE. A Drama in prose. By George Sand. Edited, with English Notes and Notice on George Sand, by Theodore Karcher, LL.B., of the Royal Military Academy and the University of London. 12mo. pp. xx. and 170, cloth. 1868. 3s. 6d.

Sanitary CONDITION OF NEW YORK. Report of the Council of Hygiene and Public Health of the Citizens' Association of New York, upon the Sanitary Condition of the City. Published, with an Introductory Statement, by Order of the Council of the Citizen's Association. 8vo. cloth, pp. cxliii. and 360. Maps, Plates. 1865. 25s.

Sanitary "REFORM." "A Model Deputation!" By A Member of the Sanitary Reform Association. Post 8vo. sewed, pp. 8. 1866. 3d.

Santorin, THE KAIMENI ISLANDS. From Observations by K. von Fritsch, W. Reiss, and A. Stübel. Translated from the German. With 4 Photographic Maps. Folio, sewed, pp. 8. 1867. 16s.

Sartorius.—MEXICO. Landscapes and Popular Sketches. By C. Sartorius. Edited by Dr. Gaspey, with Engravings by distinguished Artists. from original Sketches, by Moritz Rugendas. 4to. cloth gilt, pp. vi. and 202. 1859. 18s.

Saxe.—THE MASQUERADE and other Poems. By John Godfrey Saxe. 12mo. cloth, pp. vii. and 237. 1866. 6s.

Saxe.—THE POEMS OF JOHN GODFREY SAXE. Complete in one volume. Crown 8vo. cloth, gilt top, pp. xii. and 466. With a portrait of the author. 1868. 10s. 6d.

Scandinavia AND GREAT BRITAIN, Comparative List of the Birds of. Small Folio, pp. 18, sewed. 1859. 1s.

Scanzoni.—A PRACTICAL TREATISE on the Diseases of the Sexual Organs of Women. By Professor F. W. Von Scanzoni. Translated by A. K. Gardner. 8vo. cloth, pp. xxi. and 669. 1861. 25s.

Sceptic.—AN EXPOSITION OF SPIRITUALISM; comprising two Series of Letters, and a Review of the "Spiritual Magazine," No. 20. As published in in the "Star and Dial." With Introduction, Notes, and Appendix. By Sceptic. 8vo. cloth, pp. 330. 1862. 6s.

Schefer.—THE BISHOP'S WIFE. A Tale of the Papacy. Translated from the German of Leopold Schefer. By Mrs. J. R. Stodart. 12mo. cloth, pp. 200. 1851. 2s. 6d.

Schefer.—THE ARTIST'S MARRIED LIFE: being that of Albert Dürer. For devout Disciples of the Arts, Prudent Maidens, as well as for the Profit and Instruction of all Christendom, given to the light. Translated from the German of Leopold Schefer, by Mrs. J. R. Stodart. Post 8vo. sewed, pp. 98. 1853. 1s.

Schefer.—THE LAYMAN'S BREVIARY; or, Meditations for Every-day in the Year. From the German of Leopold Schefer. By C. T. Brookes. Square, cloth, gilt, pp. iv. and 452. With a portrait of the author. 1867. 10s. 6d.

Schoelcher.—DANGERS TO ENGLAND OF THE ALLIANCE WITH THE MEN OF THE COUP-D'ETAT. By Victor Schoelcher, Representative of the People. 12mo., sewed, pp. 190. 1854. 2s. 6d.

Schimmelfennig.—THE WAR BETWEEN TURKEY AND RUSSIA. A Military Sketch. By A. Schimmelfennig. 8vo. sewed, pp. 68. 1854. 2s.

Schlagintweit.—BUDDHISM IN TIBET: Illustrated by Literary Documents and Objects of Religious Worship. With an Account of the Buddhist Systems preceding it in India. By Emil Schlagintweit, LL.D. With a folio Atlas of 20 Plates, and 20 Tables of Native print in the Text. Royal 8vo., pp. xxiv. and 404. 1863. £2 2s.

Schlagintweit.—GLOSSARY OF GEOGRAPHICAL TERMS from India and Tibet, with Native Transcription and Transliteration. By Hermann de Schlagintweit. Forming, with a "Route Book of the Western Himalaya, Tibet, and Turkistan," the Third Volume of H., A., and R, de Schlagintweit's "Results of a Scientific Mission to India and High Asia." With an Atlas, in imperial folio, of Maps, Panoramas, and Views. Royal 4to., pp. xxiv. and 293. 1863. £4.

Schlagintweit.—Results of a Scientific Mission to India and High Asia. By Hermann, Adolphe, and Robert de Schlagintweit; undertaken between the years 1854 and 1858, by Order of the Court of Directors of the Honourable East India Company.

The Work will consist of Nine Volumes of Scientific Text, and of an Atlas, in Three Volumes Folio, containing Views and Maps, with explanatory Letterpress.

Her Majesty Queen Victoria has been most graciously pleased to accept the Dedication of the Atlas.

Vols. I. to IV. now ready (Text in 4to., Atlas in folio). 1861—1866. £4 4s. each.

Intending Subscribers may obtain Prospectuses, and every information required, of the Publishers.

Schvarcz.—The Failure of Geological attempts made by the Greeks from the Earliest Ages down to the Epoch of Alexander. By Julius Schvarcz, F.G.S. Revised and enlarged edition. 4to. pp. xx. and 154, cloth. 1868. 10s. 6d.

Sclater.—Catalogue of a Collection of American Birds belonging to Mr. Philip Linsley Sclater, M.A., Th. Doc. F.R.S., Fellow of Corpus Christi College, Oxford; Secretary to the Zoological Society of London; Editor of "The Ibis." 8vo. pp. 354, and 20 coloured Plates of Birds, cloth. 1862. £1 10s.

Scott.—Memoirs of Lieut.-General Winfield Scott, LL.D., late Commander-in-Chief of the United States Forces. Written by Himself. With two Portraits. 2 vols. crown 8vo. cloth, pp. xxii. 330 and 653. 1864. 16s.

Scully.—Brazil; its Provinces and Chief Cities; the Manners and Customs of the People; Agricultural, Commercial, and other Statistics, taken from the latest Official Documents; with a variety of useful and entertaining knowledge, both for the Merchant and Emigrant. By William Scully, editor of the "Anglo-Brazilian Times." Crown 8vo. cloth, pp. viii. and 398. 7s. 6d.

Seabridge.—Connected Poems. By Charles Seabridge. 18mo. cloth, pp. 138. 1866. 3s. 6d.

Serf (The) and the Cossack; or, Internal State of Russia. Second edition, revised and enlarged. 12mo., sewed, pp. 48. 1854. 6d.

Seyd.—California and its Resources. A Work for the Merchant, the Capitalist, and the Emigrant. By Ernest Seyd. 8vo. cloth, plates, pp. 168. 1858. 8s. 6d.

Shapurji Edalji.—A Dictionary, Gujarátí and English. By Shapurji Edalji. Second edition. 8vo. cloth, pp. xxiv. and 874. 1868. £1 1s.

Shapurji Edalji.—A Grammar of the Gujarátí Language. By Shapurji Edalji. 12mo. cloth, pp. 128. 10s. 6d.

Shaw.—Odontalgia, commonly called Tooth-Ache; its Causes, Prevention and Cure. By S. Parsons Shaw. 12mo. pp. xi. and 258, cloth, 1868. 4s. 6d.

Sherring.—The Sacred City of the Hindus: an Account of Benares in Ancient and Modern Times. By the Rev. M. A. Sherring, M.A. LL.B., and prefaced with an Introduction by Fitz-Edward Hall, Esq., D.C.L. Shortly. In a handsome 8vo. Volume of about 300 pages, with 10 Full-page Woodcut Illustrations from Photographs. Pp. xxxvi. and 388, cloth. 1868. 21s.

Simon.—THE MINISTRY OF ORIGINAL WORDS IN ASSERTING AND
DEFENDING THE TRUTH. By B. A. Simon. 8vo. cloth pp. 123. 1865. 4s.

Simonides.—Διόκλεους δαμόρου τοῦ καρυστιθοῦ ἡ περὶ ὑγιεινῶν
ἐπιστόλη, καὶ Τροφίλου πραξιάδου ὑλλαρίμεως δειψάνα. (Diokles' Letter on
Hygiene and Trophilus Recipes. Edited by Dr. Const. Simonides). Square
12mo. pp. 24, sewed. 1865. 1s.

Simonides.—'Επιστολίμαια περὶ ἱερογλυφικῶν γραμματῶν δια-
τρίβε. (A brief Dissertation on Hieroglyphic Letters. By Constantine Simonides,
Ph. D.) 8vo. pp. 58, sewed. 1863. 2s. 6d.

Simonides.—'Ορθοδοξῶν ἑλληνῶν θεολόγικαι γραφαὶ τεσσάρες.
(A. Nikolaos, Bishop of Mothone ; B. Genniadios, Archbishop of Constantinople ;
C. Gregorios, Archbishop of Thessalonich ; D. Georgios Kressios). Edited by
Constantine Simonides, Ph. D. 8vo. pp. 240, cloth (with portrait of Nicolaos).
1865. 10s.

Simonides.—CONCERNING HORUS OF NILOPOLIS, the Hierogramma-
tist of his native place, son of Amonthis and Thessais. With notices of his works.
By Constantine Simonides, Ph. D. 4to. pp. 16, sewed. 1863. 2s. 6d.

Simonides.—FAC-SIMILES of Certain Portions of the Gospel of St.
Matthew, and of the Epistles of St. James and Jude. Written on Papyrus in
the first century, and preserved in the Egyptian Museum of Joseph Mayer, Esq.,
Liverpool. Edited and annotated, etc., etc., by Constantine Simonides, Ph. D.
Folio, pp. 80, with numerous fac-similes, sewed. 1862. £1 11s. 6d.

Simonides.—REPORT OF THE COUNCIL OF THE ROYAL SOCIETY OF
LITERATURE on some of the Mayer Papyri and the Palimpsest MS. of Uranius
belonging to M. Simonides. With Letters from MM. Pertz, Ehrenberg, and
Dindorf. 8vo. pp. 27, sewed. 1863. 1s.

Simonides.—THE PERIPLUS OF HANNON, King of the Karchedo-
nians. Concerning the Lybian part of the Earth beyond the Pillars of Heracles,
which is dedicated to Kronos, the greatest God, and to all the Gods dwelling
with him. 4to. pp. 82, and two fac-similes, sewed. 1864. 10s.

Simpson.—AN INTRODUCTION TO THE PHILOSOPHY OF SHAKESPEARE'S
SONNETS. By Richard Simpson. Crown 8vo. pp. 8vo, cloth. 1868. 3s. 6d.

Smart.—AN ADDRESS to Soldiers on Leaving England for Foreign
Service. By Newton Smart, M.A. Sixth edition. 12mo. pp. 30. 1866. 3d.

Smith.—REVIEWS AND ESSAYS FOR THE MILLION, from Genesis to
Revelations. By Brooke Smith, Esq., Stoke Bishop, Gloucestershire. Fcap.
8vo. pp. 160, cloth. 1868. 3s. 6d.

Smith.—LOCAL SELF-GOVERNMENT AND CENTRALIZATION. The
Characteristics of each ; and its Practical Tendencies as affecting Social,
Moral, and Political Welfare and Progress. Including Comprehensive Outlines
of the English Constitution. With copious Index. By J. Toulmin Smith,
Esq., Barrister-at-Law. Post 8vo. cloth, pp. viii. and 409. 1851. 5s.

Smith.—SOCIAL ASPECTS. By John Stores Smith, author of
"Mirabeau," a Life History. Post 8vo. cloth, pp. iv. and 258. 1850. 2s. 6d.

Smith.—THE COMMON NATURE OF EPIDEMICS; also Remarks on Contagion and Quarantine. By Southwood Smith, M.D. 8vo. cloth, pp. vi. and 130. 1866. 3s. 6d.

Smith.—THE DIVINE GOVERNMENT. By Southwood Smith, M.D. Fifth Edition. Crown 8vo. cloth, pp. xii. and 276. 1866. 6s.

Solling.—DIUTISKA: an Historical and Critical Survey of the Literature of Germany, from the Earliest Period to the death of Göthe. By Gustav Solling. 8vo. pp. xviii. and 368. 1863. 10s. 6d.

Solling.—SELECT PASSAGES FROM THE WORKS OF SHAKESPEARE. Translated and Collected. German and English. By Gustav Solling. 12mo. cloth, pp. 155. 1866. 3s. 6d.

Somerset.—UNE CENTAINE D'INVENTIONS, OUVRAGE ÉCRIT EN 1655, par Edouard Somerset, Marquis de Worcester, traduit en Français pour la première fois, sur la texte de la première edition (Londres, 1663), et édité par Henry Dircks, C.E., LL.D., F.R.S.E. M.R.S.L., etc., autour de "The Life of the Marquis of Worcester," "Worcesteriana," etc., etc. 12mo. pp. 62, sewed, 1868. 1s.

Somerville.—EROS. A Series of Connected Poems. By Lorenzo Somerville. 18mo. cloth, pp. 142. 1866. 3s. 6d.

Sophocles.—A GLOSSARY OF LATER AND BYZANTINE GREEK. By E. A. Sophocles. 4to., pp. iv. and 624. 1860. £2 8s.

Sophocles.—ROMAIC, OR MODERN GREEK GRAMMAR. By E. A. Sophocles. 8vo., half-bound, pp. xxviii. and 196. 1866. 7s. 6d.

Spaggiari.—A LATIN, ENGLISH, ITALIAN, AND POLYGLOT ANTHOLOGY, with a variety of Translations and Illustrations. To be published once a year; designed to contribute to the cause of classical learning, as well as to forward the cultivation of the English language and literature in Italy, and that of the Italian in Great Britain, America, and Australia. Edited by John Spaggiari. Oct. 1861. No. 1, oblong 4to, sewed, pp. 10. 1861. 2s. 6d.

Spear.—ON THE POSITION OF WOMEN. By Mrs. J. H. Spear. 12mo. limp, pp. 37. 1866. 1s.

Spellen.—THE INNER LIFE OF THE HOUSE OF COMMONS. By J. N. Spellen. 12mo. sewed. 1854. 6d.

Spinoza's TRACTATUS THEOLOGICO-POLITICUS: A Critical Inquiry into the History, Purpose, and Authenticity of the Hebrew Scriptures; with the Right to Free Thought and Free Discussion asserted, and shown to be not only consistent, but necessarily bound up with True Piety and Good Government. By Benedict de Spinoza. From the Latin. With an Introduction and Notes by the Editor. 8vo. cloth, pp. 386. 1862. 10s. 6d.

Spinoza.—TRACTATUS THEOLOGICO-POLITICUS. A Theological and Political Treatise in a Series of Essays, showing that freedom of thought and of discussion may not only be granted with safety to religion and the peace of the state, but that both the public peace and piety are endangered when such freedom is denied. By Benedict de Spinoza. From the Latin, with an introduction and note by the Editor. Second edition, revised and corrected. 8vo. pp. 360. (In the press).

Spruner.—Dr. Karl Von Spruner's Historico-Geographical Hand-Atlas, containing 26 Coloured Maps engraved on copper, 22 of which are devoted to the General History of Europe, and 4 are specially illustrative of the History of the British Isles. Oblong, cloth-lettered, 15s., or half-bound morocco, 1861. £1 1s.

Stevens.—Seasoning for a Seasoner; or, the New Gradus ad Parnassum; a Satire. By Brook B. Stevens. 8vo. cloth, pp. 48. 1861. 3s.

Stewart.—Sorghum and its Products. An account of recent investigations concerning the value of sorghum in sugar production, together with a description of a new method of making sugar and refined syrup from this plant. Adapted to common use, by F. L. Stewart. Post 8vo. pp. xiv. and 240, cloth. 1867. 6s.

Stillé.—Therapeutics and Materia Medica: a Sytematic Treatise on the Action and Uses of Medicinal Agents. By Alfred Stillé, M.D. Second Edition, revised, 2 vols. 8vo., cloth, pp. xv. 776, and viii. 819. 1864. £2 8s.

Stoddard.—Grammar of the Modern Syriac Language as spoken in Oroomah, Persia, and in Koordistan. By Rev. D. T. Stoddard. 8vo. boards, pp. 180. 1865. 7s. 6d.

Storer.—First Outlines of a Dictionary of Solubilities of Chemical Substances. By Frank H. Storer. Indispensable to the practical chemist. Royal 8vo. cloth, pp. xi. and 713. 1864. £1 11s. 6d.

Story.—Commentaries on the Law of Promissory Notes, and Guaranties of Notes, and Cheques on Banks and Bankers. With occasional illustrations from the commercial law of the nations of continental Europe. By Joseph Story, LL.D., one of the Justices of the Supreme Court of the United States, and Dane Professor of Law in Harvard University. 8vo. pp. xliv. and 740. 1868. £1 11s. 6d.

Story.—Life and Letters of Joseph Story, Associate Justice of the Supreme Court of the United States, and Dane Professor of Law at Harvard University. Edited by his Son William W. Story. 2 vols., royal 8vo. cloth, pp. xx. and 1,250. 1851. £1.

Story.—The American Question. By William W. Story. 8vo. sewed pp. 68. 1862. 1s.

Stourton.—Postage Stamp Forgeries; or, the Collector's *Vade Mecum*. Containing accurate descriptions of nearly 700 Forgeries, exclusive of Essays and chymically changed Stamps. By J. M. Stourton. 12mo, sewed, pp. viii. and 66. 1865. 1s.

Stratmann.—A Dictionary of the English Language, compiled from the writings of the 13th, 14th, and 15th Centuries, by Francis Henry Stratmann. 8vo. cloth, pp. x. and 694. 1867. 25s.

Stratmann.—An Old English Poem of the Owl and the Nightingale. Edited by Francis Henry Stratmann. 8vo. cloth, pp. 60. 1868. 3s.

Strauss.—The Opinions of Professor David F. Strauss, as embodied in his Letter to the Burgomaster Hinzel, Professor Orelli, and Professor Hizig at Zürich. With an Address to the People of Zürich. By Professor Orelli. Translated from the Second Edition of the original. 8vo. sewed.

Sue.—THE RIVAL RACES; or the Sons of Joel. A Legendary Romance. By Eugène Sue. 3 vols., post 8vo. cloth. 1863. £1 11s 6d.

Sullivant.—ICONES MUSCORUM, or Figures and Descriptions of most of those Mosses peculiar to Eastern North America, which have not been heretofore figured. By William S. Sullivant, LL.D. With 129 copper-plates. 8vo. pp. 216, cloth. 1864. £4 4s.

Sullivant.—UNITED STATES EXPLORING EXPEDITION, during the years 1838, 1839, 1840, 1841, 1842, under the command of Charles Wilkes, United States Navy. Botany. Musci. By William S. Sullivant. Folio, pp. 32. With 26 folio plates, half morocco. 1859. £10 10s.

Surya SIDDHÂNTA (Translation of the); a Text-Book of Hindu Astronomy; with Notes, and an Appendix, containing additional notes and tables, calculations of eclipses, a stellar map, and indexes. By Rev. Ebenezer Burgess, formerly missionary of the A.B.C.F.M. in India; assisted by the committee of publication of the American Oriental Society. 8vo. pp. iii. and 356, Boards. 1860. 15s.

Swaab.—FIBROUS SUBSTANCES—INDIGENOUS AND EXOTIC: their Nature, Varieties, and Treatment, considered with a view to render them further useful for Textile and other purposes. By S. L. Swaab. 8vo, sewed, pp. 56. 1864. 2s.

Swanwick.—SELECTIONS FROM THE DRAMAS OF GOETHE AND SCHILLER. Translated with Introductory Remarks, by Anna Swanwick. 8vo. cloth, pp. xvi. and 290. 1846. 6s.

Taft.—A PRACTICAL TREATISE ON OPERATIVE DENTISTRY. By J. Taft, Professor of Operative Dentistry in the Ohio College of Dental Surgery. 8vo. pp. 384. With 80 illustrations. Cloth. 1859. 16s.

Taney.—HABEAS CORPUS. The Proceedings in the Case of John Merryman, of Baltimore County, Maryland, before the Honourable Roger Brooke Taney, Chief Justice of the Supreme Court of the United States. 8vo. sewed, pp. 24. 1861. 1s.

Tayler.—A RETROSPECT OF THE RELIGIOUS LIFE OF ENGLAND; or, the Church, Puritanism, and Free Inquiry. By J. J. Tayler, B.A. New Revised Edition. Large post 8vo., cloth, pp. xii. and 330. 1853. 7s. 6d.

Taylor.—TAYLOR'S SYSTEM OF SHORTHAND WRITING. Edited by Matthias Levy, author of "The History of Shorthand Writing." 8vo. pp. iv. and 16, limp cloth. 1862. 1s. 6d.

Taylor.—THE CLAIM OF ENGLISHWOMEN TO THE SUFFRAGE CONSTITUTIONALLY CONSIDERED. By Helen Taylor. Reprinted from the "Westminster Review." 8vo. pp. 16, sewed. 1867. 1d.

Taylor.—THE PICTURE OF ST. JOHN. By Bayard Taylor. 12mo cloth, pp. vii. and 220. 1866. 7s. 6d.

Taylor.—THE POEMS OF BAYARD TAYLOR. Portrait. Blue and Gold Series. Third Series. 24mo. cloth, gilt edges, pp. viii. and 419. 1865. 5s.

Technological Dictionary: French—German—English; containing the Technical Terms used in Arts and Trades, Civil, Military, and Naval Architecture, Bridges and Roads, Railways, Mechanics, construction of Machines, Artillery, Navigation, Mines and Smelting Works, Mathematics, Physics, Chemistry, Mineralogy, etc., etc. Edited by C. Rumpf and O. Mothes; preceded by a Preface by Charles Karmarsch, Chief Director of the Polytechnic School of Hanover. In one vol. 8vo. pp. vi. and 590, cloth. 1868. 10s. 6d.

Terrien and Saxton.—LIBERIEN HAG AVIELEN; or, the Catholic Epistles and Gospels for the day up to Ascension. Translated for the first time into the Brehonec of Brittany. Also, in three parallel columns, a new version of the same Breizouner (commonly called Breton and Armorican); a version into Welsh, mostly new and closely resembling the Breton; and a version Gaelic, or Manx, or Cernaweg, with illustrative articles, by Christoll Terrien and Charles Waring Saxton, D.D., Christ Church, Oxford. The penitential psalms are also added. Oblong Folio, pp. 156, sewed. 1868. 5s.

Tetraglot.—NEW UNIVERSAL DICTIONARY OF THE ENGLISH, FRENCH, ITALIAN, AND GERMAN LANGUAGES, arranged after a new system. Small 8vo. cloth. 7s. 6d.

Texas ALMANAC (THE) FOR 1868, with Federal and State Statistics; historical, descriptive, and biographical sketches, etc., relating to Texas. 8vo. pp. 314, sewed. 1868. 3s.

Théâtre FRANÇAIS MODERNE. A Selection of Modern French Plays; Edited by the Rev. P. H. Ernest Brette, B.D., Head Master of the French School in Christ's Hospital; Charles Cassal, LL.D., Professor in University College, London; and Theodore Karcher, LL.B., of the Royal Military Academy, Woolwich; former and present examiners in the University of London, and for the Civil Service of India. First Series, in one vol. crown 8vo. cloth. 6s. Containing:—

CHARLOTTE CORDAY, a Tragedy. By F. Ponsard. Edited with English Notes and Notice on Ponsard, by Professor C. Cassal, LL.D. of University College, London. Pp. xii. and 134.

DIANE, a Drama in verse. By Emile Augier. Edited with English Notes and Notice on Augier, by Theodore Karcher, LL.B., of the Royal Military Academy and the University of London. Pp. xiv. and 145.

LE VOYAGE À DIEPPE, a Comedy in prose. By Wafflard and Fulgence. Edited, with English Notes, by the Rev. P. H. Ernest Brette, B.D., of Christ's Hospital and the University of London. Pp. 104.

The Boke of NURTURE. By John Russell, about 1460—1470 Anno Domini. The Boke of Kornynge. By Wynkyn de Worde, Anno Domini 1513. The Boke of Nurture. By Hugh Rhodes, Anno Domini 1577. Edited from the Originals in the British Museum Library, by Frederick J. Furnivall, M.A., Trinity Hall, Cambridge, Member of Council of the Philological and Early English Text Societies. 4to. half-morocco, gilt top, pp. xix. and 146, 28, xxviii. and 56. 1867. £1 11s. 6d.

The Derbyites AND THE COALITION. Parliamentary Sketches. Being a second edition of the "History of the Session 1852—1853." 12mo. pp. 222, cloth. 1854. 2s. 6d.

The TRUE INTERPRETATION OF THE AMERICAN CIVIL WAR, and of England's Cotton Difficulty or Slavery, from a different Point of View, showing the relative Responsibilities of America and Great Britain. By Onesimus Secundus. 8vo. sewed, pp. iv. and 47. 1863. 1s.

The Vision of William concerning Piers Plowman, together with Vita de Dowel, Dobet et Dobest, secundum wit et resoun. By William Langland (about 1362-1380 anno domini). Edited from numerous Manuscripts, with Prefaces, Notes, and a Glossary. By the Rev. Walter W. Skeat, M.A. Pp. xliv. and 158, cloth. 1867. Vernon Text; Text A. 7s. 6d.

Θεῖα (ἡ) Λειτουργια τοῦ ἐν ἁγίοις πάτρος ἡμῶν Ἰωάννου τοῦ Χρυσοστομοῦ. Παραφρασθεῖσα κατὰ τὸ κείμενον τὸ ἐκδοθὲν ἐγκρίσει τῆς ἱερᾶς συνόδου τοῦ βασιλείου τῆς Ἑλλάδος. 8vo. pp. 76, cloth. 1865. 3s. 6d.

Thom.—St. Paul's Epistles to the Corinthians. An attempt to convey their Spirit and Significance. By the Rev. John Hamilton Thom. Post 8vo. cloth, pp. xii. and 408. 1851. 7s.

Thomas.—A Collection of some of the Miscellaneous Essays on Oriental Subjects. (Published on various occasions.) By Edward Thomas, Esq., late of the East India Company's Bengal Civil Service. Contents—On Ancient Indian Weights; The Earliest Indian Coinage; Bactrian Coins; On the Identity of Xandrames and Krananda; Note on Indian Numerals; On the Coins of the Gupta Dynasty; Early Armenian Coins; Observations Introductory to the Explanation of the Oriental Legends to be found on certain Imperial and Partho-Persian Coins; Sassanian Gems and early Armenian Coins; Notes on Certain unpublished Coins of the Sassanidæ; An Account of Eight Kûfic Coins; Supplementary Contributions to the Series of the Coins of the Kings of Ghazni; Supplementary Contributions to the Series of the Coins of the Patan Sultans of Hindustan; The Initial Coinage of Bengal, introduced by the Muhammadans, on the conquest of the country, A.H. 600-800, A.D. 1203-1397. In one vol. 8vo. half-bound, gilt edges. 1868.

Thomas.—Early Sassanian Inscriptions, Seals and Coins. By Edward Thomas, Esq., late of the East India Company's Bengal Service. 8vo. pp. viii. and 138. With numerous woodcuts, a photograph of the Hajiâbâd inscription, and a copper-plate of the Sassanian coins. Cloth, 1868. 7s. 6d.

Thomson.—Institutes of the Laws of Ceylon. By Henry Byerley Thomson, Second Puisne Judge of the Supreme Court of Ceylon. In 2 vols., 8vo. cloth, pp. xx. 647, and pp. xx. 713. With Appendices, pp. 71. 1866. £2 2s.

Thomson.—The Autobiography of an Artizan. By Christopher Thomson. Post 8vo. cloth, pp. xii. and 408. 1847. 6s.

Thoreau.—A Week on the Concord and Merrimack Rivers. By Henry D. Thoreau. 12mo. cloth, pp. 413. 1862. 7s. 6d.

Thoreau.—The Maine Woods. By Henry D. Thoreau. 12mo. cloth, pp. vi. and 328. 1864. 7s. 6d.

Thoreau.—Excursions. 12mo. cloth, pp. 319. 1864. 7s. 6d.

Thoreau.—A Yankee in Canada; with Anti-Slavery and Reform Papers. By Henry D. Thoreau. 12mo. cloth, pp. 286. 1866. 7s. 6d.

Thoreau.—Letters to Various Persons. By Henry D. Thoreau. Edited by Ralph Waldo Emerson. 16mo. cloth, Pp. 229. 1865. 7s. 6d.

A series of interesting letters selected by Mr. Emerson, with an appendix containing nine charming poems.

Thoreau.—Walden. By Henry D. Thoreau. 12mo. cloth.

Thoughts of a Lifetime; or, my Mind—its contents. An epitome of the leading questions of the day. By the author of "Utopia at Home." Crown 8vo. pp. ix. and 220, cloth. 1868. 3s. 6d.

Thoughts on Religion and the Bible. By a Layman, an M.A. of Trinity College, Dublin. Second edition, revised and enlarged. Crown 8vo. pp. x. and 42, sewed. 1865. 1s.

Thoughts on the Athanasian Creed, etc. By a Layman. 16mo. cloth, pp. vi. and 75. 1866. 2s.

Three Experiments of Living. Within the Means. Up to the Means. Beyond the Means. Fcap. 8vo., ornamental cover and gilt edges, pp. 86. 1848. 1s.

Ticknor.—A History of Spanish Literature. Entirely re-written. By George Ticknor. 3 vols. crown 8vo. pp. xxiv. 486, xiii. 506, xiv. 524, cloth. 1863. £1 4s.

Tolhausen.—A Synopsis of the Patent Laws of Various Countries. Comprising the following heads:—1. Law, Date, and where recorded; 2. Kinds of Patents; 3. Previous Examination; 4. Duration; 5. Government Fees; 6. Documents Required, and where to be left; 7. Working and Extension; 8. Assignments; 9. Specifications, Inspection, and Copies of; 10. List of Patents delivered; 11. Specifications Published; 12. Originals of Specifications (Models). By Alexander Tolhausen, Ph. D., Sworn Translator at the Imperial Court of Paris, Author of a Technological Dictionary in the English, French, and German Languages, etc. 8vo. sewed, pp. 31. 1857. 1s.

Torrens.—Lancashire's Lesson: or, the Need of a Settled Policy in Times of Exceptional Distress. By W. T. M. Torrens, Author of "The Industrial History of Free Nations," "The Life of Sir James Graham," etc. Crown 8vo. cloth, pp. viii. and 191. 1864. 3s. 6d.

Toscani.—Italian Conversational Course. A new Method of Teaching the Italian Language, both Theoretically and Practically. By Giovanni Toscani, Professor of the Italian Language and Literature in the City of London College, Royal Polytechnic Institution, etc. 12mo. cloth, pp. viii. and 249. 1867. 5s.

Tosswill.—The British and American Ready-Reckoner: consisting of Tables showing the equivalent values in Currency and Sterling at any rate for Exchange, of the following articles:—Produce, comprising butter, cheese, bacon, hams, lard, tallow, grease, hops, seeds, tobacco, sugar, beeswax, or any article whereof the Standard is the pound in America and the cwt. (of 112 lbs.) in the British Isles, with a list of net freights. Also cotton per lb.— Flour, Beef and Pork, or any article sold in both countries by the same Standard.—Wheat transferred from the bushel of 60 lbs. to quarter of 480 lbs.; likewise the equivalent value of the quarter and cental.—Indian Corn transferred from the bushel of 56 lbs. to the quarter of 480 lbs. Also freights of wheat and corn.—Oil Cake and Dye Woods, allowing, where necessary, for the difference between the 2,000 lbs. and the gross ton.—Refined Petroleum transferred from the small or wine into the imperial gallon.—Crude Petroleum transferred from the small gallon into the tun of 252 imperial or 303 small gallons. Also, Sterling Commission or Brokerage, showing the expense of placing any of the above merchandise "free on board." Computed by Edward B. Tosswill, Author of "Produce Tables from par to 400 premium." Imperial 8vo. cloth, pp. x. and 133. 1865. £1 1s.

Towler.—THE SILVER SUNBEAM: a Practical and Theoretical Text-book on Sun-Drawing and Photographic Printing, comprehending all the Wet and Dry Processes at present known. By J. Towler, M.D., Prendergast Professor of Natural Philosophy. Third Edition, enlarged. Crown 8vo. cloth, pp. viii. and 443. 1866. 10s. 6d.

Towler.—DRY PLATE PHOTOGRAPHY; or, the Tannin Process made Simple and Practical for Operators and Amateurs. By J. Towler, M.D. 12mo. sewed, pp. 97. 1865. 4s.

Towler.—THE MAGIC PHOTOGRAPH; with full Instructions How to Make it. By J. Towler, M.D. 12mo. sewed, pp. x. 1866. 1s.

Triglot.—A COMPLETE DICTIONARY, ENGLISH, GERMAN, AND FRENCH, on an entirely new plan, for the use of the Three Nations. In Three Divisions. 1 vol. small 4to, cloth, red edges. 10s. 6d.

Trimen.—RHOPALOCERA AFRICAE AUSTRALIS; a Catalogue of South African Butterflies; comprising Descriptions of all the known Species, with Notices of their Larvæ, Pupæ, Localities, Habits, Seasons of Appearance, and Geographical Distribution. By Roland Trimen, Member of the Entomological Society of London. With Illustrations, by G. H. Ford. 8vo. cloth, pp. iv. and 353. 1862-66. 18s.
Ditto Coloured, 25s.

Trübner's AMERICAN AND ORIENTAL LITERARY RECORD. A Monthly Register of the most Important Works published in North and South America, in India, China, and the British Colonies. With Occasional Notes on German, Dutch, Danish, French, Italian, Spanish, Portuguese and Russian Books. The object of the Publishers in issuing this monthly publication is to give a full and particular account of every publication of importance issued in America and the East. Vols. 1 to 3 (36 numbers) from March, 1865, to July, 1868, small quarto, 6d. per number. Subscription 5s. per annum. Continued monthly.
The object of the Publishers in issuing this monthly publication is to give a full and particular account of every publication of importance issued in America and in the East.

Trübner's SERIES OF GERMAN PLAYS, for Students of the German Language. With Grammatical and Explanatory Notes. By F. Weinmann, German Master to the Royal Institution School, Liverpool, and G. Zimmermann, Teacher of Modern Languages. No. I. Der Vetter. Comedy in three Acts, by Roderick Benedix. 12mo. cloth, pp. 125. 1863. 2s. 6d.

Trübner's GOLD AND SILVER COINS (See under Current Gold and Silver Coins).

Trübner.—TRÜBNER'S BIBLIOGRAPHICAL GUIDE TO AMERICAN LITERATURE: a Classed List of Books published in the United States of America, from 1817 to 1857. With Bibliographical Introduction, Notes, and Alphabetical Index. Compiled and Edited by Nicolas Trübner. In 1 vol. 8vo., half-bound, pp. 750. 1859. 18s.

This work, it is believed, is the first attempt to marshal the Literature of the United States of America during the last forty years, according to the generally received bibliographical canons. The Librarian will welcome it, no doubt, as a companion volume to Brunet, Lowndes, and Ebert; whilst, to the bookseller, it will be a faithful guide to the American branch of English Literature—a branch which, on account of its rapid increase and rising importance, begins to force itself daily more and more upon his attention. Nor will the work be of less interest to the man of letters inasmuch as it comprises complete Tables of Contents to all the more prominent Collections of the Americana, to the Journals, Memoirs, Proceedings, and Transactions of their learned Societies—and thus furnishes an intelligible key to a department of American scientific activity hitherto but imperfectly known and understood in Europe.

OPINIONS OF THE PRESS.

"'Trübner's Bibliographical Guide to American Literature' deserves praise for the great care with which it is prepared, and the wonderful amount of information contained in its pages. It is compiled and edited by Mr. Nicolas Trübner, the publisher, of Paternoster-row. It comprises a classified list of books published in the United States during the last forty years, with Bibliographical Introduction, Notes, and Alphabetical Index. The introduction is very elaborate and full of facts, and must be the work of a gentleman who has spared no pains in making himself master of all that is important in connection with American literature. It certainly supplies much information not generally known in Europe."—*Morning Star*, Jan. 31st, 1859.

"Mr. Trübner deserves much credit for being the first to arrange bibliography according to the received rules of the art. He began the labour in 1855, and the first volume was published in that year; constituting, in fact, the earliest attempt, on this side of the Atlantic, to catalogue American books. The present volume, of course, is enlarged, and is more perfect in every respect. The method of classification is exceedingly clear and useful.

"In short, it presents the actual state of literature, as well as the course of its development from the beginning. Into the subject-matter of this section we shall have to look hereafter, we are now simply explaining the composition of Mr. Trübner's most valuable and useful book."—*Spectator*, Feb. 5, 1859.

"Mr. Trübner's book is by far the most complete American bibliography that has yet appeared, and displays an amount of patience and research that does him infinite credit. We have tested the accuracy of the work upon several points demanding much care and inquiry, and the result has always been satisfactory. Our American brethren cannot fail to feel complimented by the production of this volume, which in quantity almost equals our own London catalogue."—*The Bookseller*, Feb. 24th, 1859.

"To say of this volume that it entirely fulfils the promise of its title-page, is possibly the highest and most truthful commendation that can be awarded to it. Mr. Trübner deserves however, something beyond general praise for the patient and intelligent labour with which he has elaborated the earlier forms of the work into that which it now bears. What was once but a scanty volume, has now become magnified, under his care, to one of considerable size; and what was once little better than a dry catalogue, may new take rank as a biographical work of first-rate importance. His position as an American literary agent has, doubtless, been very favourable to Mr. Trübner, by throwing matter in its way; and he confesses, in his preface, that it is to this source that he is mainly indebted for the materials which have enabled him to construct the work before us. Mr. Trübner's object in compiling this book is, he states, two-fold: 'On the one hand, to suggest the necessity of a more perfect work of its kind by an American, surrounded, as he necessarily would be, with the needful appliances; and, on the other, to supply to Europeans a guide to Anglo-American literature—a branch which, by its rapid rise and increasing importance, begins to force itself more and more on our attention. It is very modest in Mr. Trübner thus to treat his work as a mere suggestion for others. It is much more than this: it is an example which those who attempt to do anything more complete cannot do better than to follow a model, which they will do well to copy, if they would combine fulness of material with that admirable order and arrangement which so facilitates reference, and without which a work of this sort is all but useless.

"All honour, then, to the literature of Young America—for young she still is, and let her thank her stars for it—and all honour also, to Mr. Trübner, for taking so much pains to make us acquainted with it."—*The Critic*, March 19, 1859.

"This is not only a very useful, because well executed, bibliographical work—it is also a work of much interest to all who are connected with literature. The bulk of it consists of a classified list, with date of publication, size, and price, of all the works, original or translated, which have appeared in the United States during the last forty years; and an alphabetical index facilitates reference to any particular work or author. On the merits of this portion of the work we cannot, of course, be expected to form a judgment. It would require something of the special erudition of Mr. Trübner himself, to say how far he has succeeded or fallen short of his undertaking—how few, or how many, have been his omissions. There is one indication, however, of his careful minuteness, which suggests the amount of labour that must have been bestowed on the work—namely, the full enumeration of all the contents of the various Transaction and Scientific Journals. Thus, 'the Transactions of the American Philosophical Society,' from the year 1769 to 1857—no index to which has yet appeared in America—are in this work made easy of reference, every paper of every volume being mentioned seriatim. The naturalist, who wishes to know what papers have appeared in the Boston Journal of Natural History during the last twenty years, that is, from its commencement, has only to glance over the five closely-printed pages of this guide to satisfy himself at once."—*The Saturday Review*, April 2, 1859.

"We have never seen a work on the national literature of a people more carefully compiled than the present, and the bibliographical prolegomena deserves attentive perusal by all who would study either the political or the literary history of the greatest republic of the West."—*The Leader*, March 26th, 1859.

"The subject of my letter to-day may seem to be of a purely literary character, but I feel justified to claim a more general interest for it. That subject is connected with the good reputation of the United States abroad. It is likewise connected with the general topic of my two former letters. I have spoken of the 'friends and the antagonists of the United States among European nations, and among the different classes of European society. I have stated that the antagonists are chiefly to be found among the aristocracy, not only of birth, but 'of mind'—as it has been called—likewise; not only among the privileged classes, and those connected with the Government interests, but among those who live in the sphere of literature and art, and look down with contempt upon a society in which utilitarian motives are believed to be paramount. And I have asserted that, these differences in the opinions of certain classes left aside, the Germans, as a whole, take a more lively and a deeper interest in American affairs than in any other nation. Now, I am going to speak of a book just ready to leave the press of a London publisher, which, while it is a remarkable instance of the truth of my assertion in reference to the Germans, must be considered as serving the interests of the United States, by promoting the good reputation of American life in an uncommon degree.

"The London book trade has a firm, Trübner and Co., of whose business transactions American literature, as well as literature on America, form a principal branch. It is the firm who have lately published the bibliography of American langdages. Mr. Nicolas Trübner is a German, who has never inhabited the United States, and yet he risks his time, labour, and money, in literary publications, for which even vain endeavours would have been made to find an American publisher.

"The new publication of Mr. Trübner, to which I have referred, is a large 8vo volume of 800 pages, under the title of 'Bibliographical Guide to American Literature, A classified List of Books published in the United States of America, from 1817 to 1857. With Bibliographical Introduction, Notes, and Alphabetical Index. Compiled and edited by Nicolas Trübner.'

"This last remark has but too much truth in it. The United States, in the opinion of the great mass of even the well-educated people of Europe, is a country inhabited by a nation lost in the pursuit of material interest, a country in which the technically applicable branches of some sciences may be cultivated to a certain degree, but a country essentially without literature and art, a country not without newspapers—so much the worse for it—but almost without books. Now, here, Mr. Trübner, a German, comes out with a list of American books, filling a thick volume, though containing American publications only, upward from the year 1817, from which time he dates the period of a more decided literary independence of the United States.

"Since no native-born, and even no adopted, American, has taken the trouble of compiling, arranging, digesting, editing, and publishing such a work, who else but a German could undertake it? who else among the European nations would have thought American literature worth the labour, the time, and the money? and, let me add, that a smaller work of a similar character, 'The Literature of American Local History,' by the late Dr. Hermann Ludewig, was the work of a German, likewise. May be that the majority of the American public will ascribe but an inferior degree of interest to works of this kind. The majority of the public of other nations will do the same, as it cannot be everybody's business to understand the usefulness of bibliography, and of books containing nothing but the enumeration and description of books. One thing, however, must be apparent: the deep interest taken by some foreigners in some of the more ideal spheres of American life; and if it is true, that the clear historical insight into its own development, ideal as well as material, is one of the most valuable acquisitions of a nation, future American generations will acknowledge the good services of those foreigners, who, by their literary application, contributed to avert the national calamity of the origin of the literary independence of America becoming veiled in darkness."—*New York Daily Tribune*, Dec., 1858.

"It is remarkable and noteworthy that the most valuable manual of American literature should appear in London and be published by an English house. Trübner's Bibliographical Guide to American Literature is a work of extraordinary skill and perseverance, giving an index to all the publications of the American press for the last forty years."—*Harper's Weekly*, March 26th, 1859.

"Mr. Trübner deserves all praise for having produced a work every way satisfactory. No one who takes an interest in the subject of which it treats can dispense it with it; and we have no doubt that booksellers in this country will learn to consider it necessary to them as a shop manual, and only second in importance, for the purposes of their trade, to the London Catalogue itself. That a foreigner, and a London bookseller, should have accomplished what Americans themselves have failed to do, is most creditable to the compiler. The volume contains 149 pages of introductory matter, containing by far the best record of American literary history yet published; and 521 pages of classed list of books, to which an alphabetical index of 83 pages is added. This alphabetical index alone may claim to be one of the most valuable aids for enabling the student of literary history to form a just and perfect estimate of the great and rising importance of Anglo-American literature, the youngest and most untrammelled of all which illustrate the gradual development of the human mind."—*The Press*, of Irving and Hawthorne, of Poe and Longfellow, of Story and Wheaton, of Moses Stuart and Channing. This volume will be useful to the scholar, but to the librarian it is indispensable."—*Daily News*, March 24th, 1859.

"There are hundreds of men of moderate scholarship who would gladly stand on some higher and more assured point. They feel that they have acquired much information, but they also feel the need of that subtle discipline, literary education, without which all mere learning is the *rudis indigesta moles*, as much of a stumbling-block as an aid. To those in such a condition, works on bibliography are invaluable. For direction in classifying all reading, whether English or American, Allibone's Dictionary is admirable; but, for particular information as to the American side of the house, the recently published Bibliographical Guide to American Literature, by Nicholas Trübner, of London, may be conscientiously commended. A careful perusal of this truly remarkable work cannot fail to give any intelligent person a clear and complete idea of the whole state of American book-making, not only in its literary aspect, but in its historical, and, added to this, in its most mechanical details."—*Philadelphia Evening Bulletin*, March 5th, 1859.

"But the best work on American bibliography yet published has come to us from London, where it has been compiled by the well-known bibliophile, Trübner. The work is remarkable for condensation and accuracy, though we have noted a few errors and omissions, upon which we should like to comment, had we now space to do so."—*New York Times*, March 26th, 1859.

"Some of our readers, whose attention has been particularly called to scientific and literary matters, may remember meeting, some years since, in this country, a most intelligent foreigner, who visited the United States for the purpose of extending his business connections, and making a personal investigation into the condition of literature in the New World. Mr. Nicholas Trübner—the gentleman to whom we have made reference—although by birth a German, and by education and profession a London bookseller, could hardly be called a 'stranger in America,' for he had sent before him a most valuable 'letter of introduction,' in the shape of a carefully compiled register of American books and authors, entitled 'Bibliographical Guide to American Literature,' etc., pp. xxxii, 108. This manual was the germ of the important publication, the title of which the reader will find at the commencement of this article. Now, in consequence of Mr. Trübner's admirable classification and minute index, the inquirer after knowledge has nothing to do but copy from the Bibliographical Guide the titles of the American books which he wishes to consult, despatch them to his library by a messenger, and in a few minutes he has before him the coveted volumes, through whose means he hopes to enlarge his acquisitions. Undoubtedly it would be a cause of well-founded reproach, of deep mortification to every intelligent American, if the arduous labours of the learned editor and compiler of this volume (whom we almost hesitate to call a foreigner), should fail to be appreciated in a country to which he has, by the preparation of this valuable work, proved himself so eminent a benefactor."—*Pennsylvania Enquirer*, March 26th, 1859.

"The editor of this volume has acquired a knowledge of the productions of the American press which is rarely exhibited on the other side of the Atlantic, and which must command the admiration of the best informed students of the subject in this country. His former work on American bibliography, though making no pretensions to completeness, was a valuable index to various branches of learning that had been successfully cultivated by our scholars but, neither in comprehensiveness of plan nor thoroughness of execution, can it be compared to the elaborate and minute record of American literature contained in this volume. The duty of the editor required extensive research, vigilant discrimination, and untiring diligence; and in the performance of his task we are no less struck with the accuracy of detail than with the extent of his information. The period to which the volume is devoted, comprises only the last forty years; but within that time the literature of this country has received its most efficient impulses, and been widely unfolded in the various departments of intellectual activity. If we were permitted to speak in behalf of American scholars, we should not fail to congratulate Mr. Trübner on the eminent success with which he has accomplished his plan, and the ample and impartial justice with which he has registered the productions of our native authorship. After a careful examination of his volume, we are bound to express our high appreciation of the intelligence, fairness, and industry which are conspicuous in its pages; for exactness and precision it is no less remarkable, than for extent of research; few, if any, important publications are omitted on its catalogue, and although, as is inevitable in a work of this nature, an erroneous letter has sometimes crept into a name, or an erroneous figure into a date, no one can consult it habitually without learning to rely on its trustworthiness, as well as its completeness."—*Harper's Magazine*, April, 1859.

"Nor is the book a dry catalogue only of the names and contents of the publications of America. Prefixed to it are valuable bibliographical prolegomena, instructive to the antiquary, as well as useful to the philologist. In this portion of the work, Mr. Trübner had the assistance of the late Dr. Ludowig, whose early death was a great loss to philological science. Mr. Moran, the assistant-secretary to the American Legation, has added to the volume a historical summary of the literature of America; and Mr. Edward Edwards is responsible for an interesting account of the public libraries of the United States. To Mr. Trübner's own careful superintendence and hard work, however, the student must ever remain indebted for one of the most useful and well-arranged books on bibliographical lore ever published. In addition to this, it is right to congratulate Mr. Trübner on the fact, that his present work confirms the opinion passed on his 'Bibliotheca Glottica,' that among the booksellers themselves honourable literary eminence may exist, without clashing with business arrangements. The booksellers of old were authors, and Mr. Trübner emulates their example."—*Morning Chronicle*,

"Mr. Trübner, who is not only a bibliopole but a bibliophile, has, in this work, materially increased the claim which he had already upon the respect of all book-lovers everywhere, but especially in the United States, to whose literature he has now made so important and useful a contribution. So much larger than a former book, under a similar title, which he published in 1855, and so much more ample in every respect, the present constitutes a new implement for our libraries, as well as the most valuable existing aid for those students who, without libraries, have an interest in knowing their contents."—*Baltimore American*, 2nd April, 1859.

"Lastly, published only the other day, is Trübner's Bibliographical Guide to American Literature, which gives a classed list of books published in the United States during the last forty years, with bibliographical introduction, notes, and Alphabetical Index. This octavo volume has been compiled and edited by Mr. Nicolas Trübner, the well-known head of one of the great foreign publishing and importing houses of London, who is also editor of Ludewig and Turner's Literature of American Aboriginal Languages. Besides containing a classed list of books, with an alphabetical index, Mr. Trübner's book has an introduction, in which, at considerable fulness, he treats of the history of American literature, including newspapers, periodicals, and public libraries. It is fair to state that Mr. Trübner's Bibliographical Guide was published subsequent to Allibone's Dictionary, but printed off about the same time."—*Philadelphia Press*, April 4th, 1859.

"This is a valuable work for book buyers. For its compilation we are indebted to a foreign bibliomaniac, but one who has made himself familiar with American literature, and has possessed himself of the most ample sources of information. The volume contains:—I. Bibliographical Prolegomena; II. Contributions towards a History of American Literature; III. Notices of Public Libraries of the United States. These three heads form the introduction, and occupy one hundred and fifty pages. IV. Classed list of books; V. Alphabetical list of authors. This plan is somewhat after that adopted in Watts' celebrated 'Bibliotheca Britannica,' a work of immense value, whose compilation occupied some forty years. The classified portion of the present work enables the reader to find readily the names of all books on any one subject. The alphabetical index of authors enables the reader to ascertain instantly the names of all authors and of all their works, including the numerous periodical publications of the last forty years. Mr. Trübner deserves the thanks of the literary world for his plan, and its able execution."—*New York Courier and Enquirer*, April 11th, 1859.

"L'auteur, dans une préface de dix pages, expose les idées qui lui ont fait entreprendre son livre, et le plan qu'il a cru devoir adopter. Dans une savante introduction, il fait une revue critique des différentes ouvrages relatifs à l'Amérique; il signale ceux qui ont le plus contribué à l'établissement d'une littérature spéciale Américaine, et il en fait l'histoire, cette partie de son travail est destinée à lui faire honneur, elle est méthodiquement divisée en période coloniale et en période Américaine et renferme, sur les progrès de l'imprimerie en Amérique, sur le salaire des auteurs, sur le commerce de la librairie, les publications périodiques, des renseignements très intéressants, que l'on est heureux de trouver réunis pour la première fois. Cette introduction, qui n'a pas moins de 150 pages, se termine par une table statisque de toutes les bibliothèques publiques des différents Etats de l'Union.

"Le catalogue méthodique et raisonné des ouvrages n'occupe pas moins de 521 pages, il forme 32 sections consacrées chacune à l'une des branches des sciences humaines; celle qui donne la liste des ouvrages qui intéressent la géographie et les voyages (section xvi.) comprend près de 600 articles, et parmi eux on trouve l'indication de plusieurs ouvrages dont nous ne soupçonnions même pas l'existence en Europe. Un index général alphabétique par noms d'auteurs qui termine ce livre, permet d'abréger des recherches souvent bien pénibles. Le guide bibliographique de M. Trübner est un monument élevé à l'activité scientifique et littéraire Américaine et comme tel, il est digne de prendre place à côte des ouvrages du même genre publiés en Europe par les Brunet, les Lowndes, et les Ebert. (V. A. Malte-Brun)."—*Nouvelles Annales des Voyages*, April, 1859.

Tuder.—MY OWN PHILOLOGY. By A. Tuder. In Two Parts. 8vo. pp. iv. and 40, 60, sewed. 1866. 1s. each.

Twenty-five YEARS' CONFLICT IN THE CHURCH, AND ITS REMEDY. 12mo. sewed, pp. viii. and 70. 1855. 1s. 6d.

Uhlemann's SYRIAC GRAMMAR. Translated from the German by Enoch Hutchinson. 8vo. cloth, pp. 368. 1855. 18s.

Ullmann.—THE WORSHIP OF GENIUS, AND THE DISTINCTIVE CHARACTER OR ESSENCE OF CHRISTIANITY. By Professor C. Ullmann. Translated by Lucy Sandford. Post 8vo. cloth, pp. 116. 1840. 3s. 6d.

United States CONSULAR REGULATIONS. A Practical Guide for Consular Officers, and also for merchants, shipowners, and masters of American vessels, in all their consular transactions. Third edition, revised and enlarged 8vo. pp. 684, cloth. 1867. 21s.

United States Patent Law (The). Instructions how to obtain Letters Patent for new inventions; including a variety of useful information concerning the rules and practice of the Patent Office; how to sell patents; how to secure foreign patents; forms for assignments and licenses, together with engravings and descriptions of the condensing steam-engine, and the principal mechanical movements, valuable tables, calculations, problems, etc., etc. By Munn, and Co., Solicitors of Patents, No. 37, Park Row, New York. Third edition, 12mo., pp. 108, cloth. 1867. 1s. 6d.

Unity, Duality, and Trinity of the Godhead (a Discussion among upwards of 250 theological enquirers, clergymen, dissenting ministers and laymen, on the). With digressions on the creation, fall, incarnation, atonement, resurrection, and infallibility of the Scriptures, inspiration, miracles, future punishments, revision of the Bible, etc. The press corrected by Ranley, the Reporter of the discussion. 8vo. pp. 206, cloth. 1864. 6s.

Unity (The) of Truth. A Devotional Diary, compiled from the Scripture and other sources. By the Author of "Visiting my Relations." 18mo. cloth, pp. iv. 138. 1867. 2s.

Universal Correspondence in Six Languages. English, German, French, Dutch, Italian, and Spanish. 2 vols. 8vo. cloth, pp. 664 and 660. 1865. 20s.

Universal Church (The); its Faith, Doctrine, and Constitution. Crown 8vo. cloth, pp. iv. and 398. 1866. 6s.

Upper Rhine (The). Illustrating its finest Cities, Castles, Ruins, and Landscapes. From drawings by Messrs. Rohbock, Louis and Julius Lange, engraved by the most distinguished artists. With a historical and topographical text. Edited by Dr. Gaspey. 8vo. pp. 496. With 134 steel-plate illustrations, cloth. 1859. £2 2s.

Uricoechea. — Mapoteca Colombiana: Catalogo de Todos los Mapas, Planos, Vistas, etc., relativos a la América-Española, Brasil, e Islas adyacentes. Arreglada cronologicamente i precedida de una introduccion sobre la historia cartografica de América. Por el Doctor Ezequiel Uricoechea, de Bogóta, Nueva Granada. One vol. 8vo. cloth, pp. 232. 1860. 6s.

Uriel, and other Poems. 12mo. cloth. 2s. 6d.

Uriel.—Poems. By the Author of Uriel. Second Edition. 12mo. cloth, pp. 169. 1857. 2s.

Urquhart.—Progress of Russia in the West, North, and South, by Opening the Sources of Opinion, and appropriating the Channels of Wealth and Power. By David Urquhart. Fifth edition, pp. 490, with Map, 12mo. stiff cover. 1852. 1s. 6d.

Urquhart.—Recent Events in the East. Letters, Essays, etc. By David Urquhart. 12mo. pp. 312, 1853. 1s. 6d.

Urquhart.—The War of Ignorance; its Progress and Results: a Prognostication and a Testimony. By David Urquhart. 8vo. 1854. 1s.

Urquhart.—The Occupants of the Crimea. An Appeal from To-day and To-morrow. By David Urquhart. 8vo. sewed. 1854. 6d.

Urquhart.—The Home Face of the "Four Points." By David Urquhart. 8vo. pp. 32. 1854. 1s.

Valetta.—Ὁμήρου βίος καὶ ποιήματα. Πραγματεία ἱστορικὴ καὶ κριτική. ὑπὸ Ἰωάννου N. Βαλέττα. (The Life and Poems of Homer. A Historical and Critical Essay. By John N. Valetta). 1 vol. 4to. pp. xii. and 403, with an illustration, sewed, 1866. 21s.

Valetta.—Φωτιοῦ τοῦ σοφωτάτου καὶ ἁγιωτάτου Πατριάρχου Κωνσταντινουπόλεως Ἐπιστολαί. Αἷς δύο τοῦ αὐτοῦ παρήρτηται πονημάτια. A. Ἐρωτήματα δέκα σὺν ἴσαις ταῖς ἀποκρίσεσιν, ἤτοι συναγωγαὶ καὶ ἀποδείξεις ἀκριβεῖς, συνειλεγμέναι ἐκ τῶν συνωδικῶν καὶ ἱστορικῶν γραφῶν περὶ Ἐπισκόπων καὶ Μητροπολιτῶν, καὶ λοίπων ἑτέρων ἀναγκαίων ζητημάτων. B. Κρίσεις καὶ ἐπιλύσεις πέντε κεφαλαίων, τῷ Θεοφιλεστάτῳ, ὁσιωτάτῳ Λέοντι Ἀρχιεπισκόπῳ Καλαβρίας. Μετὰ προλεγομένων περὶ τοῦ βίου καὶ τῶν συγγραμμάτων Φωτίου κ.τ.α. ὑπὸ Ἰωάννου N. Βαλέττα. (The Epistles of Photius, the wisest and holiest Patriarch of Konstantinople. To which are attached two works of the same author: 1. Ten Questions with their answers, viz., collections and accurate descriptions gathered from the synodical and historical writings on the Bishops and Metropolitans. 2. Sentences and Interpretations, in five chapters, addressed to Leon, the Archbishop of Calabria. With an Introduction on the Life and Writings of Photius. By John N. Valetta.) 1 vol. 4to. pp. 581 sewed. 1864. £1 10s.

Van der Tuuk.—OUTLINES OF A GRAMMAR OF THE MALAGASY LANGUAGE. By H. N. Van der Tuuk. 8vo. sewed, pp. 28. 1866. 1s.

Van der Tuuk.—SHORT ACCOUNT OF THE MALAY MANUSCRIPTS belonging to the Royal Asiatic Society. By H. N. Van Der Tuuk. 8vo. sewed, pp. 51. 1866. 1s.

Van de Weyer.—CHOIX D'OPUSCULES PHILOSOPHIQUES, HISTORIQUES, POLITIQUES ET LITTÉRAIRES de Sylvain Van de Weyer. Précédés d'Avant-propos de l'Editeur. Première Série.

Table de Matières.
1. Le Roi Cobden.
2. Lettres sur les Anglais qui ont écrit en Français.
3. Discours sur l'Histoire de la Philosophie.
4. Moyen facile et économique d'être bienfaisant, proposé aux jeunes Gens, et suivi de Pensées diverses.
5. Lettre à M. Ernst Münch.

Crown 8vo. pp. 374. Roxburghe style. 1863. 10s. 6d.
Ditto. Ditto. Seconde Série. (In the Press.)

Van Laun (HENRI).—GRAMMAR OF THE FRENCH LANGUAGE. Parts I. and II. Accidence and Syntax. In one vol. crown 8vo. cloth, pp. 151 and 117. 5th edition. 1867. 4s.
Part III. Exercises. 4th Ed. Crown 8vo. cloth. pp. xii. and 285.1866.3s. 6d.

Van Laun.—LEÇONS GRADUÉES DE TRADUCTION ET DE LECTURE; or, Graduated Lessons in Translation and Reading, with Biographical Sketches, Annotations on History, Geography, Synonyms and Style, and a Dictionary of Words and Idioms. By Henri Van Laun. 12mo. cloth, pp. vi. and 476. 1863. 5s.

Varnhagen.—AMÉRIGO VESPUCCI. Son caractère, ses écrits (même les moins authentiques), sa vie et ses navigations, avec une carte indiquant les routes. Par F. A. de Varnhagen, Ministro du Brésil au Pérou, Chili et Ecuador, etc. Small Folio, pp. 120, boards. 1865. 14s.

Varnhagen.—LA VERDADERA GUANAHANI DE COLON. Memoria communicada a la facultad de humanidades. Por Don Francisco Ad. de Varnhagen, e impresa en el tomo xxvi. do los anales de Chile (Enero de 1864). 8vo. pp. xiv., with a map of the Bahaman and Antillan Archipelago, sewed, 1864. 2s. 6d.

Velasquez and Simonne's NEW METHOD TO READ, WRITE, AND SPEAK THE SPANISH LANGUAGE. Adapted to Ollendorff's System. Post 8vo.

Velasquez.—A Dictionary of the Spanish and English Languages. For the Use of Young Learners and Travellers. By M. Velasquez de la Cadena. In Two Parts. I. Spanish-English. II. English-Spanish. 12mo. pp. 680, cloth. 1864. 12s.

Velasquez.—A Pronouncing Dictionary of the Spanish and English Languages. Composed from the Dictionaries of the Spanish Academy, Terreos, and Salvá, and Webster, Worcester, and Walker. Two Parts in one thick volume. By M. Velasquez de la Cadena. Royal 8vo. pp. 1,280, cloth. 1866. 25s.

Velasquez.—An Easy Introduction to Spanish Conversation, containing all that is necessary to make a rapid progress in it. Particularly designed for persons who have little time to study, or are their own instructors. By M. Velasquez de la Cadena. New edition, revised and enlarged. 12mo. pp. 150, cloth. 1863. 2s. 6d.

Velasquez.—New Spanish Reader: Passages from the most approved authors, in Prose and Verse. Arranged in progressive order. With Vocabulary. Post 8vo. pp. 352, cloth. 1866. 6s. 6d.

Vera.—Problème de la Certitude. By Professor A. Vera. 8vo. pp. 220. 1845. 3s.

Vera.—Platonis Aristotelis et Hegelii de Medio Termino Doctrina. By Professor A. Vera. 8vo. pp. 45. 1845. 1s. 6d.

Vera.—Inquiry into Speculative and Experimental Science. By Professor A. Vera. 8vo. pp. 68. 1856. 3s. 6d.

Vera.—Logique de Hégel, traduite pour la première fois et accompagnée d'une introduction et d'un commentaire perpétuel. 2 volumes. 8vo. pp. 750. By Professor A. Vera. 1859. 12s.

Vera.—L'Hégélianisme et la Philosophie. By Professor A. Vera. 8vo. pp. 226. 1861. 3s. 6d.

Vera.—Mélanges Philosophiques (containing Papers in Italian and French. By Professor A. Vera. 8vo. pp. 304. 1862. 5s.

Vera.—Prolusioni alla Storia della Filosofia e dalla Filosofia della Storia. By Professor A. Vera. 8vo. pp. 87. 1863. 2s.

Vera.—Introduction à la Philosophie de Hégel. Deuxième édition, revue et augmentée de Notes et d'une Préface. By Professor A. Vera. 8vo. pp. 418. (The first edition appeared in 1854). 1864. 6s.

Vera.—Essais de Philosophie Hégelienne, contenant la Peine de Mort, Amour et Philosophie, et Introduction à la Philosophie. By Professor A. Vera. 12mo. pp. 203. 1864. 2s. 6d.

Vera.—Philosophie de la Nature de Hégel, traduite pour la première fois et accompagnée d'une introduction et d'une commentaire perpetuel. By Professor A. Vera. 3 volumes. 8vo. pp. 1637. 1863, 1864, and 1865. 24s.

Vera.—Philosophie de l'Esprit de Hégel, Traduite pour la première fois et accompagnée de deux Introductions et d'un Commentaire Perpetuel. Par A. Vera. Tome premiér. 8vo. sewed, pp. cxii. and 471. 1867. 12s.

Verkrüzen.—A Treatise on Muslin Embroidery in its Various Branches, including Directions for the different Styles of this Work, with eight beautiful Illustrations, a Receipt to get up Embroidery, etc. By T. A. Verkrüzen, author of a Treatise on Berlin Wool and Colours. Oblong, sewed, pp. 26. 1861. 1s.

Verkrüzen.—A Treatise on Berlin Wool and Colours; Needlework, Muslin, Embroidery, Potichomanic, Diaphanic, and Japaneric, for the use of Dealers and Amateurs in Fancy Work. By T. A. Verkrüzen. 4to. pp. 32. 1857. 1s.

Versmann and Oppenheim.—ON THE COMPARATIVE VALUE OF CERTAIN SALTS FOR RENDERING FABRICS NON-INFLAMMABLE; being the substance of a paper read before the British Association, at the meeting in Aberdeen, September 15th, 1859. By Fred. Versmann, F.C.S., and Alphons Oppenheim, Ph. D., A.C.S. 8vo. pp. 32, sewed. 1859. 1s.

Vickers.—IMAGINISM AND RATIONALISM. An Explanation of the Origin and Progress of Christianity. By John Vickers. Post 8vo. cloth, pp. viii. and 432. 1867. 7s. 6d.

Villars (De).—MÉMOIRES DE LA COUR D'ESPAGNE SOUS LE RÈGNE DE CHARLES II. 1678—1682. Par le Marquis de Villars. Small 4to. pp. xl. and 382, cloth. 1861. 30s.

Vishnu Purana.—A SYSTEM OF HINDU MYTHOLOGY AND TRADITION. Translated from the original Sanskrit, and illustrated by Notes derived chiefly from other Puranas. By the late Horace Hayman Wilson, M.A., F.R.S., thoroughly revised and edited, with Notes, by Dr. Fitzedward Hall. In 5 vols. 8vo. Vol. I. pp. 340. Vol. II. pp. 348. Vol. III. pp. 348. 10s. 6d. each. (Vols. IV. and V. in the press).

Voice from Mayfair (A). 8vo. pp. 58, sewed. 1868. 4d.

Volpe.—AN ITALIAN GRAMMAR. By Girolamo Volpe, Italian Master at Eton College. For the Use of Eton. Crown 8vo. cloth, pp. 242. 1863. 4s. 6d.

Volpe.—A KEY to the Exercises of Volpe's Italian Grammar. 12mo. sewed, pp. 18. 1863. 1s.

Von Cotta.—GEOLOGY AND HISTORY: a Popular Exposition of all that is known of the Earth and its Inhabitants in Pre-historic Times. By Bernhard Von Cotta, Professor of Geology at Freiburg. Post 8vo. cloth, pp. iv. and 84. 1865. 2s.

Voysey.—DOGMA VERSUS MORALITY. A Reply to Church Congress. By Charles Voysey, B.A. Post 8vo. sewed, pp. 12. 1866. 3d.

Voysey.—THE SLING AND THE STONE. By Charles Voysey, B.A., St. Edmund Hall, Oxford, Incumbent of Healaugh. Volume I. (12 numbers for 1866). Crown 8vo. cloth. 1866. 6s.

Voysey.—THE SLING AND THE STONE. By Charles Voysey, B.A. Volume II. (12 numbers for 1867). 8vo. cloth, pp. 176. 1867. 7s. 6d.

Voysey.—HUMANITY versus BARBARISM IN OUR THANKSGIVING. By Charles Voysey, B.A., St. Edmund Hall, Oxford, Incumbent of Healaugh, Tadcaster. 8vo., pp. 12. 1868. 3d.

Wade.—WÊN-CHIEN TZŬ-ERH CHI. A Series of Papers selected as specimens of documentary Chinese, designed to assist Students of the language, as written by the officials of China. Vol. I. and Part I. of the Key. By Thomas Francis Wade, C.B., Secretary to Her Britannic Majesty's Legation at Peking. 4to., half-cloth, pp. xii. and 455; and iv., 72 and 52. 1867. £1 16s.

Wade.—YU-YEN TZŬ-ERH CHI. A progressive course, designed to assist the Student of Colloquial Chinese, as spoken in the Capital and the Metropolitan Department. In Eight Parts, with Key, Syllabary, and Writing Exercises. By Thomas Francis Wade, C.B., Secretary to Her Britannic Majesty's Legation, Peking. 3 vols. 4to. Progressive Course, pp. xx. 296 and 16; Syllabary, pp. 126 and 36; Writing Exercises, pp. 48; Key, pp. 174 and 140, sewed. 1867. £4.

Wafflard and Fulgence.—LE VOYAGE À DIEPPE. A Comedy in Prose. By Wafflard and Fulgence. Edited, with English Notes, by the Rev. P. H. Ernest Brette, B.D., of Christ's Hospital, and the University of London. Crown 8vo. cloth, pp. 104. 1867. 2s. 6d.

Wake.—CHAPTERS ON MAN. With the Outlines of a Science of comparative Psychology. By C. Staniland Wake, Fellow of the Anthropological Society of London. Crown 8vo. cloth, pp. viii. and 344. 1868. 7s. 6d.

Wanklyn and Chapman.—WATER ANALYSIS. A Practical Treatise on the examination of potable water. By J. Alfred Wanklyn, M.R.C.S., Professor of Chemistry in London Institution, and Ernest Theophron Chapman. Crown 8vo. cloth, pp. x. and 104. 1868. 5s.

Ware.—SKETCHES OF EUROPEAN CAPITALS. By William Ware, Author of "Zenobia; or, Letters from Palmyra," "Aurelian," etc. 8vo. pp. 124. 1851. 1s.

Warning; OR, THE BEGINNING OF THE END. By the Author of "Who am I?" 1 vol., 8vo. cloth. 2s.

Watson.—INDEX TO THE NATIVE AND SCIENTIFIC NAMES OF INDIAN AND OTHER EASTERN ECONOMIC PLANTS AND PRODUCTS, originally prepared under the authority of the Secretary of State for India in Council. By John Forbes Watson, M.A., M.D., F.L.S., F.R.A.S., etc., Reporter on the Products of India. Imperial 8vo. cloth, pp. 650. 1868. £1 11s. 6d.

Watson.—THEORETICAL ASTRONOMY, relating to the motions of the heavenly bodies revolving around the sun in accordance with the law of universal gravitation, embracing a systematic derivation of the formulae for the calculation of the geocentric and heliocentric places, for the determination of the orbits of Planets and Comets, for the correction of approximate elements, and for the computation of special perturbation; together with the theory of the combination of observations, and the method of least squares. With numerical examples and auxiliary tables. By James C. Watson, Director of the Observatory at Ann Arbor, and Professor of Astronomy in the University of Michigan. 8vo. cloth, pp. 662. 1868. £1 18s.

Watts.—ESSAYS ON LANGUAGE AND LITERATURE. By Thomas Watts, of the British Museum. Reprinted, with Alterations and Additions, from the "Transactions of the Philological Society," and elsewhere. 1 vol. 8vo. (In preparation).

Watts and Doddridge.—HYMNS FOR CHILDREN. Revised and altered, so as to render them of general use. By Dr. Watts. To which are added Hymns and other Religious Poetry for Children. By Dr. Doddridge. Ninth edition. 12mo. pp. 48, stiff covers. 1837. 2d.

Way (THE) TO HAVE PEACE. By S. E. De M. 12mo sewed, pp. 16. 1856. 2d.

Way (THE) OF TRUTH; or, a Mother's Teachings from the Bible. 12mo. cloth, pp. iv. and 202. 1867. 2s.

Wedgwood.—The Principles of Geometrical Demonstration, reduced from the Original Conception of Space and Form. By H. Wedgwood, M.A. 12mo. cloth, pp. 48. 1844. 2s.

Wedgwood.—THE GEOMETRY OF THE THREE FIRST BOOKS OF EUCLID. By Direct Proof from Definitions Alone. With an Introduction on the Principles of the Science. By Hensleigh Wedgwood M.A. 12mo. cloth, pp. 104. 1856. 3s.

Wedgwood.—ON THE ORIGIN OF LANGUAGE. By Hensleigh Wedgwood, M.A., late Fellow of Christ College, Cambridge. 12mo. cloth, pp. 165. 1866. 3s. 6d.

Wedgwood.—A DICTIONARY OF THE ENGLISH LANGUAGE. By Hensleigh Wedgwood, M.A., late Fellow of Christ's College, Cambridge. Vol. I. (A to D) 8vo. cloth, pp. xxiv. 508, 14s.; Vol. II. (E to P) 8vo. cloth, pp. 578, 14s.; Vol. III., Part I. (Q. to Sy), 8vo. pp. 366, 10s. 6d.; Vol. III., Part II. (T to W) 8vo., pp. 200, 5s. 6d. complete the Work. 1859 to 1865. Price of the complete work, 44s.

"Dictionaries are a class of books not usually esteemed light reading; but no intelligent man were to be pitied who should find himself shut up on a rainy day in a lonely house in the dreariest part of Salisbury Plain, with no other means of recreation than that which Mr. Wedgwood's Dictionary of Etymology could afford him. He would read it through from cover to cover at a sitting, and only regret that he had not the second volume to begin upon forthwith. It is a very able book, of great research, full of delightful surprises, a repertory of the fairy tales of linguistic science."—*Spectator.*

Wékey.—A GRAMMAR OF THE HUNGARIAN LANGUAGE, with appropriate exercises, a copious vocabulary, and specimens of Hungarian poetry. By Sigismund Wékey, late Aide-de-Camp to Kossuth. 12mo. sewed, pp. viii. and 150. 1852. 4s. 6d.

Weller.—AN IMPROVED DICTIONARY; English and French, and French and English, drawn from the best Sources extant in both Languages; in which are now first introduced many Technical, Scientific, Legal, Commercial, Naval, and Military Terms; and to which are added, Separate Vocabularies of Engineering and Railway Terms; of those descriptive of Steam Power and Steam Navigation; of Geographical Names, and those of Ancient Mythology, and of Persons of Classical Antiquity; and of Christian Names in present use; together with an English Pronouncing Dictionary for the use of Foreigners. By Edward Weller, late Professor of the Athenæum and Episcopal College of Bruges. Royal 8vo. cloth, pp. 384 and 340. 1864. 7s. 6d.

What is Truth? Post 8vo. pp. 124, cloth. 1854. 3s.

Wheeler.—THE HISTORY OF INDIA. By J. Talboys Wheeler, Assistant Secretary to the Government of India in the Foreign Department, Secretary to the Indian Record Commission, Author of "The Geography of Herodotus," etc. Vol. I. containing the Vedic Period and the Mahá Bhárata. With a Map of Ancient India to illustrate the Mahá Bhárata. 8vo. cloth, pp. lxxv. and 576. 1867. 18s.

The Second Volume containing the Rámáyana in the Press.

Wheeler.—HISTORICAL SKETCHES OF NORTH CAROLINA, from 1584 to 1851. Compiled from original records, official documents, and traditional statements. With biographical sketches of her distinguished statesmen, jurists, lawyers, soldiers, divines, etc. By John H. Wheeler. Illustrated with engravings. Vol. I., 8vo. cloth, pp. xxii. and 480. 1851. 15s.

Whildin.—MEMORANDA OF THE STRENGTH OF MATERIALS USED IN ENGINEERING CONSTRUCTION. Compiled and edited by J. K. Whildin, Civil Engineer. Second Edition. 8vo. cloth, pp. 62. 1867. 8s.

Whipple.—LITERATURE AND LIFE. Lectures by E. P. Whipple, Author of "Essays and Reviews." 8vo. sewed, pp. 114. 1851. 1s.

Whipple.—CHARACTER AND CHARACTERISTIC MEN. By Edwin P. Whipple. 12mo. cloth, pp. 324. 1866. 9s.

Whitney.—LANGUAGE AND THE STUDY OF LANGUAGE. A Course of Lectures on the Principles of Linguistic Science. By William Dwight Whitney, Professor of Sanskrit in Yale College, New Haven, U.S.A. Crown 8vo. cloth, pp. 500. 1868. 10s. 6d.

Whittier.—SNOW BOUND. A Winter Idyl. By John Greenleaf Whittier. 12mo. cloth, pp. 52. 1866. 6s.

Whittier.—THE POETICAL WORKS OF JOHN GREENLEAF WHITTIER, Complete in 2 vols. With a Portrait. Blue and Gold Series. 24mo. cloth, gilt edges, pp. viii., 395; vi. 420. 1865. 10s.

Whittier.—MAUD MÜLLER. By John G. Whittier. With Illustrations, by W. J. Hennessy. Small 4to. extra cloth, with gilt edges; 16 leaves, printed on one side only. 1866. 12s.

Whittier.—THE TENT ON THE BEACH, AND OTHER POEMS. By John Greenleaf Whittier. Post 8vo. cloth, pp. vi. and 172. 1867. 6s.

Whittier.—THE PROSE WORKS OF JOHN GREENLEAF WHITTIER. 2 vols., crown 8vo. cloth, pp. viii., 473; viii., 395. 1866. £1 1s.

Whitty.—THE GOVERNING CLASSES OF GREAT BRITAIN. Political Portraits. By Edward M. Whitty. 12mo. boards, pp. vi. and 288. With Lord Stanley's Portrait. 1859. 3s. 6d.

Who am I? By the Author of "Warning." 1 vol., 8vo. cloth. 4s.

Wikoff.—A NEW YORKER IN THE FOREIGN OFFICE, AND HIS ADVENTURES IN PARIS. By Henry Wikoff. 12mo. cloth, pp. 299. 1858. 6s.

Williams.—FIRST LESSONS IN THE MAORI LANGUAGE, WITH A SHORT VOCABULARY. By W. L. Williams, B.A. Square 8vo. cloth, pp. 80. 1862. 3s. 6d.

Williams.—A DICTIONARY, ENGLISH AND SANSCRIT. By Monier Williams, M.A. Published under the patronage of the Honourable East India Company. 4to. cloth, pp. xii. and 862. 1855. £3 3s.

Williams.—LEXICON CORNU-BRITANNICUM. A Dictionary of the Ancient Celtic Language of Cornwall, in which the words are elucidated by copious examples from the Cornish works now remaining, with translations in English. The synonyms are also given in the cognate dialects of Welsh, Armoric, Irish, Gaelic, and Manx, showing at one view the connection between them. By the Rev. Robert Williams, M.A., Christ Church, Oxford, Parish Curate of Llangadwaladr and Rhydycroesan, Denbighshire. Sewed. 3 parts. pp. 400. 1865. £2 5s.

Williams.—THE MIDDLE KINGDOM. A Survey of the Geography, Government, Education, Social Life, Arts, Religion, etc., of the Chinese Empire and its inhabitants. With a new Map of the Empire. By S. Wells Williams, Author of "Easy Lessons in Chinese," "English and Chinese Vocabulary," "Tonic Dictionary of the Chinese Language." With Portraits, Wood-cuts, and Maps. 2 vols. 8vo., pp. viii. 614, xxii. and 590. 1861. £1 1s.

Willis.—ON THE SPECIAL FUNCTION OF THE SUDORIPAROUS AND LYMPHATIC SYSTEMS, THEIR VITAL IMPORT, AND THEIR BEARING ON HEALTH AND DISEASE. By Robert Willis, M.D. 8vo. cloth, pp. viii. and 72. 1867. 4s. 6d.

Wilson.—A BRIEF EXAMINATION OF PREVALENT OPINIONS ON THE INSPIRATION OF THE SCRIPTURES OF THE OLD AND NEW TESTAMENTS. By a Lay Member of the Church of England. With an introduction, by Henry Bristow Wilson, B.D., Vicar of Great Staughton, Hunts. 8vo. cloth, pp. lxi. and 254. 1861. 8s. 6d.

Wilson.—THE HOLY BIBLE. By the Rev. Thomas Wilson. (See under Bible.)

Wilson.—SELECT SPECIMENS OF THE THEATRE OF THE HINDUS. Translated from the Original Sanskrit. By Horace Hayman Wilson, M.A., F.R.S. Second Edition. 2 vols., 8vo. cloth, pp. lxx. and 384, 415. 15s.

CONTENTS.—Vol. I.—Preface—Treatise on the Dramatic System of the Hindus—Dramas translated from the Original Sanskrit—The Mrichchakati, or the Toy Cart—Vikrama and Urvasi, or the Hero and the Nymph—Uttara Rama Cheritra, or continuation of the History of Rama. Vol. II.—Dramas translated from the Original Sanskrit—Malati and Madhava, or the Stolen Marriage—Mudra Rakshasa, or the Signet of the Minister—Retnavall, or the Necklace—Appendix, containing short accounts of different Dramas.

Wilson.—THE PRESENT STATE OF THE CULTIVATION OF ORIENTAL LITERATURE. A Lecture delivered at the Meeting of the Royal Asiatic Society. By the Director, Professor H. H. Wilson. 8vo. sewed, pp. 26. 1852. 6d.

Wilson.—WORKS OF THE LATE HORACE HAYMAN WILSON, M.A., F.R.S., Member of the Royal Asiatic Societies of Calcutta and Paris, and of the Oriental Society of Germany, etc., and Boden Professor of Sanskrit in the University of Oxford. Vols. I. and II. Also, under this title, "Essays and Lectures" chiefly on the Religion of the Hindus, by the late H. H. Wilson, M.A., F.R.S., etc. Collected and edited by Dr. Reinhold Rost. 2 vols., 8vo. cloth, pp. xiii. 399, vi. and 416. 1861-62. £1 1s.

Wilson.—WORKS OF THE LATE HORACE HAYMAN WILSON, M.A., F.R.S., Member of the Royal Asiatic Societies of Calcutta and Paris, and of the Oriental Society of Germany, etc., and Boden Professor of Sanskrit in the University of Oxford. Vols. III., IV. and V. Also, under the title of "Essays Analytical, Critical, and Philological," on subjects connected with Sanskrit Literature. Collected and edited by Reinhold Rost. 3 vols., 8vo. cloth, pp. 408, 406, and 390. 1864-65. £1 16s.

Wilson.—WORKS OF THE LATE HORACE HAYMAN WILSON. Vols. VI. VII. and VIII. Also, under the title of the Vishnu Purana, a system of Hindu mythology and tradition. Translated from the original Sanskrit, and Illustrated by Notes derived chiefly from other Puranas. By the late H. H. Wilson, Boden Professor of Sanskrit in the University of Oxford, etc., etc. Edited by Fitzedward Hall, M.A., D.C.L., Oxon. Vols. I. to III. 8vo. cloth, pp. cxl. and 200, 344, and 344. 1864-66. £1 11s. 6d. [*Vols. IV. and V. in the press.*

Wilson.—CATHOLICITY SPIRITUAL AND INTELLECTUAL. An attempt at vindicating the Harmony of Faith and Knowledge. A series of Discourses. By Thomas Wilson, M.A., late Minister of St. Peter's Mancroft, Norwich, Author of "Travels in Egypt," etc. 8vo. cloth, pp. 232. 1850. 5s.

Wilson.—THE VILLAGE PEARL. A Domestic Poem. With Miscellaneous Pieces. By John Crauford Wilson. 12mo. cloth, pp. viii. and 140. 1852. 3s. 6d.

Wilson.—THE WATER-CURE, ITS PRINCIPLES AND PRACTICE. A Guide in the Preservation of Health and Cure of Chronic Disease. With Illus-

Wilson.—PHRASIS: a Treatise on the History and Structure of the different Languages of the World, with a comparative view of the Forms of their Words and the Style of their Expressions. By J. Wilson, A.M. 8vo. cloth, pp. viii. and 384. 1864. 16s.

Winckelmann.—THE HISTORY OF ANCIENT ART AMONG THE GREEKS. By John Winckelmann. From the German, by G. H. Lodge. Beautifully Illustrated. 8vo. cloth, pp. viii. and 254. 1850. 12s.

Winer.—GRAMMAR OF THE CHALDEE LANGUAGE, as contained in the Bible and Targums. By Dr. G. B. Winer. Translated by H. B. Hackett. 8vo. boards, pp. 152. 1845. 3s. 6d.

Winslow.—A COMPREHENSIVE TAMIL AND ENGLISH DICTIONARY OF HIGH AND LOW TAMIL. By the Rev. Miron Winslow, D.D., American Missionary, Madras, assisted by competent Native Scholars: in part from Manuscript materials of the late Rev. Joseph Knight and others. 4to. boards, pp. xiv. and 976. 1862. £3 13s. 6d.

Winthrop.—LIFE AND LETTERS OF JOHN WINTHROP, Governor of the Massachusetts' Bay Company at their emigration to New England, 1630. By Robert C. Winthrop. Two Portraits; Plate of Groton Church, Suffolk; and facsimile Autographs. 8vo. cloth, pp. xii. and 452. 1864. 14s.

Winthrop.—LIFE AND LETTERS OF JOHN WINTHROP. Vol. II. from his Embarkation for New England, in 1630, with the Charter and Company of Massachusetts' Bay to his Death, in 1649. By Robert C. Winthrop. Portrait. 8vo. cloth, pp. xv. and 483. 1867. 14s.

Winter JOURNEY FROM GLOUCESTER TO NORWAY. 18mo. sewed, pp. 100. With a Map. 1867. 1s. 6d.

Wise.—CAPTAIN BRAND, of the "Centipede;" a Pirate of Eminence in the West Indies: his Loves and Exploits, together with some Account of the Singular Manner in which he departed this Life. By Lieut. H. A. Wise, U.S.N. 12mo. fancy cover, pp. 304. 1860. 2s. 6d.

Wise.—COMMENTARY ON THE HINDU SYSTEM OF MEDICINE. By T. A. Wise, M.D., Bengal Medical Service. 8vo. cloth, pp. xx. and 432. 1845. 7s. 6d.

Witt.—AN EFFECTUAL AND SIMPLE REMEDY FOR SCARLET FEVER AND MEASLES. With an Appendix of Cases. By Charles Witt. Fourth Edition. 8vo. sewed, pp. 32. 1865. 1s.

Wolfram.—THE GERMAN ECHO. A Faithful Mirror of German Every-day Conversation. By Ludwig Wolfram. With a Vocabulary, by Henry Skelton. Third Edition. 12mo. cloth, pp. 69. 1864. 3s.

Worcester.—A PRONOUNCING, EXPLANATORY, AND SYNONYMOUS DICTIONARY OF THE ENGLISH LANGUAGE. By Joseph E. Worcester, LL.D. New Edition. 8vo. cloth, pp. 565. 1864. 7s. 6d.

Worthen.—A CYCLOPÆDIA OF DRAWING, designed as a Text-Book for the Mechanic, Architect, Engineer, and Surveyor, comprising Geometrical Projection, Mechanical, Architectural, and Topographical Drawing, Perspective, and Isometry. Edited by W. E. Worthen. Royal 8vo. cloth, pp. 410. 1864. £1 5s.

Wylie.—NOTES ON CHINESE LITERATURE; with introductory Remarks on the Progressive Advancement of the Art; and a list of translations from the Chinese into various European Languages. By A. Wylie, Agent of the British

Xenos.—EAST AND WEST; a Diplomatic History of the Annexation of the Ionian Islands to the Kingdom of Greece. Accompanied by a Translation of the Despatches exchanged between the Greek Government and its Plenipotentiary at London, and a Collection of the Principal Treaties, Conventions, and Protocols concerning the Ionian Islands and Greece, concluded between 1797 and 1864. By Stefanos Xenos. Royal 8vo. cloth, pp. iv. and 304. 1865. 12s.

Yates.—A BENGÁLÍ GRAMMAR. By the late Rev. W. Yates, D.D., Reprinted, with improvements, from his Introduction to the Bengáli Language. Edited by I. Wenger. Fcap. 8vo., boards, pp. iv. and 150. 1864. 3s. 6d.

Yates.—THE ELEMENTS OF THE SCIENCE OF GRAMMAR, put forward and explained in a totally different manner from what they have ever before been, and based on rigid definitions, incontrovertible axioms, and general principles, illustrated by a comparison of the structure of the English and Turkish languages, so as to be at once an introduction to the science of grammar, for all who wish to learn that science, and a complete Turkish grammar for the student of that language. By Edward Yates, B.A., Barrister-at-Law. Most kindly and valuably assisted by Captains Mahmood and Hussein, of the Imperial Guard of the Sultan, and by Hiry Bey. 12mo. cloth, pp. ii. and 226. 1857. 5s.

Yates.—DESCRIPTIVE CATALOGUE OF A COLLECTION OF CURRENT COINS OF ALL COUNTRIES, in the International Exhibition. Class 13, North Gallery. By James Yates, M.A., F.R.S. 12mo. sewed, pp. 69. 1862. 6d.

Zeller.—STRAUSS AND RENAN. An Essay by E. Zeller. Translated from the German, with Introductory Remarks by the Translator. Post 8vo. cloth, pp. 110. 1866. 2s. 6d.

MAGAZINES.

Anthropological REVIEW (THE). Published Quarterly, at 4s. each number.

Chess WORLD (THE). Published monthly, at 1s. each number.

Englishwoman's REVIEW (THE). Published quarterly, at 1s. each number.

Geological MAGAZINE (THE). Published monthly, at 1s. 6d. each number.

Journal OF THE ROYAL ASIATIC SOCIETY OF GREAT BRITAIN AND IRELAND (THE). Published twice a year.

Orthodox CATHOLIC REVIEW (THE). Published monthly, at 6d. each number.

Trübner's AMERICAN AND ORIENTAL LITERARY RECORD. Published monthly, at 6d. each number.

Westminster REVIEW (THE). Published quarterly, at 6s. each number.

A LIST of the PUBLICATIONS of TRÜBNER & CO., in the RUSSIAN LANGUAGE, may be had on Application.

LONDON:
PRINTED BY WERTHEIMER, LEA AND CO.
FINSBURY CIRCUS.

www.ingramcontent.com/pod-product-compliance
Lightning Source LLC
Chambersburg PA
CBHW032010300426
44117CB00008B/972